TOWARD A
DISCOURSE OF CONSENT

TOWARD A DISCOURSE OF CONSENT

MASS MOBILIZATION AND COLONIAL POLITICS IN PUERTO RICO, 1932–1948

Gabriel Villaronga

Contributions in Latin American Studies, Number 23

Westport, Connecticut
London

Library of Congress Cataloging-in-Publication Data

Villaronga, Gabriel, 1968–
     Toward a discourse of consent : mass mobilization and colonial politics in Puerto Rico,
     1932–1948 / Gabriel Villaronga.
            p.   cm.—(Contributions in Latin American studies, ISSN 1054–6790 ; no. 23)
     Includes bibliographical references and index.
     ISBN 0–313–32423–9 (alk. paper)
     1. Political participation—Puerto Rico—History—20th century.   2. Puerto Rico—Politics
and government—1892–1952.   I. Title.   II. Series.
JL1056.V55   2004
324.27295'06—dc22   2003070685

British Library Cataloguing in Publication Data is available.

Library of Congress Catalog Card Number: 2003070685
ISBN: 0–313–32423–9
ISSN: 1054–6790

First published in 2004

Praeger Publishers, 88 Post Road West, Westport, CT 06881
An imprint of Greenwood Publishing Group, Inc.
www.praeger.com

Printed in the United States of America

The paper used in this book complies with the
Permanent Paper Standard issued by the National
Information Standards Organization (Z39.48–1984).

10 9 8 7 6 5 4 3 2 1

To My Family

I leave Sisyphus at the foot of the mountain! One always finds one's burden again. But Sisyphus teaches the higher fidelity that negates the gods and raises rocks. He too concludes that all is well. This universe henceforth without a master seems to him neither sterile nor futile. Each atom of that stone, each mineral flake of that night-filled mountain, in itself forms a world. The struggle itself toward the heights is enough to fill a man's heart. One must imagine Sisyphus happy.

—Albert Camus, *The Myth of Sisyphus*

The abandonment of the aspiration to "absolute" knowledge has exhilarating effects: on the one hand, human beings can recognize themselves as the true creators and no longer as the passive recipients of a predetermined structure; on the other hand, as all social agents have to recognize their concrete finitude, nobody can aspire to be the true consciousness of the world.

—Ernesto Laclau, *Emancipation(s)*

The postmodern hero should be portrayed as a *strong poet* in the Nietzschean sense of one who both acknowledges and appropriates contingency, who both affirms the contingency of the world and knows how to take political advantage of that contingency by imagining and seeking to realize a host of new political projects that aim to make the world better and more agreeable.

—Jacob Torfing, *New Theories of Discourse*

CONTENTS

PREFACE

This book is the product of personal and intellectual concerns. My choice of research is in part the result of my preoccupations as a Puerto Rican. No only I am concerned about our national question, but I am also interested to look beyond the status issue to grasp the rich texture of the island's politics. In hindsight, the main issue that has guided my research is to study how people approach, negotiate, and agree with each other at a political level to introduce policies for their own benefit. As I narrowed the scope of my research to focus on what I now call mass mobilization and colonial politics between 1932 and 1948, I realized that the challenge to understand this topic lay not in the absence of explanations but in the sheer disposition of people to offer opinions and interpretations. Due to the myriad of passionate views, one faces not only many discrepancies but also genuine lapses of interpretation and deliberate silences about the past. In short, a political legacy that has weighed heavily in the collective memory of Puerto Ricans has led me to study a period that is important to many people but for very different reasons.

These preoccupations intertwined with the concerns proper of my academic vocation. My aim is to offer a perspective that takes into account the unequal access to political power that mass mobilization entails yet leaves room to understand how leaders and followers shaped a new political discourse based on notions of consent. Hence, this book deals with how the process of political interaction that led toward a discourse of consent produced a situation most beneficial for the individuals in power but effectively shaped by those below. I focus on the relationship between American authorities, the Popular Democratic Party—Partido Popular Democrá-tico—and its supporters to grasp how the tactics of mass mobilization and the deployment of a multifaceted discourse shaped colonial politics in Puerto Rico during the late 1930s and 1940s. Despite its mutations over time, the discourse of consent generally expressed open support for socioeconomic improvement and an agreement between multiple social groups about the need for change. The emergence of consent was above all a collective affair. This means that the study of colonial politics is not just about who did what to whom but about the exchanges between agents that enabled people to partake in political practices of their own design. It is my understanding that although people negotiated consent on unequal grounds, a two-way avenue existed to influence the haphazard process of responsiveness, dialogue, dispute, and contestation that informed the political bond among certain agents as well as the exclusion of others.

The notion of consent has been for long a pillar of liberal-democratic theory.[1] Despite being commonly accepted as a valuable concept, consent has come under fire, and few efforts have been made to counter the theoretical gap.[2] Although the writings of Antonio Gramsci[3] as well as postcolonial analysis have informed my work in the past, I prefer a conceptual approach better attuned to recent contributions of discourse analysis. Of all the works about politics that offer "new theories of discourse," I find most appealing the neo-Gramscian conceptualizations of Ernesto Laclau, Chantal Mouffe, and other contributors.[4] Although the work of Laclau and Mouffe builds upon the concept of hegemony as originally presented by Gramsci, they have developed a compelling new approach that incorporates many insights of postmodern theories.

By demolishing the idea that societies and agents embody fixed essences, Laclau and Mouffe open the way to understand that social orders and identities are constituted, organized, and imbued with meanings through the logic of articulation: the practices that establish a relation among "elements" of a given context and manage to produce a discourse. The production of discourses does not imply a free play of words or random phenomena. On the contrary, discourses emerge, compete with each other, and become dominant according to a field of political relations known as hegemony. According to Jacob Torfing, hegemony can be defined as "the expansion of a discourse, or set of discourses, into a dominant horizon of social orientation and action . . . in a context crisscrossed by antagonistic forces."[5] If I am to follow this form of analysis, consent should not be seen as the acquiescence of people toward politicians based either on deliberative processes or on an impartial standpoint above and beyond power relations. Nor should consent be understood exclusively as the result of political manipulation or social control. Instead, my notion of consent refers to a discourse that shifted over time as it expressed an agreement between disparate agents. The discourse of consent emerged from the articulatory practices that took place in a context rife with conflict, contestation, and antagonism.[6] As a field of signification without ultimate closure, consent must be grasped in the light of power relations and historical contingencies that are an inseparable part of hegemonic processes.

Since Laclau and Mouffe discard the idea of privileged agents of historical change, what furnishes coherence to a discursive formation is its "regularity in dispersion."[7] Hence, the work of Laclau and Mouffe also leads me to conclude that the discourse of consent refers to a "decentered" site of political engagement. This means that far from being the axis of a facile hierarchy between leaders and followers, consent is the manifestation of a multifaceted and multivocal political reality. In the same vein, consent should not be seen solely as the result of exogenous forces beyond the realm of a country's local affairs such as foreign intervention or the subordination of a region to relations of dependency. Political leaders and foreign interests in Latin America could provide a degree of cohesion to mobilize people but not necessarily as a "comprador class"[8] pulling the strings as they wished. That is, the need to negotiate their way to power and reach compromises with several groups can narrow the arbitrariness of a political elite that aspires to coalesce mass support. People can shape a discourse of consent despite the interference of vested interests. To a great extent, the consent of people entails not only an ambiguous zone of action but also an elasticity of meaning that allow individuals to meet eye to eye and reach an agreement. The actions and discursive practices of many agents inform each other as part of the multistranded political crossroad that is at the very heart of my notion of consent.

A discourse of consent may seem an unexpected outcome in a colonial context, which usually connotes an oppressive regime that fails to represent the interests of people and achieves its ends through coercion. Although brutal forms of domination are a fact of life in a colony, it is equally true that a range of factors not only delimits or deprives a structure of power of its determining capacity but also allows agents enough room to articulate a myriad of discursive practices, including a discourse of consent. If we are to understand social formations and identities not as essences but as constructs, then the challenge at hand is to see how the failure of final closure of any social order leaves room for dislocation, "structural undecidability," and the agency of people.[9] The Gramscian notion of "organic crisis," a pervasive form of dislocation, will help me understand the colonial instability that enabled people to articulate a new political logic in Puerto Rico. What made possible a discourse of consent was as much the erosion of the island's colonial order as the actions of agents that ushered in unexpected forms of contestation.

In addition to the impact of "traumatic events," quotidian practices can unhinge colonial forms of domination and open the way toward a discourse of consent. Recent studies stress the importance of culture to understand political formations.[10] An emphasis on cultural exchanges can help show that consent and colonialism are far from incompatible. By looking beyond institutional lines that force on observers "facile juxtapositions of 'us' and 'them,' of 'foreign' and 'local,'"[11] one can grasp the imbrication of exogenous and local factors that informed the discourse of consent in a colonial context. At a cultural level colonialism constitutes less the straightforward imposition of an invader's will than an ambiguous political order not immune to the effort of the colonized to reverse or reshape their subordinate position. Since colonial situations entail a degree of cultural permeability and diffusion not reducible to the metropolis-colonial nexus, one can find the emergence of consent and the articulation of its discourse within many blurred areas of political interaction.

Besides banking on recent contributions of discourse and cultural studies, I take issue with analyses of populist movements. Although I make no effort to revamp or salvage populism as an analytical concept, my work avoids a full-blown dismissal of notions about this type of mass politics. Many insights have been possible with the inception of discourse analysis to examine the dynamic nature of populist movements.[12] Since Ernesto Laclau presented his landmark essay about populism, many scholars have made significant strides to understand how populist movements construct new meanings, identities, and representations.[13]

Despite these gains, the concept of populism remains problematic. On the one hand, the concept can be ambiguous[14] and is inadequate to account for the multiple voices of the movement. On the other hand, taken as a set of traits that characterize a form of politics,[15] the notion of populism not only is too static but can also become an "analytical straitjacket" when historical conditions do not conform with the theoretical model. Framing the notion of consent according to the insights of discourse theory is an effective avenue to understand the elusive exchanges between agents that are part either of a populist movement or of other forms of mass politics. Moreover, analyzing consent as a discursive construct can shed light on the experience of people as they interact and negotiate with each other to implement policies for their own benefit. The discourse of consent entails not only the actions and views of individuals but also the bond between leaders and followers that can cement particular forms of mass politics.

The specific case of mass mobilization under examination here is the populist movement headed by Luis Muñoz Marín and the Popular Democratic Party—Partido Popular Democrático (PPD)—during the late 1930s and 1940s. My work considers how the PPD in conjunction with U.S. authorities coalesced the support of multiple sectors such as urban workers, rural laborers, the unemployed, religious groups, women, Communists, independentists, technocrats, and dissidents from other political parties. By defining the discourse of consent as a common aspiration for change that did not entirely preclude different courses of action and perceptions, I focus on the rise of broad support toward the PPD without denying the capacity of agents to make claims of their own and to shape the outcome of events. This means that consent is not a lineal sequence that led multiple groups to shed particular interests in favor of the same goals. Nor is there a rigid divide between consent and dissent. My notion of consent is a fluid ground of contestation that makes room for a simultaneity of agendas but without offering any guarantees about their long-term coexistence.

The analysis of the discourse of consent in Puerto Rico requires to consider the role of PPD leaders, the followers of Muñoz's party, and U.S. authorities. This is not an attempt to present a comprehensive account or "total history" of the 1930s and 1940s. Instead, my intention is to focus on what Ruth Berins Collier and David Collier refer to as "critical junctures" of regime dynamics in Latin America.[16] The concept of "critical juncture" stresses the interaction between labor and political interests that caused pivotal reorientations of Latin American politics. As an effort to study the interplay of internal and external forces in Latin America,[17] the notion of Collier and Collier do not stand far apart from what Mary Louise Pratt calls the "contact zones" of U.S. foreign relations.[18] Inspired by these concepts of politics, my work focuses on key instances of political engagement in Puerto Rico that generated a discourse of consent. My main concern is to examine the exchange between several interests that bound together PPD leaders, Muñoz's followers, and U.S. authorities.

After a brief historiographical review and some remarks about new avenues of interpretation, the first chapter examines the conditions that paved the way for the discourse of consent. I discuss the effects of the Great Depression on Puerto Rico and the political realignment caused by the economic slump that made possible the collaboration between U.S. officials and local advocates of reform. My analysis highlights how the New Deal served as a platform for the mobilization of political leaders that eventually formed the PPD. As a highly unstable context, the colonial situation in the 1930s routed any easy course of action for the advocates of reform. Puerto Rico faced an erosion of its social order and a proliferation of antagonism proper to an "organic crisis." This sort of dislocation is pervasive and upsets the most fundamental aspects that sustain a society. Although the island was at the mercy of the worst conditions imaginable in the 1930s, people tapped the possibilities that ensue from an "organic crisis." Puerto Rico became a stage for imagining a different socioeconomic and political reality. A range of alternatives promised to articulate a new political discourse subject to the power relations between the island's people, its leadership, and U.S. officials.

The political ties that developed between PPD leaders and U.S. reformers of the New Deal laid only a partial basis for the discourse of consent. Although many sectors of the island favored the U.S. policies of reform, this reality did not translate into broad support toward Muñoz and his party, the self-proclaimed representatives of the local New Deal. The second chapter examines the effort of PPD officials to insert themselves into colonial politics not only as mediators between local interests and U.S. policies but also as the "moral-intellectual leadership" of an emerging "historical bloc" in favor of social justice. That is, Muñoz and his party aimed to embody as leaders more than their own interests and aspired to lead a broad alignment of forces with reform as its main focus. This alignment or "historical bloc" included a wide range of constituencies such as workers, rural laborers, the unemployed, religious groups, women, Communists, independentists, technocrats, and dissidents from other political parties. By focusing on groups that made demands for reform or were receptive to pledges for socioeconomic improvement, I examine the political and discursive tactics of the PPD to grab the attention of people that the party perceived as its main and most accessible audience. Many claims to political legitimacy soon shaped the rhetoric of Muñoz and his peers, but the emergence of a unified discursive space (understood as "regularity in dispersion") would depend on the outcome at multiple sites of political interaction among people.

While agents engaged in a haphazard process that refashioned the island's politics as well as people's role in it, a discourse of consent took shape and became partially fixed around the idea of reform and social justice. The exchange between PPD leaders, the island's people, and U.S. officials that produced support toward reform and social justice became most evident at times of conflict. Chapter 3 discusses the sugar strike of 1942 as a political turning point that formalized the ties between a sector of labor, the PPD, and U.S. authorities. As an upheaval that took its toll among workers and haunted U.S. policymakers, the sugar strike offered the PPD a unique opportunity to consolidate its role as a mediator between local and mainland interests as well as to imagine itself as the island's "moral-intellectual leadership." Under the spell of reform and social justice, the party and its followers worked after the strike in unison, as a "collective will," even though the plurality of agents and their claims remained irreducible.

Before long, the groups that joined forces with the PPD to support U.S. policies of reform began to articulate eloquent views about their relationship to the PPD, the aim of social justice, and the future of Puerto Rico. The fourth chapter mainly focuses on the working class, advocates of independence, and Muñoz to examine what I call their visions of consent, perceptions that had in common an expressed need for comradeship and change but gave a different spin to political action and reform. My analysis of how labor and independentists nurtured their relationship to the PPD with visions and initiatives unlike those of Muñoz's party serves to highlight the elastic quality that characterized the discourse of consent. The emerging political logic not only was flexible enough to usher in amiable relations but also made way for new sorts of tension. Despite sharing a common ground of articulation, the visions of consent competed and attempted to prevail over the others as they deployed what I call the tactics of political displacement. PPD leaders, labor, and independentists tried to rearrange the terms of their coexistence by pushing to the sidelines alternative visions. Since these agents tapped unevenly the resources of political power in Puerto Rico and the mainland, the discourse of consent gradually centered on the precepts of Muñoz's party.

Although many groups had their say about consent, the partnership between the PPD and other agents soon became the domain of Muñoz's call for the "battle of production." This was the case after the PPD's landslide electoral victory of 1944, when the political balance between Muñoz's party and its supporters decisively shifted in favor of the former. In the fifth chapter, the protest of sugar workers and the labor strikes in the PPD's program of industrialization shed light on the party's policies to redefine the discourse of consent according to its own precepts. The PPD placed limits on its notion of consent, leading to the political exclusion of agents that openly eschewed the subordinate position assigned to them by the party. At this point, an ascendant discourse of consent glossed over its origins to insist on the consolidation of a political leadership that offered itself as "neutral agents" for the inscription of a broad range of political demands. While the ascendant discourse of consent suppressed alternative outlooks beyond its core of meaning, the PPD increasingly claimed political legitimacy with references to the party's heterogeneous composition. The final chapter of the book offers an overview of the process that led toward a discourse of consent. Understood as a new political logic, the discourse of consent left few lives untouched as people faced up to the challenge.

I have had the good fortune to count on the personal and intellectual support that made this book possible. It is my pleasure to acknowledge the people and institutions that provided assistance over the years. Since this book began as a doctoral dissertation, I would like to thank my Ph.D. advisers. I am especially grateful to Blanca G. Silvestrini, who never failed to offer advice, support, and encouragement to complete this project. She deserves my deepest sympathies. Acknowledgment is also due to Paul B. Goodwin, Susan Porter Benson, and Karen Spalding, who provided ample support and counsel during all stages of my research. To all of them I owe an enormous debt of gratitude. Many other people deserve my appreciation. I want to thank Luis A. Figueroa, who, as my M.A. adviser, made sound contributions to my intellectual growth. Several other scholars have influenced my work with their insights. These are Georg Fromm, Edgardo Meléndez, Francisco Moscoso, Carlos Pabón, Thomas G. Paterson, Fernando Picó, and Bruce M. Stave.

My appreciation also goes to colleagues who shared with me critical insights and many years of graduate studies. These are Alberto Arroyo (deceased), Rosa Carrasquillo, Paulo Contreras, Hilda Lloréns, Sean Moore, Ricardo Pérez, and José O. Solá. More recently, I have benefited from the invaluable knowledge of other colleagues such as Francisco García, Sigfredo García, William Ortíz, Luis Pabón, Erick Pérez (deceased), William Ríos, Nora Rodríguez, and Josefa Santiago. I am also grateful to people who, in one way or another, have had a positive effect on my life and strengthened my resolve to complete this work. I want to single out my aunt and uncle, María Isabel Villaronga and Luis Rodríguez Bachiller, as well as my cousins Luis, Juan, and Pablo. In addition, I am pleased to mention Xavier Cibes, Carlos García Gutierrez, Arnaldo González, Philip Guerreri, Laura López, Luis Lugo, Vanessa Mora, Gerardo Rodríguez, Manuel Rodríguez, Romualdo Rodríguez, Saul Rosario, Meghan Shelby, María de las Mercedes Sigüenza, José Sigüenza, Homar Torres, and Alexandra Vega.

Several libraries and archives offered me ample support to complete this project. I must extend a special thanks to the staff of the Luis Muñoz Marín Archive for their kind help and collaboration. Above all, I appreciate the assistance of archivist Julio Quirós. Likewise, I want to express my gratitude to librarian Darlene Hull at the University of Connecticut (UConn). I am also grateful to the staff of the Thomas J. Dodd Research Center at UConn, the National Archives and Records Administration, the Franklin D. Roosevelt Presidential Library, the General Archive of Puerto Rico, and both the Center of Historical Investigations and the Puerto Rican Collection at the University of Puerto Rico.

I dedicate this work to my family. My appreciation for the unlimited support of my parents, María V. Sweet and Luis M. Villaronga, is beyond boundaries. Particularly, without the affection and generosity of my mother, this work would not have been possible. My sister and grandmother, Victoria and María, also deserve my deepest appreciation. They all have been a vital source of inspiration.

NOTES

1. Douglas B. Klusmeyer, *Between Consent and Descent: Conceptions of Democratic Citizenship* (Washington, DC: Carnegie Endowment for International Peace, 1996); P. H. Partridge, *Consent and Consensus* (New York: Praeger Publishers, 1971); Jules Steinberg, *Locke, Rousseau, and the Idea of Consent: An Inquiry into the Liberal-Democratic Theory of Political Obligation* (Westport, CT: Greenwood Press, 1978).

2. Efforts to revitalize consent theory have met major obstacles of analysis. The conceptual models available today remain poor. Consider Harry Beran, *The Consent Theory of Political Obligation* (London: Croom Helm, 1987); Mark E. Kann, "The Dialectic of Consent Theory," *Journal of Politics* 40 (May 1978): 387-408; Mark E. Kann, "Consent and Authority in America," in John P. Diggins and Mark E. Kann, eds., *The Problem of Authority in America* (Philadelphia: Temple University Press, 1981), pp. 59-83; George Klosko, "Reformist Consent and Political Obligation," *Political Studies* 29 (1991): 676-690.

3. Antonio Gramsci, *Selections from the Prison Notebooks*, ed. and trans. Quintin Hoare and Geoffrey Nowell Smith (New York: International Publishers, 1971); Antonio Gramsci, *Further Selections from the Prison Notebooks*, ed. and trans. Derek Boothman (Minneapolis: University of Minnesota Press, 1995).

4. Ernesto Laclau, "The Impossibility of Society," *Canadian Journal of Political and Social Theory* 7 (1983): 21-24; Ernesto Laclau and Chantal Mouffe, *Hegemony and Socialist Strategy: Toward a Radical Democratic Politics* (London: Verso Books, 1985); Ernesto Laclau, *New Reflexions on the Revolution of Our Time* (London: Verso Books, 1991); Chantal Mouffe, "Democratic Citizenship and the Political Community," in Chantal Mouffe, ed., *Dimensions of Radical Democracy: Pluralism, Citizenship, Community* (London: Verso Books, 1992), pp. 225-239; Chantal Mouffe, *The Return of the Political* (London: Verso Books, 1993); Ernesto Laclau, "Minding the Gap: The Subject of Politics," in Ernesto Laclau, ed., *The Making of Political Identities* (London: Verso Books, 1994), pp. 11-39; Ernesto Laclau, *Emancipation(s)* (London: Verso Books, 1996); Ernesto Laclau, "Deconstruction, Pragmatism, Hegemony," in Chantal Mouffe, ed., *Deconstruction and Pragmatism* (London: Routledge, 1996), pp. 47-67; Ernesto Laclau, "Identity and Hegemony: The Role of Universality in the Constitution of Political Logics," in Judith Butler, Ernesto Laclau, and Slavoj Žižek, *Contingency, Hegemony, Universality* (London: Verso Books, 2000), pp. 44-89; Ernesto Laclau, "Constructing Universality," in Judith Butler, Ernesto Laclau, and Slavoj Žižek, *Contingency, Hegemony, Universality* (London: Verso Books, 2000), pp. 281-307; Chantal Mouffe, *The Democratic Paradox* (London: Verso Books, 2000). For a critical overview of the discourse theory of Laclau and Mouffe, see Anna Marie Smith, *Laclau and Mouffe: The Radical Democratic Imaginary* (London: Routledge, 1998); Jacob Torfing, *New Theories of Discourse: Laclau, Mouffe, and Žižek* (Oxford: Blackwell Publishers, 1999).

5. Torfing, *New Theories of Discourse*, p. 101.

6. Defined as such in my work, the term "discourse of consent" refers to what Laclau and Mouffe call a hegemonic articulation. According to these theorists, "in order to speak of hegemony, the articulatory moment is not sufficient. It is also necessary that the articulation should take place through a confrontation with antagonistic articulatory practices—in other words, that hegemony should emerge in a field criss-crossed by antagonisms and therefore suppose phenomena of equivalence and frontier effects." However, the antagonism of forces in any given context cannot be absolute for there to be a hegemonic process. Laclau and Mouffe, *Hegemony and Socialist Strategy*, pp. 135-136.

7. According to Laclau and Mouffe, this type of coherence is what characterizes the notion of discourse developed by Michael Foucault. Laclau and Mouffe, *Hegemony and Socialist Strategy*, p. 105.

8. Gilbert M. Joseph, Catherine C. LeGrand, and Ricardo D. Salvatore, eds., *Close Encounters of Empire: Writing the Cultural History of U.S.-Latin American Relations* (Durham, NC: Duke University Press, 1998), p. 13.

9. Laclau, "Deconstruction, Pragmatism, Hegemony," pp. 54-59. See also Torfing, *New Theories of Discourse*, pp. 62-66, 137-154.

10. Frederick Cooper and Ann Laura Stoler, eds., *Tensions of Empire: Colonial Cultures in a Bourgeois World* (Berkeley: University of California Press, 1997); Nicholas B. Dirks, ed., *Colonialism and Culture* (Ann Arbor: University of Michigan Press, 1992); Joseph et al., *Close Encounters of Empire*; Amy Kaplan and Donald E. Pease, eds., *Cultures of United States Imperialism* (Durham, NC: Duke University Press, 1993); Daniel H. Levine, ed., *Constructing Culture and Power in Latin America* (Ann Arbor: University of Michigan, 1995); Jan Nederveen Pieterse and Bhikhu Parekh, eds., *The Decolonization of Imagination: Culture, Knowledge and Power* (London: Zed Books, 1995); Mary Loise Pratts, *Imperial Eyes: Travel Writing and Transculturation* (London: Routledge, 1992); Edward W. Said, *Culture and Imperialism* (New York: Vintage Books, 1994).

11. Joseph et al., *Close Encounters of Empire*, p. 16.

12. Discourse analysis emphasizes the language, rhetoric, and style that are part of populist movements. Attention is given to the values that shape the populist discourse such as nationalism, popular traditions, and the influence of modernity. It is reasonable to say that Ernesto Laclau's work inspired the use of discourse analysis to understand populist movements. Consider his landmark essay, "Towards a Theory of Populism," in Ernesto Laclau, *Politics and Ideology in Marxist Theory: Capitalism, Fascism, Populism* (London: NLB, 1977), pp. 81-198. See also Ernesto Laclau, "Populist Rupture and Discourse," *Screen Education* 34 (Spring 1980): 87-93. A critical review of Laclau's work is Emilio de Ipola, "Populismo e ideología (A propósito de Ernesto Laclau: Política e ideología en la teoría marxista)," *Revista Mexicana de Sociología* 41 (1979): 925-960. See also his other work: Emilio de Ipola, *Ideología y discurso populista* (México, DF: Folios Ediciones, 1982). Laclau elaborates his theories further in Ernesto Laclau, "Populismo y Transformación del Imaginario Político en América Latina," *Cuadernos de la Realidad Nacional* 3 (1988).

13. Some cases are José Alvarez Junco, ed., *Populismo, Caudillaje y Discurso Demagógico* (Madrid: Siglo Veintiuno, 1987); José Alvarez Junco and Ricardo González Leandri, eds., *El Populismo en España y América* (Madrid: Editorial Catriel, 1994); Mariano Plotkin, *Mañana es San Perón: Propaganda, rituales políticos y educación en el régimen peronista (1946-1955)* (Buenos Aires: Ariel Historia Argentina, 1994); Felipe Burbano de Lara, ed., *El fantasma del populismo: Aproximación a un tema (siempre) actual* (Caracas: Editorial Nueva Sociedad, 1998); Carlos de la Torre, *Populist Seduction in Latin America: The Ecuadorian Experience* (Athens: Ohio University Center for International Studies, 2000).

14. A number of authors highlight the problematic nature of populism or delimit the usefulness of the concept. Consider José Alvarez Junco, "El populismo como problema," in Alvarez Junco and González Leandri, *El Populismo en España y América*, pp. 11-38; Paul W. Drake, *Socialism and Populism in Chile, 1932-1952* (Urbana: University of Illinois Press, 1978); Ian Roxborough, "Unity and Diversity in Latin American History," *Journal of Latin American Studies* 16 (May 1984): 1-26; Carlos de la Torre, "The Ambiguous Meanings of Latin American Populisms," *Social Research* 59, no. 2 (Summer 1992): 385-414; Sagrario Torres Ballesteros, "El populismo. Un concepto escurridizo," in Alvarez Junco, *Populismo, Caudillaje y Discurso Demagógico*, pp. 159-180.

15. I am referring to perspectives such as the ones collected in Michael L. Conniff, ed., *Latin American Populism in Comparative Perspective* (Albuquerque: University of New Mexico Press, 1982); Michael L. Conniff, ed., *Populism in Latin America* (Tuscaloosa: University of Alabama Press, 1999).

16. Ruth Berins Collier and David Collier, *Shaping the Political Arena: Critical Junctures, the Labor Movement, and Regime Dynamics in Latin America* (Princeton: Princeton University Press, 1991).

17. Ibid. In addition to *Shaping the Political Arena* and *Close Encounters of Empire*, other works focus on the interplay of internal and external forces to explain politics in Latin America. Consider Ruth Berins Collier, "Combining Alternative Perspectives: Internal Trajectories versus External Influences as Explanations of Latin American Politics in the 1940s," *Comparative Politics* 26 (October 1993): 1-29; David Rock, ed., *Latin America in the 1940s: War and Postwar Transitions* (Berkeley: University of California Press, 1994).

18. Mary Louise Pratts, "Arts of the Contact Zone," *Profession* 91 (1991): 33-39; Mary Louise Pratts, *Imperial Eyes: Travel Writing and Transculturation* (London: Routledge, 1992), pp. 6-7.

ABBREVIATIONS

ACPR	Asociación de Choferes de Puerto Rico (Chauffeurs' Association)
AFL	American Federation of Labor
APA	Asociación de Productores de Azúcar (Sugar Producers' Association)
ASI	Acción Social Independentista (Independentist Social Action)
CGT	Confederación General de Trabajadores (General Confederation of Workers)
CGT-A	Confederación General de Trabajadores "Auténtica" (General Confederation of Workers "Authentic")
CGT-G	Confederación General de Trabajadores "Gubernamental" (General Confederation of Workers "Governmental")
CIO	Congress of Industrial Organizations
CPI	Congreso Pro Independencia (Pro Independence Congress)
FERA	Federal Emergency Relief Administration
FLT	Federación Libre de Trabajadores (Free Federation of Workers)
FPT	Federación Puertorriqueña del Trabajo (Puerto Rican Federation of Labor)
HT	Hermandad de Trabajadores (Brotherhood of Workers)
JIRT	Junta Insular de Relaciones del Trabajo (Insular Labor Relations Board)
JSM	Junta de Salario Mínimo (Minimum Wage Board)
MIS	Movimiento de Izquierdas Sociales (Social Left Movement)
NIRA	National Industrial Recovery Act
NLRB	National Labor Relations Board
PCP	Partido Comunista Puertorriqueño (Puerto Rican Communist Party)
PPD	Partido Popular Democrático (Popular Democratic Party)
PRERA	Puerto Rico Emergency Relief Administration
PRGC	Puerto Rico Glass Corporation

PRIDCO	Puerto Rico Industrial Development Company (Compañía de Fomento Industrial de Puerto Rico)
PRPC	Puerto Rican Policy Commission
PRPPC	Puerto Rico Paper and Pulp Corporation
PRRA	Puerto Rico Reconstruction Administration
SEFRA	Sindicato de Empleados de Fomento y Ramas Anexas (Employees' Union of PRIDCO and its Annexes)
UEIC	Unión de Empleados de la Industria de Cristal (Employees' Union of the Glass Industry)
UGT	Unidad General de Trabajadores (General Union of Workers)
UIP	Unión de la Industria del Papel (Union of the Paper Industry)
UPD	Unión Protectora de Desempleados (Unemployed's Protective Union)

A STAGE FOR IMAGINING CONSENT: COLONIAL POLITICS AND U.S. POLICIES OF REFORM

I have been listening to the folk-songs of the poorest people in this country. They are the best expression of what they want. From the songs I derive three things: 1st. That love is equal in degree, if not in opportunity, regardless of economic suffering; 2nd. That inventing great lies about the world, (if a boat-load of chickens sinks in the sea, fishermen will fish eggs for many years) is an spiritual comfort here; 3rd. *That loyalty to personal leaders is the way of salvation among a very poor and harassed population.* Knowing these things, there is nothing more deeply honest than to make a program that will for the first time touch the roots of human feeling through political activity. It is not the economic man or the Marxian man that you are thus expressing, but the dreaming and poetic man, which includes economics, including Marx's. In fact, if I can get this across, I can win against all the money in the world. I want to try.[1] (emphasis added)

—Luis Muñoz Marín, 1936

At the height of social unrest and economic turmoil in Puerto Rico during the 1930s, Luis Muñoz Marín, the leader who eventually formed the "Partido Popular Democrático" (PPD), had time to ponder his political future. The words above expressed by Muñoz in a private letter to Ruby A. Black, his main lobbyist in Washington, D.C., came at a time when the collective patience of Puerto Ricans and the political aspirations of local leaders had been duly tested by the unsuccessful attempt at reform of colonial authorities. Besides expressing a romantic view of the Puerto Rican masses, the words of Muñoz revealed the enthusiasm of Latin American leaders about the possibility of a new avenue of political action to address socioeconomic maladies: to build and reaffirm a special bond with agents other than the elite that could allow constructive exchanges as well as delimit the extent of cooperation. Muñoz's perception of loyalty tells us not only about the role he assigned to himself as a leader but also about the rise of popular groups as major political actors that the elite could no longer ignore. Like other leaders of Latin

America, Muñoz fixed his thoughts on what would become the core of political consent among agents of mass politics, that is, an inexact agreement based on pledges of loyalty that would serve as a modus operandi between many groups demanding socioeconomic improvements.

The aspiration of Latin American leaders for a common understanding with nonelite groups, which entailed acknowledging their grievances and embracing them as legitimate political agents, often faced an adverse political reality in the 1930s. During the Great Depression, many among the elite in Latin America concerned about securing agricultural exports in an unstable world economy feared the consequences of including popular groups as participants in their country's political arena.[2] At best, the governments of many countries had trouble reconciling economic interests with the needs of people. Although political authorities in Latin America expressed reluctance to accommodate marginal sectors, ascendant leaders aspiring for power had few qualms about experimenting with social and economic reform to gain mass support.[3] In Puerto Rico, as elsewhere, the initiative of leaders to introduce policies of reform as a way to mobilize followers confronted political inertia and opposition.

In this chapter, I seek to understand the political project of an ascendant group of reformist leaders who tried to address socioeconomic grievances by supporting U.S. policies of reform. On the one hand, my aim is to grasp the conditions that led to broad discontent against the island's colonial order during the Great Depression. On the other hand, I want to examine the haphazard negotiation between local reformers and U.S. authorities to implement the New Deal program in Puerto Rico. Notwithstanding from what end of the political spectrum agents acted during the 1930s, all of them faced the breakdown of the island's colonial order and the steady proliferation of social conflict. The extensive and highly volatile dislocation that Puerto Ricans confronted during the economic depression exemplifies the Gramscian concept of an "organic crisis." This sort of dislocation is ample and indiscriminate, making unsustainable many institutions and practices that underpin the stability of society. According to Laclau and Mouffe, an "organic crisis" can be best under-stood as follows:

A conjuncture where there is a generalized weakening of the relational system defining the identities of a given social or political space, and where, as a result there is a proliferation of floating elements, is what we will call following Gramsci, a conjuncture of *organic crisis*. It does not emerge from a single point, but it is the result of an overdetermination of circumstances; and it reveals itself not only in a proliferation of antagonism but also in a generalized crisis of social identities.[4]

Although no facet of an "organic crisis" predetermines which agents and discourse will prevail over others, it is also true that political outcomes are not entirely the result of random events. Due to the uneven effect of the "organic crisis," people operated within a field of political forces that gave an advantage to certain articulatory practices in Puerto Rico: the engagement between agents in favor of the reform policies of the New Deal. While Puerto Ricans increasingly condemned the island's plight and became receptive to political alternatives, the advocates of the New Deal in Puerto Rico deployed a discourse that promised people an innovative framework to address their problems. By focusing on the response of political authorities toward the grievances of people, I trace the process of trial and error that led Muñoz and his supporters to conceive, modify, and fine-tune a project to usher in new political conditions. The discussion of what I call "a stage for imagining consent" sheds light on the increasing awareness of Muñoz and his peers about the Puerto Rican masses as a powerful source of political action. Far from seeing Muñoz as an agent who single-handedly discovered the basis for a discourse of consent, I consider how the pressure "from below" and the unsuccessful reforms "from above" led Muñoz to differentiate himself from other politicians as the champion of the downtrodden. Despite the increasing popularity that set apart leaders such as Muñoz in the 1930s, the discourse of consent owed much to the uneven incorporation of principles coming from various quarters of society.

This chapter examines the background of political consent and its discourse in Puerto Rico from three different angles. An understanding of the process that led toward a discourse of consent demands an examination of familiar approaches to mass politics in Latin America. After focusing on the historiography about the PPD that has reached an analytical impasse, I suggest new avenues of interpretation to explore the discourse of consent in Puerto Rico and elsewhere. In the second part of the chapter, I discuss the conditions caused by the Great Depression that left political leadership in Puerto Rico up for grabs. At the height of the economic crisis the collaboration between U.S. New Dealers and local advocates of reform began to emerge as a sound political alternative to the constant debate about the status issue in Puerto Rico. The final part of this chapter discusses the involvement of Muñoz and his adherents in the local program of the New Deal. Besides highlighting how the New Deal served to mobilize local reformers, I discuss the reverses that led Muñoz to shift his gaze toward the Puerto Rican masses as the main basis for a discourse of consent in Puerto Rico. My analysis comes full circle to the quote transcribed above by considering the motives of Muñoz and his peers in founding the PPD, the self-proclaimed "Party of the Poor."[5]

HISTORIOGRAPHICAL CONCERNS

The historiography that deals with mass politics in Puerto Rico provides two main perspectives about this topic. One of them consists of testimonies and accounts about the PPD written by leaders and followers of the party. This perspective presents the PPD as the main force behind social reform and economic progress in Puerto Rico. PPD leaders, moreover, appear as defenders of nationalist values and political sovereignty. Those who favor this view agree that the legacy of the PPD is one of triumph due to the commitment of its leadership. Luis Muñoz Marín's publications about the PPD are one of the contributions that stand out.[6] The biographies of Muñoz written by Lieban Córdova and Carmelo Rosario Natal supplement the views of the leader.[7] For Córdova, who was Muñoz's personal secretary, the sacrifice of a selected group of individuals accounts for the PPD's success in breaking with corruption and abuses from the past. The works of Antonio Fernós Isern and José Trías Monge present a similar view but from a different angle, emphasizing the efforts of the PPD to revamp the government and create better institutions.[8]

Several scholars avoid the previous interpretation by focusing on economic and social factors that explain the rise of mass politics in the form of populism.[9] With their emphasis on class analysis, authors such as Angel G. Quintero Rivera, Emilio González Díaz, and Juan José Baldrich examine the PPD by paying more attention to economic structures and social struggles than to the endeavors of party leaders. Quintero and González, for example, explain that the PPD was the result of the overwhelming social displacement caused by U.S. "imperialist capitalism." The decline of the coffee *hacienda* system and the rise of the sugar plantation economy under U.S. policies produced impoverishment in Puerto Rico. Many groups affected by this situation joined the PPD to overcome the effects of colonial rule. Quintero, in particular, does not present PPD leaders as a full-fledged upper class or bourgeoisie but as the progeny of disfranchised *hacendados* and as a "sector-of-professionals-becoming-a-class."[10] He argues that the PPD's "populist anti-imperialism" embodied national aspirations to break or at least loosen the ties of colonialism. Emilio Pantojas García also focuses on the island's socioeconomic transformation to grasp the rise of the PPD, but he reaches a different conclusion. He argues that the PPD was an alliance between a "fraction of the colonial power bloc" and U.S. agents interested in restructuring "imperialist capitalism," concluding that the PPD was largely the product of U.S. designs and that its foundation explains the continuance of Puerto Rico's colonial dependence.[11]

The works of Quintero, González, and Pantojas leave a researcher with certain problems in the analysis of the PPD. On the one hand, Quintero and González's argument, that the PPD represented an effort against colonial rule, fails to explain the continuance of Puerto Rico's integration to the United States under the aegis of Muñoz's party. On the other hand, if one argues with Pantojas that the PPD was just an extension of U.S. schemes to tighten the ties of dependency, it is difficult to explain how the PPD became a broad coalition of interests at a time when U.S. colonial rule in Puerto Rico was, to a considerable degree, discredited.

The different paths of analysis that Quintero, González, and Pantojas offer entail more than a discrepancy about the political leaning of Muñoz's party. That is, besides the issue of whether PPD leaders upheld nationalist aims or sold out to U.S. interests, these authors bring to the fore important, yet dissimilar, processes that informed the island's populist movement. Quintero, for example, extensively focuses on economic changes that set new patterns of working-class organization to understand the nature of Muñoz's party.[12] He highlights the aims and initiatives of workers who supported the PPD. Unlike Quintero and González, Pantojas gears his attention to the introduction of the New Deal to Puerto Rico. According to Pantojas, the New Deal gave a different spin to Puerto Rico's populism as compared to other cases in Latin America. The island's populist movement, Pantojas argues, "articulated the interest not of a local bourgeoisie in formation but of an imperialist bourgeoisie."[13] Although framed differently, the analyses of Quintero, González, and Pantojas should not be dismissed as altogether incompatible. Their insights suggest that the best avenue of interpretation is to explore how both the PPD's pledge to champion local values and the party's loyalty to U.S. interests shaped the island's populist movement. There is room to argue that these aspects intertwined as they informed the rise of mass politics in Puerto Rico.[14]

Neither the benevolence of populist leaders nor the demands of the capitalist system can effectively explain the mass movement headed by Muñoz and the PPD. I prefer a different approach to understand how PPD leaders and supporters informed the mobilization of people and gave shape to a discourse of consent.[15] My work banks on theories of discourse that offer innovative avenues of political analysis, particularly the neo-Gramscian notions of Ernesto Laclau, Chantal Mouffe, and other authors.[16] In contrast to the idea that people and societies embody transcendental patterns of meaning, Laclau and Mouffe argue that agents and contexts are constructed through the logic of articulation, which means "any practice establishing a relation among elements such that their identity is modified as a result of the articulatory practice."[17] What emerges from the articulatory practices of agents is called a discourse, a concept that Jacob Torfing defines as "a relational totality of signifying sequences that together constitute a more or less coherent framework for what can be said and done."[18] Since articulatory practices produce discourses in a given context, Laclau and Mouffe argue that the outcome of these practices cannot escape power relations and historical contingencies. In other words, the way a discourse emerges, competes with others, and becomes dominant is the effect of hegemony. This "type of political relation"[19] entails a plurality of agents and views as well as the disparities between them. A hegemonic process, according to Torfing, refers to "the expansion of a discourse, or set of discourses, into a dominant horizon of social orientation and action by means of articulating unfixed elements into partially fixed moments in a context crisscrossed by antagonistic forces."[20]

Following the insights of neo-Gramscian analysis, my notion of consent rejects the idea of a power-free process that enabled people to candidly identify and choose what seemed to be the best political leaders at hand. Nor do I explain the concept of consent by referring exclusively to economic forces, political manipulation, or social control. Rather, my notion of consent refers to a discourse. As the expression of an agreement about the need for reform, the discourse of consent owes its origin to a fluid ground of interaction in which agents engaged each other to herald their views about urgent issues. The articulatory practices that gave shape to the discourse of consent also account for the shifts it suffered over time. Since agents pursued their individual and collective interests in a context that never failed to introduce new forms of contestation, the discourse of consent was reconstituted over and over again according to the effects of power relations. Understood as a "partial fixation of meaning" far from immutable or predetermined, the discourse of consent must be grasped according to the island's struggle for hegemony, that is, the process that pitted different agents and discourses against each other not only to address the island's "organic crisis" but also to refashion colonial politics. Due to the competition between many agents, new forms of identities, political practices, and discourses took shape. As the successful outcome of a hegemonic process, the discourse of consent represented less a "precarious equilibrium of a negotiated agreement" and more "a stronger type of communitarian unity" among people.[21]

By keeping in mind the combined, yet uneven, influence that agents had on colonial politics, one can grasp the ascendance of certain leaders, even though the discourse of consent that gradually took shape incorporated principles from various political traditions. In terms of the leadership, my argument is that the core of the PPD consisted of a reformist sector that had the knowledge and disposition to work alongside U.S. officials. This sector was well acquainted not only with the intricacies of U.S. bureaucracy but also with the cultural values of American society. On the one hand, the experience of Puerto Rican reformers with U.S. culture and their knowledge of the island's society enabled them to act as representatives of a broad coalition of interests. This advantage, in turn, informed the PPD's conversion into a "moral-intellectual leadership"—a Gramscian term that refers to a group that, through a hegemonic process, has managed to embody a range of concerns beyond their own. On the other hand, although PPD officials played a key role in mobilizing people, they could offer a degree of cohesion to the island's mass movement and its discourse only after extensive negotiations with multiple agents. The discourse of consent owes its origin not to a single group or factor but to its "regularity in dispersion."[22] As the common theme of a multivocal constituency, the discourse of consent refers to a "decentered" site of political engagement.

My effort to understand consent as a discourse joins recent theoretical inter-ventions to revitalize the study of politics in Latin America.[23] Besides overcoming the limitations of "modernization theory" and world-system frameworks, the challenge for scholars is to avoid models that see only "domination and resistance, exploiters and victims."[24] An interpretation based on "new theories of discourse"[25] can account not only for oppression and opposition but also for forms of interaction and agency that do not fit neatly in one of the former categories. In this vein my notion of consent takes into account the uneven access to political power that mass mobilization entails, yet leaves room to grasp how leaders and followers shaped a new political discourse. As an interpretation that avoids a unilateral emphasis on the designs of political leaders and foreign interests, my perspective is similar to other recent analyses about politics in Latin America. Whether the focus is on the "contact zones"[26] of U.S. imperialism or "critical junctures"[27] of regime dynamics in Latin America, my notion of consent corresponds with theories that highlight multifaceted processes of political interaction. While conflict, contestation, and antagonism repeatedly unsettled colonial politics in Puerto Rico, the discourse of consent ushered in a fluid zone of interaction and an elasticity of meaning that allowed people to reach an agreement. By examining the exchange, dialogue, dispute, and contestation among agents that shaped the discourse of consent, one can improve the understanding of mass politics in Latin America.

My research takes issue with interpretations about populism in Latin America, a form of mass politics that pertains to my study of consent. Discourse analysis has helped to examine how populist movements construct new meanings, identities, and representations.[28] Scholars who focus on labor and popular groups have contributed to overcome perspectives that see populism as a form of elite manipulation and social control over people.[29] Although these advances cannot be easily dismissed, the notion of populism still suffers from the theoretical flaws that have eroded its usefulness.[30] A familiar problem is the ambiguity that shrouds the concept of populism. By becoming too malleable, populism makes reference to very different realities and may not account for all the voices of the movement. Another common problem is that the study of populism has become compartmentalized, embracing either a "top down" or "bottom up" approach to understand the dynamic nature of this type of mass politics.[31] In this respect, the notion of populism runs the peril of presenting self-enclosed arenas of action. To avoid these drawbacks, I prefer to focus on fluid zones of interaction where agents approach, negotiate, and agree with each other to introduce policies for their own benefits. An analysis of the elusive exchanges between agents that manage to inform a discourse of consent can shed light on aspects that are part of either a populist movement or other form of mass politics. As the expression of a multivocal political reality, the discourse of consent accounts for both a common understanding between leaders and followers of mass politics as well as the capacity of agents to make demands of their own and shape the outcome of events.

Although not framed as a debate about the theory of populism, the disagreement between Robert W. Anderson and Quintero about the degree of authority within the PPD is a good example of the analytical difficulties to understand mass politics in Latin America.[32] While Anderson stresses that Muñoz and other leaders maintained strict control of the PPD's political machinery, Quintero argues that PPD officials at the lower echelons of the party's hierarchy had room to maneuver.[33] That is, according to these perspectives, either the PPD's chain of command did not allow deviations or, on the contrary, local leaders managed certain affairs and influenced the decisions of Muñoz. Although the findings of Quintero are noteworthy, I believe the topic of political authority of PPD leaders can be approached from a different angle. Instead of focusing on the capacity of top leaders to direct the PPD or the autonomy of lower officials to make decisions of their own, my work examines the blurred boundaries that enabled people to reach a common understanding without shedding particular interests, perceptions, and goals. Shifting the focus to the diffused terrain of interaction between the PPD and multiple agents can shed light on the overlap of interests that informed the discourse of consent. Moreover, this approach can account for disparate agendas within the PPD without just seeing them as a problem of authority. With these thoughts in mind, the rest of this chapter examines the conditions that predisposed popular groups and colonial reformers to approach each other and reach an agreement to secure U.S. policies of reform.

THE QUANDARY OF COLONIAL POLITICS

In spite of the immediate impact of the Great Depression, Puerto Rico faced a turning point during the 1930s as a result of a long-term transformation at many levels of the island's society. The United States began to refashion its colonial policies toward Puerto Rico. Moreover, as the island coped with a broad realignment of political parties, new social groups entered the political scene as vigorous advocates of reform. Although these changes had a profound effect by themselves, they combined with the Great Depression to produce an explosive situation on the island. The world crisis not only made clear the severity of economic, political, and social conditions in Puerto Rico but also highlighted the urgent need to address them. Due to the pervasive and extremely unstable nature of the island's dislocation, Puerto Rico faced during the 1930s what can be best understood as an "organic crisis." This sort of dislocation meant for Puerto Rico the steady erosion of the colonial order and new forms of antagonism that wreaked havoc on all aspects of life. While the "organic crisis" weakened prevailing institutions and practices together with their capacity to define people's place in the colonial order, the island became a stage for imagining a discourse that did not hinge on any specific past experience. That is, Puerto Rico experienced a proliferation of alternatives to articulate a different political logic. The discontent of people and the crisis of political leadership in the 1930s are the focus of this part of the chapter. These conditions set the stage for the intervention of colonial reformers, even though they soon realized that their own initiative would not be enough to address the crisis.

Puerto Rico already had economic difficulties when the Great Depression struck in full force during the 1930s. Monocultural sugar production became the main model of economic growth during three decades of U.S. control of the island. While the sugar corporations were highly vulnerable to world market fluctuations, workers suffered from seasonal employment, low pay, and harsh working conditions. After the start of the Great Depression, the situation on the island deteriorated rapidly. Income levels dropped or could not keep up with rising inflation. According to James Dietz, "by 1933, per capita income was nearly 30 percent below what it had been in 1930," and "when changes in purchasing power are considered, the decline is even greater."[34] The standard of living of the majority of Puerto Ricans worsened as the price of basic necessities increased relative to wages. Besides the disparity between incomes and prices, the economic crisis became most evident with the unprecedented level of unemployment. At the height of the Great Depression unemployment surpassed 60 percent of the population.[35] As if people had not had enough with the downturn of the economy, they struggled to survive in the aftermath of two devastating hurricanes, San Felipe in 1928 and San Ciprián in 1932.[36] Both hurricanes left a high toll of deaths and damages on the island.

Other key sectors of production in Puerto Rico, besides the sugar industry, responded to the world crisis with little success. Since the economic slump came on the heels of adverse consumption patterns for the tobacco industry, the producers of this crop had little option but to phase out their operations on the island.[37]

Meanwhile, coffee producers entered the depression era already burdened by U.S. tariff laws that did not protect this crop from foreign competition in the consumer market of the mainland.[38] During the 1930s, the coffee industry reduced its production to a minimum and did not vanish altogether thanks to its precarious foothold in the local market.[39] Workers on the island suffered the brunt of economic collapse. They not only saw a reduction of wages and unemployment but also confronted malnutrition, starvation, and deteriorating health conditions.[40]

Although the needlework industry was one of the few trades that experienced an expansion in the 1930s, its labor force did not fare much better than workers in other sectors of the Puerto Rican economy. On the contrary, the fact that women filled the shopfloors of the needlework industry but consistently earned lower incomes than male workers on the island exemplifies the harsh reality that this sector of the labor force had to face.[41] In particular, women employed in domestic needlework production—about a third of working women on the island—earned the lowest wage among all workers, faced many abuses from subcontractors, and found it hard to unionize due to their isolation at home.[42] The combined effect of the economic depression and social maladies in Puerto Rico laid the base for broad protest against the colonial order during the 1930s. Besides work stoppages, labor strikes, and mass demonstrations, the island experienced popular discontent in the form of melees, riots, vandalism, and boycotts of utility bills.[43] The rise of nationalist sentiment in Puerto Rico added a political voice to the unrest of people. Many on the island increasingly questioned the legitimacy of U.S. colonial rule.[44]

Although the island's situation sent clear signals about the need for reform, Puerto Rico's political parties offered little promise of providing a leadership capable of addressing basic social and economic issues. The lack of effective leadership was partly due to a colonial form of government that gave the island's political parties a secondary role by limiting their access to power. The contradiction of U.S. efforts to "modernize" Puerto Rico with democratic institutions and its interest in keeping the island under control resulted in a colonial state in which key functions of government remained beyond the reach of Puerto Ricans. For example, the higher offices were subject not to popular vote but to the appointments of the U.S. president.[45] Although Puerto Ricans could exercise a measure of control over local affairs as members of the legislature and through lower governmental posts open to them, U.S. authorities denied the island participation in crucial policy-making processes. The colonial state placed severe limits on U.S. efforts to legitimate the values of democracy and representative government in Puerto Rico. The fact that many appointments of top officials on the island were made as paybacks for political favors undermined even further the legitimacy of the colonial administration.[46]

To explain the lack of effective leadership in Puerto Rico during the 1930s, one can place blame as much on the imposition of an inadequate colonial structure as on the constant debate among Puerto Rican leaders about the island's political future. Although U.S. colonial rule stirred problems by alienating local interests aspiring for power, political difficulties also came from a sector of the elite that had little to gain from the island's economic integration to the mainland.[47] Those who failed to benefit from U.S. policies, such as coffee producers and small landowners, opted for political accommodation or retrenchment.[48] Moreover, while U.S. policies meant advantages for workers, such as the right to organize into unions, the elite resented changes that made labor no longer an element of *la familia puertorriqueña*, the belief that all Puerto Ricans formed one great family under upper-class tutelage.[49] At the other extreme of the political divide, one can find local interests that pressured federal authorities to fully integrate Puerto Rico into the United States. This group consisted of beneficiaries of U.S. policies such as labor, public officials, and agents linked to the sugar industry.[50]

While the partial exclusion of Puerto Ricans from the colonial state hindered the effectiveness of political debate, the relentless effort of the island's leadership to find a solution to the status question displaced many other issues to the sidelines of public life. Although party leaders did address concerns other than the status issue, the latter became not only a vital feature for the internal cohesion of the island's parties but also a basis of political competition. The combination of an inadequate colonial structure and the relentless, yet futile, debate about the status had adverse consequences for Puerto Rico. Party leaders saw the government mainly as a purveyor of political patronage. Since the colonial state served U.S. interests with a thin veil of legitimacy, the island's leaders failed to see the government as more than a means for their own benefit. Meanwhile, the status issue drained time, effort, and talent that could have been better spent addressing the more urgent needs of Puerto Ricans. Debate about the political future of Puerto Rico undermined the concerns of the island's constituencies and made political parties focus on the narrow interests of their top officials.

Indicative of this situation is the fragmentation of political parties that took place in Puerto Rico during the 1920s and most of the 1930s. A series of alliances and counteralliances between disparate political factions jockeyed for an electoral majority during these years. Those who achieved a majority could then distribute among themselves governmental positions and privileges. The 1924 election saw the victory of the Puerto Rican Alliance—Alianza Puertorriqueña—a merger of the Union Party and a faction of the Republican Party. The Puerto Rican Alliance came about as an effort of elite groups to outmatch the growing strength of the Socialist Party, the political arm of the island's labor movement.[51] When the Puerto Rican Alliance won the election of 1928 by a thin margin, a dissatisfied group of leaders renounced the merger to form the Liberal Party. In 1932, after two unsuccessful electoral runs during the previous decade, a political fusion called the Coalition—La Coalición—took hold of office. The Coalition, which began as a maneuver to compete against the Puerto Rican Alliance, defeated its main opponent, the Liberal Party, in the elections of 1932 and 1936.[52]

The Coalition consisted of a bizarre pact between the Republican Party, the representative of sugar producers, and the Socialist Party, the representative of sugar workers. While Socialists joined the Coalition in a genuine effort to further the goals of labor,[53] Republicans saw the merger as a way to overpower the other parties of the island's elite.[54] The interest in political patronage informed the compromise between Socialists and Republicans. According to the preelection pact of the Coalition, the Socialist Party had the right to name its own candidates for certain positions such as the resident commissioner while the Republican Party reserved for itself other positions such as the president of the insular Senate.[55] Besides being a marriage of convenience, the Coalition can be partly explained when one considers the common aim of Socialists and Republicans to integrate Puerto Rico into the United States.[56] Both factions saw statehood as the best alternative for Puerto Rico. On the one hand, the status issue provided a source of cohesion for the Coalition vis-á-vis its political opponents. On the other hand, the alliances and counteralliances that set the rules of political competition in Puerto Rico helped to portray as an acceptable practice the Coalition's distribution of governmental posts.

While the sterile debate about the status and the parties' fixation on patronage made headway at the higher levels of government, Puerto Ricans suffered the deterioration of the island's political system. Since the colonial state seemed hardly more than a source of privileges in an era of increasing economic hardship, people used drastic means to win elections during the 1930s. For example, the electoral campaign of 1932 saw widespread violence throughout Puerto Rico. According to Ronald Fernández, "the Coalition . . . literally battled the proindependence Liberal Party."[57] One of the motives for this conflict was accusations of fraudulent registrations of voters. Several towns of the island, such as Vega Alta, Vega Baja, and Ciales, witnessed brawls, riots, and acts of disobedience against authorities.[58] In one of these riots, the police had little success in subduing Liberals throwing rocks at their opponents. The melee that ensued left three people dead. Fernández mentions that "Liberals, Republicans, and Socialists routinely used firearms, sticks, stones, and knives as a means of political persuasion."[59] The violence that tinged local politics comes as no surprise when one considers the level of political corruption during the 1930s. Deceitful electoral tactics were common such as quartering people in the so-called *corrales* (makeshift jamboree rooms) to keep them from voting, buying and selling votes, misinforming voters, and sabotaging the electoral process. Moreover, an ineffective electoral law gave an unfair advantage to parties that had a majority of votes.[60]

Ordinary people had the hardest time with the island's political situation during the 1930s. Puerto Rico had a political system that excluded them from effective means of improving their lives. Voters had value insofar as they contributed numerically to political parties in pursuit of patronage. Achieving a majority enabled a party to pressure federal authorities in favor of its demands, but this did not translate into a recognition of followers' right to political participation or real public representation. Political practices in Puerto Rico left supporters at the sidelines of public debate while party representatives engaged in discussions that failed to voice the day-to-day grievances of people. Constituencies had little input in policy-making processes at the hands of leaders who enshrouded themselves with fancy rhetoric about the status. Worst of all, the politics of alliances and counteralliances on the island recruited party followers as accomplices of a corrupt system. A good example is the contest carried out in 1940 by the newspapers *La Correspondencia* and *El Imparcial*, which offered a prize for the best account of a violation of election rules and regulations.[61] People came forward with stories about past elections that ranged from simple tactics such as stealing or invalidating ballots to complex schemes of husbands against wives to keep them from voting.[62] Practices like these shaped people's attitudes toward political leaders and the government.

The constant debate about the status question and the fight over patronage undermined the relationship between party leaders and their constituencies. In particular, the Socialist Party fell victim to the deterioration of political life in Puerto Rico during the 1930s. The past successes of the Socialist Party made its downfall lamentable. Workers had founded the party in a genuine effort to defend the rights of labor.[63] The formation of the Coalition initially responded to the aim of Socialists to improve the prolabor leverage of the party within the government.[64] However, after joining the Republicans for a third time to win the election of 1932, Socialist leaders began to distance themselves from their followers. The Socialist Party suffered as much from constant compromises with the Republicans as from leaders willing to accommodate themselves to bureaucratic positions. The initiatives of Socialists to enforce protective labor legislation failed when they came into conflict with sugar interests represented by the Republicans.[65]

The decline of the Socialist Party dragged along the island's main labor union, the Free Federation of Workers—Federación Libre de Trabajadores (FLT). As closely bound allies, both organizations suffered drawbacks that did not become fully apparent until 1933-1934. Tired of harsh conditions brought by the depression and disheartened by the inability of the Socialist Party to help them, workers took matters into their own hands. During 1933, an increase in strike activities undermined the stance of the Socialist Party and the FLT in favor of industrial peace.[66] In 1934, a dramatic strike in the sugar industry shook the island despite the lack of support from Socialist and FLT leaders. This strike is considered by many historians as a turning point in the history of Puerto Rico's labor movement.[67]

The immediate reason for the sugar strike of 1934 was an islandwide contract reached between the FLT and the Sugar Producers' Association—Asociación de Productores de Azúcar (APA)—that shortchanged workers to a considerable extent. The contract lowered wages and failed to address many grievances of workers such as company stores and long working hours.[68] This provoked spontaneous strikes by the rank and file of the FLT throughout the island. The FLT and the Socialist Party showed reluctance to join the protest. When the strike continued to grow, Socialist leaders began to defend the contract and to undermine the demands of workers.[69] This took place even when a member of the Socialist Party, Prudencio Rivera Martínez, headed the Department of Labor. It did not take a long time for the government to intervene in the strike. When it did, workers faced police repression and protection for strikebreakers.[70]

During the strike, labor had to confront the combined opposition of sugar companies, the government, and their own labor organizations. To abate the odds against them, workers invited the radical Nationalist leader, Pedro Albizu Campos, to join the strike. Workers from the town of Guayama sent a cable to Albizu expressing their willingness to have him as leader of the labor movement.[71] Albizu did not reject the offer and went to Guayama, where he spoke to a mass gathering of workers. During the next weeks, Nationalists addressed labor audiences in many other towns of the island.[72] These activities brought forth the creation of the well-intended, but ill-conceived, Association of Puerto Rican Workers—Asociación de Trabajadores de Puerto Rico—which was meant to replace the FLT. After a few weeks of activities, this organization fell apart.[73] In the end, the efforts of labor and Nationalists to form a united front did not succeed. The aim of Nationalists to become a republic did not correspond with the goal of workers to solve their immediate economic grievances.[74] Despite the unsuccessful effort of Nationalists to offer political leadership to labor, Albizu and his supporters remained militant contenders against the island's colonial order in years to come.

The sugar strike of 1934 also saw the intervention of a dissident group of workers who called themselves Socialist Affirmation—Afirmación Socialista. This organization did more than protest against the unfair contract signed by the FLT. Socialist Affirmation criticized the Coalition and the politics of patronage in an effort to address the decline of the Socialist Party.[75] At first, the leaders of Socialist Affirmation did not consider the replacement of the party as a viable solution. For them, the Socialist Party and the FLT could still function as effective representatives of workers. To correct the problems of these organizations, Socialist Affirmation called for changes to reaffirm the original prolabor stance of the Socialist Party. For example, Socialist Affirmation proposed the dismissal of party members who no longer seemed to represent the interests of workers.[76] When this plan failed, Socialist Affirmation began a campaign in 1935 to become an official party. This organizational effort entailed the creation of a new labor union to replace the FLT and the publication of a newspaper called *La Defensa del Pueblo*. Despite this challenge, the well-entrenched Socialist Party kept the upper hand.[77]

Finally, the sugar strike of 1934 informed the mobilization of Communists. Although Communist intervention in the labor movement remained indirect during the early 1930s, the organization of this group gained momentum after the labor conflict of 1934.[78] Communists acknowledged the significance of the Socialist Party for labor and the value of the FLT as a powerful union while these organizations remained true to the interests of workers.[79] When the deterioration of the Socialist Party became evident, Communists not only made a critique similar to that of Socialist Affirmation but formed their own party a couple of months after the sugar strike of 1934.[80] The Puerto Rican Communist Party—Partido Comunista Puertorriqueño (PCP)—drew support from the ranks of Socialists and Nationalists when it was officially and strategically founded on September 23, the memorial day of *El Grito de Lares*—the island's main separatist uprising in the nineteenth century.[81]

Although the PCP displayed genuine impetus as an advocate of workers, the party did not offer a well-organized network to direct the labor movement. Shortly after the formation of the PCP, a conflict between its founders weakened the party.[82]

Moreover, the political tactics of the PCP kept the party small. Communists opted not to rival the Socialist Party or the FLT.[83] Instead of garnering mass support, the PCP geared its effort toward producing a revolution on the island. That is, Communists called for the militancy of a small group of leaders to incite into action popular groups discontented with the colonial order. The party's "immediate end" was "the constitution of Puerto Rico into a Soviet Republic under the dictatorship of the proletariat."[84] The tactics of the PCP overestimated the disposition of Socialist workers to dismiss their party and union. Despite the initial setbacks of Communists, this group rethought its tactics and made a comeback in the late 1930s.[85]

The sugar strike of 1934 condensed in a single blow the pervasive impact of the island's "organic crisis." While the colonial order weakened and increasingly failed to offer itself as the only imaginable domain in the life of people, an islandwide labor conflict made evident a range of agents, agendas, and discourses eager to redefine political practices in Puerto Rico. That was the case with dissident Socialists, Nationalists, and Communists, even though their organizational drives came short of producing a broad political front. Besides these agents and their bold aims, other people took action despite having a less ambitious political project. Concerned about the island's plight, many groups mobilized themselves and embarked on their particular struggles. For example, women employed in the needlework industry took decisive steps to address their grievances. Several strikes in the needlework factories of the island exemplify the militancy of women workers during the 1930s. A similar determination became evident among women employed in home needlework production. According to historian Blanca G. Silvestrini, up to 3,000 home needleworkers formed the ranks of nine unions affiliated with the FLT in 1934.[86] In addition to these efforts, an organization called the Women's Labor Congress—Congreso Obrero de Mujeres—was formed to defend the interests of working women not just in the needlework industry but in other trades as well.[87]

While people did all they could to address their most urgent needs, the failure of colonial authorities to contain the crisis made conditions in Puerto Rico unbearable. One aspect of this situation consisted of an erosion of political leadership on the island. The constant push and pull in the contest for patronage shadowed or displaced the role of political parties as advocates of collective benefits. Leaders and parties that could not deliver at least the benefits of political patronage began to lose mass appeal. This happened to the Socialist Party, which was unable, due to Republican opposition, and disinclined, due to the lure of bureaucratic accommodation, to aid workers during the sugar strike of 1934. Despite the failure of Socialists to provide leadership, other groups such as dissident Socialists, Nationalists, and Communists did not have the prestige, organizational basis, or resources to offer an attractive alternative to workers. Meanwhile, other sectors of labor such as needleworkers had the immediate concern of securing the basic means for their livelihood.

The erosion of leadership that permeated Puerto Rico's political life became evident not only during events of social unrest such as the sugar strike of 1934. While socioeconomic problems interfered with the day-to-day affairs of people, the island's elite pondered the nature and fate of Puerto Rican society. Not for few reasons, Puerto Rico experienced the height of cultural nationalism during the 1930s.[88] As conditions worsened on the island, Puerto Ricans looked to bygone traditions and values for answers. Discussions in the intellectual circles of the elite exalted the Spanish heritage of Puerto Rico in an effort to find comfort in the past.[89] Although the elite praised Spanish customs, leading Puerto Rican scholars presented a very pessimistic portrayal of the island.

For example, Antonio S. Pedreira published a book titled *Insularismo* in 1934, an influential essay that sought to define the "ethos" of the Puerto Rican people.[90] While Pedreira presented popular classes as immature and weak, he said the elite offered little hope for improvement. The young, moreover, appeared to be "a generation of invalids."[91] Although Pedreira made a harsh critique bordering on cultural and geographical determinism, he aimed at provoking a reaction in favor of change.[92] At the end of his essay, the author included a positive note when he called on the "literate youth" of the island to lead the way toward a better future.[93] As if awaiting the populist movement of later years, Pedreira insisted on leadership that could make room for all Puerto Ricans.[94] Vicente Géigel Polanco, an outspoken advocate of independence, wrote an essay with similar conclusions.[95] Géigel's sad description of the island's "passive," "dormant," and "indifferent" masses was offset only by his own call for new leadership to transform the Puerto Rican "multitudes" into a people ready for political action.[96]

Despite growing concerns about the crisis of Puerto Rican society, the island's political scene showed few signs of change after the strike of 1934. The Socialist Party reaffirmed its role as the representative of labor while making amends to sustain its partnership with the Republicans in the Coalition. The Liberal Party stayed out of the fray of the island's labor conflicts. Meanwhile, the rank and file of the labor movement returned to work after the failed attempts of dissident Socialists, Nationalists, and Communists to provide an effective leadership. The shortcomings of these groups, however, stressed a reality of Puerto Rico's political scene. There was open ground for other pretenders to claim legitimacy as political leaders. The final section of this chapter highlights the rise of a pretender in the person of Luis Muñoz Marín.

THE NEW DEAL IN PUERTO RICO

Although Puerto Rico stood at the outskirts of the mainland crisis, the island shared the need of the U.S. economy for immediate action. As the Great Depression progressed on the island and the continent, the federal government readied itself for ample reform after the electoral victory of the Democratic Party in 1932. Franklin D. Roosevelt's pledge of a "New Deal" offered hope on the mainland to millions of people.[97] The new policies and agencies introduced by Roosevelt after taking office in March 1933 stood at a distance from the timid measures of the previous administration.[98] In Puerto Rico, too, the extension of New Deal policies produced a sympathetic reaction among the people.[99] Numerous letters reached the U.S.

president expressing an interest in reform.[100] The favorable responses of the Puerto Rican people, however, did not translate into full support for Roosevelt's program or ease the way for its implementation. Despite the promise of the New Deal and the expressions of popular approval, the federal program faced a hostile political situation on the island.

Unlike the Democratic Party's clear-cut electoral victory on the mainland, conservative interests represented by the Coalition took hold of the legislature in Puerto Rico after the election of 1932.[101] When Robert Hayes Gore, the newly appointed governor, announced the local program of the New Deal, it soon became clear that its implementation would not be an easy task. Local politicians who had received the news of Roosevelt's victory with little enthusiasm met Gore's announcement with either indifference or opposition.[102] Economic interests within the Coalition, above all the sugar corporations, perceived the New Deal as a threat to their profits. Moreover, political parties saw the New Deal as another variable in their schemes to take hold of patronage.[103] Only a small sector of the island's elite could relate to the policies of the New Deal. This sector consisted of young reformers who had few or no ties to the sugar industry. No single organization represented these reformers, but their lack of political leverage within the Coalition made many of them join the Liberal Party.

Although amorphous as a political group, Puerto Rican reformers soon found their main representative and eventually their leader in the person of Luis Muñoz Marín. The background of Muñoz can help explain the inclination of Puerto Rican reformers toward New Deal policies. Born in San Juan in 1898, Muñoz was the son of Luis Muñoz Rivera, one of the foremost political figures in Puerto Rico at the turn of the century. Muñoz's father belonged to a prominent family of Barranquitas, helped the island win concessions from Spanish authorities, and served under the short-lived autonomist regime that Spain granted in 1897. During the first years of U.S. rule in Puerto Rico, the Muñoz family frequently traveled to the mainland on official business. Those visits soon gave way to residence. Muñoz moved to the United States when his father became resident commissioner in 1910. He attended high school in Washington, D.C., and continued with law school at Georgetown University. Muñoz alternated his studies with the work he did as assistant of the resident commissioner in 1915. After the death of his father a year later and without completing a law degree, Muñoz immersed himself in the literary circles of New York. During this period, he made his first contributions to several journals and newspapers such as *The Nation, New Republic, The American Mercury, The Smart Set*, and *Baltimore Sun*. He also took courses in journalism at Columbia University. Although Muñoz traveled frequently to Puerto Rico, he lived mostly in the United States. Muñoz started a family when he married Muna Lee in 1919. Only after 1931 did he move permanently to the island to take over the editorship of *La Democracia*, his father's newspaper.[104] Before long, Muñoz also became an active leader of the Liberal Party.

Muñoz's long stay in the United States is not unique. Other members of the island's reformist elite experienced a similar cultural and educational background to that of Muñoz. Consider Carlos Chardón, who was born in 1897, a few months before Muñoz. He completed his studies in agriculture at Cornell University in 1921. Before his appointment to direct the local program of the New Deal, Chardón gained experience as commissioner of agriculture and labor. Also born in 1897, Jesús T. Piñero became a close friend of Muñoz and top official of the New Deal not long after he completed his studies in the United States. He received his education in engineering at the University of Pennsylvania during the 1920s. Another example is Antonio Luchetti, a key member of the island's reconstruction plan. He completed his studies in civil engineering at Cornell University. Also a civil engineer, Roberto Sánchez Vilella completed his degree at Ohio State University in 1934 and, subsequently, served in federal and insular relief agencies. Benigno Fernández García became attorney general and a defender of reform after he completed a law degree at Georgetown University.[105]

Although not directly involved with the New Deal, many other individuals had an interest in reform. Born in 1897, Rafael J. Cordero worked as a highschool teacher, superintendent, and professor before completing his studies in economics at Columbia University. Another example is Rafael Picó, who was born in 1912 and studied geography at Clark University in Massachusetts. Besides teaching and writing after the completion of his degree, Picó acted as consultant to federal agencies. Latecomers who joined the retinue of local New Dealers after the 1930s also deserve attention. There are several cases, such as Teodoro Moscoso, a graduate of pharmacy and chemistry from the University of Michigan; Sol Luis Descartes, a graduate of agricultural economics from Cornell University; Antonio Fernós-Isern, a graduate physician from the University of Maryland; and Jaime Benítez, a law school graduate from Georgetown University and the University of Chicago. Although younger than the rest, Roberto de Jesús Toro, who was born in 1918, graduated in economics from the University of Pennsylvania.[106]

Professionals like these became strong advocates of the local program of the New Deal. Muñoz soon recognized the political potential of these professionals after he came back to Puerto Rico. He took steps to present himself as a spokesman and leader of their cause by transforming their inclinations toward reform into a political platform. The New Deal became for Muñoz not just a call for socioeconomic improvement but also an avenue to display local reformers as agents with a sound plan for political leadership and change. Although embracing the New Deal enabled Muñoz to differentiate himself and his peers from other political groups, the U.S. policies of reform had a profound effect by leading Muñoz and his supporters to focus less on the status issue and more on socioeconomic concerns as a political agenda for the future. Muñoz's intentions became apparent in a letter he sent to Mrs. Eleanor Roosevelt in December 1933. In a concise, but powerful statement, Muñoz spelled out a vision and project of reform that he and his followers would nurture as a vital part of their political discourse during the following years:

There is in Puerto Rico a generation that is coming to power in all political parties . . . that has been educated in the United States. It is familiar and deeply sympathetic with the best in American life . . . not 100% Americanism, of course. . . . It wants to fight hunger not with doles but with social justice, operating within an economy that shall be as far as possible planned and autonomous. It wants to break the strangle-hold of land monopoly and restore the soil to the people who work it. It wants to diversify crops, plant food, emancipate the people from the constant fatal threat of Congressional action on sugar. It wants to foster industrial development to help support our relatively enormous population. It wants to give dignity and purpose to political action.[107]

On the one hand, Muñoz's words stressed the dawn of a political project and discourse that conceived the New Deal as more than a policy to address mainland grievances. For Muñoz, the reconstruction plan of the United States could be adjusted to tackle economic problems in Puerto Rico that predated the Great Depression such as monocultural sugar production and the need of a better economy to address unemployment. On the other hand, Muñoz's statement appraised the potential of individuals whom he saw as agents of his call for "social justice." His notion of a generation "sympathetic with the best in American life" highlighted his exposure and that of others to the culture and values of the mainland society. Living and studying in the United States not only enabled a sector of the Puerto Rican elite to familiarize themselves with the workings of U.S. institutions but also provided an understanding of American liberal traditions outside a colonial context.

The contrast between democratic practices on the mainland and the political realities in Puerto Rico probably influenced the mind-set of individuals who studied abroad. An education on the mainland meant a firsthand experience of political processes in the United States as much as a reappraisal of the island's colonial situation. The experience of Puerto Rican trainees with U.S. culture and their knowledge of the island's society offered a degree of cultural hybridity that Muñoz and his peers exploited to their advantage in the following years. Individuals with a cultural grasp like that of Muñoz had the opportunity to negotiate with U.S. authorities and local constituencies as well as to keep distance from those who did not share a similar cultural background. Borrowing freely from Pierre Bourdieu, one can say that Puerto Rican graduates of mainland institutions enjoyed not only the assets of "cultural capital," meaning knowledge-based acquisitions, but also of "habitus," meaning a durable disposition to act in certain ways but without an exact obedience to rules.[108] These cultural assets partly account for the head start of Muñoz and his peers when the newly formed PPD intervened in the island's politics and engaged other groups to articulate a discourse of consent.

The historiography that deals with Muñoz and his peers has trouble interpreting the rise of this new generation of leaders in Puerto Rico. While some historians such as Carmelo Rosario Natal present Muñoz and his supporters as staunch advocates of local values,[109] other scholars such as Manuel Maldonado Denis present the founders of the PPD as sell outs subordinated to U.S. interests.[110] Besides being too partial in their defense or condemnation of Muñoz, these perspectives are one-sided in that they stress mostly institutional events and the status issue. By focusing on the diffused terrain of cultural and discursive practices that informed the life of Puerto Rican reformers, one can grasp the double bind that influenced their effort to become an effective political leadership.

The imbrication of forces that shaped the life of Puerto Rican reformers became most evident in how they maneuvered to insert themselves into a blurred arena of political action. While Muñoz and his peers gained a grasp of U.S. culture during their stay in the United States, they also embraced the cultural discourse of a new generation of scholars in Puerto Rico. Muñoz, for example, became acquainted with, and participated in, the activities of intellectuals such as Pedreira, Géigel Polanco, Luis Palés Matos, and Luis Lloréns Torres.[111] Scholars like these found themselves caught between a traditional intellectual order concerned about the island's heritage and their own effort to create a new milieu to ponder the inroads of modern life in Puerto Rico.[112] As political agents trying to negotiate a middle ground between a Puerto Rican society of old and a new one under the aegis of the United States, Muñoz and his peers sought to identify themselves with both the concerns of Puerto Rican intellectuals and the New Deal policies of reform. Muñoz's prestige as the son of a well-known politician and his grasp of U.S. values ushered him in as leader of a generation trying to make room for itself in the island's political arena.

By focusing on the permeability of cultural and discursive practices to understand the rise of a new generation of leaders in Puerto Rico, my work joins recent efforts to rethink political processes in Latin America.[113] New studies about politics and U.S.-Latin American relations avoid facile contrasts between local agents and foreign interests in an effort to grasp the fluid boundaries of interaction between them.[114] To understand the role of Muñoz and his peers in the construction of consent, it is best to examine the exchanges that diluted the differences between Puerto Rican reformers, U.S. authorities, and local constituencies. Particularly useful in grasping the actions of a new generation of leaders in Puerto Rico is the notion about the "internalization" of external forces in Latin America.[115] This refers less to how subordinated societies passively assimilate conditions imposed from abroad than to how agents "internalize" foreign influences for their own purposes. In Puerto Rico, the political project of local reformers offers an example of the "internalization" of outside elements such as the U.S. policies of the New Deal. A similar perspective can be reached with Néstor García Canclini's notion of "hybrid cultures."[116] According to this concept, intercultural practices do not consist of contacts between cultural essences but of "continuous processes of transculturation (two-way borrowing and lending between cultures)."[117] The notion of cultural hybridity can help grasp how Muñoz and his peers "borrowed" from the U.S. and local culture to conceive themselves as political leaders with a promising agenda for the future. With these cultural assets in hand, local reformers engaged U.S. authorities and the island's constituencies to become intermediaries of Puerto Rico's first New Deal.

Puerto Rico's First New Deal

Governmental action to implement the New Deal offered hope to people in Puerto Rico and the United States. During the opening months of the Roosevelt administration, the U.S. Congress wasted little time to address the economic crisis. The legislative session, which came to be called the "Hundred Days," enacted many important measures such as the Banking Act, the Civilian Conservation Corps, and the Agricultural Adjustment Act.[118] Of all the early New Deal policies, Puerto Rico benefited first from the Federal Emergency Relief Administration (FERA), an agency empowered to make grants to state authorities for relief and public works projects.[119] U.S. officials created the Puerto Rico Emergency Relief Administration (PRERA) to administer the FERA program on the island.[120] Although the extension of FERA to Puerto Rico confirmed Governor Gore's announcement of the New Deal, many problems hindered the start of the relief program. Several months elapsed before Gore and the legislature made arrangements to qualify for federal aid.[121] Moreover, a conflict over political appointments delayed the implementation of the PRERA.[122] Gore's lack of experience in local affairs made him hesitate on whom to nominate to his cabinet. Finally, as a governor in charge of resources to provide relief, he became the target of local interests.[123] Before long, his administration succumbed to the pressure of political parties vying for patronage. When Gore sided with the Coalition, a systematic attack by the Liberals ensued. This conflict prompted U.S. authorities to replace Gore with General Blanton Winship in the mid-1930s.[124]

After several months of bureaucratic inertia, U.S. authorities launched the PRERA to distribute federal aid. From the start, the PRERA faced a difficult situation. Administrative confusion over the assignments of funds for the agency slowed down the implementation of relief.[125] When the funds came, the PRERA did not receive enough money to meet local needs.[126] Political rivalries compounded the problems of the PRERA. According to the Coalition, the hiring policies of the PRERA favored the Liberal minority. Since they had won the last election, Coalitionists saw as their prerogative either to seek control of the PRERA or to hinder its operations.[127] Despite the apathy of conservative interests within the Coalition toward the New Deal, Coalitionists had reasons to accuse the PRERA of favoritism toward Liberals. When work began to staff the PRERA, Muñoz successfully lobbied for the Liberals after he gained access to the higher levels of the mainland bureaucracy. Ruby A. Black, an agent for *La Democracia* and other U.S. dailies, offered Muñoz an opportunity to meet President Roosevelt.[128] As a friend of Mrs. Eleanor Roosevelt, supporter of the New Deal, and correspondent for United Press, Black attended the White House to learn and report about the activities of the first lady.[129] In one of her visits to the White House, she took Muñoz to meet Mrs. Roosevelt and the president.[130] Besides his interview with Roosevelt, Muñoz's lobbying efforts in Washington, D.C., brought him close to key New Dealers such as Harry L. Hopkins, director of FERA, and Henry A. Wallace, the secretary of agriculture.[131]

Despite the administrative delay and the political rivalries that impaired the PRERA, the agency managed to provide relief. One of the first steps of the PRERA was to dispense direct aid to poor families on the island. At the height of its operations, the PRERA handled 50,000 cases.[132] In addition to direct relief, the agency engaged in public work projects. The PRERA built roads, established community gardens, advanced a malaria control program, distributed food, and opened needlework centers.[133] An aspect that stands out about the PRERA is that it offered an opportunity to train public officials on the island. The agency recruited students and graduates of social work at the University of Puerto Rico. According to Dietz, "a core of young professionals were trained in survey, census, and other techniques which were to be vitally important skills for future development."[134] Dietz concludes that "this training ground for Puerto Rico's own 'brain trust' was perhaps the PRERA's most enduring contribution to the island."[135] During its short existence, the PRERA completed several studies including a housing survey, a plan for industrial development, and a survey of destitute families.[136]

The relief measures of the PRERA abated local needs but fell short of solving the economic problems of the island. Puerto Rico's first New Deal agency suffered the same fate of many early reform policies of the Roosevelt administration.[137] Meant as an agency with limited regulatory functions to intervene in the island's economy, the PRERA could not enforce policies that could have been beneficial. Besides its similarity to the mainland New Deal, the PRERA lacked the resources to address the magnitude of Puerto Rico's economic crisis. Policymakers designed the PRERA to provide temporary aid and not as an effort to overhaul economic grievances that predated the Great Depression, such as the monocultural model of growth.[138] In addition, although the PRERA worked effectively after overcoming initial obstacles, administrative infighting and political contentions over the distribution of patronage affected the prestige of the agency.[139] The reaction of those whom the PRERA failed to reach became evident. For example, a group of unemployed workers from Mayagüez sent a letter to the federal authorities stating that "the Council of the Unemployed asks from the great American people work not dole to address our necessities. The PRERA in Puerto Rico rehabilitates those that needed it less and the people that need it are dying of hunger."[140]

Besides the PRERA, other early measures of the New Deal produced adverse reactions. The application of the National Industrial Recovery Act (NIRA) to Puerto Rico turned out to be a disappointment. Labor lost hope in the NIRA after a brief period of enthusiasm. Although the NIRA planned to regulate industries and assist workers, this promise never materialized. News about the extension of industrial codes to Puerto Rico prompted many businesses to increase production to avoid higher costs after the application of the regulations. In the long run, the NIRA approved only three codes to regulate industries in Puerto Rico.[141] Businesses sidestepped the effects of the NIRA by cutting back on labor.[142] Workers, such as those of the needlework industry, protested against this action with strikes, marches, and mass gatherings. Unemployed needleworkers from Mayagüez, for example, announced their grievances in the local press stating that "until now we have not received the benefit of the new policies of President Roosevelt."[143]

Puerto Rico's Second New Deal

Additional policies of reform for Puerto Rico came in the wake of what has been called the "Second New Deal" of the Roosevelt administration.[144] Debate about the limitations of the early policies of reform eventually produced New Deal measures such as the Wagner Act and Social Security Act. Signs of change in Puerto Rico came with the island's transfer from the War Department to the Interior early in 1934. Another event that signaled further reform was the visit of Mrs. Eleanor Roosevelt, Rexford G. Tugwell, and other key officials of the federal administration to the island in March 1934.[145] This visit opened the ground for local reformers to discuss the needs of Puerto Rico. In a hearing held in the capital, Carlos Chardón revealed an innovative proposal to rehabilitate the economy. The exchange of ideas that Chardón and other participants had with the mainland visitors turned out to be a success. The plan proposed by Chardón impressed U.S. officials.[146] Informed by his wife, Tugwell, and other sources, President Roosevelt took action by creating the Puerto Rican Policy Commission (PRPC).[147]

The PRPC represented a radical break from past U.S. policies. It recruited local sympathizers of the New Deal as policymakers and provided an opportunity for the formulation of their ideas. The PRPC consisted of a think tank to conceive a plan for the economic rehabilitation of Puerto Rico. Federal authorities appointed Chardón and two other Puerto Ricans as members of the PRPC. Muñoz received an invitation to participate as an unofficial observer in the meetings of the PRPC, which began in the summer of 1934 in Washington, D.C.[148] After several weeks of work and much secrecy, the PRPC announced the completion of a report, popularly known as the "Chardón Plan." Although the PRPC produced a comprehensive plan to address the island's economic problems, the commission's report can be mainly understood as an effort to break up the land monopoly of sugar corporations, address the problem of absentee-ownership, and minimize the effects of mono-cultural sugar production.[149] Besides addressing agricultural problems, the Chardón Plan proposed industrial development as a solution to unemployment.[150]

Since the PRPC's proposal threatened to curtail powerful economic interests in Puerto Rico, the Chardón Plan and its implementation became the objects of contention. Outright opposition to the Chardón Plan came from sugar interests that saw the PRPC's ambitious program of land reform as a theat to their profits.[151] Sugar interests not only lobbied in Washington, D.C., against the PRPC but also attacked the integrity of supporters of the Chardón Plan on the island. Besides the opposition of sugar interests, the Chardón Plan faced the ever-present conflict among political parties over the issue of patronage.[152] While the Coalition saw the Chardón Plan as evidence of favoritism toward Liberals, Muñoz and his peers valued the PRPC report for the occasion it offered them for political action. The Chardón Plan represented more than an effort for socioeconomic improvement.

Since the island's colonial government limited the access to power of Puerto Ricans, the implementation of the Chardón Plan stood as a political opportunity without precedent. Not only had the PRPC been sanctioned by the U.S. president, but its plan gave a voice to the aspirations of local reformers. Besides forging expectations for common action between federal authorities and local reformers, the PRPC's ambitious plan to address economic grievances had the potential to coalesce the support of people in favor of reform. As an effort to mainly address economic concerns and not the status issue, the Chardón Plan embodied the project of a new generation of Puerto Rican leaders.[153]

Aware of the conflict between Coalitionists and Liberals, U.S. officials spent several months designing an agency that could sustain the onslaught of local politics and implement the Chardón Plan. Their effort gained momentum in the spring of 1935, when a plan emerged for a reconstruction agency that would fall under the direction of the Department of the Interior.[154] Although this decision promised to keep local politics at bay, it spelled difficulties from another front. Governor Blanton Winship, a general from the War Department and the successor of Gore, showed reluctance to delegate authority to mainland officials on the issue of reform.[155] To avoid a deadlock and push for reform, local supporters of the New Deal banked upon the lobbying efforts of Muñoz. As the main liaison between U.S. officials and Puerto Rican reformers, Muñoz had already taken the opportunity to inform President Roosevelt about the island's situation.[156] To deal with Winship's interference with reform, Muñoz not only relied on his mainland contacts but also concocted an ambitious political plan. In a letter Muñoz wrote to Ruby A. Black in February 1935 he explained that his plan "may have a decisive effect in kicking out racketeering and cheap politics control from Puerto Rican public life for a generation."[157] Furthermore, Muñoz explained with a hint of enthusiasm his overall goal to "break" with "cheap politics":

I believe that a break can be provoked. If a break came, all legislation in harmony with the reconstruction plan would be quickly passed. And in 1936 a new deal ticket, including liberal republicans, would sweep the island even if Winship should remain satrap, by many thousands of votes. Now mark this clearly: my position before the country is such that I would be the actual leader of that sweep, party lines within the ticket would become largely obliterated—which will never happen in the present coalition—a unitary program will be made and pushed. Therefore control by racketeering and cheap politics will disappear.[158]

While Puerto Ricans endured a colonial government that limited their access to power, Muñoz and his peers used the New Deal as a "political backdoor" for their initiatives. With their inclusion as policymakers of the New Deal in Puerto Rico, the local supporters of Roosevelt's program could envision reform as a basis for political action. By making reform a central part of his discourse, the words of Muñoz above shed light on the "contact zone"[159] that made it possible for him to imagine better conditions on the island. Although far from being the exclusive author of a new discourse centered on reform, Muñoz related his political ambitions with a socioeconomic reality around him haphazardly shaped by the contact of new forces in Puerto Rico and the mainland. On the one hand, the gradual breakdown of Puerto Rico's political order saw the rise of agents with aspirations for change such as the Nationalists, Communists, and dissident Socialists who intervened during the sugar strike of 1934. On the other hand, the extension of the New Deal to Puerto Rico opened the possibility to reformulate the relationship between the island and the United States. While the economic crisis in Puerto Rico left political leadership up for grabs, the growing collaboration between local reformers and U.S. New Dealers offered an alternative to address the problems of the island. Muñoz perceived this reality as welcoming his role as a leader. Moreover, by presenting the U.S. policies of reform as a program for political change and the Puerto Rican reformers as agents of that program, Muñoz imagined a way to build mass support beyond the restraints of party lines and the politics of patronage. According to Muñoz, the outcome of his plan would be positive:

That the end is good admits of no doubt to my mind. Good, because the socialist masses are good motive power for reform and have simply been betrayed up to this time by their leaders in coalition with reactionaries. Good because it will divide political camps along economic lines, well-defined and permanent. Good because it will in fact create one great party under the effective leadership of your humble servant, instead of a mere electoral understanding between dissimilar groups.[160]

Muñoz placed much hope on U.S. policies of reform to achieve a merger of political forces, "a new deal ticket," for the election of 1936. The relationship between local reformers and New Deal policies constituted a key element in Muñoz's effort to imagine a leadership attuned to his plan for political change. Besides imagining "a unitary program" based on the New Deal, Muñoz explored the potential of his initiative to gather mass support. Muñoz's vision of a reconfiguration of political practices in Puerto Rico assumed that the "socialist masses" would answer his call for reform without further ado and that he would easily emerge as the leader of "one great party." According to Muñoz's plan, the support of those in need of reform would be achieved once his initiative had managed to displace "cheap politics" in favor of the New Deal. Although Muñoz perceived well the problems of Socialists within the Coalition, his political plan fared no better than that of Nationalists, Communists, and dissident Socialists during the sugar strike of 1934. These groups as well as Muñoz eventually found out that building mass support for reform would require an approach devised not solely according to their own plan but in dialogue with other political agents of the island. What stands out about Muñoz's plan is that despite his aspirations, its logic did not differ much from political tactics common at the time. In a complex scheme of negotiations, Muñoz proposed to bargain certain appointments with parties of the opposition.[161] Muñoz engaged in the politics of patronage in the same way as other political leaders in Puerto Rico.

The occasion for Muñoz's plan vanished when federal authorities cleared out the final obstacles for the implementation of reform by the summer of 1935. President

Roosevelt signed an executive order in May to create the Puerto Rico Reconstruction Administration (PRRA).[162] The PRRA promised a good chance for the economic recovery of Puerto Rico. Officials from the Department of the Interior formed close ties with Muñoz and other Puerto Rican reformers during the process that led to the creation of the agency.[163] Ernest Gruening, a well-known New Dealer, became director of the PRRA. Not only did the PRRA secure the support of mainland New Dealers, but it also recruited local sympathizers of reform such as Carlos Chardón, Rafael Fernández García, Antonio Luchetti, Miguel Guerra Mondragón, and Guillermo Esteves.[164] Contrary to the PRERA, the PRRA went beyond measures of relief to include a broad program for the economic reconstruction of Puerto Rico. Besides incorporating many aims of the Chardón Plan to deal with the problems of Puerto Rico's monocultural sugar production, the PRRA included several measures such as industrial development, electrification, reforestation, and health care programs.[165] The PRRA also allocated resources to establish small farms, build cement houses, and improve educational facilities.[166]

Despite the potential of the PRRA, the agency failed to deliver its full promise. A sequence of events that pitted U.S. authorities against Puerto Rican Nationalists decided the fate of the PRRA. On the one hand, the appointment of General Winship to govern Puerto Rico entailed a policy of zero tolerance for social unrest.[167] On the other hand, Albizu and his party stepped up their militant tactics to achieve independence after their unsuccessful attempt to form a "united front" with labor during the sugar strike of 1934.[168] The opposition between U.S. authorities and Albizu's party led to bloodshed in October 1935, when a confrontation between them in Río Piedras left four Nationalists dead.[169] Nationalists retaliated by killing the island's chief of police, Elisha F. Riggs, in February 1936. Incensed by the defiance of Nationalists, policemen captured and killed at their headquarters the two men who assassinated Riggs.[170] In addition, U.S. officials responded with drastic measures toward Puerto Rico. As the head of the PRRA, Gruening started an investigation to purge his agency of politics.[171] He sought to rid the PRRA not only of radical agents but of any other individual involved in political activities. Meanwhile, Senator Millard S. Tydings introduced a bill for the independence of Puerto Rico that punished the island for the assassination of Riggs. The Tydings bill granted sovereignty under very disadvantageous conditions.[172]

Although U.S. animosity toward Nationalists undermined the impartiality of Gruening's investigation of the PRRA, the information unearthed revealed that Liberals were too close for comfort within the agency. Special agents from the Department of the Interior found that workers as well as administrators engaged in the collection of funds for the Liberal Party.[173] Federal investigators also uncovered a small organization called Renovation—Renovación—which had the main function of making political collections.[174] The Department of the Interior concluded that political favoritism toward Liberals permeated the PRRA. Gruening took it upon himself to address the problem. Far from offering a solution, Gruening's policy of purging the PRRA of political agents had a detrimental result. Gruening not only ousted the Liberals but also alienated reliable employees by centralizing authority in his office.[175] His reluctance to delegate decisions caused the mass resignation of Chardón and other top officials of the PRRA in December 1936.[176] Gruening's actions also strained his relationship with Muñoz. In December, Muñoz's role as liaison between the PRRA and local supporters of the New Deal came to an end.[177]

The crisis in the PRRA put a dent in the political future of Muñoz and his peers, but the Tydings bill compounded the problems of local reformers beyond hope. Following the introduction of the New Deal in Puerto Rico, the Liberal Party secured the support of local reformers by offering a better avenue for their political aspirations than the Coalition.[178] As a new generation of the island's elite with ambitions and perceptions of their own, local reformers coexisted with older leaders who made up the ranks of the Liberal Party. The Tydings bill brought this coexistence to an end when it forced the old and new generations within the Liberal Party to confront the issue of independence with political tactics best attuned to their own interests and beliefs. The leader of the old generation, Antonio R. Barceló, reaffirmed the stance of his party in favor of independence notwithstanding the economic costs of the Tydings bill.[179] Muñoz, as the leader of local reformers, raised his voice against the bill because it failed to provide favorable economic conditions for independence. Muñoz also insisted on boycotting the election of 1936, a tactic he called "political retreat"—*retraimiento*—to protest the Tydings bill and save the Liberal Party from defeat. For Muñoz, advocating independence when the Tydings bill was out in the open did not augur well for the Liberal Party and the implementation of reform.[180]

The question of why Muñoz opted for a "political retreat" has been the subject of different interpretations. While some scholars such as Wilfredo Mattos Cintrón present Muñoz as an agent with a plot to secure U.S. interests in Puerto Rico, other historians such as Carmelo Rosario Natal insist that Muñoz's commitment to independence wavered only after confronting unsurmountable odds.[181] On the contrary, by focusing less on status politics and more on culture, I see Muñoz's "political retreat" as the effort of an ascendant generation of leaders to find a middle ground between their own interest in reform and the Liberal Party's platform in favor of independence. The experience of Muñoz and his peers with the New Deal led them to place reform at the forefront but without dismissing their elder's concern about the status issue. This reality is evident in the conflict that ensued within the Liberal Party after the introduction of the Tydings bill.[182] At first, Barceló and Muñoz cooperated with each other to support independence. When the discrepancy of tactics between Barceló and Muñoz became obvious, the latter tried to get his proposal for "political retreat" approved by the Liberal Party. Muñoz's proposal did not prosper after Liberals rejected it a second time during an assembly.[183] With few avenues left within the Liberal Party for the initiative of local reformers and the supporters of the New Deal, Muñoz took steps that laid the groundwork of what would become the PPD.

At this stage of his political career, Muñoz wrote to Ruby A. Black the words quoted at the beginning of this chapter.[184] After explaining his difficulties in steering the Liberal Party away from the election, Muñoz commented how he visualized himself as leader of Puerto Rico. Muñoz saw a basis for his political aspiration when he remarked "that loyalty to personal leaders is the way of salvation among a very poor and harassed population."[185] Far from surprising, the words of Muñoz corresponded with the reverses of Puerto Rican reformers after the assassination of Riggs. Since Muñoz had placed his hope so squarely on the New Deal and local reformers, the purge in the PRRA and the Tydings bill made him ponder his political future. Besides being a reflection of his difficulties and misgivings, the words of Muñoz stressed the development of his political thought and actions. Muñoz began to realize that broad support for reform would depend on more than his own effort to extend the New Deal to Puerto Rico. It would require an initiative carried out in conjunction with the island's constituencies. Muñoz perceived this initiative as a special bond based on "loyalty" between himself and the "poor" people of Puerto Rico.[186]

To provide impetus to his aspiration, Muñoz formed a political organization within the Liberal Party called Independentist Social Action—Acción Social Independentista (ASI).[187] ASI vowed not to interfere with the electoral campaign of the Liberal Party but to push for an economically sound proposal for the island's independence.[188] Despite the fact that ASI took little action, this organization is important for two reasons. First, far from being either part of a plot to use the independentist cause for ulterior motives or evidence of Muñoz's zealous defense of sovereignty, as some historians argue,[189] ASI embodied a stage in the political ascendance of Muñoz and his peers. In their effort to build support for reform in Puerto Rico, local reformers tied together in one organization their interest in "social justice" and the Liberal Party's call for independence.[190] Instead of being a clear-cut platform for change, ASI exemplified the haphazard and ambiguous maneuver of an ascendant group of leaders trying to make room for themselves in the island's political arena. A second point of importance is that ASI, by distancing Muñoz from the upper echelons of the Liberal Party, led him to spread his cause with an intense campaign aimed at the rank and file.[191] Muñoz drew on this experience when he formed the PPD less than two years later.

The defeat of the Liberal Party during the election of 1936 deepened the divide between the followers of Muñoz and those of Barceló. ASI quietly disappeared from the island's political scene soon after the defeat of the Liberals.[192] For Muñoz and his peers, the electoral aftermath vanquished the possibility of local reformers to represent the New Deal forces in Puerto Rico. Muñoz regretted this situation. Two days after the election, Muñoz wrote to Ruby A. Black saying that "it is like a breath of fresh air to receive the news of the tremendous victory of Roosevelt and the New Deal. A somewhat similar victory would have been achieved in Puerto Rico by the supporters of the New Deal if it had not been for the monstrous Tydings Bill."[193] For the followers of Barceló, Muñoz and his peers contributed to the electoral defeat of the Liberal Party.[194] Barceló not only blamed the supporters of "political retreat" but also saw their stance as incompatible with that of Liberals. In May 1937, after several months of recriminations between the two Liberal factions,

Barceló arranged a meeting in a rural property called "Naranjales" to expel Muñoz and his supporters from the party.[195]

The time that elapsed between Muñoz's expulsion from the Liberal Party and the formation of the PPD turned out to be one of doubt and indecision for local reformers. Not long after the assembly at "Naranjales," Muñoz and his followers formed a political organization named the Pure, Authentic, and Complete Liberal Party—Partido Liberal Neto, Auténtico y Completo.[196] As a party that flaunted Liberal insignias but failed to mobilize support, it stood as no more than a political statement against Barceló and his group.[197] Little more than a year passed before Muñoz and his supporters made another attempt to form a party. The names taken into consideration for the new party ranged from Democratic Party of the New Deal—Partido Democrático del Nuevo Trato[198]—to Popular Party—Partido Popular.[199] In the end, Muñoz settled for Popular Democratic Party—Partido Popular Democrático (PPD)—which he soon nicknamed the "Party of the Poor."[200]

The process of selecting a name for Muñoz's party exemplified the effort of Puerto Rican reformers to find a middle ground between the New Deal program and the support of local constituencies. By appealing to broad sectors of society with the all-inclusive word "popular" and presenting the PPD as the local counterpart of Roosevelt's party and the New Deal, Muñoz and his followers strove to build support for reform with themselves as intermediaries between Puerto Rican and U.S. interests. As of July 1938, when Muñoz founded the PPD, little besides the name of the party stood as political credentials of the new organization. Only after a prolonged process of interaction between the PPD and multiple agents did the party gain shape and become the locus of mass support and a discourse of consent.

NOTES

1. Letter from Luis Muñoz Marín to Ruby A. Black, August 5, 1936, Colección Ruby A. Black, Centro de Investigaciones Históricas, Universidad de Puerto Rico. Hereafter referred to as CRB, CIH/UPR.

2. Ruth Berins Collier and David Collier, *Shaping the Political Arena: Critical Junctures, the Labor Movement, and Regime Dynamics in Latin America* (Princeton: Princeton University Press, 1991), pp. 100-157.

3. Ibid., pp. 100-157.

4. Ernesto Laclau and Chantal Mouffe, *Hegemony and Socialist Strategy: Toward a Radical Democratic Politics* (London: Verso Books, 1985), p. 136.

5. Lieban Córdova, *7 años con Muñoz Marín, 1938-1945* (Arecibo: Editora Corripio, 1988; orig. 1945), p. 90.

6. Luis Muñoz Marín, *La Historia del Partido Popular Democrático* (San Juan: Editorial El Batey, 1984); Luis Muñoz Marín, *Memorias: Autobiografía pública, 1898-1940* (San Juan: Universidad Interamericana de Puerto Rico, 1982); Luis Muñoz Marín, *Memorias: Autobiografía pública, 1940-1952* (San Germán: Universidad Interamericana de Puerto Rico, 1992).

7. Córdova, *7 años con Muñoz Marín, 1938-1945*; Lieban Córdova, *Luis Muñoz Marín y sus campañas políticas: Memorias de su secretario-taquígrafo personal* (Río Piedras: Editorial de la Universidad de Puerto Rico, 1983); Lieban Córdova, *¿Cómo era Muñoz*

Marín?, 2 vols. (Arecibo: First Book Publishing of Puerto Rico, 1996); Carmelo Rosario Natal, *La juventud de Luis Muñoz Marín: Vida y pensamiento, 1898-1932* (San Juan: Editorial Edil, 1989); Carmelo Rosario Natal, *Luis Muñoz Marín y la independencia de Puerto Rico* (San Juan: Producciones Históricas, 1994); Carmelo Rosario Natal, ed., *Luis Muñoz Marín: Servidor Público y Humanista (Cartas)* (San Juan: Producciones Históricas, 1998). Other works in the same vein are R. Elfren Bernier, *Luis Muñoz Marín: Líder y Maestro, Anecdotario Mumarino I* (San Juan: Ramallo Bros. Printing, 1988); R. Elfren Bernier, *Luis Muñoz Marín: Anecdotario Mumarino II* (San Juan: Fundación Luis Muñoz Marín, 1999); Enrique Bird Piñero, *Don Luis Muñoz Marín: El poder de la excelencia* (San Juan: Fundación Luis Muñoz Marín, 1991); Ernesto Juan Fonfrías, *Historia de mi vida política en la fundación del Partido Popular Democrático* (Río Piedras: Imprenta ESMACO, 1986); Manuel de Heredia, *Luis Muñoz Marín : Biografía abierta* (Río Piedras: Ediciones Puerto Rico, 1973); Carlos R. Zapata Oliveras, *"Nuevos Caminos hacia Viejos Objetivos": Estados Unidos y el Establecimiento del Estado Libre Asociado de Puerto Rico, 1945-1953* (San Juan: Editorial Edil, 1991); Carlos R. Zapata Oliveras, *De independentista a autonomista:La transformación del pensamiento político de Luis Muñoz Marín (1931-1949)* (San Juan: Fundación Luis Muñoz Marín, 2003).

8. Antonio Fernós Isern, "From Colony to Commonwealth," *The Annals of the American Academy of Political and Social Studies* (January 1953); Antonio Fernós Isern, *El Estado Libre Asociado de Puerto Rico: Antecedentes, creación, y desarrollo hasta la época presente* (Río Piedras: Editorial Universitaria, 1973); José Trías Monge, *Historia constitucional de Puerto Rico* (Río Piedras: Editorial Universitaria, 1980); Arturo Morales Carrión, *Puerto Rico: A Political and Cultural History* (New York: W. W. Norton, 1983). These authors were governmental officials of the PPD. Fernós Isern was resident commissioner in the U.S. capital. Trías Monge was a judge of the island's Supreme Court. Morales Carrión was the assistant secretary of state of the Commonwealth of Puerto Rico.

9. Among the main works in Puerto Rico that use class analysis to understand the island's populism are Juan José Baldrich, "Class and State: The Origins of Populism in Puerto Rico, 1934-52" (Ph.D. diss., Yale University, 1981); Emilio González Díaz, "El populismo en Puerto Rico: 1938-1952" (Ph.D. diss., U.N.A.M., 1977); Emilio González Díaz, "Class Struggle and Politics in Puerto Rico during the Decade of the 40's: The Rise of P.D.P.," *Two Thirds* 2, no. 1 (1979): 45-57; Emilio González Díaz, "La lucha de clases y la política en el Puerto Rico de la década del '40: El ascenso del PPD," *Revista de Ciencias Sociales* 22, no. 1-2 (March-June 1980): 37-69; Emilio González Díaz, "Muñoz, el populismo y el ELA," *Claridad*, July 25-31, 1980, pp. 2-3; Emilio González Díaz, *La política de los empresarios puertorriqueños* (Río Piedras: Ediciones Huracán, 1991); Angel G. Quintero Rivera, "La desintegración de la política de clases: De la política obrera al populismo," Part IV-2, *Revista de Ciencias Sociales* 20, no. 1 (1976): 3-47; Angel G. Quintero Rivera, *Conflictos de clase y Política en Puerto Rico* (Río Piedras: Ediciones Huracán, 1977); Angel G. Quintero Rivera, "Bases sociales de la transformación ideológica del Partido Popular en la década del '40," in Gerardo Navas Dávila, ed., *Cambio y desarrollo en Puerto Rico: La transformación ideológica del Partido Popular Democrático* (San Juan: Editorial de la Universidad de Puerto Rico, 1980), pp. 35-119; Angel G. Quintero Rivera, *Patricios y plebeyos* (Río Piedras: Ediciones Huracán, 1988); Angel G. Quintero Rivera, "Base clasista del proyecto desarrollista del 40," in Eduardo Rivera Medina and Rafael L. Ramírez, eds., *Del cañaveral a la fábrica: Cambio social en Puerto Rico* (Río Piedras: Ediciones Huracán, 1985), pp. 139-145; Angel G. Quintero Rivera, "La ideología populista y la institucionalización universitaria de las ciencias sociales," in Silvia Alvarez Curbelo and María Elena Rodríguez Castro, eds., *Del Nacionalismo al Populismo: Cultura y Política en Puerto Rico* (Río Piedras: Ediciones Huracán, 1993), pp. 107-145. These works

are part of a broad historiography about populism in Latin America that includes key publications such as Octavio Ianni, *La formación del estado populista en América Latina* (México, DF: Editorial Era, 1975); Francisco Weffort and Anibal Quijano, *Populismo, marginalización y dependencia: Ensayos de interpretación sociológica* (Costa Rica: Editorial Universitaria Centroamericana, 1973).

10. Quintero Rivera, "Bases sociales de la transformación ideológica del Partido Popular en la década del '40," p. 94. See also Angel G. Quintero Rivera, "Background to the Emergence of Imperialist Capitalism in Puerto Rico," in Adalberto López and James Petras, eds., *Puerto Rico and Puerto Ricans* (Cambridge: Schenkman, 1974), pp. 87-117.

11. Emilio Pantojas Garcia, "Puerto Rican Populism Revisited: The PPD during the 1940s," *Journal of Latin American Studies* 21 (October 1989): 522-523, 557. See also Emilio Pantojas García, "Estrategias de desarrollo y contradicciones ideológicas en Puerto Rico, 1940-1980," *Revista de Ciencias Sociales* 21, no. 1-2 (March-June 1979): 73-119; Emilio Pantojas García, "Desarrollismo y luchas de clases: Los limites del proyecto populista en Puerto Rico durante la década del cuarenta," *Revista de Ciencias Sociales* 24, no. 3-4 (July-October 1985): 355-391; Emilio Pantojas García, *Development Strategies as Ideology: Puerto Rico's Export-Led Industrialization Experience* (Río Piedras: Editorial de la Universidad de Puerto Rico, 1990).

12. In particular, see Quintero Rivera, "Bases sociales de la transformación ideológica del Partido Popular en la década del '40," pp. 35-119.

13. Pantojas Garcia, "Puerto Rican Populism Revisited," p. 557. According to Pantojas, "the characterization of the PPD as a movement of the middle sectors and the working classes with a national project can only be based on an inadequate extrapolation to Puerto Rico of the Latin American populist experience."

14. My approach has been informed in part by the theories of Ruth Berins Collier and David Collier. Collier and Collier, *Shaping the Political Arena*; Ruth Berins Collier, "Combining Alternative Perspectives: Internal Trajectories versus External Influences as Explanations of Latin American Politics in the 1940s," *Comparative Politics* 26 (October 1993): 1-29.

15. My work joins recent efforts to rethink the history of the PPD. Consider the following contributions. One work emphasizes the history that preceded the formation of the PPD: Rafael Alberto Bernabe, "Prehistory of the 'Partido Popular Democrático': Muñoz Marín, the Partido Liberal and the Crisis of Sugar in Puerto Rico, 1930-1935" (Ph. D. diss., State University of New York at Binghamton, 1989). Another work highlights the role of women during the emergence and consolidation of the PPD: Mary Frances Gallart Calzada, "Mujeres, aguja y política en el Siglo 20 en Puerto Rico: Obdulia Velázquez de Lorenzo. Alcaldesa de Guayama, 1952-1956" (Ph.D. diss., Universidad de Puerto Rico, 1992). The contribution of Luis A. López Rojas is based on the theories of Michel Foucault: Luis Alfredo López Rojas, *Luis Muñoz Marín y las estrategias del poder, 1936-1946* (San Juan: Editorial Isla Negra, 1998). Consider also the analysis of José J. Rodríguez Vázquez, which uses the notions of Partha Chatterjee to examine the nationalist rhetoric of Muñoz: José J. Rodríguez Vázquez, "El Sueño que no cesa: La nación deseada en el debate intelectual y político puertorriqueño, 1920-1940" (Ph.D. diss., Universidad de Puerto Rico, 1998). Other important contributions are the essays in Fernando Picó, ed., *Luis Muñoz Marín: Ensayos del Centenario* (San Juan: Fundación Luis Muñoz Marín, 1999); Fernando Picó, ed., *Luis Muñoz Marín: Perfiles de su gobernación, 1948-1964* (San Juan: Fundación Luis Muñoz Marín, 2003). Finally, Silvia Alvarez Curbelo provides useful hints to understand the discursive practices of the PPD: Silvia Alvarez Curbelo, "La Casa de Cristal: El Ejercicio Senatorial de Luis Muñoz Marín, 1932-36," in Fernando Picó, Silvia Alvarez Curbelo, and Carmen Raffucci, eds., *Senado de Puerto Rico, 1917-1992: Ensayos de historia institucional*

(San Juan: Senado de Puerto Rico, 1992), pp. 105-135; Silvia Alvarez Curbelo, "La conflictividad en el discurso político de Luis Muñoz Marín: 1926-1936," in Silvia Alvarez Curbelo and María Elena Rodríguez Castro, eds., *Del Nacionalismo al Populismo: Cultura y Política en Puerto Rico* (Río Piedras: Ediciones Huracán, 1993), pp. 13-36; Silvia Alvarez Curbelo, "Populismo y autoritarismo: reflexiones a partir de la experiencia muñocista," in Irma Rivera Nieves and Carlos Gil, eds., *Polifonía Salvaje: Ensayos de cultura y política en la postmodernidad* (San Juan: Editorial Postdata, 1995), pp. 319-327; Silvia Alvarez Curbelo, "La década del '40 y el movimiento populista," in Carlos Di Núbila and Carmen Rodríguez Cortés, eds., *Puerto Rico: Sociedad, cultura y educación* (San Juan: Editorial Isla Negra, 1997), pp. 91-104.

16. Laclau and Mouffe, *Hegemony and Socialist Strategy*; Ernesto Laclau, *New Reflexions on the Revolution of our Time* (London: Verso Books, 1991); Chantal Mouffe, "Democratic Citizenship and the Political Community," in Chantal Mouffe, ed., *Dimensions of Radical Democracy: Pluralism, Citizenship, Community* (London: Verso Books, 1992), pp. 225-239; Chantal Mouffe, *The Return of the Political* (London: Verso Books, 1993); Ernesto Laclau, "Minding the Gap: The Subject of Politics," in Ernesto Laclau, ed., *The Making of Political Identities* (London: Verso Books, 1994), pp. 11-39; Ernesto Laclau, *Emancipation(s)* (London: Verso Books, 1996); Ernesto Laclau, "Identity and Hegemony: The Role of Universality in the Constitution of Political Logics," in Judith Butler, Ernesto Laclau, and Slavoj Žižek, *Contingency, Hegemony, Universality* (London: Verso Books, 2000), pp. 44-89; Ernesto Laclau, "Constructing Universality," in Judith Butler, Ernesto Laclau, and Slavoj Žižek, *Contingency, Hegemony, Universality* (London: Verso Books, 2000), pp. 281-307; Chantal Mouffe, *The Democratic Paradox* (London: Verso Books, 2000); Anna Marie Smith, *Laclau and Mouffe: The Radical Democratic Imaginary* (London: Routledge, 1998); Jacob Torfing, *New Theories of Discourse: Laclau, Mouffe, and Žižek* (Oxford: Blackwell Publishers, 1999).

17. Laclau and Mouffe, *Hegemony and Socialist Strategy*, p. 105. The theoretical approach of Laclau and Mouffe owes much to the definition of discourse of Jacques Derrida. According to Torfing,

Derrida's definition of discourse as a differential system in which the absence of a transcendental signified, in terms of a priviledged centre, extends the play of signification infinitely. This definition emphasizes the moment of unfixity in the construction of meaning. Discourse can thus be defined as a decentered structure in which meaning is constantly negotiated and constructed. This broad conception of discourse in terms of an ensemble of signifying sequences allows for the inclusion of both physical objects and social practices as meaningful parts of discourse. (Torfing, *New Theories of Discourse*, p. 40)

18. Torfing, *New Theories of Discourse*, p. 300.

19. Laclau and Mouffe, *Hegemony and Socialist Strategy*, p. 141.

20. Torfing, *New Theories of Discourse*, p. 101.

21. Laclau, *Emancipation(s)*, pp. 43-44.

22. Ibid., p. 105.

23. Jeremy Adelman, *Colonial Legacies: The Problem of Persistence in Latin American History* (New York: Routledge, 1999); José Alvarez Junco and Ricardo González Leandri, eds., *El Populismo en España y América* (Madrid: Editorial Catriel, 1994); Marjorie Becker, "Lázaro Cárdenas and the Mexican Counter-Revolution: The Struggle over Culture in Michoacán, 1934-1940" (Ph.D. diss., Yale University, 1988); Marjorie Becker, *Setting the Virgin on Fire: Lázaro Cárdenas, Michoacán Peasants, and the Redemption of the Mexican Revolution* (Berkekey: University of California Press, 1995); John Beverly and José Oviedo, eds., *The Postmodernism Debate in Latin America* (Durham, NC: Duke University Press, 1993); Felipe Burbano de Lara, ed., *El fantasma del populismo: Aproximación a un tema*

(siempre) actual (Caracas: Editorial Nueva Sociedad, 1998); Collier and Collier, *Shaping the Political Arena*; Lilliam Guerra, *Popular Expression and National Identity in Puerto Rico: The Struggle for Self, Community, and Nation* (Gainesville: University of Florida Press, 1998); Gilbert M. Joseph and Daniel Nugent, eds., *Everyday Forms of State Formation: Revolution and the Negotiation of Rule in Modern Mexico* (Durham, NC: Duke University Press, 1994); Gilbert M. Joseph, Catherine C. LeGrand, and Ricardo D. Salvatore, eds., *Close Encounters of Empire: Writing the Cultural History of U.S.-Latin American Relations* (Durham, NC: Duke University Press, 1998); Daniel H. Levine, ed., *Constructing Culture and Power in Latin America* (Ann Arbor: University of Michigan Press, 1995); Mariano Plotkin, *Mañana es San Perón: Propaganda, rituales políticos y educación en el régimen peronista, 1946-1955* (Buenos Aires: Ariel Historia Argentina, 1994); Carlos de la Torre, *Populist Seduction in Latin America: The Ecuadorian Experience* (Athens: Ohio University Center for International Studies, 2000).

24. Joseph et al., *Close Encounters of Empire*, p. 578.

25. Torfing, *New Theories of Discourse*.

26. Mary Louise Pratts, "Arts of the Contact Zone," *Profession* 91 (1991): 33-39; Mary Louise Pratts, *Imperial Eyes: Travel Writing and Transculturation* (London: Routledge, 1992), pp. 6-7.

27. Collier and Collier, *Shaping the Political Arena*, p. 161; Ruth Berins Collier, "Combining Alternative Perspectives," pp. 1-29.

28. José Alvarez Junco, ed., *Populismo, Caudillaje y Discurso Demagógico* (Madrid: Siglo Veintiuno, 1987); Alvarez Junco and González Leandri, *El Populismo en España y América*; Burbano de Lara, *El fantasma del populismo*; Emilio de Ipola, "Populismo e ideología (A propósito de Ernesto Laclau: Política e ideología en la teoría marxista)," *Revista Mexicana de Sociología* 49 (1979): 925-960; Emilio de Ipola, *Ideología y discurso populista* (México, DF: Folios Ediciones, 1982); Ernesto Laclau, "Towards a Theory of Populism," in Ernesto Laclau, *Politics and Ideology in Marxist Theory: Capitalism, Fascism, Populism* (London: NLB, 1977), pp. 81-198; Ernesto Laclau, "Populist Rupture and Discourse," *Screen Education* 34 (Spring 1980): 87-93; Ernesto Laclau, "Populismo y Transformación del Imaginario Político en América Latina," *Cuadernos de la Realidad Nacional* 3 (1988); Plotkin, *Mañana es San Perón*; de la Torre, *Populist Seduction in Latin America*.

29. Perspectives that stress the manipulation and social control of populist leaders over the masses hark back to modernization theory. Dependency theory and more recent interpretations also suffer from this view. Some examples are Youssef Cohen, *The Manipulation of Consent: The State and Working-Class Consciousness in Brazil* (Pittsburgh: University of Pittsburgh Press, 1989); Robert H. Dix, "Populism: Authoritarian and Democratic," *Latin American Research Review* 20, no. 2 (1985): 29-52; Kenneth Paul Erickson, "Populism and Political Control of the Working Class in Brazil," in June Nash, Juan Corradi, and Hobart Spalding, eds., *Ideology & Social Change in Latin America* (New York: Gordon and Breach, 1977), pp. 200-236; Gino Germani, *Authoritarianism, Fascism and National Populism* (New Brunswick, NJ: Transaction Books, 1978); James M. Malloy, ed., *Authoritarianism and Corporatism in Latin America* (Pittsburgh: University of Pittsburgh Press, 1977); Steve Stein, *Populism in Perú: The Emergence of the Masses and the Politics of Social Control* (Madison: University of Wisconsin Press, 1980). Some studies that have made important revisions are John D. French, "Industrial Workers and the Birth of the Populist Republic in Brazil, 1945-1946," *Latin American Perspectives* 63, no. 4 (Fall 1989): 5-27; John D. French, *The Brazilian Worker's ABC: Class Conflict and Alliances in Modern São Paulo* (Chapel Hill: University of North Carolina Press, 1992); John D. French, "The Populist Gamble of Gertúlio Vargas in 1945: Political and Ideological Transitions in

Brazil," in David Rock, ed., *Latin America in the 1940s: War and Postwar Transitions* (Berkeley: University of California Press, 1994), pp. 141-165; Daniel James, *Resistance and Integration: Peronism and the Argentine Working Class, 1946-1976* (Cambridge: Cambridge University Press, 1988); Daniel James, "October 17th and 18th, 1945: Mass Protest, Peronism and the Argentine Working Class," *Journal of Social History* (Spring 1988): 441-461; Joel Wolfe, *Working Women, Working Men: Sao Paulo and the Rise of Brazil's Industrial Working Class, 1900-1955* (Durham, NC: Duke University Press, 1993).

30. Several authors highlight the problems of the notion of populism. Consider José Alvarez Junco, "El populismo como problema," in José Alvarez Junco and Ricardo González Leandri, eds., *El Populismo en España y América* (Madrid: Editorial Catriel, 1994), pp. 11-38; Paul W. Drake, *Socialism and Populism in Chile, 1932-1952* (Urbana: University of Illinois Press, 1978); Ian Roxborough, "Unity and Diversity in Latin American History," *Journal of Latin American Studies* 16 (May 1984): 1-26; Carlos de la Torre, "The Ambiguous Meanings of Latin American Populisms," *Social Research* 59, no. 2 (Summer 1992): 385-414; Saguaro Torres Ballesteros, "El populismo. Un concepto escurridizo," in Alvarez Junco, *Populismo, Caudillaje y Discurso Demagógico*, pp. 159-180.

31. Besides perspectives that employ a "top down" or "bottom up" approach, there are notions that are too static or refer to a list of traits to set apart populist movements. For example, consider Michael L. Conniff, ed., *Latin American Populism in Comparative Perspective* (Albuquerque: University of New Mexico Press, 1982); Michael L. Conniff, ed., *Populism in Latin America* (Tuscaloosa: University of Alabama Press, 1999).

32. Robert W. Anderson, *Party Politics in Puerto Rico* (Stanford, CA: Stanford University Press, 1965); Angel G. Quintero Rivera, *El liderato local de los partidos y el estudio de la política puertorriqueña* (Río Piedras: Universidad de Puerto Rico, 1970).

33. Anderson, *Party Politics*; Quintero Rivera, *El liderato local*.

34. James Dietz, *Economic History of Puerto Rico* (Princeton: Princeton University Press, 1986), p. 139.

35. Quintero Rivera, "Bases sociales de la transformación ideológica del Partido Popular en la década del '40," p. 54; Francisco Scarano, *Puerto Rico: Cinco Siglos de Historia* (San Juan: McGraw-Hill, 1993), p. 673.

36. Dietz, *Economic History of Puerto Rico*, p. 137.

37. Ibid., p. 173. See also Juan José Baldrich, *Sembraron la no siembra: Los cosecheros de tabaco puertorriqueños frente a las corporaciones tabacaleras, 1920-1934* (Río Piedras: Ediciones Huracán, 1988).

38. Ibid., p. 100.

39. Ibid., p. 174.

40. Kelvin Santiago-Valles, *"Subject People" and Colonial Discourses: Economic Transformation and Social Disorder in Puerto Rico, 1898-1947* (New York: State University of New York Press, 1994), p. 169; Blanca G. Silvestrini, *Violencia y criminalidad en Puerto Rico* (Río Piedras: Editorial Universitaria, 1980), pp. 73-74.

41. Dietz, *Economic History of Puerto Rico*, pp. 175-176, 142-143.

42. Ibid., p. 142. See also María del Carmen Baerga, ed., *Género y trabajo: La industria de la aguja en Puerto Rico y el Caribe Hispánico* (San Juan: Editorial de la Universidad de Puerto Rico, 1993); Lydia Milagros González García, *Una Puntada en el tiempo: La industria de la aguja en Puerto Rico, 1900-1929* (Río Piedras: CEREP, 1990).

43. Santiago-Valles, *"Subject People,"* p. 188.

44. Dietz, *Economic History of Puerto Rico*, p. 160.

45. Lyman Gould, *La Ley Foraker: Raíces de la política colonial de los Estados Unidos* (Río Piedras: Editorial Universitaria, 1969); María Dolores Luque de Sánchez, *La ocupación norteamericana y la ley Foraker* (Río Piedras: Editorial de la Universidad de Puerto Rico,

1986); Carmen I. Raffucci de García, *El gobierno civil y la ley Foraker* (Río Piedras: Editorial Universitaria, 1981).

46. Lester D. Langley, *The United States and the Caribbean in the Twentieth Century* (Athens: University of Georgia Press, 1989), p. 142; Muñoz Marín, *Memorias, 1898-1940*, p. 97; Thomas Mathews, *Puerto Rican Politics and the New Deal* (New York: Da Capo Press, 1976), p. 13.

47. Dietz, *Economic History of Puerto Rico*, pp. 90-91, 99.

48. Ibid., pp. 99-102.

49. Ibid., p. 95. See also Juan G. Gelpí, *Literatura y paternalismo en Puerto Rico* (Río Piedras: Editorial de la Universidad de Puerto Rico, 1993); Quintero Rivera, *Conflictos de clase y Política en Puerto Rico*.

50. Dietz, *Economic History of Puerto Rico*, pp. 103-106.

51. Edgardo Meléndez, *Movimiento anexionista en Puerto Rico* (Río Piedras: Editorial de la Universidad de Puerto Rico, 1993), p. 66.

52. Reece B. Bothwell, *Orígenes y Desarrollo de los Partidos Políticos en Puerto Rico* (San Juan: Editorial Edil, 1988), pp. 168-170; Antonio Quiñones Calderón, *Trayectoria Política de Puerto Rico* (San Juan: Ediciones Nuevas de Puerto Rico, 1988), pp. 37-44.

53. Quintero Rivera, "Bases sociales de la transformación ideológica del Partido Popular en la década del '40," p. 77.

54. Meléndez, *Movimiento anexionista en Puerto Rico*, p. 78.

55. Mathews, *Puerto Rican Politics and the New Deal*, p. 26; Blanca G. Silvestrini, *Los trabajadores puertorriqueños y el Partido Socialista, 1932-1940* (Río Piedras: Editorial Universitaria, 1979), p. 28.

56. Silvestrini, *Los trabajadores puertorriqueños y el Partido Socialista*, pp. 26-27.

57. Ronald Fernández, *The Disenchanted Island: Puerto Rico and the United States in the Twentieth Century* (New York: Praeger, 1992), p. 111.

58. Ibid.

59. Ibid.

60. Mathews, *Puerto Rican Politics and the New Deal*, pp. 301-304.

61. Domingo Targa, *El Modus Operandi de las Artes Electorales* (San Juan: La Correspondencia, 1940). This book contains the responses of the contest carried out by *La Correspondencia* and *El Imparcial*. Puerto Rican Collection, Thomas J. Dodd Research Center, University of Connecticut.

62. Ibid.

63. Gervasio García and Angel Quintero Rivera, *Desafío y solidaridad: Breve historia del movimiento obrero puertorriqueño* (Río Piedras: Ediciones Huracán, 1986).

64. Quintero Rivera, "Bases sociales de la transformación ideológica del Partido Popular en la década del '40," p. 77.

65. César A. Rey, "Parlamentarismo Obrero y Coalición, 1932-1940," in Fernando Picó, Silvia Alvarez Curbelo, and Carmen Raffucci, eds., *Senado de Puerto Rico, 1917-1992: Ensayos de historia institucional* (San Juan: Senado de Puerto Rico, 1992), pp. 137-160; Silvestrini, *Los trabajadores puertorriqueños y el Partido Socialista*, pp. 91-94.

66. Taller de Formación Política, *Huelga en la caña, 1933-34* (Río Piedras: Ediciones Huracán, 1982), pp. 41-78. Besides the sugar industry, many other sectors of the economy experienced labor strikes in 1933. According to Dietz, the island saw eighty-five strikes during the second half of 1933 that affected the tobacco, sugar, needlework, baking, and transport industry. Dietz, *Economic History of Puerto Rico*, p. 163.

67. García and Quintero Rivera, *Desafío y solidaridad*, pp. 106-107; Juan Angel Silén, *Apuntes para la historia del movimiento obrero puertorriqueño* (Río Piedras: Editorial Cultural, 1978); Scarano, *Puerto Rico: Cinco siglos de historia*, p. 692; Silvestrini, *Los*

trabajadores puertorriqueños y el Partido Socialista, pp. 72-73; Taller de Formación Política, *Huelga en la caña.*

68. Silvestrini, *Los trabajadores puertorriqueños y el Partido Socialista*, p. 68; Taller de Formación Política, *Huelga en la caña*, pp. 65-78.

69. Taller de Formación Política, *Huelga en la caña*, pp. 65-78.

70. Ibid., pp. 79-118.

71. Silvestrini, *Los trabajadores puertorriqueños y el Partido Socialista*, pp. 72, 168.

72. Taller de Formación Política, *Huelga en la caña*, pp. 14, 123-139, 183.

73. Ibid., pp. 124-125.

74. Ibid. See also Taller de Formación Política, *La cuestión nacional: El Partido Nacionalista y el movimiento obrero puertorriqueño* (Río Piedras: Ediciones Huracán, 1982).

75. García and Quintero Rivera, *Desafío y solidaridad*, pp. 106-108.

76. Silvestrini, *Los trabajadores puertorriqueños y el Partido Socialista*, pp. 77-119.

77. Ibid.

78. García and Quintero Rivera, *Desafío y solidaridad*, pp. 110-113; Silén, *Apuntes para la historia del movimiento obrero puertorriqueño*, pp. 96-98.

79. García and Quintero Rivera, *Desafío y solidaridad*, pp. 110-111.

80. Ibid.

81. Ibid. See also Wilfredo Mattos Cintrón, *La política y lo político en Puerto Rico* (México, DF: Ediciones ERA, 1980), pp. 202 n.155; Luis Angel Ferrao, *Pedro Albizu Campos y el nacionalismo puertorriqueño* (San Juan: Editorial Cultural, 1990), pp. 292-302.

82. Ferrao, *Pedro Albizu Campos y el nacionalismo puertorriqueño*, pp. 297–298.

83. García and Quintero Rivera, *Desafío y solidaridad*, pp. 110-113; Silén, *Apuntes para la historia del movimiento obrero puertorriqueño*, pp. 96-98.

84. Ferrao, *Pedro Albizu Campos y el nacionalismo puertorriqueño*, p. 296.

85. García and Quintero Rivera, *Desafío y solidaridad*, pp. 110-113; Silén, *Apuntes para la historia del movimiento obrero puertorriqueño*, pp. 96-98.

86. Blanca G. Silvestrini, "La mujer puertorriqueña y el movimiento obrero en la década de 1930," in Edna Acosta Belén, ed., *La mujer en la sociedad puertorriqueña* (Río Piedras: Ediciones Huracán, 1980), p. 85.

87. Ibid., p. 86.

88. Ferrao, *Pedro Albizu Campos y el nacionalismo puertorriqueño*, pp. 43-65; Luis Angel Ferrao, "Nacionalismo, hispanismo y élite intelectual en el Puerto Rico de los años treinta," in Silvia Alvarez Curbelo and María Elena Rodríguez Castro, eds., *Del Nacionalismo al Populismo: Cultura y Política en Puerto Rico* (Río Piedras: Ediciones Huracán, 1993), pp. 37-60.

89. Ibid.

90. Antonio S. Pedreira, *Insularismo* (Río Piedras: Editorial Edil, 1985).

91. Ibid., p. 147.

92. A close analysis of Pedreira's *Insularismo* can be found in: Juan Flores, *"Insularismo" e ideología burguesa (Nueva lectura de A. S. Pedreira)* (Río Piedras: Ediciones Huracán, 1979).

93. Pedreira, *Insularismo*, p. 170. Pedreira stated: "The literate youth must stretch their fraternal hands toward the working and bureaucratic bunch that needs to exchange their anxieties and expand the zones of their guild. One must be generous and open the tent of enthusiasm so that all would fit."

94. A number of studies focus on the relationship between Pedreira's *Insularismo* and the island's populist movement. See, for example, Gelpí, *Literatura y paternalismo en Puerto Rico*; Jorge Rodríguez Beruff, "Antonio S. Pedreira, la Universidad y el Proyecto

populista," *Revista de Administración Pública* 18, no. 2 (1986): 5-20.

95. Vicente Géigel Polanco, "Puerto Rico: ¿Pueblo o Muchedumbre?" (1936), in *El despertar de un pueblo* (San Juan: Biblioteca de Autores Puertorriqueños, 1942), pp. 27-59.

96. At one point in his essay, Géigel stated, "It is, thus, urgent to form a new governing class linked to the legitimate interest of the people, capable of kindling in our multitudes the sense of self worth and rightly conduct them to the achievement of their collective destiny." Ibid., p. 56.

97. Roger Biles, *A New Deal for the American People* (De Kalb: Northern Illinois University Press, 1991), p. 1.

98. Alan Brinkley, "The New Deal and the Idea of the State," in Steve Fraser and Gary Gerstle, eds., *The Rise and Fall of the New Deal Order, 1930-1980* (Princeton: Princeton University Press, 1989), pp. 85-121.

99. Mathews, *Puerto Rican Politics and the New Deal*, pp. 44-45.

100. Many letters that Puerto Ricans wrote to Roosevelt can be found in the record groups that follow: Democratic National Campaign Committee 1928-1933, U.S. Possessions, Before Elections (Puerto Rico); After Elections (Puerto Rico). Franklin D. Roosevelt Library, Hyde Park, New York. Hereafter referred to as FDRL.

101. Bothwell, *Orígenes y Desarrollo de los Partidos Políticos en Puerto Rico*, pp. 168-170; Quiñones Calderón *Trayectoria Política de Puerto Rico*, pp. 37-44.

102. Mathews, *Puerto Rican Politics and the New Deal*, pp. 44, 58-116.

103. Scarano, *Puerto Rico: Cinco siglos de historia*, pp. 670-693.

104. Charles T. Goodsell, *Administration of a Revolution, Executive Reform in Puerto Rico under Governor Tugwell, 1941-1946* (Cambridge: Harvard University Press, 1965), pp. 9-15. See also Amalia Lluch Vélez, *Luis Muñoz Marín: Poesía, periodismo y revolución, 1915-1930* (San Juan: Universidad del Sagrado Corazón, Fundación Luis Muñoz Marín, 1999); Muñoz Marín, *Memorias, 1898-1940*; Carmelo Rosario Natal, *La juventud de Luis Muñoz Marín*.

105. Useful information about these individuals can be found at the Fundación Luis Muñoz Marín, Archivo Luis Muñoz Marín, Sección IV, Serie 3 (Individuos). Hereafter referred to as FLMM/ALMM, IV-3. Goodsell, *Administration of a Revolution*, pp. 61-89.

106. Ibid.

107. Copy to Ruby A. Black of a letter sent by Luis Muñoz Marín to Eleanor Roosevelt, December 8, 1933, CRB, CIH/UPR. The changes that informed the generational shift of leadership in Puerto Rico were evident not only to Muñoz. For example, a mainland observer with residence on the island stressed the rise of a new generation of leaders in the late 1930s. While urging the appointment of a colleague for the Supreme Court of Puerto Rico, Herbert S. McConnell, an attorney with a law firm in San Juan, commented to an acquaintance in the United States as follows:

The entire Puerto Rican scene has been and continues to be profoundly affected by the impact of ideas from the North. Instead of diminishing this impact seems to grow stronger from year to year. The younger generation of Puerto Ricans . . . is able to cope with it, as its elders are not. The outstanding figures in the Island at the present time are still those who were born before the American occupation, and who have resisted, perhaps not wilfully but inevitably, ideas from the North. . . . On the other hand, there are hundreds of young men, now in their twenties and early thirties, who in the course of time will take over the leadership of the island, and who were educated in the North, and have been wrested from their natural insularity. (Letter from Herbert S. McConnell to James M. Landis, February 4, 1938, President's Official File, Series 400, Puerto Rico: Appointments, FDRL. Hereafter referred to as POF 400, FDRL). As if to confirm these observations, in the late 1930s and early 1940s, key leaders of the island's political parties passed away such as Antonio R. Barceló, Santiago Iglesias Pantín, and Rafael Martínez Nadal. Juan Angel Silén, *Historia de Puerto Rico* (Santo Domingo: SUSAETA, 1993), p. 205.

108. Pierre Bourdieu, *Language and Symbolic Power* (Cambridge: Harvard University Press, 1991), pp. 51-52, 61-62, 123, 172.

109. Rosario Natal, *La juventud de Luis Muñoz Marín*; Rosario Natal, *Luis Muñoz Marín y la independencia de Puerto Rico*. See also Bird Piñero, *Don Luis Muñoz Marín*; Córdova, *Luis Muñoz Marín y sus campañas políticas*; Córdova, *7 años con Muñoz Marín*; Zapata Oliveras, *"Nuevos Caminos hacia Viejos Objetivos"*; Zapata Oliveras, *De independentista a autonomista*.

110. Manuel Maldonado Denis, *Puerto Rico: Una interpretación histórico-social* (México, DF: Siglo Veintiuno, 1974); Manuel Maldonado Denis, *Hacia una interpretación marxista de la historia de Puerto Rico y otros ensayos* (Río Piedras: Editorial Antillana, 1977); Juan Mari Brás, *El Independentismo en Puerto Rico: Su pasado, su presente y su porvenir* (San Juan: Editorial CEPA, 1984); Mattos Cintrón, *La política y lo político en Puerto Rico*.

111. Other individuals to consider are Samuel R. Quiñones and Antonio J. Colorado. Many of these scholars contributed to a journal called *Indice*, which had a major impact in the literary discourse of the island during the 1930s. *Indice* called upon scholars to define the personality of Puerto Ricans. Many did with extensive essays such as Pedreira's *Insularismo*. Scarano, *Puerto Rico: Cinco siglos de historia*, pp. 683-685.

112. Gelpí, *Literatura y paternalismo en Puerto Rico*, pp. 40, 48-49; María Elena Rodríguez Castro, "Tradición y modernidad: El intelectual puertorriqueño ante la década del '30," *Op. Cit.* 3 (1987-1988): 45-65.

113. I have found most appealing the approach suggested by the contributors of the volume that follows: Joseph et al., *Close Encounters of Empire*. For additional references about new approaches to politics see my historiographical review in this chapter.

114. Ibid.

115. Ibid., pp. 14, 519.

116. Néstor García Canclini, *Hybrid Cultures: Strategies for Entering and Leaving Modernity* (Minneapolis: University of Minnesota Press, 1995).

117. Ibid., p. xv. The quote is from Renato Rosaldo's "Foreword."

118. Biles, *A New Deal for the American People*, pp. 33-56.

119. Ibid., pp. 98-105.

120. Dietz, *Economic History of Puerto Rico*, p. 146. For a detailed account of the PRERA, see Manuel R. Rodríguez Vázquez, "Power and Development: The Puerto Rico Emergency Relief Administration and the Emergence of a New Colonial Order, 1933-1936" (Ph.D. diss., Temple University, 2001); Manuel R. Rodríguez Vázquez, "Representing Development: New Perspectives about the New Deal in Puerto Rico, 1933-36," *Journal of the Center for Puerto Rican Studies* 14, no. 2 (Fall 2002): 148-179.

121. Dietz, *Economic History of Puerto Rico*, p. 146.

122. Mathews, *Puerto Rican Politics and the New Deal*, pp. 58-116.

123. Ibid.

124. Ibid.

125. Ibid., pp. 127-128.

126. Dietz, *Economic History of Puerto Rico*, pp. 146-147. According to Dietz, "During 1933, the PRERA did manage to receive $770,000, but with barely one third of the population employed, this amount was wholly inadequate to the magnitude of the problem, as is indicated by the number of people applying for assistance."

127. According to Mathews, after building enough pressure, the Coalition was given a free hand by the authorities to introduce a spy in the main offices of the PRERA. Although the plan for a spy did not materialize, the Coalition managed to steal a payroll list. The party used it to make demands on who should be eliminated from the agency. Mathews, *Puerto*

Rican Politics and the New Deal, pp. 129-130.

128. Muñoz Marín, *Memorias, 1898-1940*, p. 97. The role of Ruby A. Black in Muñoz's political campaigns of the 1930s is discussed in Lorraine de Castro, "Ruby Black y las campañas de los treinta (1933)," in Juan M. García Passalacqua, ed., *Vate, de la cuna a la cripta: El nacionalismo cultural de Luis Muñoz Marín* (San Juan: Editorial LEA), pp. 61-89. See also Mary Frances Gallart, "Las mujeres en la discursiva de Luis Muñoz Marín: Primeras décadas," in Fernando Picó, ed., *Luis Muñoz Marín: Ensayos del Centenario* (San Juan: Fundación Luis Muñoz Marín, 1999), pp. 187-207.

129. Ibid., pp. 97-99.

130. Ibid., p. 99. Mathews, *Puerto Rican Politics and the New Deal*, pp. 104-105. Muñoz went to the White House with Ruby A. Black on November 7, 1933. He revisited the executive mansion before long. Ibid., p. 225.

131. Ibid., p. 148.

132. Ibid., p. 130.

133. Ibid., pp. 130-131.

134. Dietz, *Economic History of Puerto Rico*, p. 147.

135. Ibid.

136. Ibid.

137. Biles, *A New Deal for the American People*, pp. 55, 91-94; Brinkley, "The New Deal and the Idea of the State," pp. 88-89.

138. Dietz, *Economic History of Puerto Rico*, pp. 147-149.

139. Mathews, *Puerto Rican Politics and the New Deal*, pp. 129-142.

140. Letter from Alejandro Silva, President of the National Council of the Unemployed, to Ernest Gruening, August 19, 1935, File 9-8-76, Records of the Division of Territories and Insular Possessions, Department of the Interior (Record Group 126). National Archives and Records Administration.

141. Silvestrini, *Los trabajadores puertorriqueños y el Partido Socialista*, pp. 95-98.

142. Ibid., pp. 95-98.

143. *El Mundo*, July 17, 1934, p. 7.

144. Steve Fraser, "The 'Labor Question,'" in Steve Fraser and Gary Gerstle, eds., *The Rise and Fall of the New Deal Order, 1930-1980* (Princeton: Princeton University Press, 1989), pp. 55-84.

145. Mathews, *Puerto Rican Politics and the New Deal*, pp. 154-173.

146. Ibid., p. 162. Tugwell, who was then assistant secretary of agriculture, presented the ideas of Chardón to his superiors. Tugwell also prepared his own report about conditions in the Caribbean. Rexford G. Tugwell, Assistant Secretary of Agriculture, "Report on American Tropical Policy with Special Reference to Puerto Rico and the Virgin Islands." Submitted to the President in 1934. POF 400, FDRL.

147. Dietz, *Economic History of Puerto Rico*, p. 150.

148. Ibid, p. 150.

149. Puerto Rican Policy Commission, *Report*, 1934, POF 400, FDRL.

150. Ibid. Dietz offers a good review of the major points of the Chardón Plan. Dietz, *Economic History of Puerto Rico*, pp. 149-154. See also Miles H. Fairbank, "The Chardón Plan and the Puerto Rico Reconstruction Administration, 1934-1954" (Manuscript). Miles H. Fairbank Files, FDRL.

151. Mathews, *Puerto Rican Politics and the New Deal*, pp. 175-188.

152. Ibid., pp. 180-198. The Coalition attempted to approve a bill to establish a rehabilitation corporation to take charge of the Chardón Plan (ibid., p. 211). See also César A. Rey, "Parlamentarismo obrero y Coalición: 1932-1940," p. 146.

153. Puerto Rican reformers did not stay idle while sugar interests and their political allies attacked the Chardón Plan. As opposition to their proposal grew, Chardón and the PRPC insisted on the viability of reform by presenting additional data to U.S. officials. Meanwhile, Muñoz took the opportunity to step in as a strong advocate of reform. He felt confident about his association with President Roosevelt when he wired the White House several times in 1934. Muñoz sent cables to the president on June 27, August 14, and December 24, 1934. These efforts failed to speed up the implementation of the Chardón Plan. Although U.S. officials reaffirmed their commitment toward economic reconstruction, it took most of the fall of 1934 for a concrete program to take shape. During a visit to Washington, D.C., in December, Muñoz made some progress when he secured from President Roosevelt a Christmas message for Puerto Rico expressing his support for reform. Back on the island, Muñoz made good use of this valuable source of political capital when he read the message over the radio. According to Mathews, "The liberal party on the island was prepared for the event. A radio was placed on every plaza and crossroad so that an estimated half million people received the message." Mathews, *Puerto Rican Politics and the New Deal*, pp. 176, 185, 201.

154. Mathews, *Puerto Rican Politics and the New Deal*, pp. 197-222.

155. Ibid., p. 217.

156. Besides meeting with Roosevelt at the White House in November 1933, Muñoz wrote several telegrams to the president during the fall of 1934. Ibid., pp. 176, 185, 201.

157. Letter from Muñoz Marín to Ruby A. Black, February 16, 1935, CRB, CIH/UPR. Although this letter has drawn the curiosity of several historians, I believe further examination is needed to grasp the full implication of Muñoz's plan. Alvarez Curbelo, "La Casa de Cristal: El Ejercicio Senatorial de Luis Muñoz Marín, 1932-36," p. 130; Mathews, *Puerto Rican Politics and the New Deal*, pp. 218-219; Rosario Natal, *Luis Muñoz Marín y la independencia de Puerto Rico*, p. 95.

158. Letter from Muñoz Marín to Ruby A. Black, February 16, 1935, CRB, CIH/UPR.

159. Pratts, "Arts of the Contact Zone"; Pratts, *Imperial Eyes*, pp. 6-7.

160. Ibid.

161. Ibid.

162. Mathews, *Puerto Rican Politics and the New Deal*, pp. 224-225.

163. Ibid., pp. 222-225. On May 7, 1935, Muñoz and Ernest Gruening met with President Roosevelt to discuss the creation of the PRRA and other issues.

164. Ibid., p. 238. Fairbank, "The Chardón Plan and the Puerto Rico Reconstruction Administration," p. 37, Miles H. Fairbank Files, FDRL.

165. Mathews, *Puerto Rican Politics and the New Deal*, pp. 243, 282-283, 324.

166. Ibid., pp. 282-283.

167. Ferrao, *Pedro Albizu Campos y el nacionalismo puertorriqueño*, pp. 149-155.

168. Ibid., p. 155.

169. Ibid., pp. 157-159.

170. Ibid., p. 161.

171. Mathews, *Puerto Rican Politics and the New Deal*, pp. 263-265.

172. Besides being a close friend of Riggs, Tydings nominated him for the island's post of Chief of Police. Dietz, *Economic History of Puerto Rico*, p. 169.

173. According to Mathews, "the Liberal Party expected to receive on payday from 10 per cent to 15 per cent of . . . wages or salaries." Persons unwilling to contribute faced the possibility of losing their job. Mathews, *Puerto Rican Politics and the New Deal*, pp. 264-265.

174. Ibid., p. 271.

175. Ibid., pp. 270-273.

176. Ibid., p. 276.

177. Dietz, *Economic History of Puerto Rico*, p. 169. When Gruening asked Muñoz to condemn the murder of Riggs, Muñoz expressed his unwillingness to do so unless U.S. authorities made a similar statement condemning the killing of the two Nationalists under police custody. This exchange accentuated unsurmountable differences between Gruening and Muñoz. After the ouster of Puerto Rican reformers from the PRRA, the reconstruction agency lost momentum. According to Dietz, "in mid-1937, funds were cut back, and in 1939, the PRRA received only $7 million. Some aspects of the PRRA's activities (e.g., health care, sanitation, and education) were then turned over to the local government, but the lack of funds at that level led to reductions in service, anyway." Ibid., p. 156.

178. Refer to the discussion in the previous section of this chapter about political parties in Puerto Rico. Sugar interests and their political allies within the Coalition hindered the implementation of reform. In contrast to the Coalition, the Liberal Party sheltered the political aims of Puerto Rican reformers.

179. Barceló's recalcitrant stance reached new heights when he defended independence by stating the well-known words, "even if we die of hunger." Rosario Natal, *Luis Muñoz Marín y la Independencia de Puerto Rico*, p. 85; Zapata Oliveras, *De independentista a autonomista*, p. 48. Barceló also approached Albizu in an effort to form a "united front" in favor of sovereignty. Fernández, *The Disenchanted Island*, pp. 126-127. Later on, Barceló tuned down his call for independence.

180. Bothwell, *Orígenes y Desarrollo de los Partidos Políticos en Puerto Rico*, p. 174; Quiñones Calderón *Trayectoria Política de Puerto Rico*, pp. 44-45.

181. Mattos Cintrón, *La política y lo político en Puerto Rico*; Rosario Natal, *Luis Muñoz Marín y la independencia de Puerto Rico*.

182. Bothwell, *Orígenes y Desarrollo de los Partidos Políticos en Puerto Rico*, p. 175; Quiñones Calderón *Trayectoria Política de Puerto Rico*, pp. 44-45.

183. Ibid.

184. Letter from Muñoz Marín to Ruby A. Black, August 5, 1936, CRB, CIH/UPR.

185. Ibid.

186. Ibid.

187. *El Imparcial*, September 11, 12, 29, 1936; *El Mundo*, September 11, 1936.

188. *El Imparcial*, September 26, 1936; *El Mundo*, October 15, 1936.

189. Mattos Cintrón, *La política y lo político en Puerto Rico*, pp. 100-103, 112-113; Rosario Natal, *Luis Muñoz Marín y la independencia de Puerto Rico*, pp. 94-106.

190. Ernesto Juan Fonfrías, a follower of Muñoz, emphasizes that ASI placed aside the call for independence and focused on socioeconomic issues during the Liberal Party's electoral campaign of 1936. Fonfrías, *Historia de mi vida política en la fundación del Partido Popular Democrático*, pp. 97-101.

191. Alvarez Curbelo, "La Casa de Cristal: El Ejercicio Senatorial de Luis Muñoz Marín, 1932-36," p. 134; Rosario Natal, *Luis Muñoz Marín y la independencia de Puerto Rico*, pp. 90, 99.

192. Rosario Natal, *Luis Muñoz Marín y la independencia de Puerto Rico*, pp. 94-106.

193. Copy of a letter from Muñoz Marín to Ruby A. Black, November 5, 1936, President's Secretary's Files, Series 48, FDRL.

194. Fonfrías, *Historia de mi vida política en la fundación del Partido Popular Democrático*, p. 103.

195. Ibid., p. 104.

196. Quiñones Calderón, *Trayectoria Política de Puerto Rico*, pp. 48-49.

197. Muñoz and his supporters confronted legal difficulties to inscribe their new party. Barceló and his group impugned the initiative of Muñoz. Reece B. Bothwell, *Orígenes y Desarrollo de los Partidos Políticos en Puerto Rico*, p. 178; Quiñones Calderón, *Trayectoria Política de Puerto Rico*, pp. 48-49. According to Muñoz, the "Partido Liberal, Neto, Auténtico y Completo" adjourned just after it was formed. Muñoz Marín, *Memorias, 1898-1940*, p. 163.

198. Juan M. García Passalacqua, *Los secretos del patriarca: Memorias secretas de Luis Muñoz Marín* (San Juan: Editorial Cultural, 1996), p. 52. Although scant, the sources consulted indicate that steps were taken to organize the "Partido Democrático del Nuevo Trato." Elmer M. Ellsworth, who later on joined the PPD as a senator, acted as president of Muñoz's Party of the New Deal. He gathered petitions to register with electoral authorities the "Partido Democrático del Nuevo Trato" at the offshore town of Culebra. See the folder titled "Partido Democrático del Nuevo Trato," Box #637, Colección "La Fortaleza," Archivo General de Puerto Rico.

199. Córdova, *7 años con Muñoz Marín*, p. 90.

200. Ibid.

2

DEMANDS FOR REFORM AND THE RISE OF POLITICAL LEADERSHIP

To be a citizen of the universe one has to be first a citizen of a particular and determinate place.

—Antonia Sáez

I dream of a new concept of Puerto Ricanness . . . that can reciprocate high universality and conscious particularity to the spiritual traffic of the world.

—Emilio S. Belaval

Although social and economic conditions in the late 1930s spared few sectors of Puerto Rican society, no common plan existed to address the grievances of the island. Disadvantaged groups that received little or no relief from federal authorities tackled socioeconomic difficulties as best they could with their own strategies. After many years of protest, certain groups such as transport workers and unemployed laborers made significant strides in mobilizing their forces and making themselves heard in Puerto Rico. Meanwhile, elite groups that sought to overcome a hostile climate to their political aspirations attempted to solve the island's crisis with pledges that catered to a range of interests. That was the case of Muñoz and his peers after they transformed their role as advocates of the New Deal into political action with the formation of the PPD.

This chapter seeks to understand how the pressure "from below" that had mounted since the start the Great Depression and the political transformation "from above" that brought forth the PPD informed the political campaign of Muñoz's party in the late 1930s. On the one hand, disadvantaged sectors sought to improve their chances for a better livelihood by either approaching or heeding elite groups less likely to turn down their demands for reform. That is, many sectors affected by the island's crisis perceived and incorporated the PPD as part of their strategies for tackling socioeconomic grievances. On the other hand, Muñoz and his peers geared the campaign of the PPD to address key groups that had proven to be or promised to become powerful political agents. By studying the contact between the PPD and other sectors of the island's society, this chapter focuses on the conditions that informed the rise of a new discourse in favor of reform. During the late 1930s, agents in Puerto Rico began to generate a discourse of consent by acting on a common aspiration for change that did little to preclude different avenues of action and perceptions.

It is not my aim to see the island's mass movement as the turf of a party boss but rather to understand the demands for reform of people as the result of a multivocal political reality. Instead of asking who favored reform first, I focus not only on the articulation of a discourse about socioeconomic grievances but also on how that discourse enabled people to confront their situation and envision improvements. This is far from saying that a discourse of consent took shape above and beyond the relations of power between the PPD and other groups. A myriad of inequalities in Puerto Rico must be kept in mind to grasp how the process that led to a discourse of consent also informed the consolidation of PPD officials. The island's mass movement vigorously demanded improvements and achieved many successes, but it also enabled a group of leaders to impose their own goals and come forth as the authors of favorable changes.

The role played by the PPD in colonial politics can be best understood through the Gramscian concept of hegemony, a type of political relation in which a group transcends its narrow interests and becomes the "moral-intellectual leadership" of society through the expansion of a discourse. In its final form, the discourse that emerges from a hegemonic process is not circumscribed to any specific group but becomes "a dominant horizon of social orientation and action."[1] As the product of many exchanges between people, hegemony does not take place entirely at the expense of particular agents and aims. According to Ernesto Laclau, "if the hegemony of a *particular* social sector depends for its success on presenting its own aims as those realizing the *universal* aims of the community, it is clear that this identification is not the simple prolongation of an institutional system of domination but that, on the contrary, all expansion of the latter presupposes the success of the articulation between universality and particularity."[2] In the case at hand, this means that the discourse of consent and the rise of the PPD cannot be grasped without heeding particular agents and claims in Puerto Rico.

To be sure, the exchange that took place between the PPD and other agents of the island's political scene included a myriad of sectors such as workers, rural laborers, small landowners, teachers, and professionals. This chapter, however, is selective in that it focuses on key cases that exemplify the points of contact between the PPD and other groups in Puerto Rico. In this sense, I agree with the observation of Judith Butler when she says that "social transformation occurs not merely by rallying mass numbers in favour of a cause, but precisely through the ways in which daily social relations are rearticulated, and new conceptual horizons opened up by anomalous or subversive practices."[3] As a result of Puerto Rico's organic crisis in the 1930s, social and political practices on the island not only changed but eased the way to what Laclau and Mouffe call "nodal points"[4]—privileged discursive elements that produce partial fixations of meaning. While a variety of agents entered the fray of political contestation and carried on with their particular demands, they soon incorporated into their rhetoric a number of key signifiers such as *justicia social* (social justice), *pueblo* (the people), *jíbaro* (subsistence farmer), *vergüenza contra el dinero* (shame on money), and *colmillús* (fanged ones, i.e., corporations). These and many other "nodal points" did not efface the differences between agents and their claims, even though they helped "create and sustain the identity of a certain discourse by constructing knots of definite meaning."[5] Indeed, the discourse of consent owes much to how different groups accommodated to their needs a range of ideas that people shared as supporters of reform.

By focusing on groups that made demands for reform or were receptive to pledges for socioeconomic improvement, this chapter examines the political and discursive tactics of the PPD to grab the attention of people that the party perceived as its main and most accessible audience. First, I study the activities of specific sectors such as *público* drivers, unemployed laborers, dockyard workers, Communists, women, and religious groups and how the PPD targeted them as potential supporters of the party. Second, I discuss the campaign tactics of Muñoz aimed at spreading the PPD's propaganda mostly, but not exclusively, in rural areas. Finally, this chapter examines the messages that Muñoz delivered during special occasions to appeal to U.S. authorities. On the one hand, the activities and organizational drive of several groups drew the attention of Muñoz and his peers. On the other hand, the PPD appraised people not so much as agents with claims of their own but as audiences to which the party could make fervent avowals of its commitment to change. The challenge is to understand how different groups and the PPD tailored their expressions and strategies to bridge the gap between them. Many discrepancies existed between the PPD and other groups, but the call for reform and social justice offered a common ground for a discourse of consent in Puerto Rico.

Despite the variations on how the PPD addressed its audiences, it is clear that party leaders sought to become intermediaries between local and mainland interests. In doing so, the PPD made room for itself as the "moral-intellectual leadership" of an emerging "historical bloc" in Puerto Rico—meaning the broad alignment of forces held together by the call for social justice. To become that sort of leadership, PPD officials appropriated the ideals and values of people not just for banal campaign purposes but to articulate their own interests as embodying those of all Puerto Ricans. The alignment of agents in favor of reform offered a point of departure to the PPD but under conditions beyond their party's grasp. That is, what expedited the formation of a new "historical bloc" in Puerto Rico was not merely the hegemonic pretensions of PPD officials but the merger of particular interests and common aims as part of a nascent discourse of consent.

By articulating their consent toward social justice as a "political language" accessible to a wide range of interests, disparate groups of the island's mass movement created what Laclau and Mouffe call a "chain of equivalences"[6]—a linkage between the demands for reform coming from several quarters of society.

Although this linkage promised to broaden the scope of demands in Puerto Rico, its potential to introduce significant change faced the effort of Muñoz and his peers to steer the mobilization of people in a certain direction. In this respect, my analysis focuses on the practices that limited the possibility of an extensive "chain of equivalences"—that is, greater solidarity between multiple groups—but leaves room to imagine what would have been the outcome without the constraint of vested interests.

PÚBLICO DRIVERS

Long before the PPD entered the island's political scene, transport workers took the initiative to address the deplorable conditions caused by the Great Depression. Just like the needleworkers, sugar workers, Socialists, Nationalists, and Communists studied in Chapter 1, transport workers joined labor strikes and other forms of protests to counteract the ills affecting their lives.[7] Labor groups in the public and private sectors of the transport industry helped each other as they moved along a shared path of mobilization.[8] Of all transport workers, *público* drivers (the *público* is a private vehicle operated along a regular transit route by an independent driver-owner)[9] made headway to organize labor into a union of its own under the name of Chauffeurs' Association—Asociación de Choferes de Puerto Rico (ACPR).[10] The ACPR welcomed *público* drivers, truck owners, mechanics, and other wage workers of the transport industry.[11] *Público* drivers, in particular, could hope for better representation as part of the ACPR. As owners of their own vehicle, *público* drivers did not quite fit the definition of workers (i.e., wage earners lacking control of the "means of production") offered by some labor leaders and governmental authorities. Moreover, although the FLT helped to mobilize transport workers, Socialists had proven less inclined to represent labor in the service sectors of the economy.[12]

The PPD realized the potential of addressing the grievances of transport workers. Although PPD officials targeted several sectors of the working class as an audience, the party focused its attention on *público* drivers. As owners of small buses and cars, these workers supplied most of the jitney-based transportation to labor in Puerto Rico. *Público* drivers also provided oral communication to the working-class public throughout the island.[13] This promised a potential network for the growth of Muñoz's party. Shortly after the formation of the PPD, the party aligned its newspaper, *La Democracia* in favor of *público* drivers. The problems of transportation on the island received close attention. For example, *La Democracia* focused on the inefficient service of companies such as the White Star Bus Line in San Juan and the Ponce Star Line. The PPD voiced its protest against the monopoly held by these companies over transport routes and the reluctance of authorities to uphold competitors such as *público* drivers. According to the PPD, transport workers who engaged in the practice of *velloneo* (randomly picking passengers for a nickel) in routes covered by company buses were jailed or fined or had their license revoked. Moreover, the PPD argued, *público* drivers throughout the island faced police harassment, excessive taxes, and high gasoline prices.[14]

The expressions of *La Democracia* appealed to workers who had made the same claims as the PPD many times in the past. Transport workers dissatisfied with the inefficiencies of public transportation—especially, with the service provided by the White Star Bus Line in San Juan—visited Muñoz in September 1938.[15] They offered their cooperation for the inscription of the PPD. Muñoz welcomed their offer and in turn promised to address the problems of all transport workers on the island. The PPD not only announced this meeting with enthusiasm but took the opportunity to elaborate the goals and ideals of the party. Muñoz defined the PPD as a party of "free men."[16] He said that the party's leadership could act freely because it owed nothing to corporations and was adamantly opposed to buying votes. Moreover, according to Muñoz, the PPD could implement legislation in favor of the people because the party had no interests of its own. Although as a newcomer the PPD lacked exploits that could be easily impugned by its rivals, Muñoz obviated the fact that he and other party leaders belonged to the island's elite, had previously engaged in politics, and thus had particular aims in mind. To win the support of labor, Muñoz downplayed the origin of his party and conceived it as an organization above petty politics. Other PPD officials mirrored Muñoz's rhetoric by presenting themselves as a special breed of leaders above the limitations of colonial politics.

What promised an advantage to labor is that the newly formed PPD lacked a clear base of support and was bound to engage in negotiations. While the PPD moved to form a partnership with labor by presenting itself as a trustworthy ally, transport workers assessed and used the resources of Muñoz's party to further their demands for reform. The ACPR kept *La Democracia* well informed about the organizational drive of the union. *Público* drivers also sent press releases to the newspaper of the PPD for publication. For example, a long note sent to *La Democracia* by union leaders Gerardo Ferrao, Alberto E. Sánchez, and Francisco Colón Gordiany explained the grievances of *público* drivers in colorful terms. ACPR leaders lamented that in Puerto Rico the *público* driver was viewed as a "social trifling," "disassociating element," and "jail meat." According to them, "the 'público' driver lives like a gipsy. The 'público' driver does not have someone to defend him. Sometimes he is robbed and exploited without mercy."[17] By stating their claims in detail and with great zest, ACPR leaders made good use of *La Democracia* to stir the readers's imagination and bring to the fore the problems of *público* drivers. Besides the rapport between the ACPR and the PPD press, a key element in this relationship is that the expressions of *público* drivers did not stand far apart from those of Muñoz's party. PPD leaders also highlighted the abuses against labor with dazzling phrases such as "the miserable ones," "the exploited masses," "down with the fanged ones!" (a reference to large propertied interests), and the "barbaric and condemnable outrages" of corporations.

The ACPR worked fast to expand its ranks during November and December of 1938. Leaders of the ACPR sponsored conferences in several towns and organized local branches of the union. In January of 1939, preparations began for the annual congress of the ACPR.[18] A major concern of the ACPR was to decide the political position of the union for the next election. Despite debate on this issue, ACPR leaders explained that consensus existed in favor of a nonpartisan stance. *Público* drivers proved to be well aware of the difficulties faced by labor as a consequence of the political ties between the FLT and the Socialist Party. After the failed attempt of "Afirmación Socialista" to reform their party and union, the decline of the FLT served as a warning for other sectors of labor.

The ACPR annual congress enabled Muñoz to catch up with the unionization impetus of *público* drivers. He accepted an invitation to address the audience. Muñoz's message to workers searched for common points between the PPD and the ACPR. The leader of the PPD distanced himself from politics by expressing regret about the "little games" that politicians play as if they stood beyond the will of the people.[19] After noting the disastrous effects of politics on Puerto Rico's social classes, Muñoz expressed that "I would feel better here as a 'público' driver, as a worker, than as a political leader."[20] Moreover, he explained the need of *público* drivers to act as workers and not as members of political parties to avoid obstacles to their cause. The ardent denunciations of Muñoz aimed to discredit political exploits and exalt working-class concerns in an effort to assuage the misgivings of labor about the PPD. Muñoz's background as one of the foremost representatives of the island's political elite—an advantage bestowed on him thanks to his late father's position in colonial politics—did not stop him from appealing to *público* drivers with claims that seemed to sacrifice his interests in the name of labor.

By displacing his role as a politician and identifying himself as a worker, Muñoz took a significant step toward forming a partnership with *público* drivers. Moreover, by telling the ACPR about the need for nonpartisanship, Muñoz searched for a common ground on which workers and the PPD could meet. This is consistent with the overall propaganda of the PPD at that time. The party saw itself not as a political entity representing the people but as the embodiment of the people themselves. An example is the editorial of *La Democracia* commenting on the ACPR congress.[21] It contrasted that event and a political activity that had been held to honor the governor. According to the PPD, the ACPR congress, which included the participation of Muñoz's party, belonged to the people, while the homage to the governor was a bureaucratic event sponsored by parties that excluded the people. That is, *La Democracia* saw no contrast between the PPD and what it perceived as the people in Puerto Rico. With that sort of bold claim, the PPD hoped to prove itself worthy of mass support despite the deterioration of political conditions in the 1930s, meaning the erosion of credibility among leaders and the loss of faith among followers. After several years of economic depression, in a context where parties seemed to aggravate the problem with their squabbles, many groups hoped for an arrangement limiting the effects of partisanship. As groups such as the ACPR took a nonpartisan stance and PPD leaders offered a party "free of interests" in return, the initial steps were taken to define a "political language" centered on reform.

The ACPR congress brought to light many of the grievances of *público* drivers. Union leaders passed several resolutions demanding from the government better conditions for transport workers. The ACPR complained against vicious arrests, arbitrary revocation of licenses, unjust taxes, and excessive regulations over transit routes.[22] After the annual congress of the ACPR, the PPD made public several legislative projects to address the problems of *público* drivers.[23] Proposing legislation, however, was not enough for the PPD. In an effort to take issue with the problems of *público* drivers, the PPD press kept reporting many of the activities of the ACPR during the spring and summer of 1939.[24] Due to the adverse conditions faced by labor in the transport industry, the PPD had its chance to reaffirm its commitment toward *público* drivers. Although ACPR representatives made frequent demands for reform to the legislature, their protest fell on deaf ears. Even after a successful appeal to the federal court to ease the restrictions over transit routes, little action was taken by the local authorities.[25]

In May 1939, Ramón Barreto Pérez, treasurer of the ACPR and president of the Ponce local of the union, suggested a tax strike to boycott the collection of revenues from *público* drivers.[26] He also suggested an islandwide stoppage as another alternative to protest against the inaction of the government. The following week, Muñoz made a strong pledge to support the demands of the ACPR. He said that Rodolfo Ramirez Pabón, "floor" leader of the PPD in the House of Representatives, would request the governor to introduce legislation to improve the conditions of transport workers. He proposed laws to break up the monopoly of bus companies and to ensure the rights of *público* drivers to feed their families.[27]

Muñoz's ideas fell short of solving the problem. Governmental inaction and further abuse from the police convinced the ACPR to follow the suggestions of Barreto Pérez. After several weeks of preparations,[28] *público* drivers declared a 24-hour islandwide stoppage on June 14, 1939. The PPD press offered good coverage of the stoppage. According to the party, the stoppage spread to several cities and towns of the island to include ACPR members, nonunionized drivers, gas stations, and the general public. Muñoz did not miss this opportunity to reinforce his support for *público* drivers. He sent a message to the ACPR to express grief about the abuses suffered by transport workers. Muñoz also expressed irritation at the refusal of the legislature to consider the proposals of the PPD. He concluded by saying that the "exploited classes" are perfectly aware that political parties subject to the money of big corporations become "slaves" of those entities.[29] Muñoz asserted that the PPD could act freely because it did not have those ties. As on other occasions, Muñoz erased from view the interests of the PPD by portraying the party as a "blank slate" able to assimilate the concerns of labor.

Muñoz argued that the PPD and the "exploited classes" had reasons to cooperate with each other. According to Muñoz, while the PPD stood free of interests, the "exploited classes" knew that other political parties did not offer a good alternative. Muñoz appealed to the working class by presenting them as thoughtful observers able to discern the higher values and ideals of the PPD. This idea filled the pages of *La Democracia* after the labor stoppage of *público* drivers. For example, an editorial made the point that the PPD represented "sacrifice" and "unconditional solidarity" toward *público* drivers.[30] The editorial added that, on the other hand, the protest of the ACPR had to be understood as a transcendent event. According to the PPD, it offered a timely warning about the need to "respect" transport workers as a vital economic sector. The PPD also argued that the protest had significance because workers grasped who their "true allies and friends" were at times of trouble.

One of the aims of the PPD's propaganda was to provoke and mobilize *público* drivers by making references to their role as political actors. The party explained that *público* drivers embodied "conscious electors" who did not need to be told for whom they should vote.[31] According to the PPD, workers were "awakening" and learning about their "defenders" and "oppressors."[32] The PPD also appealed to the sense of dignity and manhood of workers. *La Democracia* often pictured *público* drivers in the most adverse situations such as being persecuted like "animals" or being used as "cannon fodder" during elections. According to an editorial, suffering men and women found themselves ready to fight for a better life, "in which men would be men and not pariahs, in which workers would be men and not beasts, in which 'público' drivers would be men, living as men and not persecuted like fiends."[33] With its fancy rhetoric, the PPD conjured feelings of indignation and retribution to befriend transport workers. Muñoz also promised a new era of self-esteem for labor.

The PPD's propaganda and the ACPR's expressions of protest often presented the same concerns about the island's grievances. The similarities between the statements of ACPR leaders and PPD officials illustrate that both sides not only listened well to the expressions of the other but also incorporated them as part of their discourses. A key aspect to consider is the precepts articulated by both *público* drivers and PPD officials to denounce poor conditions. For example, the idea of not selling the vote on which the PPD hammered relentlessly during its campaign was used by ACPR leaders in their own fashion. They announced that *público* drivers would use "the vote as a weapon to punish those responsible for their situation and to help their friends."[34] In a different vein, Alberto E. Sánchez, a key ACPR official and leader of the Communist Party, voiced the need to unite the people under a "popular democratic front." According to Sánchez, this longtime goal of Communists explained their support toward the PPD.[35] Besides adopting the words "don't sell your vote" and "popular democratic" as part of their rhetoric, many groups on the island came to share other expressions such as "the people," "social justice," "fanged ones," and "shame on money." Although the notions shared by many groups did not efface the differences between them, they informed a series of "nodal points"—the partial fixations of meaning of a new "political language" on the island. As people grasped in their own way a set of ideas shared by others, they gradually laid the basis for a discourse of consent.

Instead of being slogans that belonged exclusively to any one group, the expressions shared by PPD leaders and supporters owed their existence to the engagement between multiple agents. Such was the case with transport workers and PPD officials, whose rapport experienced few pauses before the election of 1940. The efforts of PPD leaders and *público* drivers to form a partnership took another turn in the ACPR annual congress in January 1940. Muñoz accepted again an invitation to address the audience. As on previous occasions, the leader of the PPD distanced himself from politics.[36] Muñoz said that, contrary to other politicians present in the congress, he did not come to address the ACPR because it had now acquired an important place in public opinion. To prove his point, Muñoz reviewed his actions in favor of *público* drivers. He also explained that the best defense of workers was found not in political parties but in their own organization. According to Muñoz, *público* drivers should act "less as politicians and more like workers, less as politicians and more like citizens, less as members of parties and more like fathers of their sons that need the bread they can provide through justice."[37]

One more time, Muñoz's advice led the way toward the PPD, a party that proclaimed itself free of interests and ready to address the demands of labor. Despite the interest of PPD officials to take charge of colonial politics, Muñoz searched for a realm beyond politics to befriend ACPR leaders and *público* drivers. In this way, the PPD attempted to align itself with political changes on the island. Tired of an economic crisis that had as its political counterpart the barren machinations of the island's parties, people hoped for reform without the impairments of partisanship. As people lost faith in political leadership, the PPD sought to present itself as a special organization with little resemblance to the other political parties. In this effort to sidestep the immobility of partisanship, PPD officials and other groups conceived reform as the basis of fruitful exchanges between them. With the demand for reform of different groups and the pledges of PPD leaders, a discourse of consent began to take shape in Puerto Rico.

UNEMPLOYED LABORERS

As in the case of *público* drivers, unemployed laborers on the island wasted little time to address the grievances caused by the Great Depression. Before the PPD had a chance to target unemployed laborers as an audience, this group had shown its potential for mobilization throughout the 1930s. Many mass gatherings of unemployed laborers produced impressive demonstrations of protest. In 1934, for example, close to 10,000 unemployed laborers met at the city of Ponce to demand reforms.[38] Besides joining their own demonstrations of protest, the vast numbers of unemployed laborers offered support to workers during labor strikes and stoppages. Despite the rise of unemployed laborers as key agents of the working class, few organizations valued individuals devoid of the means to earn a living. Moreover, unemployed laborers faced the troublesome stance of the Socialist Party and the FLT. The craft-oriented thrust of the FLT gave secondary importance to the demands of unskilled workers. When it came to unemployed laborers, FLT leaders wasted few words on their needs. For example, Socialist leader Santiago Iglesias Pantín downplayed the protest of unemployed laborers.[39] Faced with these difficulties, unemployed laborers took the same initiative as *público* drivers. They began to organize their own union under the name of Unemployed's Protective Union—Unión Protectora de Desempleados (UPD).

The PPD press tried to keep up with the organizational drive of the UPD during the late months of 1938 and early 1939. Muñoz's party made accessible the pages of *La Democracia* to leaders of the UPD. A. I. Felicci, for example, reported the efforts of unemployed laborers to mobilize forces in different towns of the island.[40] Local assemblies had been promoted to coordinate the activities of the movement and to elect delegates of the union. Pilar Llanos, president of the UPD, detailed a meeting organized by unemployed laborers in December 1938. The UPD condemned U.S. corporations and the government for the "hunger and misery suffered by the people."[41] Unemployed laborers also discussed the plan for a hunger march to be held during the next year. After the meeting, UPD members marched through the streets demanding work and direct aid to labor. The protesters made clear with their statements and demonstration that the UPD would not be easy to dismiss as an inconsequential actor of colonial politics. Despite the lack of indispensable resources such as a steady income and support from a major labor union, the UPD highlighted the failure of colonial authorities to address the island's crisis. Also, the UPD probably surprised political leaders that had a low expectation about what unemployed people could achieve with their protest.

The activities of the UPD gathered momentum in 1939. Unemployed laborers scheduled a congress to be held on February 28 to make official the creation of the UPD. While preparations began for the congress, the UPD engaged in a campaign to pressure local and federal authorities by sending them several letters of protest.[42] Unemployed laborers addressed many of their messages to President Roosevelt. The UPD complained about all sorts of problems, including unemployment, bad working conditions, corporate monopolies, "imperialist" banks, limited relief, government corruption, and abuse from the police. The remedies proposed by the UPD focused on the need to extend New Deal measures to Puerto Rico such as the Works Progress Administration (after 1939, Works Projects Administration), the Social Security Act, the Fair Labor Standards Act, the National Youth Act, and the Slum Clearance and Housing Program. Industrial development also received the consideration of the UPD.

Besides sending letters to President Roosevelt and other officials, many of the demands of unemployed laborers appeared in a periodical titled *Justicia Social* in 1940.[43] In this periodical, which was edited by Communist and labor leader Juan Sáez Corales, the UPD explained what "social justice" meant for the unemployed population in Puerto Rico. According to the UPD, "social justice" entailed not only economic improvements in urban and rural areas of the island but also conditions to ensure the sense of worth and dignity of labor. To avoid the grievances that impinged on the self-esteem of workers, *Justicia Social* offered several solutions. The periodical, for example, focused on the advantages of industrial development to overcome unemployment on the island.

Since the UPD used the term "social justice" at a time when other groups also employed the same expression, unemployed laborers contributed to the efforts of many agents to inform a new political discourse in Puerto Rico. On the one hand, the effort of different agents to improve their lives with calls for social justice converted this term into a "nodal point"—a partial fixation of meaning that led toward a discourse of consent. On the other hand, as people warmed up to a discourse centered on social justice, they helped create a "chain of equivalences"—a linkage between the demands for reform coming from several quarters of society. This became evident among workers of different industries. Although the UPD strongly voiced its support toward the New Deal and social justice, other sectors of labor expressed their interest to extend U.S. policies of reform to Puerto Rico. An example that merits attention is the short "Memorandum and Petition" sent to federal authorities by several labor organizations, including unemployed laborers, *público* drivers, and dockyard workers. The "Petition" demanded the extension of the Social Security Act, National Labor Relations Act, and the Fair Labor Standards Act to Puerto Rico.[44]

While the bond between the UPD and other sectors of labor seemed imminent, the relationship between unemployed laborers and the PPD took another turn. The first congress of the UPD on February 28, 1939, gave Muñoz a chance to sell the program of the PPD to unemployed laborers. Muñoz and other political leaders who received an invitation to attend the congress had the opportunity to address a large audience. A crowd of 598 union delegates assisted the congress under the leadership of Communist Juan Sáez Corales.[45] In his message to the UPD, Muñoz lamented the "misery," "anguish," and "hunger" suffered by the people of Puerto Rico.[46] He also expressed optimism at seeing people acting according to their needs and not according to political affiliations. Muñoz claimed that if unemployed laborers voted for a party that did not buy votes and that owed nothing to big interests, the government would belong to those who suffered.

The PPD press made public Muñoz's participation in the congress. Party officials stressed the fact that Muñoz had been the only political leader to accept the invitation of the UPD. To identify Muñoz with unemployed laborers, the PPD commented as follows: "All of you know Muñoz Marín. You know that he has never lied to you. You know that to this day he is poor, despite having the chance to maliciously use the name of Muñoz Rivera to become rich."[47] Despite the resources and prerogatives that placed Muñoz squarely in the camp of the island's elite, the PPD portrayed its leader as a poor person who could relate well to the difficulties of unemployed laborers. Notwithstanding Muñoz's background, the PPD also pictured its leader as a loyal comrade with no intention of bailing out from the ranks of the poor by making use of his social assets.

The PPD addressed unemployed laborers in the same way it did *público* drivers. On the one hand, the party tried to win over unemployed laborers by presenting Muñoz as one of them. On the other hand, the PPD addressed unemployed laborers as observers capable of discerning a common ground between the PPD and the UPD beyond mere politics. Overall, the PPD's propaganda tailored the image of both the party and its audience to gain the support of marginal or disadvantaged groups of society. Moreover, the constant references made by the PPD to the value of democracy, elections, votes, and parties sought to persuade a broad sector of labor that had remained at the sidelines of political representation. Despite much fanfare, Muñoz's proposal to the UPD about relying on votes to bring a progressive party to power was not entirely original. As in the case of *público* drivers, the ideas of the PPD developed vis-á-vis the expressions of unemployed laborers. In this sense, trying to pinpoint the originality of the PPD's or UPD's notions and rhetoric is not necessarily the best way to understand how they gained acceptance as part of a new political discourse on the island.

A good example is a press release of the UPD announcing its first congress. Notwithstanding the UPD's radical tone, the values and ideals of the union comprised many tenets voiced by PPD officials. The UPD not only expressed hope in democracy and elections but proposed to form a new political party. The union warned the "powerful"and the "well-fed" about what would happen if "the legions of hungry people . . . decided to fight the battle for happiness to which they were unarguably entitled. By making use of the right of suffrage, they could take over the government. And by making use of their force, they could shake the hoarders of the wealth that should be within their reach."[48] Although the PPD softened its discourse, the party mirrored the expressions and style of UPD leaders when it addressed unemployed laborers as an audience. Even if their choice of words set them apart, the PPD and UPD coincided on the need to mobilize people, organize a party in favor of "social justice," and introduce New Deal policies in Puerto Rico. Another similarity between the PPD and UPD is the energetic and forceful way in which they couched their aims. In the case of unemployed laborers, for example, the UPD made a point by asking people: "will the [legions of the unemployed] continue dispersed, letting the privileged ones, the ones who have everything in excess, to have their way?"[49] Since the UPD saw the government as "totally irresponsible" and with "nothing to offer," the union insisted that unemployed laborers faced a "battle of existence" and the urgent need to organize themselves in a "militant" fashion.

Just two weeks after the UPD congress, Muñoz had another opportunity to present himself and the PPD in favor of unemployed laborers. A major gathering of business interests and civic groups took place in San Juan under the name of the Economic Congress—Congreso Económico.[50] The goal of the Economic Congress was to discuss the problems of the island in an open forum and to demand remedies from federal authorities. Unemployed laborers attended the activity and selected Muñoz as their representative. Muñoz embraced his role as delegate of the UPD to the Economic Congress. He not only emphasized to the public the importance of the convention but made clear that he had "the honor to represent in the assembly the most numerous class but possibly the most defenseless: the unemployed."[51] The PPD press supplemented the claims of Muñoz when it announced that the "democratic forces" on the island had a majority in the Economic Congress. Most participants, the PPD argued, defended the "people's cause" and recognized the need to alleviate "hunger" and "misery."[52] Although as usual the PPD exalted its audience, this time Muñoz downplayed the impetus of unemployed laborers by visualizing them as "defenseless" and as needing to be rescued. This rhetorical subtlety, portraying marginal sectors more as victims than as agents, soon became a major tactic of PPD leaders. Under the guise of sympathy, Muñoz and his colleagues assigned a subordinate role to supporters by presenting them either as passive or as completely loyal to their party.

Despite the enthusiasm of the PPD for the Economic Congress, the UPD became disillusioned with the result of the convention during the following months. Unemployed laborers had good reasons for their misgivings. The committee nominated by the Economic Congress to demand reforms in Washington, D.C., did not include the UPD. Pilar Llanos, president of the UPD, wrote to federal representative Vito Marcantonio in April 1939 accusing the Economic Congress of being a sham. She said that the committee consisted of "reactionary elements, enemies of the working class . . . all of them are members of the chamber of commerce, of the sugar interest, and fascist persons, enemies of all democratic rights."[53] Muñoz did not express his opinion about the activities of the Economic Congress until the summer. In July, he recalled his role as representative of unemployed laborers.[54] Muñoz regretted that workers were being used as a "parapet" for the defense of big economic interests in Puerto Rico. He added that the omission of the UPD from the committee greatly reduced the "moral force" of the Economic Congress. Muñoz also excused himself, saying that he was unable to leave for Washington, D.C., to represent the UPD. Besides making sure to stress his zeal for the UPD, Muñoz minimized the initiative of unemployed laborers when he portrayed them mostly as the prey of economic interests. By presenting the UPD as a victim, Muñoz prepared the way for the PPD to proclaim itself as the champion of the poor.

The fiasco of the Economic Congress was one of many factors that added to the discontent of unemployed laborers. To protest conditions on the island, the UPD scheduled a "hunger march" for September 21, 1939, to receive the newly appointed governor, Admiral William D. Leahy. *La Democracia* informed the public about the preparations being made for the demonstration.[55] The hunger march was well received by *público* drivers. The ACPR insisted on being part of the march despite opposition from local authorities.[56] The PPD also reported the requests for support made by the UPD to political parties and the general public. Although the Socialist and the Communist Party came forward as supporters of the march, Muñoz insisted most vehemently on the PPD's commitment to the UPD. Muñoz claimed political legitimacy as a defender of unemployed laborers by recalling once again his role as a UPD delegate in the Economic Congress.[57] On the one hand, the preparations for the hunger march made clear the solidarity between different sectors of labor such as *público* drivers and unemployed laborers. This disposition for mutual cooperation informed the rise of an "equivalential chain"[58] or linkage between the demands for reform of many groups. On the other hand, the steps taken to organize the hunger march left few doubts about the determination of the PPD to become a representative of disadvantaged sectors in Puerto Rico. With their effort to engage different groups on the island, Muñoz and his party hoped to embody a myriad of interests besides their own and become what can be best understood as the "moral-intellectual leadership" of Puerto Rican society.

If the preparation for the march demonstrated the concern of PPD leaders and other groups, the event itself shed light on the strength of unemployed laborers. The hunger march of the UPD turned out to be a success. Several thousand participants filled the streets of San Juan. The demonstration culminated at the house of the governor, where the UPD and Communist leaders turned in a memorandum demanding better conditions for the island.[59] Besides the usual call for the New Deal, the UPD included other issues such as better expenditure of public funds, action against the speculation of food prices, access to vacant lands, and the elimination of excessive taxes. The UPD stated one of its concerns as follows: "we ask that running water and electric lights, first aid stations, schools and school lunch rooms be extended to these zones where most of our people live. We are against slums; we are for a program of building hygienic houses for the people."[60] Besides highlighting a set of grievances that impinged the most basic needs of the island's population, this statement is valuable because it made a call for reform with which the PPD could agree. Moreover, the improvement of public utilities appealed as much to local residents and political parties as to colonial authorities that not long ago gave their approval to form the first New Deal agencies in Puerto Rico—the PRERA and PRRA.

Eager to emphasize the common ground between the PPD and UPD, the party saw the hunger march as an opportunity it could not miss. The same day of the march, the PPD announced the decision of Muñoz to participate in the demonstration.[61] After the event, the PPD lamented the collapse of a tired woman who had being carrying a black flag—a sign of protest against the "complete indifference of the Legislature and . . . the governmental machinery" toward the people, "victims of the most painful misery."[62] Muñoz also wrote in *La Democracia* about the meaning of the demonstration.[63] He followed the same approach that the PPD used to describe the islandwide stoppage of *público* drivers during the summer. According to Muñoz, the hunger march was a significant event because it highlighted the need to take unemployed laborers seriously as a significant sector of the economy. Muñoz added that the march should be of special concern to commerce, industry, and professionals because one could not expect prosperity from an unemployed people.[64]

By taking issue with the hunger march, the PPD emphasized once again its role as a party free of interests that could pledge its support to marginal sectors of society. Despite the PPD's constant promise to provide support without sacrifices to political interests, the ties that developed between the PPD and UPD never stood unaffected by the ambitions of Muñoz and his party. While the call for reform offered a common ground for the PPD and UPD, the fixation of Muñoz and his peers in seeing unemployed laborers as "defenseless victims" introduced the seeds of future conflict. Far from perceiving themselves as passive actors, UPD leaders and supporters banked upon their capacity to negotiate successfully the murky waters of colonial politics.

DOCKYARD WORKERS AND COMMUNISTS

Many years of protest and organization informed the rise of dockyard workers and Communists as key agents of colonial politics. The activities of these groups climaxed during the final years of the depression era. Dockyard workers and

Communist leaders loudly voiced their demands for better conditions during the explosive strike that shook Puerto Rico in the spring of 1938. Contrary to the sugar strike of 1934, well-organized forces not only secured the support of U.S. labor leaders but also repudiated with a degree of success the representation of Socialists and FLT officials during the conflict.[65] The dockyard strike of 1938 heralded the rise of new labor organizations in Puerto Rico under the guidance of the Congress of Industrial Organizations (CIO) and the influence of Communists. Several labor groups saw a better future as part of the CIO. Not only the orientation but also the deterioration of the FLT diminished the appeal of Socialists. Not surprisingly, *público* drivers responded to the call for support of CIO leaders during the dockyard strike.[66] The extent of the conflict and its impact on the island's economy heightened the concern of political leaders and colonial authorities. Few officials remained silent about the best way to solve the labor strike.

Although Muñoz shared the concerns of other leaders and offered his thoughts in an editorial, he took a cautious position. Muñoz aligned *La Democracia* with the labor strike but did not participate in the protest of workers.[67] Muñoz explained to Ruby A. Black his decision to avoid close contact with the strike as follows: "I can not go directly into the CIO work unless I decide that that end and not political leadership is my job. As long as I do not take this decision I shall be careful not to involve CIO activities with my party. A labor movement adjoined to one political party is just as bad as a labor movement adjoined to another."[68] By supporting the labor strike from a distance, Muñoz took steps to secure the sympathy of dockyard workers without making political compromises. Labor's repudiation of Socialists probably influenced the mind-set of Muñoz, a political leader yearning for mass support but fearful of sharing the same fate as that of the Socialist Party. Besides being aware of the organizational difficulties of labor, Muñoz understood the problems to secure an effective course of political action in Puerto Rico. Since more than one political party had proven inadequate to address economic grievances or stand above petty quarrels, people on the island favored reform but feared the encroachment of partisanship. As more Puerto Ricans expressed this concern, Muñoz and his colleagues sought to place themselves squarely in the camp of social justice and far from the political practices of other parties. This situation helped to define a "political language" centered on reform. That is, with social justice as its centerpiece, a discourse of consent began to take shape.

During the PPD's electoral campaign, Muñoz addressed dockyard workers in similar ways as he appealed to *público* drivers and unemployed laborers. Compared to the previous cases, however, dockyard workers and PPD leaders either met on few occasions or their relationship did not receive much press coverage. The PPD publicized two cases of exchanges between the party and dockyard workers. In June 1939, Muñoz, Ernesto Ramos Antonini, and other PPD officials spoke to a large crowd of dockyard workers in the town of Ponce. Before addressing the concerns of labor, PPD leaders clarified that their party stood for the independence of Puerto Rico as long as the means to achieve this goal meant "order," "peace," and "friendship" with the United States.[69] Ramos Antonini then explained the effort of party officials to defend the minimum wage of workers.

After PPD officials delivered their usual speech about not selling the vote and the party's decision to avoid political alliances, dockyard workers complained to Muñoz about the deductions to their paycheck that went to certain political parties. Muñoz made an offer of legal assistance that received the approval of dockyard workers. Not long after his intervention in Ponce, Muñoz announced his meeting with the attorney general, Benigno Fernández García, to address the grievances of labor.[70] To clarify the details of this meeting, a press release narrated the encounter between PPD leaders and dockyard workers in Ponce and how the latter selected Muñoz as their representative before the Department of Justice. Two months later, *La Democracia* announced the first court hearings in Ponce to address what seemed to be "open violations" to the Wagner Act.[71] Even though it was a local and brief encounter, the exchange in Ponce enabled PPD leaders and dockyard workers to approach each other, assess the merits of negotiation, and reach a favorable understanding.

In October 1939, Muñoz had a better opportunity to intervene in favor of dockyard workers and display political bravado. When the authorities of San Juan prohibited a picket line during a strike of dockyard workers, Muñoz joined the stoppage to uphold the rights of labor.[72] Muñoz voiced his disposition to be arrested if necessary to defend the strikers' picket line as a legal form of protest. Muñoz also publicized his effort to assist two workers arrested during the strike. After conveying to the public what he saw as a prolonged and tortuous process to seek legal recourse for the two detainees, Muñoz called governmental procedures "anti-democratic, anti-American, and anti-civilian." The arrest of the two workers and the legal system they had to confront confirmed to Muñoz the "great helplessness in which workers find themselves with respect to their most elemental rights before great capitalist organizations."[73] Muñoz pledged to join the picket line of as many strikes as needed to defend the rights of labor. Notwithstanding the odds that Muñoz perceived against him and dockyard workers, he announced with satisfaction that the PPD managed to free from jail the two detainees. According to Muñoz, this represented a great victory in favor of the fundamental rights of labor.

While Muñoz produced an image of labor as a victim of great atrocities, workers formed in turn an opinion about Muñoz. After the strike, dockyard workers sent a letter of gratitude to Muñoz for defending strikers who had been "stepped upon by men that were brought to power by those same workers."[74] In their letter, workers expressed discontent toward Socialists and sympathy toward Muñoz. They stressed that the Department of Labor under the direction of the "ominous" FLT was largely to blame. According to labor, the actions of Muñoz during the strike made evident by comparison how a cadre of "false labor leaders" profited from "the ignorance, the hunger, and the needs of Puerto Rican laborers." If Muñoz saw an advantage in portraying workers as "helpless," labor in turn found it useful to contrast the commitment of Muñoz and the failure of Socialists. While PPD leaders desired legitimacy as the ones capable of offering improvements to their passive followers, workers sought a degree of accountability from those with resources beyond the grasp of labor. Despite the disparate interests that informed the views of Muñoz and dockyard workers, they found a ground of common action in their demand for better conditions in Puerto Rico.

Although the PPD engaged labor groups with Communist ties such as dockyard workers, *público* drivers, and unemployed laborers, the relationship between Communists and the PPD was elusive at best. As a recently formed party facing the urgent need to expand its ranks, the PPD's discourse incorporated many values, symbols, and expressions not entirely of its own creation. Even the slogan of the PPD, "Bread, Land, and Liberty," was far from original due to the fact that it mirrored the slogans of several revolutionary movements. Besides resembling the words of Bolsheviks—"Peace and Land"—and Mexican revolutionaries—"Land and Liberty"[75]—the PPD's slogan echoed the call for "bread and liberty" made by the American Popular Revolutionary Alliance in Peru.[76] Most important of all, the motto of the PPD comprised almost the exact words used by Communists in Puerto Rico. A case that stands out is the Communist periodical *Verdad*, which included on its front page the words "For Bread, Land, and Liberty!" in the early 1940s.[77]

The elusive origin of the PPD's slogan has led to a disagreement among scholars. According to Lieban Córdova and other authors, Muñoz and his supporters came up with the phrase "Bread, Land, and Liberty."[78] Juan Angel Silén and Kenneth Lugo argue that Communists deserve credit for the motto of Muñoz's party. Silén mentions that *Lucha Obrera*, the main periodical of the PCP, used the words "Bread-Land-Liberty" in 1935.[79] Lugo asserts that Communist leader César Andreu Iglesias conceived the PPD's slogan.[80] Despite the disagreement among scholars, it is clear that both Communists and the PPD used the same words during the political campaign of 1940. The expression "Bread, Land, and Liberty" not only has a similar history to that of "social justice" but also suffered the same fate as part of a new political discourse in Puerto Rico. Instead of owing its appeal to the authorship and originality of a single actor, the PPD's slogan gained significance thanks to the haphazard interaction between multiple agents on the island. While different groups made demands for reform and the PPD promised to take action in return, people articulated according to their needs many ideas that were not exclusively their own. By sharing a range of notions without forfeiting their particular interests, many groups made their contribution to a nascent discourse of consent. This is the case with PPD leaders and Communists, both of whom made innovative appropriations of the phrase "Bread, Land, and Liberty."

Besides sharing the same slogan and a similar interest in reform, Communists and PPD leaders left few trails that can help us understand the ambiguous relationship between them. Communists voiced their decision to support the PPD[81] not out of loyalty toward Muñoz but to coalesce a "popular democratic front" in favor of their revolutionary aims. This plan obeyed the decision of the Communist International to enter into coalitions with advanced liberals and other political groups to combat fascist forces. When the Seventh World Congress met in Moscow in 1935, the Puerto Rican Communist Party (PCP) not only gained admission to the

Comintern but also abandoned its hard-line revolutionary zeal in favor of the "popular front" strategy.[82] Besides adopting a tactic that became common among Communist Parties in Latin America,[83] the PCP operated under the influence of Earl Browder and U.S. Communists.[84] Browder, who led the American Communist Party after being chosen by U.S.S.R. premier Joseph Stalin,[85] introduced the "united" or "popular front" policy to the United States. This policy reoriented the activities of mainland Communists, who were busy assisting local branches of their party, the labor movement, and distant affiliates such as the PCP. Lizabeth Cohen explains the situation of the U.S. Communist Party during the 1930s: "As the thirties wore on, the party's influence on workers, black and white, grew, reflected somewhat in larger membership but much more so in the way the party cooperated with the mainstream institutions that workers most identified with, the Democratic Party and the CIO unions."[86]

The PCP followed the lead of mainland Communists but only to a certain extent. While PCP leaders welcomed the pledges of Muñoz, they still had fresh in their mind the decline of Socialists. Thus, the PCP kept some distance from political parties and did not rush into alliances. Despite their political misgivings, Communists did all they could to mobilize workers. After abandoning their hard-line revolutionary stance, PCP organizers understood that to attract labor they had to subordinate their more radical agenda to the practical concerns of the rank and file, whose dissatisfaction with capitalism tended to focus more on securing improvements soon than promoting an alternative system for the future. By targeting reform as the solution to people's troubles, the PCP helped workers to look beyond their specific aims and form a "chain of equivalences"—a linkage between the demands for reform of different groups. It is not a surprise that Communists figured in the ranks of labor such as *público* drivers, unemployed laborers, and dockyard workers. Although labor did not join the PCP in massive numbers, many workers were inspired by Communist leaders to take to the streets in protest against hunger, deprivation, unemployment, and the lack of relief.

The PPD dealt with PCP organizers at least informally when the party appealed to labor groups with Communist ties. Officially, however, Muñoz and his supporters distanced themselves from Communists. In February 1940, PPD leaders made public their decision to reject the support of the PCP.[87] The PPD's statement came shortly after Communists announced their endorsement of Muñoz's party.[88] Fearful of leaving unanswered the assertions of Communists, PPD leaders offered reasons to reject the PCP's offer of support. Muñoz's party stressed above all its policy against political pacts. To make clear that the PPD did not take this position only with Communists, party leaders stressed that their policy echoed "the unequivocal rejection of the people against the entire system of alliances, coalitions, and arrangements" that have had "ill-fated" consequences for the island since the formation of the Puerto Rican Alliance. Besides stating its views about colonial politics, the PPD also claimed that its stance mirrored the decision of President Roosevelt to turn down the support of Communists in the United States. After offering justifications for their position, PPD leaders did not restrain themselves from criticizing the PCP. Among the issues that the PPD found disturbing, the party mentioned the PCP's ties to the dictatorship of Russia, its hostility toward private property, and its enmity toward religion. According to PPD leaders, their party was against the "system of exploitation" prevalent in Puerto Rico but favored the right of the people, other than abusive corporations, to become owners of property and engage in religious activities.[89]

Faced with the apathy of the PPD, PCP leaders soon expressed their disappointment and downplayed the appeal of Muñoz's party.[90] Communists stressed the importance of their own party in the creation of the PPD. According to the PCP, Communists first proposed the idea of a "popular democratic front" of "anti-imperialist" forces. Since Communists saw the need to unite all the progressive forces on the island, PCP leaders regretted the steady drift of the PPD toward an undesirable direction. Hence, Communist leader César Andreu Iglesias not only announced that the PCP would run in the election of 1940 but also unveiled a plan to focus on the candidacy of only one member, Alberto E. Sánchez, for the House of Representatives. For the Communists, their campaign for a single representative promised a fail-safe approach to introduce a staunch advocate of reform into the island's government. The breach between the PCP and PPD—a setback that hardly cut short future exchanges between them—had to do with issues not limited to an ideological incompatibility. In the case of Communists, international events should be taken into consideration. Probably, the PCP's decision to eschew the PPD had to do in part with the Nazi-Soviet Pact of 1939, which baffled Communists in the West. After Adolf Hitler and Stalin signed their nonaggression treaty, Communists distanced themselves from World War II. PCP leaders did so at first when they criticized the approval of the PPD and other parties toward the war plans of President Roosevelt. For them, the war did not augur well for labor, reform, or the fight for the island's independence—all major concerns of the PCP and its followers since the mid-1930s.[91]

In the case of Muñoz and his party, at the other end of the PCP-PPD breach, one finds a different set of issues. The PPD's repudiation of Communists responded in part to the accusations of political opponents. Although the rivals of Muñoz often raised issues more imagined than real, the accusations to red-bait the PPD were frequent during the political campaign for the election of 1940.[92] In some instances, the apprehension of PPD members and followers about the accusations of political rivals became evident. In October 1940, for example, the president of the local committee of Gurabo wrote a letter to Muñoz about the circulation of an inflammatory leaflet in his town and Caguas. According to this letter, the leaflet charged PPD officials of being "communist incendiaries and assassins." The rivals of Muñoz also said the PPD's slogan stood for "ANTI-CHRISTIAN COMMU-NISM" and the party was a "WOLF disguised as a lamb."[93] Another person wrote to Muñoz with similar concerns stating that, according to a farmer of his town, the leader of the PPD wanted to establish Communism in Puerto Rico.[94] Hence, PPD leaders distanced themselves from Communists and appeased followers with statements in favor of property and religion. Even though they sacrificed the support of Communists in favor of other constituencies, PPD leaders probably recognized the potential of the PCP in mobilizing large numbers of workers.[95] Despite the estrangement between Communists and the PPD, later events showed that these agents did not cut their political ties as much as conceal them. As will be seen, the PCP and PPD found more than a few occasions for common action.

WOMEN

As a sector that gained a greater stake in the island's economic life, women had reason to protest in the 1930s. In spite of the Great Depression, women joined the Puerto Rican labor force in large numbers as teachers, nurses, tobacco workers, and needleworkers. As of 1930, women represented 70% of teachers in public education.[96] Women also significantly augmented the island's labor force as part of the needlework industry, the second economic sector of importance during the 1930s.[97] Besides contributing with their work to their family's income, women offered their support to the island's unions and launched their own organizational drive. For example, home needleworkers became members of nine unions affiliated with the FLT in 1934.[98] Another case is the activities of the Women's Labor Congress—Congreso Obrero de Mujeres—to defend the minimum wage law.[99] The labor strikes of women in the tobacco and needlework industries also stood out during the 1930s. Despite these gains, a long way lay ahead for women to overcome economic hardships and achieve gender equality. For example, home needleworkers faced an industry that remained largely unregulated, made unionization difficult, and did not correspond to the organizational aims of the island's labor unions.[100] The fact that women joined the labor force in great numbers but consistently earned lower incomes than male workers makes clear the difficulties they had to face.[101]

In addition to their efforts against economic disadvantages, women struggled to surmount their poor participation in politics during the 1930s. To achieve genuine political representation, women faced challenges no less formidable than the ones that beset them in the economic sector. Only after building enough pressure did women gain a limited right to vote in 1929 and universal suffrage in 1935.[102] Despite the difficulties to secure the right to vote and many other odds against them, women took actions that left an indelible mark of their political endeavors. Many women became members of political parties on the island and contributed to their electoral campaigns. In some cases, women formed organizations such as the Republican Union Women's Association—Asociación de Mujeres de la Unión Republicana—and the Sisterhood of Liberal Women—Hermandad de Mujeres Liberales—to assist their parties in raising funds and securing votes.[103] In other cases, women had the opportunity to run as party candidates. For example, Adela Ramírez de Ramírez and Isabel Andreu de Aguilar of the Liberal Party ran, respectively, for the House and Senate of the island's legislature. Socialists, too, encouraged the membership of women in their party. One of their leaders, legislator Bolívar Pagán, deserves credit for having introduced the bill of universal suffrage for women that became law in 1935. Before the end of the decade, Republican

María Luisa Arcelay and Liberal María Martínez de Pérez Almiroty became legislators in Puerto Rico.[104] The latter was the first female senator of the island.

Notwithstanding the inroads of women in Puerto Rico, the PPD failed to address many of their grievances. To a great extent, the PPD compartmentalized its search for the support of women. Muñoz's party mostly appealed to women according to their assigned task within the domestic sphere. Even more, on rare occasions the PPD addressed women directly as it did other sectors of the island's population. Almost always the PPD defined and appealed to women in terms of their relationship to men. This approach is evident in the pages of *El Batey*, a small newspaper the PPD published to spread the party's propaganda to rural areas. For example, one of the first messages of *El Batey* to its female audience assumed that women's awareness of social grievances derived from the pains they faced at home in nurturing their sons and feeding their husbands.[105] In their role as housekeepers, the PPD argued, women saw up close from "dawn to dusk" the cry of children, the constant hunger, the lack of food, the empty stove, the illnesses of their offsprings, and medical resources out of their reach. The point here is not that the PPD fantasized about the concerns of women and their dire situation at home. Rather, the point is that the PPD's depiction vanished from view the problems of women beyond the household such as wage disparities, unequal employment opportunities, their precarious foothold in politics, and their overall subordination to men.

Despite the evidence of women's activities outside the home, the PPD depicted its female audience mostly as wives and mothers with few other concerns. That is, the contributions of women to the island's economy and politics did not preclude the women-as-housekeepers and women-as-victims approach of the PPD. Again, the party saw women and their domestic chores in narrow terms when *El Batey* claimed that "it is possible to win against [corporate] interests if women—mothers, wives, girlfriends, and daughters—tell their men every day that they must have shame and not sell themselves to politicians."[106] As if to prove that women had this very same concern, *El Batey* quoted at length the words that Muñoz heard from a rural woman who stopped him in mid-road during his campaign.[107] For the PPD, these words proved that women mostly lamented in Puerto Rico the impossibility of feeding their family and caring for their homes. Besides expressing her lamentations, the woman who spoke to Muñoz emphasized her solution. No longer she would accept the buying of votes, which availed her family of food stocks and petty commodities on election day but led to misery the rest of the year. Instead, she would not let her husband sell his vote in the next election and would follow Muñoz, the "only hope" on the island.

By using this woman's words as a point-by-point confirmation of the PPD's precepts, the party offered a good understanding of what it expected from women. Since the PPD alleged that "through the mouth of this desperate woman spoke all women, all wives, and all mothers," the party left no doubt about the importance of their duty in caring for, and guiding, men. Moreover, once the PPD placed its female audience within a limited sphere of domestic chores, the party felt free of restraints to venerate women. The island's female population, the PPD argued, had the "sacred obligation of defending with their votes the prosperity of their sons."[108] Women also had to demand "shame, valor, and honesty" from men weak enough to sell their votes. As housekeepers, the PPD assigned women a higher moral task. The party implored women to make their husband "behave like men and not as a beast sold against their own sons." Since the PPD insisted that selling the vote equaled selling one's offspring, the party told women with a sense of urgency "save your home and save your sons!"[109] With gender constructs that emphasized the moral superiority of women and the banal weaknesses of men, the PPD hoped to empower women, but just to a certain extent. They could make claims of their own and join the demands for reform on the island as long as they did not overstep their realm of legitimate action—the domestic sphere. A discursive subtlety that seemed to place men on a lower moral ground only served to impose limitations on women in accordance with prevalent boundaries of gender inequality in Puerto Rico.

Since the identity of any subject does not develop in isolation or constitute immutable essences, the PPD's notion of women hinged on broader interpretations of gender that gave an advantage to men. Instead of being fortuitous utterances or the expressions of a neutral bystander, the gender-biased conceptions of PPD leaders developed hand in hand with practices that reinforced certain discourses about women and men in the island's society. As Anna Marie Smith points out, "the very categorization of human bodies in the supposedly given biological categories, 'male' and 'female,' depends upon the normalizing work of a historically specific political apparatus."[110] This means for the case of Puerto Rico in the 1930s-1940s the conditions that gave an edge to the employment of men over that of women. A favorable job market for men ensued as a result of policies that strengthened the definition of men as wage earners and women as homemakers.

In his analysis of the Women and Children's Bureau, Félix O. Muñiz-Mas demonstrates that certain New Deal agencies in Puerto Rico subordinated the work of women to that of men by defining the latter as the head of the household.[111] Moreover, according to Muñiz-Mas, the notion of the male breadwinner of some federal programs in turn influenced the reforms of the PPD. Since female employment was not the priority of policymakers, the government stressed, for example, the protection of labor in the sugar industry but not in home needlework production. This bias had dire consequences for the effort of women to meet their needs as part of the island's labor force. While *público* drivers, unemployed laborers, dockyard workers, and Communists made room for mutual cooperation or "chain of equivalences," working-class women did not have the same opportunity to form a linkage with the demands for reform of other agents. Even upper- and middle-class women would have to contend with definitions that placed them at home or at the service of men so common in the PPD press.

While the PPD's campaign represented a step backward from the inroads of women in previous years, the initial discourse of the party suffered enough inconsistencies so as to leave a door open for the participation of women. Despite addressing its female audience mostly as housekeepers and servants of men, the PPD issued remarks about the initiatives of women beyond the domestic sphere.

Perhaps prodded by female activists, Muñoz's party publicized some women's endeavors. For example, *La Democracia* reported a PPD meeting that had as its aim the formation of the Local Committee of Ladies in Yabucoa. The PPD also paid attention to the activities of the Association of Graduate Women of the University of Puerto Rico.[112] In the United States as well PPD leaders tried to follow the activities of women when, for example, party representative Antonio J. Colorado joined a conference of the U.S. Section of the Women's International League for Peace and Freedom in March 1940. Although the information at hand about the PPD's involvement in this activity is minimal, no doubt exists that the league made an earnest effort to address the problems of Puerto Rico by inviting key speakers to the conference such as Congressman Vito Marcantonio, Dr. Rafael Picó, and Earl P. Hanson, former planning consultant for the PRRA.[113]

Besides commenting on the activities of different organizations, the PPD also made sporadic references about its female representatives. For instance, the party boasted that Muñoz's mother, Amalia Marín, and the president of the Municipal Committee of San Juan, Felisa Rincón, had joined other PPD officials to address women.[114] In an effort to broaden their ranks, these female leaders extended an invitation to their peers not only in San Juan but also in several towns of the island. The PPD defined the significance of the activity with words that stressed not the initiative of women but the party's usual outlook about the island's quandary: "the fight is not of men of parties but between the exploited people of all parties and the exploiters and their servants in all parties."[115] As they moved within the boundaries of the PPD's rhetoric, women reproduced the party's propaganda but did not foreclose their participation in mobilizing the female population of Puerto Rico.

Although Muñoz and his peers did not embrace their female audience as they did other groups, women left their mark as part of the PPD by running as candidates of the party. As one of the candidates for the Municipal Assembly of Guayama, María Vaquer Santiago issued a statement in *La Democracia* about her political commitment.[116] According to Vaquer, the PPD recognized women as indispensable supporters of reform. Alma Delgado, who aimed to become a member of the House of Representatives for the towns of Añasco, Aguada, and Rincón, appeared in the PPD press as a lawyer well aware of the island's problems.[117] Finally, María Libertad Gómez, who also aspired to be part of the House of Representatives, claimed political legitimacy as a teacher, farmer, and collaborator of the New Deal from Utuado.[118] Gómez had a range of experiences that could help the PPD. Besides her service as an organizer and functionary of tobacco workers in her town, she worked as a teacher and accountant after completing a degree in the YMCA College of Washington, D.C. Although the PPD press issued few statements about these candidates, it is possible to assume that women engaged in the political campaign of female candidates of diverse backgrounds such as the lawyer and teacher mentioned above.

The inclusion of female candidates as part of Muñoz's party did not shift the burden of the PPD's discourse in favor of women. Nevertheless, Muñoz's party failed to produce a monolithic discourse free of exceptions and contradictions. After the electoral victory of its female candidate for Utuado, the PPD relied mainly on Gómez to articulate its perception about women's role in the public domain. Probably on her own initiative, Gómez made provocative remarks about the expectations of the PPD. Instead of replaying the PPD's narrow perception of women and their domestic tasks, Gómez stressed in one of her messages the need to consider women for key governmental positions as well as for posts of lesser importance.[119] On another occasion, Gómez pronounced a discourse to the Club of Women of the University of Puerto Rico that begged intellectual women to reach out toward "their sisters in the countryside."[120] To achieve this goal, Gómez suggested public conferences to bridge the gap between women across the island. According to Gómez, by bringing together female graduates and women from rural areas, they had a better chance of achieving political representation. Gómez believed that, according to the principle of democracy, "women should impose themselves as men are imposed in the direction and management of Government."[121]

As a representative of the PPD, Gómez also took the opportunity to highlight the value of education for children and women.[122] Since better access to educational resources promised to improve the life of these sectors, she promised to introduce legislation to this effect. For her, while the school system found itself detached from "real and practical life" on the island, divorce and instability at home aggravated the problems of children. She had strong words for those responsible: "unfortunately for our beloved Puerto Rico, the vices of those above have been legalized for the protection—they say—of those below."[123] Gómez did not elaborate further on this statement, but the nuance of her words corresponds well with her awareness of class differences in Puerto Rico.

Finally, Gómez honored the contribution of women to the program of food production during the war effort.[124] Regardless of the progress already made, Gómez argued that women could do even more to increase the food supply in Puerto Rico. She said women could improve the program in many other ways, particularly if they joined the government's propaganda efforts. Another suggestion of Gómez urged city women to harvest food in their backyard. She emphasized that "social rank" or "economic situation" should not hinder this effort. Clearly, this last appeal referred to female sectors other than the working class. What seemed to be a trait in the expressions of Gómez is her concern about the gap between women of different social classes. Perhaps Gómez's concern is an offshoot of a populist discourse intent on uniting different groups under the rubric of "the people." This, however, was not incompatible with, or made less plausible, an alternative perspective: the genuine preoccupation of Gómez in addressing the immediate grievances of women.

Notwithstanding the support of women for the PPD, the party failed to fully acknowledge their involvement in politics. For example, women remained an "invisible" task force beyond the official purview of Muñoz's party, even though they significantly contributed to distribute *El Batey* and other pieces of PPD propaganda in rural areas of Puerto Rico.[125] Women did not miss the fact that much more could be done for the female population. Worthy of mention is the letter that

Carmen García sent to Muñoz after the election of 1940.[126] García valued Muñoz's defense of the New Deal but lamented the absence in Puerto Rico of a feminist movement like that of the United States. While Puerto Rican women asked only for "little things and clerical work," on rare occasions they focused on "executive positions that could honor women." García highlighted the possibility of "equal representation of men and women in all spheres of government."[127] She concluded that although "a Miss Perkins would be too much to ask for now," it could be possible to nominate a Puerto Rican women for sub-commissioner of labor. The suggestion of García to Muñoz banked upon "the fundamental principles of democracy" and entailed an opportunity for women to prove their capacity in administration. She made a demand that broadened the scope of reforms of PPD officials. Whether or not this message appealed to the leader of the PPD, it voiced a reasonable step to overcome the wide gap of gender inequality in Puerto Rico.

RELIGIOUS GROUPS

Like other sectors of society, religious groups expressed intense concerns about the island's socioeconomic needs and the urgency of reform. Aside from sharing with others an interest in reform, religious groups gave free rein to different practices, visions, and alternatives to deal with grievances in the 1930s. A central aspect that set this group apart from other sectors is how the beliefs of devotees underscored a drastic outlook about the Great Depression. Even if we keep in mind as a caveat that Puerto Rico had a myriad of congregations with dissimilar precepts, the fact remains that the economic crisis combined with spiritual notions to produce extreme perceptions among the people of faith on the island. According to Nélida Agosto Cintrón, the impact of the Great Depression led to movements of religious revival and spiritual fervor that centered on beliefs about the end of the world and the Second Coming of Christ. Agosto Cintrón explains that these movements included charismatic manifestations, the use of "languages" to unveil revelations, the invocation of prophecies, and up-close experiences with the Holy Ghost.[128]

What took place in the island's religious community can be properly described as "millenarianism."[129] On the one hand, millenarianism portrays an evil social order of unprecedented magnitude that could very well jeopardize the spiritual well-being of people. On the other hand, millenarianism foreshadows not only the actions of purified forces and the destruction of evil but also the salvation and moral regeneration of society. While millenarianism became common among devotees, religious groups did not lose focus on reform. In particular, religious authorities on the island centered their attention on the New Deal. A case that deserves attention is the study carried out by the U.S. Catholic Church at the request of the bishops of Puerto Rico.[130] When the PRRA began operations on the island, Catholics produced a long report to support the reconstruction plan of federal authorities. Not unlike U.S. officials, Catholics proposed a broad plan to revamp the island's economy that included changes to agricultural production and a program of industrial development. Initiatives of this sort heightened the political appeal of religious groups as well as Muñoz's drive to bring them into the fold of his party. Millenarianism would also play a vital role in the political maneuvers of the PPD.

Religious groups did not remain for long beyond the scope of the PPD's propaganda. Key aspects of the island's Christian faith figured prominently in the pages of *El Batey*. In the first issues of *El Batey*, the PPD included statements that left no doubt about the party's pledge to religious groups. Since a strict reference to Catholicism or Protestantism could not do justice to different denominations or other religions on the island, the PPD faced a challenge in its attempt to appeal to as many religious groups as possible. In an effort to negotiate a middle ground, the PPD promised to cooperate with all the creeds on the island but hinted at its inclination toward the Catholic Church.[131] This did not sit well with all religious groups. It soon became evident that the PPD touched a nerve among Protestant devotees by calling Catholicism the main faith on the island.

A case that sheds light on this issue is a letter that a Baptist missionary, Narciso Cosillos Piñero, sent to Muñoz on May 8, 1939.[132] It was a message of protest against the PPD's statements on religion. Cosillos made a provocative assertion when he explained that the *jíbaro* (subsistence farmer) of old, when Spain controlled the island, had been replaced by the *jíbaro* of today, "a person that is not asleep." His next observations did not pale in comparison. On the one hand, Cosillos explained that most people in the countryside belonged to the Evangelical Church, the one that best catered to the interests of the rural population. On the other hand, he criticized the Catholic Church for being the church of the "aristocracy" and expressed little sympathy for priests who seldom visited rural homes. The message of Cosillos raised issues far from trivial and offered an assessment close to reality. Recent studies stress that while Protestantism made headway among lower- and middle-class groups, the island's elite mostly identified with the Catholic Church despite the institution's broad popular base.[133]

Although the inroads of Protestantism made this faith hard to miss to the PPD, the heritage and prestige of the Catholic Church carried much weight for the party. The influence of the Catholic Church, however, explains only in part the priorities of PPD leaders. When addressing religious groups, the campaign of the PPD did not hinge entirely on matters of faith. Another aspect to consider is the convergence between Catholicism and nationalism in Puerto Rico.[134] Before the Great Depression but especially during the crisis, when a debate about Puerto Rican identity ensued, many groups exalted past traditions such as Catholicism and made them part of their notion of a national "ethos." Since the PPD wanted the support of Nationalists and other groups with such a definition of Puerto Rican identity, the party made ample room for Catholicism in its rhetoric.

The PPD showed little reluctance to use religious values, symbols, and expressions as a source of political legitimacy. Shortly after *El Batey* began to circulate, the PPD praised Holy Week as an important event to overcome "hunger," "misery," and "exploitation" in Puerto Rico.[135] While the PPD attempted to align itself with religious groups during a key period of spiritual fervor, the party offered a version of Christ that demanded the political mobilization of all Puerto Ricans.

Overt expressions of support for religious groups to promote "genuine Christian customs" in Puerto Rico made the political strategies of the PPD somewhat unusual. But the PPD's use of religious motifs truly broke many conventions when the party established a parallel between its own agenda and the values of the church. According to *El Batey*, the PPD and the church fought for a common goal: to "save the people" and bring "equality and justice" to the island. The only difference lay in the arena of their fight. One took place in politics, and the other in a spiritual realm. Despite this fact, *El Batey*'s Manichaean rhetoric presented the PPD and the church as interchangeable entities. Whether addressing political corruption or the frailties of the soul, *El Batey* placed the PPD and the church on a moral high ground that blurred the distinctions between them.

Besides the PPD's ingratiation with religious groups and their beliefs, the party did the most it could with the "millenarian" manifestations in Puerto Rico. With "millenarianism" as a sounding board for the party, the PPD's rhetoric was not an aberration or out of sync with reality but emerged as an effort of Muñoz and his peers to insert themselves into people's imagination as the harbingers of salvation against an evil social order. While the religious community experienced visions of the Apocalypse and the advent of Christ, the PPD stepped in to provide an answer to their concerns. The most powerful religious motif incorporated into the PPD's discourse centered around Luis Muñoz Marín. The PPD constructed an image of its leader by presenting him as a figure of messianic proportions. *El Batey* not only informed the public about ways to "save the people" but also offered a redeemer in the person of Muñoz. This was done through rhetorical subtleties and innuendos, like placing two articles with suggestive titles side by side. Worthy of attention is an article by Muñoz titled "God created bread for every mouth" placed next to a article titled "From Muñoz Rivera to Muñoz Marín."[136] By making reference to the real and religious symbolism of the father-son nexus, the second article presented Muñoz as the rightful heir to political authority on the island. According to the PPD, Muñoz was a messenger of hope ushering in a new era of progress to overcome the decades of political stagnation that followed his father's death.

The relationship between Muñoz and his father, as presented by the PPD, implied an analogy to the relationship between God and Jesus. This rhetorical strategy was far from incidental. Muñoz backed up his religious aura with a yearly ritual that became widely publicized by the PPD. Each summer, Muñoz traveled to his hometown, Barranquitas, to visit the tomb of his father. The leader of the PPD paid homage to Muñoz Rivera by pronouncing a discourse. In his visit of 1938, Muñoz made a dramatic claim: "we come to rescue your sepulcher so many times visited by ambition. We come with a high and noble battle cry to rescue your sepulcher from impious businessmen. We come to swear to you, before the heart of our people, that we will throw out from the temple of your sepulcher the marketeers of your name."[137] Like Jesus in Jerusalem, Muñoz aimed his wrath at individuals whom he perceived as unworthy of his father's mercy. In this case, the "impious businessmen" were Muñoz's political opponents. Despite the specificity of his political concern, Muñoz portrayed the issue as the ultimate spiritual crusade.

During the electoral campaign of 1940, Muñoz repeated the previous phrase and made further claims as the rightful messenger of his father and God: "The intelligence that God wanted to give me, I pass forward to you! Through my word you see as clearly as I see. God gave me intelligence so that the humble ones among my people can see—not to blind them or confuse them."[138] With statements of this sort, Muñoz could do no other than target even the most extreme devotees of "millenarian" visions in Puerto Rico. By emphasizing his impersonation of Jesus and the gift that God bestowed upon him, Muñoz promised to enlighten people against the worst kind of evil. From a political standpoint, this tactic of Muñoz was consistent with the objectives of his party. Since the PPD aimed not just to represent its own interests but to embody the needs of all people—that is, to become the island's "moral-intellectual leadership"—the party focused on issues in such a way that it made dissent an affront to common sense and to the basic moral values of Puerto Ricans. Before long, questioning the PPD would require an assault against claims that sided the party with the downtrodden, the incorruptible, and even God.

The populist discourse of the PPD incorporated religious motifs to get its message across to the island's population. The aim of the PPD was not only to communicate its program to a broad audience but also to present it as one of transcendent importance. *El Batey* and *La Democracia* never understated the material benefits of the social and economic measures proposed by the PPD. However, the PPD press made clear that the party's policies of reform were significant insofar as they belonged to an overall plan of "moral cleansing" of Puerto Rican society. In other words, to get the attention of workers, rural laborers, the unemployed, and others, the PPD did more than aim its discourse at their back pockets where the money is kept. Besides focusing on monetary needs, the PPD solicited a response from people based on their notion of dignity, deference, fairness, and even spiritual self-esteem. In this respect, the religious motifs of the PPD attempted to create a sense not only of participation but also of communion between the party and its audience. Leaders and followers of the PPD could embrace as one in a new era of "salvation" for Puerto Rico. With Muñoz as the rightful redeemer of society, communion with the PPD was less an option than a moral and imperative need.

Instead of feeling pressured, many supporters of the PPD either informed or played along with the line laid by the party's religious motifs. For example, in April 1939, a person wrote to Muñoz as follows: "Our compatriot Mr. Marín, each time I preach you as a Christ to my peasants so they can hear the voice of a man like you that wishes us good and bread and land for all those unemployed."[139] Also, on February 20, 1940, a woman who wrote to President Roosevelt compared Muñoz and his men with "Him, the one from Nazareth and his apostles."[140] Although these men did well by "preaching in the towns and countryside," she begged protection for Muñoz against "very perverse people," who, if left unchecked, could "crucify him as they did with Jesus Christ." At a later date, a similar view came from the writings of Lieban Córdova, Muñoz's personal secretary. For Córdova, Muñoz resembled Jesus at the Golgotha. That is, "while the Son of God already carried a cross along, the son of Muñoz Rivera was preparing to cast another over his shoulders."[141] Armando Miranda, who wrote the prologue of one of Córdova's book, saw in the Holy Scriptures "the prophecy of Puerto Rican salvation" and pictured Muñoz as the "*caudillo* assigned by God to guide his people."[142]

As the island approached the election of 1940, the PPD secured the support of representatives of the Catholic Church to present itself as a legitimate advocate of religious values. Members of the church, on the other hand, had no objection to allying themselves with a party that defended higher moral values for the island. The bishop of Ponce, Father Aloysius J. Willinger, joined the populist bandwagon early on when he made public his support for the PPD. *El Batey* took the opportunity to compare Willinger's sermons with the political discourse of Muñoz. The point was made that both leaders demanded an end to the "exploiters of men," the "perverse principle" of governmental neglect, and the abuses against the people. For the PPD, "hope for social justice and faith in God are fused as one."[143]

Two other representatives of the church, Father Ramón M. Stadta and Father Juan Rivera Viera, also spoke up in favor of the PPD. The former wrote and then visited Muñoz after one of his sermons was used by political opponents to attack the PPD for being a Communist party. Stadta assured the public in *El Batey* that his attack against the "false prophets" and Communism did not apply to the PPD. Father Rivera also wrote to *El Batey* expressing that Muñoz, far from being a Communist, was the "only politician willing to speak as a Christian, considering men as God's beings, and not as things."[144] By siding with the church and God, the PPD took a significant step toward presenting itself as an omnipresent entity. That is, the PPD's effort to reach all sorts of audiences in Puerto Rico could be understood as an act of God. Moreover, the support that Muñoz received from religious leaders enabled the PPD to visualize its political campaign as a sacred mission or crusade and not just as another effort to win the election.

MUÑOZ'S CAMPAIGN AND THE PPD'S RURAL PROPAGANDA

The significance of Muñoz's campaign lay not only in its scope but also in its effort to transform political practices in Puerto Rico. Like other populist leaders, Muñoz and his party portrayed public spaces as legitimate areas for the discussion of social grievances.[145] According to the PPD, political debate could no longer be an exchange between leaders at the expense of followers. Politics, the PPD argued, demanded more than discussions behind the closed doors of saloons occupied by the elite. To back the PPD's claims, Muñoz toured the island extensively. He visited many towns in Puerto Rico and traveled to remote rural areas. Muñoz tried to address people wherever he could find them: in public plazas, streets, cane fields, and homes. Muñoz's meetings with people often took the form of a dialogue that undermined the usual distance between leaders and their audience. More often than not, Muñoz's message would be a repetition of the basic slogans of the PPD such as "don't sell your vote" or "shame on money." The way Muñoz delivered his message, however, helped create a sense of participation among the audience. At times, fraternization between Muñoz and his listeners completely sidestepped political issues or the discussion of problems. These exchanges helped produce a bond between PPD leaders and followers.

The distribution of pamphlets, leaflets, flags, and even phonograph recordings to the population became a common practice during Muñoz's campaign.[146] At the most basic level, Muñoz became a purveyor of propaganda by handing out literature and other tokens during his meetings with people. Muñoz and the PPD widely distributed a printout called *The People's Catechism—Catecismo del Pueblo.*[147] Besides being a key piece of the religious motifs of Muñoz's party, *The People's Catechism* consisted of simple questions and answers that publicized the PPD's program. This pamphlet also served as a guideline to party members engaged in propaganda for the PPD. In case of doubt about their party's program, PPD members could use *The People's Catechism* as a reference. Overall, the news releases of the PPD became an integral part of Muñoz's tour throughout the island. The party closely followed the movements of Muñoz and reported them to the public. The PPD not only provided information about Muñoz but portrayed him with almost superhuman qualities. According to *La Democracia*, for example, Muñoz was able to offer several meetings that lasted for hours, one after the other.[148] The distance between towns or the number of meetings did not hinder Muñoz. The PPD also magnified Muñoz's campaign by presenting the party as an omnipresent entity. Every day, *La Democracia* informed the public about the growth of the party. Editors filled the pages of the PPD press with news about the inscription of Muñoz's party in different towns of Puerto Rico and with notes about people who became members of local committees.[149]

By presenting himself as larger than life through propaganda and his touring campaigns, Muñoz became a celebrity whom people hoped to see in person. Clifford Geertz's notion of charisma, which regards this trait as a cultural construct, applies well to the leader of the PPD.[150] Muñoz's charisma depended on cultural practices that placed him at the center of events. By becoming part of the daily scene of people's lives, Muñoz became an object of interest. People wrote to Muñoz asking him about his itinerary. Some letters requested Muñoz to notify rural communities of his visit in advance.[151] Muñoz answered these letters as best he could, sometimes specifying the day and hour of his visit.[152] The expectations of Muñoz and his audience before a meeting intensified the bond that developed between them. The meeting itself established a precedent for the generation of a new "political "language"—a nascent discourse of consent— by portraying such opportunities for direct contact with Muñoz as a key access to political participation. This situation, however, did not amount to a total freedom of choice for Muñoz or his supporters. On the one hand, while different groups informed an emerging discourse of consent, Puerto Ricans faced the effort of PPD officials to steer the mobilization of people in a certain direction. On the other hand, PPD officials could hope to transcend their own interests and become a "moral-intellectual leadership" only after extensive interaction with a myriad of sectors.

Despite Muñoz's efforts to address his audience through personal tours, the leader of the PPD faced limits on how many people he could reach. To fill in the gap, the PPD began the publication of *El Batey* in March 1939. The name of the newspaper, which refers to the meeting place in front of a peasant's house, highlights the idea of dialogue and interaction that Muñoz strove to achieve during his campaign. *El Batey* was free of charge, short, and easy to understand. It was meant to be read aloud in front of large gatherings of rural people. The newspaper explained all sorts of problems that affected the countryside, ranging from low wages to the policies of land reform. In the first issues of *El Batey*, Muñoz explained the goal of the newspaper. He presented the rural laborer as the "forgotten man" of Puerto Rico by emphasizing his exclusion from political debate. According to Muñoz, although rural laborers produced most of the riches in Puerto Rico, the island's leadership did not consult or inform them about governmental affairs. Instead, rural laborers were exploited by "big corporations" and "abhorred like a beast useful for work."[153] Muñoz proposed to discuss rural issues in *El Batey*, the same way "the problems of a family are discussed in the *batey* of their house." The leader of the PPD explained that "from the thousand *bateyes*, from the thousand poor homes in Puerto Rico, must emerge a government that expresses the will of the suffering people."[154]

Muñoz's opening words in *El Batey* highlight how the PPD employed this publication, together with *La Democracia*, to create a sense of inclusion and participation among its rural audience. The PPD incorporated the motifs and symbols of rural people's everyday life into the writings of *El Batey* and *La Democracia*. Besides using the term *batey* to set the tone of its rural newspaper, the PPD made frequent references to other popular motifs such as *la pava* (peasant's hat), *machete* (cane-cutting utensil), and *tiempo muerto* (season between harvests). The PPD's insignia, the head of a *jíbaro* (subsistence farmer) outlined in red, became the most obvious popular symbol of the party. At times, the PPD was outspoken and went into detail about incorporating popular motifs as part of the party's rhetoric. For example, *La Democracia* published an article about Rafael Hernández's song, "Lamento Borincano," saying that it was an accurate representation of rural problems.[155] The song is about a *jíbaro* who went home disillusioned after failing to sell his products in a depression-stricken town. The article explains that "Rafael got inspired by the 'jíbaro' that lives ignored in his hut . . . and it appears that Luis Muñoz Marín had the same vision as our composer when he founded, together with a group of patriots, the glorious Popular Democratic Party."[156] The author of the article proposed "Lamento Borincano" as a "hymn" to be played during the manifestations of the PPD. A song that, according to historian Ruth Glasser, had been an "unofficial Puerto Rican national anthem" since its composition in 1930 became an icon of the PPD.[157]

The appropriation of cultural values of the island's population enabled the PPD to display itself as an advocate of reform. Although Muñoz had the resources to publish two newspapers and built a party, he had to rely on people and their culture to provide content, texture, and feeling to his political campaign. The PPD backed up its rhetorical maneuvers with concrete ways to stress the openness of the party. The PPD constantly encouraged people to write to *El Batey* and *La Democracia*. Both newspapers published letters, poems, notes, and suggestions sent by readers. Moreover, to leave no doubt about the PPD's pledge toward rural people, *El Batey* announced one month prior to the 1940 election that many rural laborers and farmers planned to run as candidates of the party.[158] The PPD, for example, published a picture of a cane cutter running for one of the island's rural districts.[159] Whether or not these candidates made it to the election, subsequent issues of *El Batey* did not say.

At the editorial desk of *La Democracia* and *El Batey* Muñoz gave the final word about the news releases of the PPD. Even so, tailoring the PPD's image for maximum effect with the countless messages of people introduced a degree of indeterminacy to the party's propaganda. On what ground exactly PPD leaders and supporters embraced as partners would depend on a political process that no one could yet foresee. Although the call for social justice offered a basis for common action, the meaning and extent of reform remained elusive and subject to further exchanges between the PPD and multiple groups. Hence, the PPD press gained an advantage by lending its pages to many advocates of reform but upped the stakes against any specific version of social justice.

Besides incorporating the cultural values of popular groups, the PPD welcomed the demands for reform of people. An example is the controversy over the application of the Fair Labor Standards Act to Puerto Rico.[160] The PPD took issue with the failure of federal authorities to apply minimum wages to agricultural production.[161] The party not only announced that two of its lawyers, Ernesto Ramos Antonini and Victor Gutierrez Franqui, were hard at work in court to change the law,[162] but also devised a strategy to include laborers as participants in this process. *El Batey* urged rural laborers to "use democratic action, IMMEDIATELY."[163] For this purpose, *El Batey* printed a small coupon that workers could fill out and send to Congressman Vito Marcantonio, who represented the American Labor Party and had proven to be a strong advocate for Puerto Rican workers, Nationalists, and the island's independence.[164] The coupon included a statement in favor of minimum wages and provided space for the name and town of the sender. Although many workers already knew about Marcantonio and wrote to him directly,[165] the PPD's invitation to address the congressman helped to bring people into the fold of the party. Some workers used the coupon of *El Batey*. On one occasion, Muñoz himself wrote to Marcantonio on behalf of labor.[166]

Despite the unidirectional line of communication that the PPD's propaganda may have produced, the party and its audience found ways to interact with each other. Another of Muñoz's strategies to create a sense of participation among followers would be to exchange letters with them. *El Batey* explained to readers that they could ask Muñoz any question and that he would answer it personally. The PPD couched this offer with words that stressed the importance of the matter. *El Batey* proclaimed that the PPD is "the party of the people" and that there is no other "salvation" in Puerto Rico than to establish a "government of the people" free of big interests. For the PPD to achieve this goal, *El Batey* said that "it is necessary that the people understand all of its problems."[167] With lofty words, the PPD portrayed the exchange of letters between Muñoz and his audience as an initiative well above day-to-day events: the common effort of "the people" to save Puerto Rico. For Muñoz, having an audience to keep in touch with allowed him to deliver the promise he made in *El Batey* about the need to inform and consult "the people." Muñoz's personal letters to individuals banked upon the charismatic image that the PPD fashioned about its leader through propaganda. The letters of Muñoz tried to cause an impression by making it clear that a leader of his stature would no longer tolerate the exclusion of people from political debate. Moreover, addressing individuals through personal letters allowed Muñoz to reproduce the interaction he had with people during his campaign tours. Muñoz hoped to form a direct bond with his audience even as he addressed them from afar with his letters.

The answers that Muñoz gave to the questions of people did not add much to the information available in *El Batey* and *La Democracia*. When asked about the endeavors of the PPD, Muñoz stressed that his party did not buy votes, opposed big interests, and favored a government in the hands of "the people."[168] When asked about poor conditions in Puerto Rico or the lack of relief, Muñoz blamed corporations that exploited "the people" and Socialist leaders who showed indifference toward reform.[169] More than information, Muñoz offered reassurance to his audience about the PPD's legitimacy by dividing society into two antagonistic camps: "the people" and "the big interests." Or, as Muñoz expressed it in a letter to José Flores from Maricao, "we represent today clarity before obscurity, and we should not permit the obscurity to tinge the clear light we uphold."[170] Muñoz's Manichaean rhetoric placed the PPD and "the people" in the same camp of moral virtue. The leader of the PPD acted on this pretension when he concluded many of his letters by telling people to spread the righteous message of his party. As Muñoz wrote to Flores, by "preaching" the PPD's ideals, "you would be doing in your *barrio* the same work I am trying to do in all Puerto Rico."[171]

People responded with enthusiasm to Muñoz's offer to address their questions. As agents who desired better socioeconomic conditions and had made steady demands for reform throughout the 1930s, Puerto Ricans probably saw Muñoz's invitation to exchange words with him as yet another tactic to improve their lot that deserved a try. Such a direct avenue of communication represented an opportunity for marginal groups to loudly voice their concerns to a sector of the island's political elite. Despite much fanfare, people's enthusiasm toward Muñoz did not necessarily have the same meaning for the Puerto Rican population as it had for the PPD. As Carlos de la Torre points out, it is important to grasp that populism in Latin America had "ambiguous meanings" for the actors involved.[172] Although leaders and followers shared certain principles that bound populist movements together, the actual experiences of agents produced at best an elusive relationship between them.

The exchange of letters between Muñoz and his audience allowed the PPD to present itself as a benefactor of people suffering grievances. It also offered the PPD a way to recruit many individuals as part of the propaganda machinery of the party. Not all people, however, wrote to Muñoz in search of an answer to their problems. Instead of seeing the PPD as a purveyor of information or a palliative to their grievances, many people saw the party as an opportunity to express their views and to contribute as best they could to improve conditions on the island. Numerous individuals sent messages simply to voice their appreciation at the work being done by the PPD and to offer their cooperation.[173] Other letters proposed to Muñoz how the PPD could better address certain issues. Many messages sent to Muñoz expressed the disposition of individuals to join the campaign of the PPD. For example, people volunteered themselves to distribute *El Batey* in their rural communities, to establish local committees of the PPD, or to assist in the membership drive of the party.[174]

What is significant about the exchange of letters between the leader and supporters of the PPD are not only Muñoz's effort to grab the attention of people with his claims but also his attempt to define the basis for social justice: to form a direct bond between himself and the island's population. This tactic had a broader counterpart. The means of communication of PPD officials—handouts, news releases, phonograph records, and radio announcements—equated the particular concerns of different groups with the aims of party leaders. Despite what the PPD hoped to achieve with propaganda, conditions remained too fluid in 1940 for party leaders to impose a strict criterion on supporters. Besides being a newly formed party and out of power, the PPD depended on many groups and the exchanges between them to sustain its rhetoric of social justice. Hence, PPD leaders and supporters interacted without having yet a precise basis of common action. Under these circumstances the discourse of consent remained latent or, to use the term of Raymond Williams, at the stage of "pre-emergence." That is, the discourse was "active and pressing but not yet fully articulated."[175] Since it lacked an a priori logic, the discourse of consent would emerge through a process of trial and error as the agents of the island's mass movement negotiated the terms of reform.

MUÑOZ AND HIS U.S. AUDIENCE

One vital concern informed the early campaign of Muñoz to incorporate U.S. officials as an audience of his party. Muñoz focused all his efforts to recover his role as an advocate of U.S. reform in Puerto Rico. After being ousted from the New Deal, Muñoz maintained contact with U.S. policies by making his voice heard through the press. Instead of seeing his exclusion from U.S. affairs as a hindrance or as reason for resentment, Muñoz used the occasion to his advantage. While affirming his support for mainland authorities, Muñoz distanced the PPD from the worst aspects of U.S. policies such as the governorship of Blanton Winship.[176] The leader of the PPD portrayed himself as a New Dealer of better, but vanished, times. This approach is evident in Muñoz's discourse before the tomb of his father on July 17, 1939.[177] Besides stressing his political legitimacy as Muñoz Rivera's son, the leader of the PPD called attention to his role in bringing the New Deal to Puerto

Rico. Muñoz visualized the past in romantic terms. The early program of the New Deal did not fail because of political infighting, lack of cooperation between local politicians, or the miscalculations of U.S. officials. It failed because anti-New Deal forces, including General Winship, sabotaged the program of reform. Muñoz and his followers belonged to a different camp. They represented unconditional supporters of President Roosevelt and the New Deal.

By framing his message as a bipolar conflict between progressive and backward forces, Muñoz provided a degree of coherence and veracity to the PPD's discourse. When the PPD addressed its audience beyond the confines of the island, meaning federal authorities, the party focused on the New Deal to rationalize its advocacy of U.S. policies. When the PPD addressed its local audience, meaning all potential sources of mass support, the party focused on the "exploitation" and abuses of U.S. colonialism to highlight the authenticity of its message. The discursive maneuvers of the PPD constructed a Janus-faced leadership in the person of Muñoz and his party.[178] The PPD did not acknowledge the contradictions of its discourse. Despite being pro-U.S. and anti-U.S. simultaneously during its electoral campaign, the PPD eschewed the need to present a consistent position toward colonial rule. On the one hand, the PPD included the word "liberty" in its slogan, and, on the other hand, the party officially declared that the political status of the island was not an issue. The PPD downplayed this ambiguity by insisting that Puerto Rico's main dilemma consisted of a struggle between the defenders and the opponents of reform.

The early program of the New Deal in Puerto Rico was not the only theme touched upon by the PPD to present itself favorably to the United States. The menace of war in Europe had a catalytic effect on U.S. policies toward the island and on how the PPD addressed its mainland audience. Puerto Rico became a key outpost of U.S. military plans.[179] Besides improving Puerto Rico's defenses, the United States reconsidered its colonial policies. Winship's repressive measures had proven impractical and seemed inappropriate at a time when authoritarian powers in Europe prepared for war. Puerto Rico under Winship tarnished Roosevelt's Good Neighbor Policy toward Latin America at the worst possible moment. In order to lift Puerto Rico's morale and prepare the population for the impending world crisis, the United States announced in the summer of 1939 that Admiral William D. Leahy would be the new governor of the island.[180]

While federal plans remained on the drawing board, the PPD made cautious remarks about the advantages of U.S. policies. When Washington, D.C., decided to go ahead with its agenda, the PPD pulled out all the stops to make clear its loyalty toward the United States. In August 1939, for example, Muñoz revealed the traits that made the PPD a valuable ally of U.S. officials.[181] The leader of the PPD explained that so far the tensions between Puerto Rico and the United States ensued from a misunderstanding. Muñoz blamed local politicians, lackeys, and subordinates for this situation. He concluded that "when the PPD, which is the party of the people, takes power our people and that of the United States will understand each other perfectly."[182] Contrary to other parties, Muñoz argued, only the PPD could help the United States because it had "clean hands" and opposed the "oppressors" of "the people." Once again, Muñoz used his notion of "the people" to blur the line between the PPD and its audience—this time U.S. officials—and to portray both sides as the embodiment of ideals untarnished by narrow interests.

The PPD's pro-U.S. discourse negotiated a middle ground between being supportive and being critical of federal authorities. Muñoz's party wanted to become an intermediary of U.S. policies in Puerto Rico but without alienating its local base of support. To achieve this goal, the PPD aligned itself with what it perceived as the best policies of the United States toward the island. According to the PPD, the New Deal and Leahy not only underscored Muñoz's initial role in favor of Roosevelt's program but also the PPD's pro-U.S. stance since its inception. By making reference to the New Deal and Leahy, the PPD bridged its involvement in what the party perceived as two "progressive eras" of U.S. activities on the island. Moreover, this perspective helped the PPD express support for U.S. policies without mentioning the "unfortunate episode" of Winship's governorship.

Shortly after the start of World War II and the arrival of Leahy to Puerto Rico, Muñoz had an opportunity to meet the new governor. According to *El Batey*, Muñoz and Leahy had a friendly exchange of ideas.[183] Muñoz offered the cooperation of PPD officials to pave the way for social reform. He insisted that the PPD never asked for public offices or privileges of any kind. Muñoz concluded that Leahy is a "sensible man and that he has good intentions to improve the conditions of our people."[184] According to the PPD, Leahy agreed with the points raised by Muñoz. The new governor and Muñoz met again in February 1940. This time they discussed certain deficiencies of the island's electoral law.[185] Despite the rapport established between Muñoz and Leahy, the leader of the PPD told Ruby A. Black that he could not tell whether the new governor was a "conservative or a liberal."[186] Nevertheless, Muñoz decided to take his chances with Leahy, even though he had met him "only two or three times" and did not know his political leaning. Not all PPD officials felt comfortable with the direction being taken by Muñoz. Vicente Géigel Polanco voiced his misgivings in a long letter he sent to other key leaders of the PPD, including Samuel R. Quiñones and Ernesto Ramos Antonini. Géigel's main point of contention centered on the PPD's decision to postpone the solution of Puerto Rico's political status. Géigel saw this decision as inconsistent with the PPD's program and its official slogan, "Bread, Land, and Liberty."[187]

Muñoz felt the need to assuage the uneasiness of his peers. He offered words of comfort during an event already familiar to the PPD. When the day came in 1940 to honor Muñoz Rivera, Muñoz journeyed to his father's tomb to pronounce a long and carefully worded discourse.[188] The leader of the PPD avoided an "either/or" dead end that would require him to chose between favoring U.S. colonial policies and advocating liberty for the island. Instead, Muñoz redefined Puerto Rico's political dilemma by stressing the significance of international events. It made no sense, Muñoz argued, to demand liberty at a time when democratic forces fought dictatorial ones in the name of freedom. In this context, according to Muñoz, liberty could be achieved by Puerto Rico not by cutting its ties with the United States but by joining Americans and other democratic nations in the fight for world freedom.

For Muñoz, liberty meant overcoming the regional narrow-mindedness or *insularismo* of Puerto Ricans in an effort to become one with the rest of the Western Hemisphere. This was the basis of Muñoz's vision of an American Confederation including Canada, the United States, and Latin America. From this perspective, regional unity, not divisiveness, was the policy that could ensure liberty for Puerto Rico. Muñoz phrased it well when he asked his audience: "Can we believe . . . that Puerto Rico's well-being can be considered exclusively in relation to the values of Puerto Rico alone? Or do we have to confront the reality that Puerto Rico is part of a hemisphere, of a world, and of a great fight for human liberty?"[189]

The leader of the PPD conceived a vision of international affairs that did not differ from his depiction of Puerto Rican society. Muñoz repeated "ad nauseam" that Puerto Rico's problem arose from an ominous fight between "the people" and the "enemy of the people." The former included *público* drivers, the unemployed, dockyard workers, rural laborers, farmers, teachers, shopkeepers, professionals, and mainland New Dealers. The latter was an ambiguous category that encompassed at times sugar corporations, their lawyers, FLT leaders, Socialists, Republicans, the Coalition, and U.S. policymakers. By presenting a Manichaean view of society, the PPD not only urged its audience to decide between two irreconcilable camps but also stressed the party's own choice to embody the forces of good against evil. The PPD used the same discursive strategy to portray world events. The international arena consisted of a bipolar conflict between progressive forces and reactionary ones. Although Puerto Rico's fate depended on choosing between these two forces, the island could follow the footsteps of the PPD and Muñoz, who had already sided with the democratic nations in defense of "freedom" and "human dignity."

After the election of 1940, PPD officials celebrated their precarious victory[190] by comparing it to Roosevelt's success in the United States. Muñoz's party argued that in Puerto Rico, as in the United States, "the battle of the people was being fought to claim their rights and happiness."[191] According to the PPD, the outcome of both elections embodied the dawn of a new era. It meant that the "dignity of the people" triumphed over "money" and "corporate interests." For the PPD, both elections also made clear that the unity of the "Puerto Rican people" and the "American people" was at hand. One month after the elections, the PPD made further claims when it announced the plan of President Roosevelt to visit Puerto Rico.[192] Since the itinerary of the president could be interpreted as a reassurance for reform, the PPD aligned itself with the U.S. executive. The party made arrangements in Barranquitas, the hometown of Muñoz, to celebrate the "Day of President Roosevelt."[193] In mid-December, Muñoz pronounced a discourse in his name. The message that Muñoz delivered, which he called a "Panamerican homage" to President Roosevelt, resembled his discourse of July to honor his father. The leader of the PPD developed further his idea of hemispheric unity to form one America. President Roosevelt commanded a significant part of this vision not just as a representative of U.S. democracy but as "a great leader" and "symbol of democracy in all America."[194]

To leave no doubt about how he viewed Puerto Rico's relationship to the United States, Muñoz repeated his ideas six months later during the Fourth of July celebration of 1941. The leader of the PPD delivered a speech in which he emphasized the importance of U.S. values for Puerto Rico.[195] Muñoz's message saw no contradiction between the United States as an independent country and Puerto Rico as a colonial territory subordinated to the former. The leader of the PPD explained that with the Declaration of Independence, the United States established a precedent that embodied all other celebrations of freedom. Again, the defense of democracy took place for Muñoz not just in the Unites States but "in all of America, in all of the democratic areas of the world."[196] Muñoz specified Puerto Rico's role in the "great fight for human liberty." The leader of the PPD demanded more than sacrifice from Puerto Ricans during the war effort. He insisted that Puerto Rico should participate as a leader in world affairs by serving as a bridge between U.S. and Latin American societies. For Muñoz, Puerto Rico had the exceptional task of establishing a dialogue between both of these cultures in the Western Hemisphere.

NOTES

1. Jacob Torfing, *New Theories of Discourse: Laclau, Mouffe, and Žižek* (Oxford: Blackwell Publishers, 1999), pp. 101, 302.

2. Ernesto Laclau, "Identity and Hegemony: The Role of Universality in the Constitution of Political Logics," in Judith Butler, Ernesto Laclau, and Slavoj Žižek, *Contingency, Hegemony, Universality* (London: Verso Books, 2000), pp. 44-89, p. 50.

3. Judith Butler, "Restaging the Universal: Hegemony and the Limits of Formalism," in *Contingency, Hegemony, Universality*, p. 14.

4. Ernesto Laclau and Chantal Mouffe, *Hegemony and Socialist Strategy: Toward a Radical Democratic Politics* (London: Verso Books, 1985), p. 112.

5. Torfing, *New Theories of Discourse*, p. 98.

6. Laclau and Mouffe, *Hegemony and Socialist Strategy*, pp. 127-134; Ernesto Laclau, "Constructing Universality," in *Contingency, Hegemony, Universality*, pp. 281-307.

7. Particularly, the protest of *público* drivers against high gasoline prices made headlines in Puerto Rico during 1933 and 1934. Blanca G. Silvestrini, *Los trabajadores puertorriqueños y el Partido Socialista, 1932-1940* (Río Piedras: Editorial Universitaria, 1979), pp. 55-56, 80; Silvia Alvarez Curbelo, "La Casa de Cristal: El Ejercicio Senatorial de Luis Muñoz Marín, 1932-36," in Fernando Picó, Silvia Alvarez Curbelo, and Carmen Raffucci, eds., *Senado de Puerto Rico, 1917-1992: Ensayos de historia institucional* (San Juan: Senado de Puerto Rico, 1992), pp. 119-120. According to Silvia Alvarez Curbelo, as senator of the Liberal Party, Muñoz defended the protest of *público* drivers in 1934.

8. Transport workers included drivers of public buses and trucks as as well as *público* drivers. Silvestrini, *Los trabajadores puertorriqueños y el Partido Socialista*, p. 45.

9. James Dietz, *Economic History of Puerto Rico* (Princeton: Princeton University Press, 1986), p. 163.

10. The ACPR brought together several smaller unions already in operation. See the explanations of labor leader Gerardo Ferrao in *La Democracia*, July 11, 1939.

11. Gervasio García and Angel Quintero Rivera, *Desafío y solidaridad: Breve historia del movimiento obrero puertorriqueño* (Río Piedras: Ediciones Huracán, 1986), p. 128.

12. The craft-oriented trust of the FLT resembled the orientation of its counterpart in the United States, the American Federation of Labor (AFL). This explains in part the rise of labor organizations in Puerto Rico more attuned with the industrially-oriented trust of the Congress of Industrial Organizations. The local CIO-type unions, include not only the ACPR but also the organizations created by unemployed laborers and dockyard workers. Angel G. Quintero Rivera, "Bases sociales de la transformación ideológica del Partido Popular en la década del '40," in Gerardo Navas Dávila, eds., *Cambio y desarrollo en Puerto Rico: La transformación ideológica del Partido Popular Democrático* (San Juan: Editorial de la Universidad de Puerto Rico, 1980), pp. 35-119; Silvestrini, *Los trabajadores puerto-rriqueños y el Partido Socialista*, pp. 18-20. Despite the gulf between the FLT and *público* drivers, Socialists cooperated with the former. Ibid., p. 45.

13. Miles Galvin, *The Organized Labor Movement in Puerto Rico* (London: Associated University Presses, 1979), p. 94; Quintero Rivera, "Bases sociales de la transformación ideológica del Partido Popular en la década del '40," p. 85.

14. *La Democracia*, July 30, August 13, September 30, 1938, February 14, 24, 1939.

15. *La Democracia*, September 30, 1938; *El Mundo*, September 30, 1938. Besides trying to improve labor conditions with their strikes, transport workers aimed their protests against the shortcomings of companies in charge of public transportation. Labor unrest in this service sector of the economy highlighted the fact that people urgently needed the cars and jitneys of *público* drivers. In 1937, for example, a labor strike against the White Star Bus Line in San Juan halted the transit of buses for three days and provoked a harsh response from the government. Despite the government's effort to neutralize the militancy of labor, the protests of transport workers proved vital to the process of unionization. Labor leaders stepped up their efforts to coalesce all transport workers on the island. Also, several individuals such as Francisco Colón Gordiany, Gerardo Ferrao, and Alberto E. Sánchez enhanced their role as representatives of labor. *La Democracia*, July 11, 1939; *El Mundo*, March 18, 1939. Useful information about this conflict can be found in U.S., Congress, House, Subcommittee of the Committee on Insular Affairs, C. Jasper Bell of Missouri, Chairman, Hearings, *Investigation of Political, Economical, and Social Conditions in Puerto Rico*, 78th Cong., 1st. Sess., 1943, parts 1-14; 78th Cong., 2nd. Sess., 1944, parts 15-19.

16. *La Democracia*, September 30, 1938; *El Mundo*, September 30, 1938.

17. *La Democracia*, October 7, 1938, July 11, 19, 1939.

18. *El Mundo*, November 30, December 21, 27, 1938, January 17, 20, 25, 1939.

19. *La Democracia*, January 30, 1939; *El Mundo*, January 31, 1939.

20. *El Mundo*, February 1, 1939. According to *La Democracia*'s version of Muñoz's discourse, he stated that "my desire would have been to assist [the ACPR Congress] as a delegate or simply as a 'público' driver, as one of you. The politicians of all parties and the petty politics that the country has been suffering for so many years have done so much harm to the workers of all crafts and to the people in general; it is lamentable to come here as a politician." *La Democracia*, January 30, 1939.

21. *La Democracia*, February 13, 1939.

22. *La Democracia*, January 30, 1939; *El Mundo*, January 31, 1939. The claims of *público* drivers highlighted the unusual problems of these workers. As independent "contractors" who owned the means of their livelihood (i.e., their vehicle), *público* drivers faced high taxes and other grievances not common to other sectors of labor. Legal ambiguities about the right and obligations of *público* drivers complicated the issue during the 1930s. See *El Mundo*, March 18, 1939.

23. *El Mundo*, February 1, 1939.

24. *La Democracia*, February 14, 24, May 31, 1939.

25. *El Mundo*, February 11, March 12, 17, 18, April 22, 1939.

26. *El Mundo*, May 6, 10, 1939. This form of protest seems to highlight one of the aspects that set *público* drivers apart from other workers. A question to consider is how many sectors of labor could rely on a tax strike to demand better conditions in the 1930s.

27. *El Mundo*, May 12, 1939.

28. *La Democracia*, May 31, 1939; *El Mundo*, June 1, 1939.

29. *La Democracia*, June 14, 1939.

30. Ibid.

31. *La Democracia*, July 1, 1939.

32. Ibid.

33. *La Democracia*, July 13, 14, 1939.

34. *La Democracia*, January 21, 1940. See also *La Democracia*, July 11, 1939.

35. *El Mundo*, July 17, 1939.

36. *La Democracia*, February 1, 1940.

37. Ibid.

38. Juan Angel Silén, *Apuntes para la historia del movimiento obrero puertorriqueño* (Río Piedras: Editorial Cultural, 1978), p. 107.

39. For example, Socialist leader Santiago Iglesias downplayed the protest of unemployed laborers. According to historian Blanca G. Silvestrini, "instead of analyzing why they [the unemployed and dissident Socialists] searched for alternatives outside the circle of the Socialist Party, Iglesias preferred to ignore them as a 'multitude' of 'limited preparation.'" Silvestrini, *Los trabajadores puertorriqueños y el Partido Socialista*, p. 95.

40. *La Democracia*, August 13, 1938.

41. *La Democracia*, December 27, 1938.

42. Letter from the UPD to Franklin D. Roosevelt, January 13, 1939, File 9-8-107; Letter from the UPD to Franklin D. Roosevelt, January 28, 1939, File 9-8-76; Letter from the UPD to Franklin D. Roosevelt, Vito Marcantonio, Santiago Iglesias, and the Governor of Puerto Rico, February 13, 1939, File 9-8-59, Records of the Division of Territories and Insular Possessions, Department of the Interior (Record Group 126), National Archives and Records Administration. Hereafter referred to as DTIP, RG 126, NARA. See also Memorandum from the UPD to the Insular Legislature, February 1939; Letter from the UPD to Franklin D. Roosevelt, February 28, 1939, Colección Vito Marcantonio, Centro de Investigaciones Históricas, Universidad de Puerto Rico. Hereafter referred to as CVM, CIH/UPR.

43. *Justicia Social* 1940, Microreels S95A and F-S450, Colección Puertorriqueña, Biblioteca José M. Lázaro, Universidad de Puerto Rico. Hereafter referred to as CPR/UPR.

44. "Memorandum and Petition on Conditions of Labor in Puerto Rico," April 1939, File 9-8-76, DTIP, RG 126, NARA.

45. Silén, *Apuntes para la historia del movimiento obrero puertorriqueño*, p. 107.

46. *El Batey*, March 1939, No. 2.

47. Ibid.

48. Reproduction of *Prensa Libre*, "El Congreso de los Desempleados," February 25, 1939, CVM, CIH/UPR.

49. Ibid.

50. *El Mundo*, March 14, 1939.

51. Ibid.

52. *El Batey*, April 1939, No. 1.

53. Letter from the UPD to Vito Marcantonio, April 11, 1939, CVM, CIH/UPR.

54. *El Mundo*, July 3, 1939.

55. *La Democracia*, August 24, 29, September 14, 1939.

56. *La Democracia*, August 29, 1939.

57. *La Democracia*, September 19, 1939.

58. Laclau, "Constructing Universality," p. 304.

59. Memorandum, "Hunger Marchers Welcome Leahy to Puerto Rico," September of 1939, File 9-8-59, DTIP, RG 126, NARA. Several leaders signed the petition: Juan Sáez Corales, Luis Arquinzoni, Juan Santos, Sergio Kuilan, José Antonio Huertas, Francisco Montalvo, Pilar Llanos, and Nicolas Méndez.

60. Ibid.

61. *La Democracia*, September 21, 1939.

62. *La Democracia*, September 22, 1939.

63. *La Democracia*, September 21, 1939.

64. Ibid.

65. Taller de Formación Política, *No estamos pidiendo el cielo: Huelga portuaria de 1938* (Río Piedras: Ediciones Huracán, 1988).

66. Ibid., p. 106. Also see Silvestrini, *Los trabajadores puertorriqueños y el Partido Socialista*, p. 144.

67. Ibid., pp. 153-155, 164.

68. Letter from Luis Muñoz Marín to Ruby A. Black, April 5, 1938, Colección Ruby A. Black, Centro de Investigaciones Históricas, Universidad de Puerto Rico.

69. *La Democracia*, June 22, 1939. The position of the PPD toward independence is discussed in greater detail in Chapter 4.

70. *El Mundo*, July 29, 1939.

71. *La Democracia*, September 29, 1939.

72. *El Mundo*, October 10, 1939.

73. Ibid.

74. *El Mundo*, October 19, 1939.

75. Rexford G. Tugwell, *The Stricken Land: The Story of Puerto Rico* (New York: Doubleday, 1947), p. 7.

76. Paul W. Drake, "International Crises and Popular Movements in Latin America: Chile and Peru from the Great Depression to the Cold War," in David Rock, ed., *Latin America in the 1940s: War and Postwar Transitions* (Berkeley: University of California Press, 1994), pp. 109-140.

77. *Verdad*, May 1, 1941, File 9-8-82, DTIP, RG 126, NARA.

78. Lieban Córdova, *7 años con Muñoz Marín, 1938-1945* (Arecibo: Editora Corripio, 1988), p. 90; Juan M. García Passalacqua, ed., *Vate, de la cuna a la cripta: El nacionalismo cultural de Luis Muñoz Marín* (San Juan: Editorial LEA, 1998), p. 143.

79. Silén, *Apuntes para la historia del movimiento obrero puertorriqueño*, p. 92.

80. Kenneth Lugo, "Un peculiar manifiesto obrero puertorriqueño - época Confederación General de Trabajadores," *Homines* 13, no. 1 (February-July 1989): 226-235.

81. *El Mundo*, February 1, 1940. Georg Fromm emphasizes the relationship between Communists and the labor movement to understand the tactics of the PCP. Georg Fromm, *César Andreu Iglesias: Aproximación a su vida y obra* (Río Piedras: Ediciones Huracán, 1977), pp. 28-34.

82. Wilfredo Mattos Cintrón, *La política y lo político en Puerto Rico* (México, DF: Ediciones ERA, 1980), pp. 121-123, 199 n.143; Luis Angel Ferrao, *Pedro Albizu Campos y el nacionalismo puertorriqueño* (San Juan: Editorial Cultural, 1990), pp. 300-301.

83. Leslie Bethell and Ian Roxborough, "The Postwar Conjuncture in Latin America: Democracy, Labor, and the Left," in Leslie Bethell and Ian Roxborough, eds., *Latin America between the Second World War and the Cold War* (Cambridge: Cambridge University Press, 1992), pp. 1-32.

84. Juan Angel Silén, *We, the Puerto Rican People: A Story of Oppression and Resistance* (New York: Monthly Review Press, 1971), pp. 68-69.

85. Dumas Malone and Basil Rauch, *Empire for Liberty: The Genesis and Growth of the United States of America* (New York: Appleton-Century-Crofts, 1960), p. 615; David M. Kennedy, *Freedom from Fear: The American People in Depression and War, 1929-1945* (New York: Oxford University Press, 1999), p. 315.

86. Lizabeth Cohen, *Making a New Deal: Industrial Workers in Chicago, 1919-1939* (Cambridge: Cambridge University Press, 1990), p. 262.

87. *El Mundo*, February 1, 1940; *El Imparcial*, February 1, 1940.

88. *El Mundo*, February 1, 1940.

89. Ibid. The PPD also distanced itself from Communism in *La Democracia*, January 27, 1940; *El Batey*, September, 1940, No. 15, October, 1940, No. 17. See also Juan Angel Silén, *Historia de Puerto Rico* (Santo Domingo: SUSAETA , 1993), pp. 202-203.

90. *El Mundo*, July 30, 1940.

91. Ibid.

92. *El Mundo*, August 2, September 30, 1940; *Los Tres* (Semanario Político Unitivo), January 27, 1939, File 9-8-82, DTIP, RG 126, NARA. Also, the U.S. military feared the political ties that seemed to exist between Muñoz and Communists. Jorge Rodríguez Beruff, "La pugna entre dos grandes sistemas: la guerra en el discurso político de Luis Muñoz Marín hasta Pearl Harbor," in Fernando Picó, ed., *Luis Muñoz Marín: Ensayos del Centenario* (San Juan: Fundación Luis Muñoz Marín, 1999), pp. 136-137. U.S. officials in Puerto Rico voiced their worries about Communist influence within the PPD. According to Rexford G. Tugwell, the island's governor in the early 1940s, Guy J. Swope "thought there was [a] group, very influential, who would force Muñoz to the most extreme radical and anti-American measures. They were, in spirit, communists—that is, they had learned communist tactics. They lived on for trouble, anywhere and everywhere; they wanted riots and disorders. These tactics were aimed not only at the upper class, the landlords, and so on, but at the Continentals in Puerto Rico." Tugwell, *The Stricken Land: The Story of Puerto Rico*, p. 76; see also p. 7. Hence, U.S. concerns also informed the PPD's distanciation from Communists.

93. Letter from Miguel González to Muñoz Marín, October 4, 1940, Gurabo, Fundación Luis Muñoz Marín, Archivo Luis Muñoz Marín, Sección IV, Serie 7 (Pueblos). Hereafter referred to as FLMM/ALMM, IV-7 (Pueblos).

94. Letter from Daniel Piñero to Muñoz Marin, October 30, 1939, Juncos, FLMM /ALMM, IV-7 (Pueblos).

95. The news about the organizational drive of PCP officials demonstrates that the party did not rest during the political campaign of 1940. *El Mundo*, November 9, 11, 18, 1939, May 30, July 30, August 10, 14, 26, September 21, October 31, 1940.

96. Marcia Rivera, "El Proceso educativo en Puerto Rico y la reproducción de la subordinación femenina," in Yamila Azize Vargas, ed., *La mujer en Puerto Rico: Ensayos de investigación* (San Juan: Ediciones Huracán, 1987), p. 133.

97. María del Carmen Baerga, "La articulación del trabajo asalariado y no asalariado: hacia una reevaluación de la contribución femenina a la sociedad puertorriqueña (el caso de la industria de la aguja)," in *La mujer en Puerto Rico: Ensayos de investigación*, p. 98.

98. Blanca G. Silvestrini, "La mujer puertorriqueña y el movimiento obrero en la década de 1930," in Edna Acosta Belén, ed., *La mujer en la sociedad puertorriqueña* (Río Piedras: Ediciones Huracán, 1980), p. 85.

99. Yamila Azize Vargas, "Cronología: La mujer y el cambio social en el Puerto Rico del Siglo XX," in Azize Vargas, *La mujer en Puerto Rico*, p. 44.

100. María del Carmen Baerga, ed., *Género y trabajo: La industria de la aguja en Puerto Rico y el Caribe Hispánico* (San Juan: Editorial de la Universidad de Puerto Rico, 1993); Lydia M. González García, *Una Puntada en el tiempo: La industria de la aguja en Puerto Rico, 1900-1929* (Río Piedras: CEREP, 1990).

101. Dietz, *Economic History of Puerto Rico*, pp. 175-176, 142-143.

102. María de Fátima Barceló-Miller, "Halfhearted Solidarity: Women Workers and the Women's Suffrage Movement in Puerto Rico during the 1920s," in Félix V. Matos Rodríguez and Linda C. Delgado, eds., *Puerto Rican Women's History: New Perspectives* (Armonk, NY: M. E. Sharpe, 1998), pp. 126-142.

103. Ibid.

104. Unfortunately, as owner of needle workshops in Mayagüez, Arcelay opposed labor legislation that promised better conditions to women workers. Yamila Azize Vargas, *La mujer en la lucha* (San Juan: Editorial Cultural, 1985), pp. 162-164; Azize Vargas, "Cronología: La mujer y el cambio social en el Puerto Rico del Siglo XX," p. 133; Silvestrini, *Los trabajadores puertorriqueños y el Partido Socialista*, p. 39.

105. *El Batey*, April 1939, No. 2. See also *La Democracia*, January 14, 1940.

106. *El Batey*, April 1939, No. 2.

107. *El Batey*, August 1939, No. 7.

108. *El Batey*, November 1940, No. 18.

109. Ibid.

110. Anna Marie Smith, *Laclau and Mouffe: The Radical Democratic Imaginary* (London: Routledge, 1998), p. 153.

111. Félix O. Muñiz-Mas, "Gender, Work, and Institutional Change in the Early Stage of Industrialization: The Case of the Women's Bureau and the Home Needlework Industry in Puerto Rico, 1940-1952," in *Puerto Rican Women's History*, pp. 181-205.

112. *La Democracia*, February 23, 1940, March 21, 27, 1941.

113. The topics of the conference, which was titled "Puerto Rican Problems," ranged from state repression and the economy to civil liberties and the liberation of political prisoners in U.S. custody. Letter from Heloise Brainerd to Muñoz Marín, November 29, 1940, File 9-8-104, DTIP, RG 126, NARA. See also Sen. 76A-F24, RG 46, NARA. During the following years, the league addressed again the problems of Puerto Rico. Alfredo Montalvo Barbot, *Political Conflict and Constitutional Change in Puerto Rico, 1898-1952* (Lanham, MD: University Press of America, 1997), pp. 114-115.

114. *La Democracia*, February 23, 1940.

115. Ibid.

116. *La Democracia*, October 5, 1940.

117. *La Democracia*, October 31, 1940.

118. *La Democracia*, November 12, 1940, February 11, 1941.

119. *La Democracia*, February 11, 1941.

120. *La Democracia*, March 13, 1941.

121. Ibid. Instead of falling on deaf ears, the words of Gómez inspired an activity in her honor sponsored by the Association of Graduate Women of the University of Puerto Rico. *La Democracia*, March 27, 1941. For graduate women, Gómez represented an appropriate spokesperson of their cause. Not long before, the association had endorsed her for a position on the Board of Trustees of the University of Puerto Rico. *La Democracia*, March 21, 1941.

122. *El Mundo*, April 13, 1941.

123. Ibid.

124. *La Democracia*, June 12, 1941.

125. Mary Frances Gallart, "Mujeres, aguja y política en el Siglo 20 en Puerto Rico: Obdulia Velázquez de Lorenzo. Alcaldesa de Guayama, 1952-1956" (Ph.D. diss., Universidad de Puerto Rico, 1992), p. 193; Mary Frances Gallart, "Las mujeres en la discursiva de Luis Muñoz Marín: primeras décadas," in *Luis Muñoz Marín: Ensayos del Centenario*, pp. 187-207; Mary Frances Gallart, "Political Empowerment of Puerto Rican Women, 1952-1956," in *Puerto Rican Women's History*, pp. 227-252.

126. Letter from Carmen Ma. García de Socorro to Muñoz Marín, September 8, 1941, FLMM/ALMM, IV-2-9.

127. Ibid.

128. Nélida Agosto Cintrón, *Religión y cambio social en Puerto Rico, 1898-1940* (Río Piedras: Ediciones Huracán, 1996), pp. 143-160; Nélida Agosto Cintrón, "Género y discurso religioso en dos movimientos carismáticos en Puerto Rico," *Fundamentos* 5-6 (1997-1998): 97-124.

129. Todd A. Diacon, *Millenarian Vision, Capitalist Reality: Brazil's Contestado Rebellion, 1912-1916* (Durham, NC: Duke University Press, 1991).

130. "The Church and Reconstruction in Puerto Rico," 1935, Report prepared by Rev. R. A. McGowan, Assistant Director of the Social Action Department of the National Catholic Welfare Conference. Requested by the Bishops of Puerto Rico: Rev. Edwin V. Bryne, Bishop of San Juan; Rev. Aloysius J. Willinger, Bishop of Ponce. Franklin D. Roosevelt Library, President's Official File, Series 400, Puerto Rico: Appointments, FDRL Hereafter referred to as POF 400, FDRL.

131. *El Batey*, March 1939, No. 2.

132. Letter from Narciso Cosillos Piñero to Muñoz Marín, March 8, 1939, Canóvanas; Letter from Muñoz Marín to Narciso Cosillos Piñero, March 27, 1939, Canóvanas, FLMM /ALMM, IV-7 (Pueblos).

133. Agosto Cintrón, *Religión y cambio social en Puerto Rico*; Samuel Silva Gotay, *Protestantismo y política en Puerto Rico, 1898-1930* (Río Piedras: Editorial Universidad de Puerto Rico, 1997), pp. 189-90.

134. Agosto Cintrón, *Religión y cambio social en Puerto Rico*, pp. 147-148; Ferrao, *Pedro Albizu Campos y el nacionalismo puertorriqueño.*

135. *El Batey*, April 1939, No. 2.

136. *El Batey*, August 1939, No. 1.

137. Luis Muñoz Marín, "Discurso ante la tumba de Luis Muñoz Rivera," July, 17, 1938, FLMM/ALMM, Sección III, Serie 3, Cart. 10, Doc. 1. Hereafter referred to as FLMM/ALMM, III-3. These words appear in other texts of the PPD. See, for example, Jaime Benítez's prologue in Luis Muñoz Marín, *Memorias: Autobiografía pública, 1898-1940* (San Juan: Universidad Interamericana de Puerto Rico, 1982), p. vii. That Muñoz had an interest to become a sort of religious icon can be ascertained, to some extent, by the poems he wrote in the 1920s. In one poem, Muñoz wrote about the "agitator of God." Another poem is titled "Psalm of the Downtrodden God." Ibid., pp. 221-224.

138. Luis Muñoz Marín, "Discurso," November 4, 1940, FLMM/ALMM, III-2, Cart. 3, Doc. 1. Other populist movements used religious values in a similar fashion. For example, see Mariano Plotkin, *Mañana es San Perón: Propaganda, rituales políticos y educación en el régimen peronista, 1946-1955* (Buenos Aires: Ariel Historia Argentina, 1994).

139. Letter from Macario Burgos to Muñoz Marín, April 19, 1939, Juncos, FLMM/ ALMM, IV-7 (Pueblos).

140. Letter from Flora López to the President of the United States, February 20, 1940, File 9-8-82, DTIP, RG 126, NARA.

141. Córdova, *7 años con Muñoz Marín, 1938-1945*, p. 53. Besides words of support, Muñoz received messages just before the election of 1940 warning him about the activities of his political rivals. For example, the president of the local committee of Las Piedras wrote to Muñoz about some Catholics who employed an "effigy" of Christ to "combat" the PPD. Letter from José Marquéz Borrás to Muñoz Marín, s.f., Las Piedras, FLMM/ALMM, IV-7 (Pueblos). According to another letter, the rivals of Muñoz said the PPD represented "Anti-Christian Communism." Letter from Miguel González to Muñoz Marín, October 4, 1940, Gurabo, FLMM/ALMM, IV-7 (Pueblos). Aside from the fact that opponents also used

religious motifs in imaginative ways, these messages stress the dilemma that Communism and religion represented for the PPD. Regardless of the PPD's effort to distance itself from Communists and embrace Christian values, the party did not persuade all Catholics or preempt with its tailored image the accusations of political rivals that saw the PPD as a Communist haven. Two studies that offer key insights about the religious motifs of Muñoz are Juan José Baldrich, "Class and State: The Origins of Populism in Puerto Rico, 1934-52" (Ph.D. diss., Yale University, 1981); José J. Rodríguez Vázquez, "El Sueño que no cesa: La nación deseada en el debate intelectual y político puertorriqueño, 1920-1940" (Ph.D. diss., Universidad de Puerto Rico, 1998).

142. Córdova, 7 años con Muñoz Marín, p. 29.

143. El Batey, June 1939, No. 1; El Batey, June 1939, No. 2. See also La Democracia, June 15, 1939. It should be noted that Rev. Aloysius J. Willinger was one of the bishops who requested the report quoted above, "The Church and Reconstruction in Puerto Rico."

144. El Batey, February 1940, No. 11; El Batey, October 1940, No. 16-17.

145. Carlos de la Torre, "Velasco Ibarra and 'La Revolución Gloriosa': The Social Production of a Populist Leader in Ecuador in the 1940s," Journal of Latin American Studies 26 (October 1994): 683-711; Carlos de la Torre, "Populism and Democracy: Political Discourses and Cultures in Contemporary Ecuador," Latin American Perspectives 94, no. 3 (May 1997): 12-24.

146. According to Muñoz, he urged the PPD to "record and distribute hundreds of discs throughout the country to be played on personal phonographs or borrowed ones. The records repeated time and time again that the insignia of the Popular Party was . . . the suffering face of a Puerto Rican peasant with the typical hat of the countryside, which is familiarly called the 'pava.'" Muñoz Marín, Memorias, 1898-1940, p. 195.

147. Partido Popular Democrático, Catecismo del Pueblo, 1940, FLMM/ALMM, IV-2 and IV. See also Muñoz Marín, Memorias, 1898-1940, pp. 265-267.

148. Consider not only the press releases of the PPD in La Democracia and El Batey but also in El Mundo. For example, El Mundo, November 24, 1939.

149. Ibid.

150. Clifford Geertz, "Centers, Kings, and Charisma: Reflections on the Symbolics of Power," in Sean Wilentz, ed., Rites of Power: Symbolism, Ritual, and Politics since the Middle Ages (Philadelphia: University of Pennsylvania Press,1984), pp. 13-38.

151. See, for example, the letter from José Díaz to Muñoz Marín, August 5, 1939, Juana Díaz, FLMM/ALMM, IV-7 (Pueblos).

152. Letter from Muñoz Marín to José Díaz, August 11, 1939, Juana Díaz; Letter from Muñoz Marín to Santiago Alvarez, September 7, 1939, Lares; Letter from Muñoz Marín to Juan Ortiz Ramos, March 23, 1940, Maunabo, FLMM/ALMM, IV-7 (Pueblos).

153. El Batey, March 1939, No. 1.

154. Ibid.

155. La Democracia, October 1, 1940.

156. Ibid.

157. Ruth Glasser, My Music Is My Flag: Puerto Rican Musicians and Their New York Communities, 1917-1940 (Berkeley: University of California Press, 1995), p. 163. Unsurprisingly, when the PPD bought airtime for a radio program in 1942, the party used Hernández's sound track, "El Jibarito," as a theme song to start its broadcast. FLMM /ALMM, IV-4 (Empresas Comerciales: Diario Hablado de La Democracia y El Batey).

158. El Batey, October 1940, No. 17. See also El Mundo, August 16, 1940.

159. Ibid.

160. The difficulties to apply the Fair Labor Standards Act in Puerto Rico are discussed in Silvestrini, Los trabajadores puertorriqueños y el Partido Socialista, pp. 121-151.

161. The application of the law mainly affected the needlework industry. Ibid., p. 130.

162. *La Democracia*, July 6, 1939, August 25, 1939.

163. *El Batey*, April 1939, No. 2.

164. Félix Ojeda Reyes, *Vito Marcantonio y Puerto Rico: Por los trabajadores y por la nación* (Río Piedras: Ediciones Huracán, 1978), p. 12.

165. A review of the papers of Vito Marcantonio reveals this reality (CVM, CIH/UPR). Many sectors of labor wrote to Marcantonio such as *público* drivers, mechanics, agricultural laborers, and workers from the needlework industry.

166. Muñoz wrote to Marcantonio as follows:

This letter is written in the name of carpenters, masons and other construction workers employed by the WPA. Their delegation, consisting of more than fifty, sign this letter jointly with me. They protest against a cut in their wages.... These workers have appealed in vain to the organization of their trades, which, as you know, is so involved in political combinations with the big interests that cannot render them the normal services that labor organizations should render. It is for this reason that they have appealed to me here and to you there as the only forces in which they have confidence. They feel that you are free to defend them there as I am free to defend them here, because we have no connection with powerful interests that gain millions every year from low wages in Puerto Rico. (Letter from Muñoz Marín to Vito Marcantonio, September 5, 1939, CVM, CIH/UPR). This letter offers a partial account of the concerns of labor since only the words of Muñoz reached Marcantonio. Despite being one-sided, Muñoz's message to the congressman sheds light on the relationship between labor and the leader of the PPD. Inconvenienced by a reduction in their wages, workers made a favorable assessment of the help Muñoz could provide to solve their grievance. Eager to incorporate labor into the ranks of his party, Muñoz not only heeded the problems of workers but also took the opportunity to flesh out his image as a benefactor. As on other occasions, by portraying labor's request for help not as a discrete event but as a political occurrence of great significance, Muñoz displaced to an arena of his liking the relationship he began to develop with his supporters.

167. *El Batey*, April 1939, No. 1.

168. For example, Letter from Muñoz Marín to José García Colón, November 16, 1939, Canóvanas; Letter from Muñoz Marín to Custodio Pérez Cardisel, April 12, 1939, Luquillo; Letter from Muñoz Marín to Macario Burgos, April 20, 1939, Juncos; Letter from Muñoz Marín to Carlos Guzmán, March 13, 1939, Juana Díaz; Letter from Muñoz Marín to Andrés Rodríguez, May 21, 1939, Naranjito; Letter from Muñoz Marín to Inés López Guzmán, June 5, 1939, Juncos; Letter from Muñoz Marín to Rafael Resto, June 13, 1939, Las Piedras; Letter from Muñoz Marín to Miguel Vázquez, July 5, 1939, Juncos; Letter from Muñoz Marín to Andrés Rivera, July 10, 1939, Canóvanas; Letter from Muñoz Marín to Santiago Alvarez, September 7, 1939, Lares; Letter from Francisco Cruz Miranda, September 11, 1939, Juncos; Letter from Muñoz Marín to Luis H. Lugo, September 26, 1939, Lajas, FLMM/ALMM, IV-7 (Pueblos).

169. For example, Letter from Muñoz Marín to Jesús María López, May 21, 1939, Las Piedras; Letter from Muñoz Marín to Jesús Rodríguez Torres, April 22, 1939, Manatí; Letter from Muñoz Marín to Euligio Colón, May 31, 1939, Manatí; Letter from Muñoz Marín to Pablo Rosario Martínez, October 4, 1939, Manatí; Letter from Muñoz Marín to Gertrudis Rivera, September 15, 1939, Juncos, FLMM/ALMM, IV-7 (Pueblos).

170. Letter from Muñoz Marín to José Flores, May 21, 1939, Maricao, FLMM/ALMM, IV-7 (Pueblos).

171. Ibid. See also Letter from Muñoz Marín to Clotilde Matos Colón, May 29, 1939, Naranjito, FLMM/ALMM, IV-7 (Pueblos).

172. Carlos de la Torre, "The Ambiguous Meanings of Latin American Populisms," *Social Research* 59, no. 2 (Summer 1992): 385-414. Indeed, the response of the Puerto Rican population to the discourse of PPD officials demands a careful reading to avoid

simplistic interpretations. Although people made enthusiastic remarks about the PPD, this did not necessarily mean a blind adherence toward Muñoz or a response entirely consistent with the intentions and expectations of party officials. Probably, on a few occasions PPD followers extracted, absorbed, or constructed the same exact meaning intended in the original text of the party's discourse. I find particularly useful the theories of Roger Chartier to understand the relationship between texts and the "consumers" of those texts. According to Chartier,

Defined as 'another production,' cultural consumption—for example, the reading of a text—can . . . escape the passivity traditionally attributed to it. Reading, viewing and listening are, in fact so many intellectual attitudes which, far from subjecting consumers to the omnipotence of the ideological or aesthetic message that supposedly conditions them, make possible reappropriation, redirection, defiance, or resistance. Awareness of this should lead to a thoroughgoing rethinking of the relationship between a public referred to as 'popular' and the historically diverse products . . . offered for its consumption. (Roger Chartier, *Cultural History: Between Practices and Representations* (Ithaca, NY: Cornell University Press, 1988), p. 41).

173. For example, Letter from José Negrón to Muñoz Marín, April 24, 1939, Naranjito; Letter from Andrés Rodríguez to Muñoz Marín, May 5, 1939, Naranjito; Letter from Clotilde Matos Colón to Muñoz Marín, May 29, 1939, Naranjito; Letter from Luis Lugo to Muñoz Marín, September 26, 1939, Lajas. FLMM/ALMM, IV-7 (Pueblos).

174. For example, Letter from Alejandrino Torres Colón to Muñoz Marín, April 12, 1939, Juana Díaz; Letter from Daniel Piñero to Muñoz Marín, June 9, 1939, Juncos; Letter from José Díaz to Muñoz Marín, August 5, 1939, Juana Díaz; Letter from José García Colón to Muñoz Marín, November 16, 1939, Canóvanas. FLMM/ALMM, IV-7 (Pueblos).

175. Raymond Williams, *Marxism and Literature* (Oxford: Oxford University Press, 1977), p. 126.

176. Repression became commonplace during the governorship of Blanton Winship. Although the Nationalist movement became Winship's main target, his authoritarian style permeated every aspect of life. Winship equipped the police with machine guns, pepper gas, and antiriot weapons. He also prohibited peaceful protests, the circulation of certain books, criticism against the government, raising the Puerto Rican flag, and public meetings. Winship's repressive policies culminated with the massacre of a group of Nationalists during a peaceful march in Ponce. Ferrao, *Pedro Albizu Campos y el nacionalismo Puertorriqueño*, pp. 152-153.

177. *La Democracia*, July 17, 1939.

178. The ambiguities of the PPD's pro-U.S. and anti-U.S. discourse can be compared to other cases in Latin America. Consider Laura Ruíz Jiménez, "Peronism and Anti-imperialism in the Argentine Press: 'Braden or Perón' Was Also 'Perón Is Roosevelt,'" *Journal of Latin American Studies* 30 (October 1998): 551-571. Jorge Rodríguez Beruff offers key insights about the reorientation of Muñoz's discourse before Pearl Harbor. Rodríguez Beruff, "La pugna entre dos grandes sistemas," pp. 126-152.

179. María del Pilar Argüelles, *Morality and Power: The U.S. Colonial Experience in Puerto Rico from 1898 to 1948* (Lanham, MD: University Press of America, 1996), pp. 91, 93; Humberto García Muñiz, "El Caribe durante la Segunda Guerra Mundial: El Mediterráneo Americano," in Carmen Gautier Mayoral, Angel I. Rivera Ortiz, and Idsa E. Alegría Ortiz, eds., *Puerto Rico en las relaciones internacionales del Caribe* (Río Piedras: Ediciones Huracán, 1990), pp. 161-191.

180. Several congressmen hoped that Leahy would help overcome Puerto Rico's instability. The secretary of state, Harold L. Ickes, clarified that the economic situation of the island would receive close attention despite the plans of defense. Eleanor Roosevelt added her opinion by saying that "with Leahy, there will be an era of reconstruction on the island." It soon became public knowledge that Leahy would implement the relief measures

of the Works Progress Administration in Puerto Rico. *El Mundo*, May 14, 29, August 21, 1939. See also Jorge Rodríguez Beruff, ed., *Las memorias de Leahy: Los relatos del Admirante William D. Leahy sobre su gobernación de Puerto Rico, 1939-1940* (San Juan: Fundación Luis Muñoz Marín, 2002).

181. *La Democracia*, August 26, 1939.

182. Ibid.

183. *El Batey*, October 1939, No. 8.

184. Ibid.

185. *El Mundo*, February 6, 1940.

186. Letter from Muñoz Marín to Ruby A. Black, January 8, 1940, in Reece B. Bothwell González, ed., *Puerto Rico: Cien Años de Lucha Política*, vol. 3 (Río Piedras: Editorial Universitaria, 1979), pp. 220-221.

187. Letter from Vicente Géigel Polanco to Samuel R. Quiñones, Ernesto Ramos Antonini, Victor Gutiérrez Franqui, and Francisco Susoni, February 9, 1940, in *Puerto Rico: Cien Años de Lucha Política*, pp. 222-223.

188. *El Mundo*, July 18, 1940.

189. Ibid.

190. By overwhelming its audience with constant repetitions about the PPD's great victory of 1940, the party created a political myth. A quick glance at the ballot returns of that year shows that the party elected its candidates by a slim margin. Antonio Quiñones Calderón, *Trayectoria Política de Puerto Rico* (San Juan: Ediciones Nuevas de Puerto Rico, 1988), p. 51; Fernando Bayrón Toro, *Elecciones y partidos políticos de Puerto Rico 1809-2000* (Mayagüez: Editorial Isla, 2000), p. 194.

191. *La Democracia*, November 7, 13, 1940.

192. *La Democracia*, December 4, 14, 1940.

193. *La Democracia*, December 17, 1940.

194. *El Mundo*, December 17, 1940; *La Democracia*, December 18, 1940. Other aspects of the event in Barranquitas highlighted the symbolism of the PPD's message. During the celebration of "the Day of Roosevelt," Muñoz was photographed holding together the hands of a girl representing South America and another girl representing North America. He was also photographed shaking hands with a little boy dressed up as Uncle Sam. *El Mundo* published both of these photographs on December 18, 1940. It seems Muñoz pulled the same stunt several months later, in November 16, 1941, to honor once again President Roosevelt. Photographs of the event on 1941 can be found in: Rodríguez Beruff, "La pugna entre dos grandes sistemas," pp. 126.

195. *El Mundo*, July 5, 1941.

196. Ibid. It seems that by this time U.S. officials felt confident about Muñoz's loyalty toward the United States. According to the PPD, federal authorities transmitted by radio Muñoz's speech to other Latin American countries. *El Batey*, July 23, 1941, No. 21.

FROM TURMOIL TO TURNING POINT: POLITICAL CHANGE AND THE SUGAR STRIKE OF 1942

> Politics in our country has always been a back-room politics. One thing is what is placed on display and another what is expedited under the counter.
>
> —César Andréu Iglesias

As participants of a restless political arena, no single agent in Puerto Rico could exclusively account for the discourse of consent during the 1940s. In this sense, far from being the protagonist of change, the PPD formed part of a broad lineup of forces grappling with the challenges of a new local and international reality. As World War II progressed, the defense priorities of the United States and the wartime concerns of Latin American societies forced people to deal with conditions that either unhinged or buttressed the socioeconomic and political order of their country.[1] For Puerto Rico, the international conflict unarguably shifted the balance of political forces in favor of local supporters of the New Deal. While the wartime policies of U.S. officials meant an effort to avoid social unrest and political instability, the defense priorities of federal authorities represented an opportunity for local agents to make forceful demands for socioeconomic improvement. Indeed, the groups that pleaded the full extension of the New Deal to Puerto Rico, such as workers, the unemployed, rural laborers, and the PPD, finally found during wartime a promising context to make their demands. As people raised their voice in favor of reform and the authorities responded to them at least partially, a process was set in motion that transformed colonial politics and led the way toward a discourse of consent. Although the rise of this discourse must be understood as the outcome of a gradual transition, at each step of the way agents embraced practices that evidenced its consolidation.

This chapter focuses on the sugar strike of 1942 to understand the shift of political forces that informed the discourse of consent in Puerto Rico. Although the 1942 sugar strike fell short of being a "moment of significant structural change,"[2] the events surrounding it had a strong impact on the island's political development. People mobilized themselves in large numbers and eagerly lent an ear to the calls for reform during the strike. The labor conflict brought into action key agents of colonial politics and touched upon issues not limited to labor. As workers couched their aims according to broad demands for reform and envisioned the best benefits of social justice, the labor conflict also made evident that the mobilization of people on the island had entered a new phase.

Instead of representing a mere equilibrium of forces, the mass movement came to embody "a stronger type of communitarian unity"[3] among its participants in 1942. In the initial stages of the movement—especially during the PPD's electoral campaign—the call for social justice simply encouraged the convergence of interests and aims that otherwise would not have been possible. During the sugar strike, however, leaders and supporters of the PPD did more than form a "chain of equivalences"[4] or a linkage between their demands for reform. They broadened the scope of the mass movement in Puerto Rico and articulated their aims as part of a "collective will"—meaning the contingent articulation of a plurality of subjects into an organized totality capable of instituting a new social order.[5] The sugar strike made evident this process as workers, Communists, dissident Socialists, PPD leaders, and mainland New Dealers acted in unison to secure a favorable outcome for labor. These prolabor forces informed the discourse of consent not only through their common action but also by introducing an "us and them," "friend and foe" rhetoric into the political scene. That is, the reformist sectors on the island distanced themselves and demonized an opposing "chain of equivalences"—the one that grouped FLT workers, Socialist leaders, sugar producers, and their mainland allies.

This chapter discusses the sugar strike of 1942 as a political turning point that formalized the ties between a sector of labor, Muñoz's party, and U.S. authorities. As an upheaval that took its toll among workers and haunted U.S. policymakers, the sugar strike offered PPD officials a unique opportunity to act as mediators between local and mainland interests. Because their actions as mediators offered only a partial solution to the labor conflict, the strike exacted from PPD officials a level of commitment beyond the tussles of everyday politics. Hence, the labor strike also enabled the PPD to take further steps as the "moral-intellectual leadership" of a new "historical bloc" in Puerto Rico. On the one hand, the PPD became such a leadership because it managed to condense the values and practices of many supporters as well as ensure the dominance of Muñoz and his peers. On the other hand, the formation of a "historical bloc" on the island depended only to a degree on the PPD's insistent pursuit for hegemony. Besides the hegemonic pretensions of PPD leaders, the political outcome would greatly depend on how different groups negotiated the terms of reform.

Since the call for social justice could hardly succeed without compromises between agents, disadvantaged groups as well as the elite paved the way toward a discourse of consent. Jacob Torfing makes a theoretical assessment that applies well to the hegemonic process that the island experienced under the "moral-intellectual leadership" of the PPD. According to Torfing, "hegemony does not take the form merely of a precarious agreement between different political forces that 'strike together, but march separately.' Neither does it take the form of an imposition upon other political groups of a pre-given organizational principle provided by a political vanguard. Rather, hegemony involves the construction of a collective will, in the Gramscian sense of a political project that is shaped in and through the political struggles for hegemony."[6] While agents engaged each other to secure reforms in Puerto Rico, they did not respond to any specific pact or to the strict requisites of PPD officials. Instead, people informed a "collective will" in favor of reform only after a prolonged process of interaction and conflict between particular interests. Although this process gave an advantage to certain groups over others, few political practices and identities on the island remained untouched.

The discourse of consent in Puerto Rico had as much to do with the effort of people to engage PPD officials and U.S. policymakers as with the attempt of these functionaries to assuage the concerns of local constituencies. At the political crossroad that ensued from the appeal of reform and social justice, people constantly interacted with each other to find relief for their needs. Although the day-to-day exchanges between U.S. officials, PPD leaders, and party supporters account for the discourse of consent, the initiatives of these agents became most evident at times of conflict. To understand the sugar strike of 1942, I focus first on the main agents who participated in the labor conflict. Then I discuss the outbreak, course, and outcome of events. On the one hand, the strike entailed sequences of dialogue, deliberation, decision, and action that set it apart from similar labor conflicts in the past. On the other hand, the sugar strike of 1942 enabled PPD officials, along with the strikers, to envisage interaction and responsiveness as their modus operandi and to perceive their rivals as the embodiment of exclusion, nonincorporation, and repression. In this respect, fact and fiction formed the locus of consent during the strike not only as they became entangled to reshape the past but also as they set high expectations about the future.

THE MAIN ACTORS INVOLVED

To some extent, the sugar strike of 1942 offers a microcosm of the changes that shaped politics in Puerto Rico after the start of World War II. Local demands for reform combined with the war efforts of the United States to create an explosive situation on the island. The strike stands out in that it contributed to a broad redefinition of political practices, meanings, and code of conduct in Puerto Rico. As will be seen, both the agency of people and the context of their actions informed a sharp divide during the conflict. The sources of frictions and divergences have to be found within the ranks of labor and their political supporters and not just between workers and employers. The impact of the sugar strike can be better understood by considering first the main actors involved, which include labor, the PPD, its political rivals, and U.S. authorities.

General Confederation of Workers

By 1940, many sectors of the working class had expressed their antipathy toward the FLT and Socialist Party. *Público* drivers led the protest against the lack of representation suffered by workers. During the ACPR annual congress of 1940,[7] *público* drivers made clear their opposition to FLT leaders. Although ACPR officials credited the early FLT for its valuable contribution to mobilize workers, they highlighted the "decomposition" suffered by the union.[8] *Público* drivers believed that FLT leaders abandoned workers to reap benefits as allies of employers. According to a statement of the ACPR, "the Free Federation is today a cadaver that can be remembered by what it did in life, but that the proletariat cannot revere, living from the past, because that does not respond to the dictates of the moment." The leaders of *público* drivers offered a solution. Their statement included the words that follow: "The working class needs a live, young, vigorous, strong organ that, structured on sane principles of organization and class struggle, can indicate to workers the sane and judicious path to follow."[9]

The ACPR backed its statement with a proposal to form a new labor organization to replace the FLT. PCP and UPD leaders joined the initiative of the ACPR. Communists, in particular, bolstered the unionization drive of labor with their support and leadership.[10] In March 1940, one month after the ACPR congress, *público* drivers announced the formation of the General Confederation of Workers—Confederación General de Trabajadores (CGT).[11] This name echoed the one of trade unions in Mexico, Argentina, and other Latin American countries. At its first convention on March 31, the CGT began operations with a total of 42 affiliate unions and 112 delegates representing approximately 72,000 workers in Puerto Rico. These numbers skyrocketed in a short time. Two years later, the CGT vaunted 1,115 delegates, 159 affiliate unions, and an estimate of 150,000 members.[12]

Besides revealing the strength of the CGT, these numbers exemplified the appeal and openness of the union. The CGT became a safe haven to many labor groups dissatisfied with the FLT. In addition to *público* drivers, the CGT included workers from the dockyards, needlework industry, liquor industry, restaurants, commerce, and to some extent agriculture.[13] Unemployed laborers also joined the CGT in great numbers. The CGT was different from the FLT not only in its composition but also in its political orientation. From the very beginning, the CGT insisted on nonpartisanship.[14] CGT leaders sought to protect their union from the political quandaries that troubled the FLT. The CGT expressed its strong determination to maintain a neutral position several times to union members. However, despite the effort of CGT officials to keep their organization away from politics, the new labor union could not avoid developing close ties to the PPD.

Ramón Barreto Pérez, a key organizer of the ACPR, became the most obvious link between the CGT and the PPD. Barreto Pérez not only assisted during the campaign of the PPD but accepted to run as candidate of the party.[15] The support of the CGT toward the PPD became evident during election day. The union encouraged *público* drivers to mobilize potential voters of the PPD by transporting them to the electoral centers of the island.[16] Although CGT leaders expressed concern about its ties to the PPD, the union could not hide its jubilation after the precarious victory of the party. In a note to *La Democracia*, the CGT congratulated the members of the union who ran successfully as candidates of the PPD.[17] Besides Barreto Pérez, who won as senator for Ponce, the CGT could claim three legislators in the House of Representatives and many officials in the towns of the island.[18]

Throughout 1941, the CGT had two main objectives: to secure the labor policies promised by the PPD and to expand the ranks of the union by recruiting workers from rural areas. The first goal gained momentum. Under the pressure of workers,[19] the PPD moved fast to improve the welfare of one of its most important political allies. In March, the PPD informed the public about its project to waive the tax paid by *público* drivers for their car license.[20] According to the PPD, *público* drivers should not be defined as property owners but as workers who use cars as a tool of their trade. Muñoz's party also announced that passengers would benefit from a public insurance fund in case of accident. Besides *público* drivers, the Senate paid attention to unemployed laborers, another important constituency of the CGT and supporter of the PPD. Barreto Pérez took the time to assure this sector of the working class that a project to establish a social security fund to address unemployment was already under way.[21]

The CGT wanted to represent not only urban workers but rural laborers as well. By 1941 it became evident that the CGT had the potential to become a dominant labor union on the island. Shortly after its creation, the CGT managed to organize more than 300 local branches.[22] Union leaders of the CGT welcomed labor from many sectors of industry, including, for example, construction workers, laborers in button manufacturing, cinema operators, booth tellers, street peddlers, and other self-employed persons.[23] Labor in the service sector of the island's economy was well represented in the union. The CGT also showed little reluctance to carry out strikes when other options had failed. Many of the strikes initiated by the CGT proved successful such as the one that took place at a hat factory in Ponce.[24] From the very beginning, the CGT emerged as a progressive labor union and as a viable alternative to workers dissatisfied with the FLT. The contrast between the CGT and the FLT could not be overlooked by labor. Contrary to the FLT, in the early 1940s, the CGT projected a commitment toward labor issues with its rapid growth and eager disposition to organize workers in large and small sectors of the economy. Moreover, as Miles Galvin explains, the CGT's "working class leadership personified by the legendary Juan Sáez Corales, left a record of honesty, dedicated militance, class consciousness, and political awareness."[25]

Despite the CGT's impetus, the effort of the union to expand its ranks into rural areas turned out to be a difficult task. Contrary to the urban scene, the CGT's organizational drive in the countryside no longer addressed "gray areas" of labor that had been overlooked by the FLT. By recruiting rural workers, the CGT impinged directly on the FLT's main turf of labor support. Moreover, despite the reverses of the FLT, this union still possessed a powerful base of support. Many years of labor organization produced a well-developed network throughout the island. FLT leaders secured important connections locally and on the mainland. Finally, the FLT relied on its long history of labor militancy to justify its actions. Besides its past glories, the FLT could bank upon its traditional role as labor representative during negotiations with sugar producers.

Since its creation, the CGT expressed several times its interest to expand into rural areas. The union took a decisive step when it demanded a role in negotiating, along with the FLT, the 1941 collective agreement in the sugar industry.[26] Neither the sugar producers nor the FLT took seriously the demands of the CGT. The main representative of sugar interests on the island, the Sugar Producers' Association—Asociación de Productores de Azúcar (APA)—and the FLT reached an agreement without consulting the CGT.[27] The latter, which affirmed to represent a majority of sugar workers,[28] not only protested against its exclusion but sent an ultimatum to the APA. CGT leaders said they would hold the APA responsible for any labor conflict that might arise in the sugar industry.[29] The CGT dared to challenge the APA and FLT, but it did not follow up on its claims.[30] Perhaps CGT leaders felt the union was not yet strong enough to confront the APA and FLT. Although the CGT held back its decision to strike, the seeds of conflict were laid with the collective agreement of 1941. On the one hand, as a union that had proven to be of importance, the CGT did not get a chance to be heard during the APA-FLT negotiations. On the other hand, the protest of CGT officials highlighted a problem already brewing in the sugar industry. Workers made evident their dissatisfaction with problems in the sugar industry such as the shortcomings of labor legislation, adverse work conditions, their meager salaries, and the rising cost of living. The collective agreement signed by the APA and FLT did not solve these grievances. The problems of workers snowballed and climaxed with the sugar strike of 1942.

The PPD and Its Political Rivals

The PPD did not ease its production of propaganda after the election of 1940. Instead, the PPD strove to enhance the circulation of its message and to elaborate even further its claims to political legitimacy. The discourse of the party constructed an image of the election that would lend credence to the PPD as a representative of a broad coalition of interests. According to *La Democracia*, the coming to power of the PPD signaled a new era of progress for Puerto Rico.[31] The PPD insisted that its victory embodied the unity of all people in favor of social justice. By overwhelming its audience with constant repetitions about the PPD's victory of 1940, the party created a political myth about its rise to power. A quick glance at the ballot returns of that year shows that the party elected its candidates by a slim margin.[32] This fact helps explain the agitated campaign of the PPD after the election of 1940. The PPD discourse constituted less the expression of the party in power than the pledges of a political faction in need of strengthening its precarious position. With great fervor, the PPD assured the public that legislation would be forthcoming. Also, Muñoz constantly announced his discussion of local issues with President Roosevelt and U.S. officials.[33]

On the one hand, the weak position of PPD leaders informed the party's disposition to go out of its way to secure political allies throughout 1941. On the other hand, the rivalry between Muñoz's party and the Coalition—composed of Republicans and Socialists—imperiled the PPD's claim to be above petty politics and questionable tactics. For instance, under pressure to deliver the legislation promised by Muñoz to his audience, the PPD violated its pledge to avoid pacts with other political parties. Although Muñoz's party won ten of the nineteen seats in the Senate, there was a tie between the PPD and the Coalition in the House of Representatives.[34] To break the deadlock of votes and implement legislation, the PPD secured the support of the Tripartite Unification, a party that included Laborists, Liberals, and Republicans.[35] This meant that the Coalition represented a major force to contend with, as it held almost half of the seats in the legislature.

Far from leading to inaction, the discrepancy between the political tactics of Muñoz and the campaign pledges of his party spurred the PPD's effort to produce an evasive discourse. At one point, for example, when the PPD faced an impasse in the legislature, Muñoz took the issue to the public, calling on "policemen, teachers, businessmen, farmers, workers, and the suffering people" to claim their rights as citizens.[36] The PPD's discourse tried to make sense of what the party could not account for in reality. Although weak and sometimes outmatched, the PPD conceived politics after the election as a Manichaean confrontation between a moral majority, the forces of good, and a mischievous minority, the forces of evil. In this sense, the discourse of consent entailed the constant effort of PPD officials to offer a definition of themselves as selfless individuals vis-à-vis their rivals. Real or imagined, the opposition became an indispensable element for Muñoz's party to construct an image of itself as well as to build mass support around its own program of reform.

Despite the statements of PPD officials to the contrary, the antagonism between Muñoz's party and the Coalition pitched two agents equally driven to undermine their opponent with their discourse. However, the tactics of PPD officials and the Coalition to foil each other did not have the same effect. After the election of 1940, the strength of the PPD and Coalition depended not only on their effort to shape the island's public opinion but also on their respective place in the political context of the time. The wartime conditions that produced a common interest in reform between U.S. authorities and local constituencies gave an edge to Muñoz's party over the Coalition.[37] The United States left no doubt in 1941 about its interest to implement reform when it appointed Rexford G. Tugwell, one of the foremost New Dealers of the Roosevelt administration, to the governorship of Puerto Rico. As the self-proclaimed advocate of the local New Deal, the PPD suited the new aims of U.S. officials toward the island. The Coalition, on the other hand, suffered an erosion of support among the officials of the federal bureaucracy.

In particular, Socialist leaders within the Coalition had a difficult time with the changes in colonial politics. Besides facing the misgivings of labor toward the FLT, Socialists fell out of favor after the shift of U.S. priorities during wartime. When U.S. officials switched their support toward the PPD, a party better attuned to their policies, Socialists faced yet another hindrance against their position as labor representatives. This became evident during the political campaign and after the election of 1940, when Socialists suffered overt forms of dissension. Dissatisfied with the Socialist Party's decision to remain within the Coalition, Prudencio Rivera Martínez and other FLT leaders formed a new political organization under the name of Pure Laborist Party, which eventually joined the Tripartite Unification.[38] In response, Bolivar Pagán and the Socialist Party created a new labor union, the Puerto Rican Federation of Labor—Federación Puertorriqueña del Trabajo (FPT)—which was, according to Quintero Rivera, a "dismal failure."[39] Although Socialists elected Pagán as resident commissioner in 1940, they had a difficult time during the next years to make themselves heard at the higher echelons of the U.S. bureaucracy. Hence, political changes in the early 1940s entailed not only the fluctuation of loyalties between the island's parties and their constituencies but also the gradual realignment of interests between local leaders and federal officials.

The rivalry between Muñoz's party and the Coalition played itself out most clearly in the Puerto Rican press. Republicans and Socialists secured the support of *El Mundo*, which gave ample coverage to their allegations against the policies of Muñoz's party and Tugwell. The PPD responded to the attacks of the Coalition by acquiring the newspaper *El Imparcial*. Muñoz became director of this daily after party members working for the government gave a month's salary to pay for its acquisition.[40] The PPD got hold of *El Imparcial* just in time to defend the newly appointed governor of Puerto Rico, Rexford G. Tugwell, against the Coalition.[41] Muñoz used his new journal and the rest of the PPD press to provide ample coverage of Tugwell's inauguration in September 1941. The PPD described the whole event in detail, even a stunt that Muñoz pulled when he brought to the inauguration parade a large group of marching laborers "for ovation purposes."[42]

Besides the most overt maneuvers of Muñoz's party, the private expressions of PPD leaders underscored their zeal and animosity against the opposition. The perception about a clash between progressive forces and reactionary ones informed the conviction of party officials. Jesús T. Piñero, for example, wrote to Ruby A. Black saying that "the fight with *El Mundo* has been very acrid and if Luis had not had *El Imparcial* those nasty Sons of Bs. would have done quite some harm. They have subsided lately when they have felt blows in their bellys [*sic*] but I think they won't behave for a long time as they are the voice of Big Business which stands back of them covered by a smoke screen."[43] As will be seen, the conflict between PPD officials and their political rivals climaxed during the sugar strike of 1942. Also, the Manichaean streak of the PPD's discourse reached new heights.

Besides facing the opposition at the front lines of colonial politics, the PPD also engaged in a different sort of contestation as an advocate of labor. Since the election of 1940, the mobilization of labor involved as much the interest of the PPD and CGT to reach a mutual understanding as the effort of both organizations to produce dissent among workers toward the Coalition. In this respect, PPD leaders and CGT workers found a basis for common action not merely by denouncing the lack of relief or the problems of political representation on the island. Instead of stepping into the political scene without designs or animosities, the PPD and CGT shaped their rhetoric in a context full of antagonism. Hence, what gave rise to a discourse of consent entailed the defense of reform as well as the displacement of political rivals. Since mass mobilization went hand in hand with a shift of political alliances in Puerto Rico, it made the generation of dissent an intrinsic part of the process.

Although the CGT contributed in generating dissent among workers toward the Coalition, the PPD took the lead against its political rival. Besides acquiring *El Imparcial* to counter the attacks of Republicans and Socialists in 1941, the PPD bought airtime to broadcast a radio program not long after the labor strike.[44] The PPD's radio program and *El Imparcial*, together with *La Democracia* and *El Batey*, furnished party officials with a formidable array of media to spread their message. With these resources at hand, the sugar strike of 1942 acquired significance for the PPD not only as an event that made possible the joint action of labor and Muñoz's party but also as a political stage on which party officials could voice most strongly the appeal of the PPD and the lackluster of the Coalition. Indeed, as will be seen, the PPD partly unhinged the strike from its historical context and framed it as part of a clash between the forces of good against evil.

U.S. Authorities

As Ruth Berins Collier explains, it is important to grasp not only "internal trajectories" of change but also "external influences" to understand Latin American politics in the 1940s.[45] Like other countries of Latin America, Puerto Rico experienced at the time new patterns of labor activism and political mobilization as well as the effects of an unstable international conjuncture. While changes in the organization of labor and parties introduced new actors into the island's political arena, international events dealing with World War II prompted a modification of U.S. policies toward Puerto Rico. Although these processes informed the island's "critical juncture"[46] in distinctive ways, they cannot be set apart. The priorities of the United States worldwide intertwined with the concerns of local agents such as the PPD and CGT. External influences and internal conditions eased the interaction between the advocates of reform and social justice in Puerto Rico.

At the eve of World War II, the deficiency of federal policies toward Puerto Rico came into sharp relief. Not only had little progress been made to introduce reform to the island, but also longtime flaws of U.S. colonial policies became evident. Rexford G. Tugwell stated it well when he said that the "underemphasis [of career men], careless staffing and general lack of equipment for the task of colonial government was obviously the result of our confused policy."[47] Indeed, according to Tugwell, the decisions of federal authorities toward the island amounted to no policy at all.[48] Puerto Rico's haphazard pace of change exacerbated the problem. As economic conditions worsened, they eroded the tolerance of people toward the unassertive steps of federal authorities to introduce reform. After recalling the island's governor, Admiral William D. Leahy, to perform diplomatic service in Europe, U.S. officials tried to ease local tensions with the appointment of Guy J.

Swope to the executive branch in 1941.[49] The new governor brought into office what he had learned during his brief tenure as auditor of Puerto Rico. Swope, however, perceived the PPD as an inauspicious challenge to U.S. authority. Instead of viewing the PPD as a potential collaborator, Swope expressed mistrust about the conglomerate group held together by Muñoz's party.[50] He feared that as a result of Puerto Rico's phase of unrest, certain PPD affiliates such as Communists and Nationalists would take a stab at U.S. interests. Moreover, U.S. officials could still recall Muñoz's dismissal from the island's early program of the New Deal.

Although Leahy's governorship did not last long, the one of his successor, Guy J. Swope, was even shorter. He replaced Leahy in January 1941 to stay in Puerto Rico for scarcely more than six months.[51] The uncertainty of U.S. policies toward the island, as exemplified by this rapid turnover of appointments, tell us less about the interest of federal officials to solve the oversight of local problems and more about their urgent concerns on how to best address Puerto Rico's instability in case of war.[52] U.S. authorities recognized the need to make substantial improvements on the island to secure its defenses. Turmoil in other regions of the Caribbean seemed to confirm that an outbreak of civil war was not a distant fear.[53] Federal authorities made a significant change of policy when they assigned Rexford G. Tugwell as governor of Puerto Rico.[54] This decision marked a sharp break with the usual practice of the United States toward the island. Instead of assigning a military official or businessman, as had often been the case in the past, U.S. authorities appointed a well-trained administrator and academician. The coming of Tugwell confirmed the decision of the United States to align itself with political changes in Puerto Rico, ease the introduction of reforms, and prepare the island for war.

Undoubtedly, federal authorities appointed Tugwell to safeguard U.S. military interests in Puerto Rico. Tugwell knew that military defense was the main priority of his governorship.[55] This concern, however, explains only in part the role of Tugwell in colonial politics. It is important to focus on Tugwell to understand the rise of a new style of political leadership on the island. Besides being a representative of U.S. foreign policies, Tugwell gained renown as an innovator of public administration and as a staunch New Dealer.[56] During Roosevelt's first term in office, Tugwell became a White House adviser, supplying the president with ideas and helping to draft key policies to rehabilitate the economy. He also acquired valuable experience as assistant secretary and later undersecretary of agriculture. Equally significant, Tugwell proved to be a close observer of Puerto Rican affairs. He visited the island more than once before becoming governor and participated in the initial proceedings for land reform.[57]

Besides his training, Tugwell had a better disposition than other U.S. officials to tackle arduous conditions in Puerto Rico. Tugwell's record as a federal agent had shown him to be a dynamic administrator when the circumstances demanded unconventional measures. This proved advantageous to local advocates of reform. Either by chance or intention, the United States appointed a governor who would be able to work hand in hand with Muñoz and the PPD. The leader of the PPD and Governor Tugwell worked together as a team, introducing a peculiar form of leadership to the island.[58] To some extent, Tugwell and Muñoz had their own areas of expertise, focusing correspondingly on what Anthony Giddens calls "allocative resources" and "authoritative resources."[59] As governor, Tugwell administered the former—meaning "the dominion over material facilities"—while Muñoz, as leader of the PPD, focused on the latter—meaning the "dominion over the activities of human beings themselves." Although Tugwell and Muñoz did not strictly adhere to this unusual division of authority, which entailed an intricate overlap of responsibilities, they reached some sort of arrangement about their functions. Tugwell concerned himself with administrative issues and bureaucratic details while Muñoz oversaw the flow of decisions, information, and the performance of officials. As a politician yearning for mass support, Muñoz also worried about the best way to render understandable to the public the policies of Tugwell and federal authorities.

The Tugwell-Muñoz team worked best during moments of crisis such as the sugar strike of 1942. The relationship between these two leaders, however, suffered tensions and even estrangement. Conflict developed over several issues, but the most problematic divergences revolved around Tugwell's effort to revamp the executive office. In colonial politics, public officials faced a fact of overriding importance: legislative interference in executive affairs had become the preferred way by which partisan manipulation of the government took place. As noted in Chapter 1, a weak governmental machine shot through with partisan interests hindered reform. Tugwell expressed the problem well when he said that "this left the real power in the hands of a boss, a backstairs dictator, a legislator whom all Puerto Ricans acknowledged, but who, so far as official recognition was concerned, did not exist."[60] Tugwell's goal entailed a broad plan to strengthen an "executive office emasculated by legislative attrition" and to create agencies that would take from the legislature its pervasive control over the executive branch.

It may be assumed that Tugwell's goal placed his administration on a collision course with Muñoz and the PPD. In many ways it did, but the fact remained that Muñoz needed Tugwell. Despite all the electoral fireworks and fanfare about the PPD's commitment toward reform, the institutional framework to carry out the party's broad program did not exist. To overcome this deficiency of governance, the PPD had to rely on the administrative know-how of Tugwell and his advisers. Muñoz welcomed the policies of Tugwell, even though he may have resented the governor's intrusion into his realm of political action. That is, although cooperating with Tugwell meant losing some control as a "legislative boss," Muñoz saw the advantages of bureaucratic expansion and the centralization of authority. Tugwell, on the other hand, began to trust Muñoz after hearing his Fourth of July speech in 1941. He came to believe that "Muñoz and Muñoz' people were wholly with us."[61]

THE OUTBREAK OF THE STRIKE

The CGT raised a legitimate issue during the negotiations of the 1941 collective agreement in the sugar industry. After its rapid expansion and its disposition to address unionization problems in Puerto Rico, the CGT not only had a stake in the sugar industry but also gained credibility to fend off accusations about its weak position. The CGT counterbalanced its recent formation with swift actions in favor of labor. Despite the inroads of CGT organizers and workers, the union was not allowed to participate in the hearings between the APA and the FLT. Moreover, the CGT stressed the grievances of labor in the sugar industry, but the union's protests did not receive attention. Workers believed that the favorable prospect of the sugar industry warranted better wages.[62] They also demanded a raise to keep up with the cost of living. The collective agreement signed by the FLT and the APA in 1941 failed to address these issues. According to the island's Department of Labor, "said agreement fixed $1.51 daily for sugar-cane cutters and the strikers demanded $1.91. They also asked for an increase in the different works done at the sugar-cane plantation."[63] To the dissatisfaction of workers, FLT leaders accepted the same wage rate as the past year's harvest.[64] The CGT saw the agreement as too advantageous for employers and demanded substantial benefits for labor.

At a glance, the circumstances that led to the sugar strike of 1942 seemed unremarkable. Labor faced the continuation of a yearlong dispute between the CGT and FLT. As the 1942 harvest neared, the CGT raised again its demand to be included in the negotiations for the next collective agreement. The CGT also asked for better salaries and labor conditions.[65] As before, the FLT and APA excluded the CGT from the hearings. In this respect, the sugar strike that broke out at the end of January escalated a conflict already familiar to workers. It represented another episode of a protracted jurisdictional conflict between two labor unions.

To leave it at that, however, would be deceptive. While labor tensions before the strike drew the concerns of party leaders, the strike itself became deeply enmeshed in politics. Puerto Rico's uncertain political situation after the election of 1940 displaced the CGT-FLT conflict from the public limelight for a short time. A long sequence of quarrels between representatives of the PPD and Coalition became the main focus of attention during the next months. The line was somewhat drawn after PPD leaders achieved a foothold in power with their first reforms and Tugwell became governor of the island in September. The growth of the CGT, moreover, brought to the forefront the grievances of labor. By 1942, the CGT, PPD, and Tugwell cast their role as newcomers to the island's political scene by affirming their decision to stay. While the CGT pushed ahead its demands, the PPD and Tugwell opted not to remain at the sidelines of the labor dispute. Due in large measure to the strike, what appeared to be merely an overlap of labor and political interests soon became a bond or "chain of equivalences" in favor of reform.

To relate the concerns of the PPD to those of labor, the party used a strategy already familiar to the public. The PPD published an editorial in the newspaper *El Imparcial* in December 1941 expressing its concern about the continuing dispute between the CGT and the FLT.[66] Muñoz's party emphasized the drawbacks of a labor conflict during wartime. The PPD feared that interference with basic war industries would seriously affect the economy of the country, meaning not just Puerto Rico but the United States. The editorial of the PPD asked for cooperation from all groups involved in the conflict. Briefly and with moderate words, the editorial concluded that the rise in the cost of living justified a substantial increase of salaries. The lack of improvement in the CGT-FLT dispute prompted PPD officials to write another editorial a couple of weeks later, in mid-January 1942.[67] Although the PPD repeated the same ideas of its previous editorial, the party expressed high concern about the CGT's decision to strike if its demands were not met. The full impact of World War II in the Caribbean loomed on the horizon. Before long, the island would experience a shortage of basic supplies due to the hostilities of German submarines.[68] Since the ties between the CGT and PPD could not be denied, Muñoz's party had reasons to worry about the consequences of a labor strike during a critical moment of the war, more so when major trade unions on the mainland promised to uphold "industrial peace" during the war effort.[69]

Besides cautiously articulating a prolabor discourse, the PPD helped workers by mobilizing governmental functionaries loyal to the party. One of them was Benigno Fernández García, a key leader of the PPD and a local advocate of the New Deal, who headed the Department of Labor. His intervention in the CGT-FLT dispute meant that workers could expect a friendly attitude toward their grievances from an important quarter of the government. Fernández García welcomed the demands of the CGT. This became clear during the second week of January, when Martín Avilés Bracero, a legal assistant of the commissioner of labor, joined CGT leaders to inspect labor conditions throughout the island.[70] Juan Sáez Corales, the secretary of the CGT, reported the tour as a success. The joint visit made by the CGT and the Department of Labor to several towns of the island confirmed workers' discontent toward the FLT-APA agreement. The tour also disclosed watchmen armed with carbines to supervise workers and the formation of company unions at sugar mills to hinder the demands of the CGT.

The favorable disposition of the Department of Labor under Fernández García proved to be a valuable gesture toward workers. It is vital to notice that, perhaps to labor, Fernández García's background was as relevant as, or even more important than, his political affiliation or his position in government. As attorney general, Fernández García intervened in the explosive dockyard strike that unsettled the island in 1938.[71] He showed a genuine concern toward workers when he defended them against Governor Winship's repressive tactics. At that time, moreover, the conflict between the FLT and other labor groups that eventually formed the CGT was already in gestation. Fernández García supported dockyard workers who, dissatisfied with the FLT, later joined the CGT. While the support of CIO and Communist leaders proved critical during the dockyard strike, the intervention of Fernández García offered effective assistance to workers. In his memoir, Tugwell made a candid description of Fernández García and the Department of Labor under his direction:

Mr. Fernández García hated the reactionaries so much and felt so kindly toward anyone who fought them that he soon had his Department peppered with the most radical *Populares*, suspected communists many of them, and as little susceptible to governmental discipline as communists usually are. They were, in fact, completely out of hand. Much of their time was spent in soap-boxing. It was claimed by the employers that they were "fomenting" strikes; and actually they were. However much these were justified, it was scarcely an activity in which employees of the Government ought to engage. Mr. Fernández García was the decentest and kindest of men and he could believe no wrong of anyone—except perhaps of an employer.[72]

Socialists viewed Fernández García as an affront to the interests of their party. FLT leaders also had strong reservations about the attorney general. His intervention in the dockyard strike of 1938 established an unpleasant precedent for Socialists and their union. Moreover, Fernández García's position in government meant that the Department of Labor, which had been a stronghold of FLT leaders, was no longer in their hands. The actions of Fernández García exacerbated a recent setback still fresh in the mind of union leaders. In 1941, the process to appoint the commissioner of labor produced an agitated political battle.[73] While FLT officials favored a member of their ranks such as Prudencio Rivera Martínez, CGT and PPD leaders demanded a candidate of their own. Muñoz's party, with the support of Tugwell, had the upper hand. After much negotiation, Fernández García filled a position that had been claimed over and over again by the FLT and Socialists.

This turn of events helps explain the bitter resentment among FLT leaders against the Department of Labor. For example, Nicolás Nogueras Rivera, the secretary-general and treasurer of the FLT, aimed his attacks against Fernández García's subaltern, Avilés Bracero, for touring the island with the CGT. The secretary-general accused Avilés Bracero of cooperating with Communists in a "perturbation campaign" against industry. Moreover, Nogueras scorned Fernández García's legal assistant when he said that Avilés Bracero "had confused his actual position with the position he had held in the Nationalist Party."[74] That is, he had confused his position with that of a "politician." Far from unconventional, the accusations of Nogueras Rivera fed on notions that reversed the Manichaean streak of Muñoz's party. While CGT and PPD leaders did the most they could to present their political opponents as the reactionary henchmen of "big business," FLT and Socialist leaders moved to portray Muñoz's party as a murky conglomerate of careless radicals. In their own way, the CGT, PPD, FLT, and Socialists informed what became the main discursive divide during the strike by pulling the attention of their audiences into diametrically opposed directions.

The indifference of Socialists, union officials, and sugar producers toward the CGT turned to outright opposition by mid-January 1942. The FLT, FPT, and APA announced that they had already signed a collective agreement and that no changes would be made to it.[75] CGT leaders responded to this aggravation by inviting all workers of the island to form a single trade union. Lawyer Francisco Colón Gordiany, president of the CGT, presented this proposal in *El Imparcial*.[76] He stressed the damage done by the pact between Socialists and Republicans and the advantages of uniting workers "under one flag" free of "personal selfishness." The CGT proposal mirrored the call for a "united front" of labor made by Fernández García a week earlier.[77] Despite the last-minute efforts of the CGT and the PPD to solve the labor dispute, the stage had been set for the strike. Although the CGT's decision to strike remained unequivocal, the FLT and APA did not flinch. On January 19, 1942, a long-awaited labor conflict broke out in the sugar industry.

THE COURSE OF THE STRIKE

The sugar strike lasted little more than two weeks, yet in this short period the CGT, PPD, and Governor Tugwell took decisive actions in favor of labor. Moreover, despite their disparate backgrounds, the participants in the strike first glimpsed the full potential of their political power. On the one hand, the strike enabled PPD leaders to discover that labor mobilization could be an effective source of political leverage. On the other hand, labor leaders learned that allies from outside the ranks of workers could be a valuable asset. CGT leaders knew the risks of making common cause with political parties. An alliance of this sort entailed the possibility of serving interests other than those of workers. During the sugar strike, however, the benefits of accepting the support of the PPD seemed to outweigh the inconveniences or dangers. In short, a bond coalesced among the CGT, PPD, and Tugwell due in large measure to a labor conflict that touched upon a myriad of interests. Supporters of the strike exemplified the genesis of a "collective will" in favor of reform in Puerto Rico.

The limited number of workers who joined the first days of the strike made support from outside the ranks of labor critical from the start. According to the first police reports that poured in from the island, labor stoppages had spread to eleven towns during the first two days of the conflict.[78] The number of workers on strike totaled 2,470. Construction workers at air bases that joined the strike raised the number to 6,370. On January 23, five days after the conflict started, the number of workers on strike reached 4,358.[79] Although workers in the sugar industry joined the strike in greater numbers, labor stoppages in the construction sector came to an end. The critical stage of the sugar strike, when it began to spread rapidly, did not start until the second week of the conflict.

Despite the weak number of workers during the first days of the strike, which may have been in part due to the police's inability to account for all protesters, the labor conflict spelled difficulties from the start. First, according to historian Juan Giusti Cordero, the initial stoppages mostly concentrated in the northeast region and, thus, struck with force that part of Puerto Rico.[80] Second, Giusti argues, the bulk of the strike coincided with labor unrest at U.S. naval and air bases in close-by areas such as Isla Grande, Vieques, Fajardo, and Ceiba. Since workers in these bases lacked affiliation with any union, U.S. officials not only feared the impact of labor unrest on the war effort but also the incursion of CGT activists and their organizational drive into military installations. Barely two months after the attack of Pearl Harbor and the entry of U.S. forces into World War II, a labor strike threatened key U.S. bases in the Caribbean.

As soon as the strike started, the CGT and PPD lent each other a hand. The first day of the strike, Avilés Bracero blasted away against Nogueras Rivera in *El*

Imparcial.[81] He asserted that no conflict existed between his role as Fernández García's legal assistant and his effort to help the CGT. Avilés legitimated his actions by stressing "a new form of politics that manifests the renovated conscience of our great masses."[82] According to Avilés, the votes of workers brought to an end a sad epoch still embraced by Nogueras and the "feudal lords of sugar." With his statements, the legal assistant of Fernández García mirrored the accusations spearheaded by CGT leaders against Socialists who had become too comfortable in governmental positions. Avilés, however, touched upon a different issue when he stressed being the son of a cane cutter and having no animosity against Communists, who in "a sixth part of the world had liquidated the oppressive and inhumane capitalist regime."[83] The FLT president, Prudencio Rivera Martínez, counterattacked Avilés by recalling the legal assistant's turbulent past as a follower of radical Nationalist leader Pedro Albizu Campos.[84] He also labeled the Department of Labor an "incubator of vipers." For Rivera Martínez, the extremism of governmental officials robbed them of legitimacy. Infuriated by these words, Fernández García replied that 80% of the employees of his department belonged to the FLT and that they had the freedom to defend their union. Moreover, Fernández García criticized Nogueras for presenting himself as the only rightful labor leader on the island and for wanting to dictate the "few employees" of the Department of Labor affiliated with the CGT.[85]

The CGT welcomed the support of PPD officials. Strikers lost no time in seeking to bolster their position with help from outside the ranks of labor. Given the hostility of the FLT and APA toward the protest, workers made a sensible move. From the start of the strike, the CGT expressed concern about the presence of the police in the zones of conflict. Many past experiences involving clashes with the police brought unpleasant memories to workers. Police brutality during the sugar strike of 1934 stood out as a woeful instance of repression that the CGT wanted to avoid. Workers informed Muñoz about their preoccupation. The leader of the PPD received many telegrams during the strike telling him about incidents with the police. For example, a cable from Yabucoa and one from Luquillo alerted Muñoz that policemen in those towns patrolled the picketing areas on horses provided by the sugar employers. Another cable from Salinas explained to Muñoz that a police sergeant took the names of 100 workers picketing in front of the town hall. The strikers ended up in jail after a municipal judge set a bail they could not pay. Many other cables simply asked of Muñoz to transfer policemen interfering with picket lines and gatherings of strikers.[86]

Workers encountered a government willing to intercede on their behalf. One reason that explains the administration's receptiveness toward workers is that labor's concern about the police coincided with that of the PPD. According to Tugwell, the independentist sector within the PPD not only resented the past actions of the Police Department but demanded the removal of General Winship's chief of police, Colonel Orbeta. Tugwell stressed in his memoir that "many of Muñoz' followers had been *independentistas* in the old demonstration days and had in person felt the heavy hand of the law."[87] Consequently, PPD leaders demanded a tactful chief of police as a "symbol of renewed liberty" on the island.

Another reason explaining the government's prolabor stance is that Tugwell favored a change of policy toward "one of protection for traditional American liberties." The governor made clear that strikes "were not illegal and that strikers were not lawbreakers; they would be protected in picketing, speechmaking, organizing—everything, in fact, except disorder, the invasion of property, or the use of force."[88] Tugwell's insistence was such that even the Federal Bureau of Investigation cooperated during the strike.[89] Placed within a broader context, the new policy of law enforcement in Puerto Rico exemplified the shift of U.S. priorities during wartime that gave an edge to Muñoz's party over the Coalition. On the one hand, the halt of repression promised local solidarity with U.S. defense and mass support toward the PPD's New Deal-based program. On the other hand, the new policy of law enforcement ended the context that warranted cooperation between Socialists, Republicans, and federal authorities during the previous decade.

The chief of police under Tugwell, Colonel Antonio R. Silva, detailed his department's policies in a circular he sent to local police stations the second day of the strike. Silva demanded impartiality from his officers in their duty to maintain the law. He noted that policemen should not accept gratuities such as the use of horses, vehicles, food, or lodging from those involved in the strike. The chief of police stressed labor's irrefutable right to strike "with the aim of improving its living standards."[90] The right to strike included recruiting supporters, celebrating assemblies, public manifestations, and picketing. Throughout the strike, Muñoz answered many telegrams that asked him about the police by disclosing the chief's guidelines.[91] The leader of the PPD quoted Silva's circular in his cables as evidence of his efforts in favor of workers. Moreover, the PPD announced the government's policies in *El Imparcial* one day after Silva sent out his circular.[92] The newspaper said that Muñoz contacted the appropriate authorities to ensure labor's right to strike. It was Muñoz's aim to see that no employer catered to the needs of policemen. *El Imparcial* reminded the public that two years ago Muñoz participated in a picket line of dockyard workers to defend their rights.[93]

The PPD kept a close watch on police activities throughout the island. A newsman for *La Democracia*, for example, reported a guard oiling a carbine in a police station near a strike zone.[94] He felt surprised, recalling that not long ago policemen unjustly treated the workers in that area. Meanwhile, as the strike progressed, sugar workers and PPD followers wrote to Muñoz about all kinds of concerns. Muñoz received cables asking him to send people to direct the strike movement. Other cables invited Muñoz to the picket lines. For example, a cable sent from Salinas petitioned Muñoz to attend a meeting of 5,000 workers to be held that evening in front of the Aguirre sugar mill.[95] A similar message sent from Fajardo invited Muñoz to a local union's assembly to take place in the town's theater.[96] Yet another cable came from Guayama urging Muñoz's presence.[97] Workers kept reporting incidents with the police. One message informed Muñoz about policemen who remained unaware about Silva's circular while the nearby sugar mill closed its gates, cutting access to a public mail station, telegraph, and telephone.[98] Finally, many other cables asked Muñoz to improve the salaries of workers.

The strike produced a short-term arena of legitimation in which the CGT, PPD, and Tugwell confronted the FLT and its political allies in a fight to win over the confidence of workers. When the CGT pulled out all the stops with its decision to strike, the PPD faced a challenge of its own: to make good its promise about being a champion of labor. The PPD's effort during the electoral campaign to pledge an earnest commitment toward reform and secure the participation of people reverted back, becoming a real issue to a party that was still in a process of formation. The obligation toward workers placed upon the PPD pressured the party to go out of its way during the strike. As leader of the PPD, Muñoz used all the resources at his disposal. He communicated with the chief of police to investigate questionable arrests of workers or police interference with picket lines.[99] Muñoz called upon Fernández García to address workers' inquiries about wages and labor conditions. Muñoz also delegated many tasks to loyal colleagues. Jesús T. Piñero, for example, took care of labor leaders wishing to meet with high-ranking party officials.[100]

Each time workers asked the PPD for help and the party responded in kind, people inched along a path that made possible a "collective will" in favor of reform. While this process remained volatile and offered no guarantees about the consolidation of the islands's new "historical bloc"—the combination of forces held together by the call for social justice—the PPD, workers, and other groups gave free rein to the exchanges that had proven beneficial to them. During the labor conflict of 1942, PPD leaders realized the importance of leaving their desks and offices to join the protest. Workers in turn saw the benefits of political support. On several occasions, the PPD made its presence felt in the labor front of the strike. Party affiliates frequented picket lines and repeatedly spoke at improvised meetings in the streets and at local headquarters of the CGT. PPD legislators kept pace with events at major zones of conflict. One case is Senator Ramón Barreto Pérez, who informed the public about conditions in Ponce. The town's mayor, Andrés Grillasca, assisted Barreto Pérez.[101] Other PPD legislators engaged in the strike include Jesús T. Piñero, Cruz Ortiz Stella, and Luis Sánchez Franqueri.

Certain areas of the island became hot spots of CGT-PPD activities. A good example is the sequence of events at the town of Yabucoa. The PPD and CGT addressed close to 3,000 workers one day before the strike. Four days later, leaders of the CGT and PPD met again to address a large assembly of workers at the local theater. Ernesto Carrasquillo, a local schoolteacher[102] who now served as town mayor under the PPD, started the ceremony. After the mayor's opening words, CGT leaders Juan Sáez Corales, Luis Sánchez Negrín, and Francisco Colón Gordiany spoke to the crowd. Avilés Bracero also delivered a speech. Senators Barreto Pérez and Ortiz Stella had the opportunity to attend the event. On January 29, another mass assembly gathered in Yabucoa under the auspices of the CGT and PPD.[103] Instead of being an oddity, this sort of joint assembly would be a common feature throughout the labor conflict.

The strike became as much an arena of legitimation for the FLT and Socialist Party as it did for the CGT and PPD. However, even as they moved to mend their differences to confront the strike—in an effort, that is, to reconcile the alternative paths of action initiated by the FPT and Pure Laborist Party—Socialists and FLT officials did not fare as well during the conflict as did their competitors. Their actions and discourse made clear that they fought a losing battle. As the strike progressed, the expressions of FLT and Socialist leaders turned desperate and even vitriolic. They realized the odds were stacked against them. The CGT strike meant that a new and more aggressive union supported by the government threatened to erode even further the declining hegemony of the FLT and FPT over labor. FLT and Socialist leaders focused on this fact in their attempt to present themselves as victims of the strike. On the one hand, Socialists viewed governmental policies as flawed because of the PPD's influence. It was said that the PPD manipulated Governor Tugwell in an effort to displace the Socialist Party. Tugwell was pictured as an "American Quisling" completely subordinated to Muñoz.[104] On the other hand, the FLT insisted that Communists and Nationalists manipulated the PPD and CGT. To prove their point about the infiltration of extremists, FLT leaders named people such as Avilés Bracero, Father Severo Ramos, and Lizardo Lizardi.[105]

Besides their warning against the "radical" CGT, which they called the "Communist and Nationalist Confederation," the opponents of the strike compared the island's government with the fascist dictatorships of Hitler and Mussolini.[106] FLT leaders accused the government of lacking neutrality. According to the FLT, the government's favoritism toward the CGT caused indignation among laborers that did not believe in the strike and had a right to work. The FLT constantly argued that the strike was a political affair concocted by the PPD. Although the FLT produced ample evidence of PPD involvement in the strike, one cannot help but notice that this tactic had the opposite effect of that desired by the union. Instead of undermining the PPD as an instigator, FLT leaders serviced their competitors by proving something else: the existence of a government that, according to Tugwell, "for the first time in Puerto Rico the workers considered to be their own."[107]

In their effort to question the government, FLT leaders censured employees of the legislature, Department of Labor, Interior, and Police who joined the strike. FLT leaders went as far as to accuse clerical workers, archivists, landscapers, road keepers, a school janitor, and a secretary of the municipal court.[108] Union officials, moreover, kept track of governmental cars being used to help strikers. The efforts of FLT leaders to win over workers with these sorts of accusations, which only confirmed governmental support toward labor, illustrates the extent of their alienation from the rank and file. FLT leaders not only stood at a distance from workers but also defended the APA's call for "industrial peace." Both the FLT and APA argued that "industrial peace" offered the best way to cooperate with the war effort. Also, both organizations said the police should stay out of the conflict. To a great extent, the discourse of the FLT addressed not workers but employers and federal authorities. With their alarmist outcries about the CGT's violation of "industrial peace," FLT leaders targeted those sectors most worried about a possible state of "anarchy" in Puerto Rico.[109]

The FLT legitimated its position during the strike in ways that the CGT and PPD could not. FLT leaders made reference to the long history of their union. They claimed that historically the FLT had proven to be the authentic representative of workers. Union officials said that their range of experience had no comparison since it amounted to more than forty years of work. Rivera Martínez, the president of the FLT, presented himself as an open-minded leader. He claimed to be ready to step aside voluntarily if the time had come for other labor leaders to replace him. Rivera Martínez also said he would support the government if it meant improvement for labor.[110] Although not long ago Socialists and FLT officials suffered a double split over a conflict about party politics—when Rivera Martínez formed the now defunct Pure Laborist Party and another faction created the FPT—they made amends to welcome back former supporters into their organization. Besides Rivera Martínez and his group, Socialists in charge of the FPT aligned their small and recently formed union with FLT officials. Senator Lino Padrón Rivera, a Socialist and FPT leader, backed the FLT, saying that "no one is more radical than us to defend the conquests of labor."[111] For Padrón, the participation of Socialist leaders in a "hundred combats" of labor served as proof of their claim.

FLT leaders made especial reference to the 1934 sugar strike to confirm the prestigious legacy of their union. Their version of that event presented an outcome favorable to workers. According to FLT leaders, the 1934 sugar strike established the benefit of an islandwide collective agreement to be signed each year by the FLT and APA. FLT leaders said that the collective agreement had been advantageous to workers for eight years. The creation of the Department of Labor was also claimed as one of the achievements of Socialists. Finally, FLT and FPT leaders presented the PPD as an agent outside the ranks of labor. The opponents of the strike viewed PPD officials as "theoreticians," "writers and poets."[112] Padrón Rivera even compared Muñoz's role in the 1942 strike to that of Albizu in one of his anti-American strikes some years back.[113] The FLT also accused the PPD of welcoming as party members sugar producers, such as Senator Juan Dávila Díaz, who underpaid workers.[114] Overall, FLT and FPT leaders found no flaws with their actions or any dissatisfaction among followers of their unions.

Although the CGT did not have the prestige of a lengthy legacy, the sugar strike of 1942 became a time of reckoning for the union. CGT leaders forwarded reports to the press about labor stoppages throughout the island to counter the FLT's and APA's claims that only minor walkouts had taken place.[115] On January 29, Fernández García backed the CGT when he officially declared as commissioner of labor that a strike existed in the sugar industry and that it had stopped production.[116] To correct the FLT's assertion that PPD agents initiated the strike, CGT leaders insisted that as a policy their union did not have a political affiliation with any party. PPD officials corroborated the CGT's claim in an editorial of *El Imparcial*, which distanced the former from labor issues and credited the latter for the strike.[117] Unarguably, party and union officials mirrored each other with their insistence of being groups at arm's length. Even so, none of the avowals about their lack of ties, earnest as they might have been, corresponded with events so far, which showed otherwise. The CGT and PPD obviated with their remarks the close relationship between them. This oversight, however, does not shed that much light on an ineffective form of cover up as it does on the self-perception of CGT and PPD officials during the strike. Besides treading an uncertain ground and loathing the adverse political pacts of the 1930s, the CGT and PPD saw their partnership as capable of reaping mutual benefits without cutting short the union's and party's particular interests. In this sense, while they could definitely act as a "collective will," the PPD, CGT, and other groups could hardly rid the island's new "historical bloc" of its heterogeneity.

Aside from fending off the attacks of the FLT and APA representatives, CGT leaders had the support of Communists and the PCP when they took the offensive and passed judgment on Socialists. The CGT and PCP mocked Socialists by calling them "political cadavers," "feudal lords," or by mimicking the socialist slogan of "labor leaders of 40 years." For these organizers of the strike, the recent past of the FLT offered no reasons to be proud. FLT leaders, according to CGT and PCP officials, had proven to be cohorts of sugar interests after selling out to the APA. In this respect, Colón Gordiany felt outraged to see "traditional leaders of workers and their institutions fighting in the same trenches as those of employers."[118] Juan Santos Rivera, the president of the PCP, aimed his wrath at Nogueras for his "treason . . . at the side of the most reactionary exploiters as the fascists are" and for "unconditionally delivering workers to the claws of corporations."[119] CGT leaders and Communists made clear that they would not tolerate the abuses of FLT agents willing to accommodate themselves to bureaucratic positions. The judgment passed on the FLT entailed more than rash words. When confronted with the FLT's claims about its lengthy background, CGT leaders turned out to be considerate and even tactful. They acknowledged that the FLT had been vital to labor's cause and that Socialists had achieved major victories in their defense of workers. CGT leaders asked Socialists to honor their past and join the strike.[120]

The CGT countered its lack of a long history by presenting itself as a youthful and vigorous organization. The secretary of the CGT, Juan Sáez Corales, for example, described his fellow leaders as young men who had been in close contact with the rank and file for many years before the creation of their union. He argued that the young men of the CGT had proven to old Socialist leaders that they were born within the labor movement. According to Sáez Corales, these "authentic sons of the working class" had been seen in action by the FLT for no less than eight years. As he said to Rivera Martínez, the president of the FLT, "you came to know us at one strike or another." Several cases merited attention for Sáez Corales such as the strikes that struck the sugar industry in 1934, the Sunoco button factory in 1937, the dockyards in 1938, and the ones of *público* drivers. He also mentioned the boycott against gas companies and the "struggle" to secure federal legislation.[121] With his words, Sáez Corales cut across organizational lines to emphasize that the vitality of his union lay in the commitment of individuals who had taken action even before the creation of the CGT. Implicit was the fact that some CGT leaders had belonged and gained experience as part of the FLT.

The PPD supplemented the statements of the CGT with its own discourse about labor. One example is the comment of columnist Antonio Pacheco Padró in *El Imparcial*.[122] After recalling Fenández García's former position in the House of Representatives and the labor legislation he introduced at the time, Padró applauded the commissioner of labor for his initiative to reconcile the CGT and FLT. According to Padró, "the unity of the working-class in front of fascism and its diverse forms of exploitation is indispensable at this critical moment of the world."[123] To prove his point about the perils workers faced internationally, Padró warned about the detrimental consequences of labor disunity in Cuba, México, and Spain. Padró also stressed the situation on the mainland. He compared the conflict between the FLT and CGT to that between the AFL and CIO in the United States, saying that mainland workers would have been imperiled if President Roosevelt had not intervened. This statement hinted at Muñoz's role in the labor strike. Padró also acclaimed the CGT for its attempt to organize rural workers.

Santiago Iglesias, Jr., wrote a similar piece to that of Padró for *El Imparcial*, in which he referred to Puerto Rico as the "new Gibraltar in the Caribbean."[124] After a quick glance at the international conflict, Iglesias, Jr., focused on local events. He said that while certain "political cadavers" had been driven to anger and despair after losing power and the confidence of the people, the CGT came into being as a union free of political influences and truly committed to the needs of labor. Iglesias, Jr., validated Colón Gordiany as a leader, saying that he came from the same school of leaders as Santiago Iglesias Pantín, the founder of the FLT. Iglesias, Jr., underlined the difference between the CGT and FLT by commenting that "leaders are made with years of struggle in the countryside, factories, and shops, and not in the aristocratic saloons."[125] As a "cofounder" and former member of the FPT, Iglesias, Jr., discredited this union by saying that it came into being only so that Bolívar Pagán could call himself a labor leader before Congress.

Local and international concerns merged during the strike and informed the actions of participants. The strike enabled the CGT to strongly voice its discontent about the FLT, a concern that had been expressed before but without such resonance. On the one hand, the grievances of labor that had been bottled up until the strike suddenly exploded during the period of conflict. On the other hand, the strike allowed CGT leaders to legitimate themselves before workers. Their constant visits to picket lines, makeshift assemblies, and hot spots of conflict provided the best proof of the CGT's commitment. In addition to the rank and file, the true combatants of the strike included leaders who did not rest, such as Colón Gordiany, Sáez Corales, and Sergio Kuilan Báez. Besides affirming their legitimacy before the eyes of labor, CGT officials took care to maximize their chances of winning support from the federal administration. The CGT left no doubt that it aligned itself with Governor Tugwell, President Roosevelt, and the Allies at the front lines of World War II. At the height of the strike, the CGT bombarded the executive mansion with telegrams expressing sympathy toward the governor and the war effort.[126] During manifestations in strike zones, Roosevelt's and Tugwell's names came up often in clamors, ditties, banners, and makeshift signs. From the outset, the CGT portrayed its demands as moderate and the sugar strike as a peaceful event to avoid accusations of hindering U.S. wartime policies. The CGT argued that the APA was the real enemy of the war effort for not paying enough for labor to work.[127]

Concerns about the war effort and the spread of labor walkouts prompted the search for a quick solution of the strike.[128] Fernández García and Governor Tugwell proposed several alternatives to solve the conflict. As soon as the strike started, the commissioner of labor offered the services of the Commission of Meditation and Conciliation.[129] The CGT rejected the offer because some members of the commission belonged to the FLT. Fernández García tried again to solve the conflict by calling CGT and FLT leaders to a meeting on January 22.[130] The presence of several CGT and Communist leaders during the meeting made clear their desire to negotiate. The CGT and FLT, however, could not reach an agreement on Fernández García's proposal for a "united front" of labor. Communist leader Alberto E. Sánchez expressed his support to fuse the CGT and FLT. The PPD also applauded the commissioner's efforts and held on for a while to the idea of a "united front." Unfortunately, the appraisals of the CGT, PCP, and PPD were to no avail.

Tugwell and the PPD asked federal authorities to intervene in the CGT-FLT dispute even before the strike began. The governor made arrangements to bring Father Francis Haas to the island, an experienced mediator of the National Labor Relations Board (NLRB).[131] Teodoro Moscoso, the coordinator of insular activities for Puerto Rico and the island's future leader of industrial development, wrote to the NLRB about the urgency of Tugwell's initiative saying that "it would be extremely regrettable to have a serious labor controversy delay the grinding season with the consequent curtailment of our sugar supply."[132] Tugwell explained in greater detail his decision to request help from federal authorities in a letter he sent to the secretary of the interior, Harold L. Ickes, shortly after the strike ended.[133] First, Tugwell mentioned the limits of what he or local agencies could do to solve the conflict. Second, Tugwell expressed to Ickes his interest to address a legitimate labor issue and the contradictions he faced as governor during the strike:

I am convinced that it is a mistake for the Governor to get into these labor troubles. We not only have a Federal Labor Department, with a conciliation service, but a National Labor Relations Board, and certain war-time agencies. Only the National Labor Relations Board has an office here and that is no good to us because it only enforces the Wagner Act and that does not apply to agriculture. . . . The sugar people have never made as much money as they will make this year and who can blame the workers for trying to share in it, especially since the cost of living here has gone up 36% in one year without corresponding wage increases. The effort is to use the war as a club to prevent wage increases. But if I object to that I shall certainly be reported by all the military people—no doubt I already have—as "fomenting disorder." That was screamed at me by the press throughout the troubles. . . . I am not very well fitted to handle situations of this sort, perhaps, because I have an overwhelming sympathy with the workers.[134]

Fernández García backed Tugwell's effort to bring a federal mediator to the island, more so after his unsuccessful meeting with the CGT and FLT. As if to prove the need for federal mediation, an informal meeting between Rivera Martínez, CGT leaders, the PCP president, and eight CIO representatives on January 25 failed to produce favorable results.[135] The PPD placed much hope on Father Haas and explained the reason for his visit.[136] An important goal would be to establish a regional office of the NLRB under the direction of Melton Boyd. Father Haas arrived on the island on January 27. He met with the CGT, FLT, APA, and Tugwell during the next three days. Although Haas revived the idea of uniting the CGT and FLT, the plan did not prosper. Another option, however, gained public attention and the support of Tugwell. Workers would cast a vote in a referendum for their union and the one with most followers would be permitted to negotiate with the APA. CGT leaders accepted the idea and felt confident about having a majority. The FLT questioned the legal validity of the referendum. This was consistent with the FLT's lack of enthusiasm for Haas' visit and its claim that credit should go to its ally, the AFL, for requesting help from the NLRB. Of all options, the FLT accepted only its own call for the Minimum Wage Board, a project that had been passed by the legislature but not by Tugwell, who wanted to amend it.[137]

While local and federal agents debated how to solve the conflict, the strike gathered force as more workers came to support the CGT. The labor conflict also became more intense as the moderation and restraint of the emboldened strikers began to erode. During the second week of the strike, the police reported a steady increase of labor stoppages throughout the island. Over ten towns were added to the list of strike zones. The number of strikers totaled 4,659 on January 26; 5,439 on January 27; and 5,996 on January 28. The total number of strikers jumped to 8,926 on January 30 and 9,326 on January 31. On February 5, the number of workers on strike reached an all-time high with a total of 11,241. During the ensuing days, the number of strikers began to subside, only after the CGT agreed to call off the strike.[138] Although the strike certainly gained momentum during the second week, an incongruence became evident at this point. Given the large workforce and extent of grievances in the sugar industry, the number of strikers reported by the police is low in comparison and at odds with the situation in that sector of the economy. Since the strike came at a critical point of the war effort, perhaps the police underplayed the labor conflict by hollowing out the numbers in their reports.

Whether that was the case or not, Colón Gordiany disputed the information handed by the police.[139] Even though the estimates at his disposal did not account for the entire island, Colón Gordiany was able to set the numerical force of the strike between 50,000 and 80,000 workers. Iglesias, Jr., placed the strength of the CGT over 75,000 workers.[140] At one time or another, labor had a glimpse of the strike's real size when a single picket line, rally, or meeting produced a high turnout, which usually ranged—even with a cautious margin of error—from 3,000-5,000, to 10,000 protesters.[141] Moreover, the strike spread to many towns, including Juncos, Canóvanas, Fajardo, Ceiba, Humacao, Yabucoa, Arroyo, Guayama, Salinas, Ponce, Guánica, Lajas, Aguada, and Camuy. In Humacao, the labor conflict gathered such force that even FLT workers were swept away and joined the protest. Fearful of the strike's strength, an employer of the southeast, Agripino Roig, broke ranks with the APA and attempted to negotiate on his own with the CGT.[142] Also concerned about the magnitude of the strike, another employer in Ponce, Pedro Juan Serrallés, opted to inform Tugwell in a telegram about the threats made by labor to destroy the tires of company buses and transport vehicles.[143]

Besides the increase in the number of workers on strike, tensions grew at the zones of conflict. The antagonism between the CGT and FLT gave way to open confrontations between workers. Information about distressing incidents in many towns reached U.S. officials, local authorities, and the public. On the one hand, the CGT complained about policemen and armed thugs who broke up picket lines to introduce strikebreakers. On the other hand, the FLT reported the unwarranted actions of the CGT and the government.[144] Socialists said that the police escorted strikers during illegal entries of private property and dispatched laborers who wanted to work. Moreover, the opponents of the strike—not only the FLT but also the Coalition and APA—accused CGT workers of violent acts. They reported, for example, that CGT workers shot, stoned, and attacked with pipes FLT workers at the town of Juncos. For FLT leaders, this represented the actions of a "savage mob."[145] A frequent charge of the FLT and APA was that government employees and strikers blocked the way to plantations and invited FLT workers to strike by claiming to have official authorization to do so. On many occasions, according to the opponents of the strike, peaceful bystanders had little protection and became victims of protesters armed with stones, sticks, pipes, knives, and guns.

Undoubtedly, the FLT, Coalition, and APA instigated difficulties with false accusations and exaggerations about the conduct of CGT workers. Too many times they portrayed strikers as hardly above petty thieves and criminals. Yet, there is evidence that some CGT workers did engage in the sort of activities denounced by the FLT and others. The police reported many incidents during the strike. Several cases consisted of threats made by CGT workers to nonstrikers or company employees. More often than not, CGT workers acted on these threats. In Juncos, workers stopped "in a disorderly manner" the car of a white-collar employee headed toward a sugar mill. A worker of the same town assaulted a nonstriker with a *machete* (cane-cutting utensil). In another incident, workers derailed two wagons hauled by a locomotive belonging to a sugar company. In the towns of Guánica and Lajas, workers filled the road with nails to cripple company trucks. Workers also jammed railroad switches and set fire to sugarcane fields. Another sort of situation ensued in the town of Juana Díaz when workers placed an American flag on the ground to block the transit of five tractors of a sugar plantation.[146]

Besides assaulting individuals, damaging property, and obstructing production, strikers targeted laborers still at work. They stopped the drivers of trucks and trains carrying sugarcane. Moreover, groups of strikers entered sugarcane fields to drive workers out. In one of these cases, a worker seized a shotgun from an overseer and fired once at him. He was uninjured, but his mare was badly wounded. The chief of police and Governor Tugwell received several cables about incidents in various districts of the island. A number of telegrams expressed the concern of managers about the constant trespasses made on their company's property and the failure of the police to deal with the situation. Other messages warned about the activities of political agitators at the picket lines, the destruction of property, and threats to individuals.[147]

The actions of strikers against FLT workers and company employees did not differ much from labor practices at previous conflicts in the sugar industry. However, the strike's rapid growth and intensity indicate that the actions of CGT workers entailed more than an effort to defend their cause by hindering production or inducing other laborers to join them. As Daniel James has shown, intense forms of public violence and unruly behavior may carry a heavy load of symbolic meaning. In his analysis of Argentina's mass protest in support of Juan D. Perón on October 17, 1945, James demonstrates that the "carnivalesque festive behavior" of workers was less a random event than a form of action that deliberately targeted institutions and symbols that had been known to marginalize labor.[148]

The sugar strike of 1942 stopped short of becoming the sort of "secular iconoclasm" experienced during Argentina's "October 17." On the other hand, the strike is similar to Argentina's case in that it was a form of payback time for workers. CGT followers expressed through actions what their leaders had said with words. Strikers made clear the limits of their tolerance toward the FLT and APA either by pushing nonparticipants around or destroying property. Not all, however, consisted of unruly behavior. The public conduct of strikers also suggest a degree of relief and jubilation among workers who no longer had to face the repressive conditions of the depression era. To continue the comparison with Argentina's case, the steps taken by workers to shed unpleasant memories about the 1930s meant overcoming Puerto Rico's very own Infamous Decade—Década Infame. Strikers expressed their newly gained right to protest through street parades, marches, night vigils, and spontaneous meetings at public plazas.[149]

The strike began to get out of hand at the end of its second week. The growth and intensity of the conflict menaced to engulf the entire island and to cause unprecedented levels of violence. On January 30, a bloody event at the town of Guayama marked the climax of the strike and precipitated its conclusion. A collision occurred between strikers and employers at the Luce & Co.'s "colonia Josefa," a sugarcane field near the Aguirre sugar mill. About 9:00 A.M., a group of fifty strikers or more carrying the American flag paraded along the road from Guayama to Ponce, next to an area known as "barrio Jobos." When the men and women of the group reached the company's plantation, they entered the property with the American flag upfront and invited other workers to strike.[150]

To their surprise, the strikers encountered the general administrator of Luce & Co., Marcelo J. Obén, and about fifteen employees or more carrying firearms and tear-gas pistols. Obén warned that if the strikers' march continued through the company's property, he would order his men to shoot. Moreover, according to witnesses, Obén degraded the American flag by saying that "for him it was a furnace's rag." When the company employees saw that the strikers invited other workers to walk out, they shot their tear-gas pistols, forming clouds of stinging smoke. Thereupon, as the strikers lay on the ground coughing, Obén and his men fired pistols, revolvers, and a double-barrel shotgun at them. Over eight strikers suffered serious injuries from the shots fired by Obén's men. Justino Ortiz Aponte, who had been carrying the flag, lost his life moments after the pellets from a shotgun shell pierced his head. Although Delfín Alicea Sánchez survived the bullet that smashed his left eye, he died in the hospital three days later after doctors operated on his head to extract a second projectile.[151]

By firing at will a burst of bullets, employers wreaked havoc among strikers. Blood smeared the American flag, which lay on the floor with "8 to 10 perforations." Besides the first two casualties of the tragedy, many other workers faced the possibility of death. José Alvarado had "13 perforations in the intestine." Two other workers, José Almodóvar and Vicente Martínez, "were badly wounded with very probable fatal consequences."[152] That a terrible incident was waiting to happen in Guayama can be ascertained in hindsight. Strikers had warned several days before the tragedy that they would enter the grounds of Luce & Co. They not only set foot on "colonia Josefa" the day before the shooting but also entered several nearby properties such as "Central Guamaní," "Hacienda Melania," "Hacienda Algarrobos," and "Hacienda Reunión."[153] Meanwhile, Obén expressed his vexation about the strike to Tugwell and the police in over five separate telegrams before and on January 30. For the last five days, according to Obén, 100 to 200 strikers yelled to him, hurled stones, and threatened to enter the company's property. A more emphatic cable came from Leo R. O'Neill, who protested "against [the] use of [the] American flag by racketeers, men working in cane fields. The flag of my country guarantees civil liberties to all groups not only [to] leeches who live off others."[154]

Shortly after the "Aguirre Massacre," the name given to the tragedy, Muñoz received a telegram asking for help.[155] He replied that a high-ranking police officer had been sent to Guayama.[156] The leader of the PPD also informed workers that Representative Piñero would go to the scene of the crime. Next day, agents from the legislature, Department of Labor, and Police went to Guayama. PPD Representatives Elmer M. Ellsworth and Piñero examined the place of the shooting, interviewed witnesses, and visited the home of the dead worker.[157] Meanwhile, a large crowd of laborers gathered in front of the town's police station to demand justice. On February 1, according to El Imparcial, over 2,000 workers paid their last respects to Ortiz Aponte after joining the funeral procession to the cemetery.[158]

Several CGT and PPD officials joined the ceremony such as Colón Gordiany, Sáez Corales, Kuilan Báez, Piñero, and Representative Pedro A. Cordero. Muñoz also paid homage to Ortiz when he visited Guayama to pronounce a few words at the worker's funeral. He lamented that some people still saw workers as "slaves" but guaranteed to labor a victory "because there is a government that backs them."[159] That same day, the widow of the victim received Muñoz at her home. Muñoz also stopped at the hospital to see the wounded workers. Soon, the authorities began to investigate the shooting. A preliminary report of the Department of Labor concluded that "the striking workers on parade were unarmed. They walked . . . in a peaceful way and did not make any provocation to the employees who shot at them."[160] The district attorney of Guayama, Luis R. Polo, reached a similar conclusion.[161]

FLT officials and sugar producers quickly denied responsibility for the shooting in Guayama. The president of the FLT blamed the government for the tragedy.[162] According to Rivera Martínez, the partiality of the police and the lack of safety for labor allowed an armed group of strikers to assault private property. As a consequence, company employees had been forced to defend themselves and provide the protection that the government had failed to guarantee. Rivera Martínez portrayed the shooting as a rare event that stood in contrast to several years of industrial peace. In his view, the FLT put an end to tragedies, jails, and assassinations for more than ten years. Rivera Martínez said the government "wanted to stain with blood once again" the history of labor. The president of the FLT also mocked the chief of police, alleging that sixty policemen poured into Guayama, even though the chief previously said to have none available. After the shooting, Ramón Ramos Casellas, the secretary of the APA, let loose his wildest thoughts. With a "pistol in hand," Ramos argued, governmental functionaries hatched a scheme to impose the CGT, an "instrumental type" of labor organization and a breeding ground of Communists. Ramos warned about the "painful history" that would be written if Puerto Rico became a "sovereign republic" according to the designs of the PPD. For Ramos, no room existed for workers carrying the American flag.[163]

For the PPD, Fernández García, CGT leaders, and Communists nothing seemed further from the truth. On January 31, the PPD expressed its sympathy with workers in an editorial of El Imparcial.[164] On the one hand, according to the editorial, workers could count on the support of the PPD. On the other hand, El Imparcial made clear that the labor conflict had "absolutely nothing to do with the Popular Party." The PPD laid the success of the strike on workers. Distressed by the news of the shooting, the commissioner of labor remarked that sugar producers had failed to see that the situation on the island no longer allowed their abuses. Fernández García accused sugar producers, saying that "these gentlemen have not noticed that things in Puerto Rico have changed as in other parts of the world. These gentlemen are the same barons that previously had been accustomed to command from the most high-ranking official in the government to the most humble policeman."[165] Fernández García concluded that "they believe themselves to be above the law."

CGT and Communist leaders had a vigorous reaction to the news of the shooting in Guayama. The president of the CGT regretted that labor's demands for bread had been met with "close-range gunshots" and that workers suffered mortal wounds for refusing "salaries of hunger and misery." Colón Gordiany presented a different view of the island's history from that of Rivera Martínez. He said that under Tugwell, the government did not show unconditional support toward employers, as had been the case so many times in the past. That is, "in other times of sad recollection, there would have been an infinitude of thrashings and brutalities against the workers on strike."[166] According to Colón Gordiany, instead of being in vain, the blood spilled in Guayama offered new hope to win democratically the "crusade of social justice."

Juan Santos Rivera, the president of the PCP, answered the statements of Ramos Casellas.[167] According to Santos Rivera, the leader of sugar producers believed that he could still count on the repressive tactics of Winship. Under the actual circumstances, Santos Rivera argued, workers would defend the precepts of President Roosevelt "to their last drop of blood." Santos Rivera blamed the APA for lumping the burden of the war effort on labor, hindering the work of Tugwell, and aiding with "subversive" tactics the "nazifascist powers."[168]

With words nothing short of spectacular, calling for attention with their gigantic typeset, the headlines of the PPD press magnified the tragedy in Guayama. To leave no doubt about the meaning of the shooting, *La Democracia* published many details of what it called a "savage monstrous" act and an event "without precedent in the history of labor struggle in all the world."[169] On February 1, the PPD press ran a front cover underscoring the fact that a peaceful group of workers carrying the American flag had been massacred "in cold blood by a sort of GESTAPO of the Aguirre sugar mill."[170] Federal agents were called upon to investigate the "shooting and rape" of the American flag by the assailants. With the greatest shock and alarm they could possibly muster, the editors of *La Democracia* reported on February 4 that, among other weapons, the police seized a German gun at the Aguirre sugar mill. According to the PPD, the gun could have been used in the shooting of the "National flag." *La Democracia* let it be known that the weapon came from "the dominions of Adolf Hitler, the current beast of Berlin" and that it belonged to employees who had no respect for the "sacred national symbol."[171] While the PPD conveniently demonized the German pistol of sugar employees, the party failed to condemn another weapon that the police confiscated at the scene of the crime, a U.S.-made Colt revolver,[172] which also could have been used against the strikers.

The discourse of the PPD absorbed and transformed a local event of much significance for workers into an occurrence of major political consequences for the island's authorities. According to the PPD, the worldwide forces of good and evil had their counterparts in Puerto Rico. The discourse of Muñoz's party implied that Tugwell, the PPD, and CGT had to form an alliance to fight successfully against the enemies of democracy, meaning the FLT, APA and the Coalition. The former reserved for themselves the role of the Allies while portraying the latter as a homegrown version of the Axis. Despite the ingenuity of the PPD's discourse, the party did not have a monopoly over the symbolic meaning of the war. People in favor of, and against, the strike attacked each other with equal frequency and intensity using words such as "totalitarian," "fascist," and "Nazi." Although the arguments varied, two basic allegations became familiar during the labor conflict. Opponents of the strike accused their rivals of debilitating the home front with demands that could only bring chaos. In turn, supporters of the strike accused their contenders of handing over the country by using the same repressive and reprehensible tactics of the enemy.

Only a combination of factors can explain the effectiveness of the CGT's and PPD's discourse over that of their rivals. The FLT and Socialists not only lost support after their pact with the Coalition turned sour but also faced the indisposition of U.S. authorities. The CGT and PPD had the opportunity to pick up the broken pieces of colonial politics after Washington, D.C., revamped its policies toward Puerto Rico during wartime. While the opponents of the strike faced many discrepancies that robbed even their most fervent avowals of credibility, the advocates of the strike had an edge over their opponents as part of a new "historical bloc" in favor of social justice. This does not mean that the PPD, CGT, and other participants of the strike lacked specific interests. Although the labor conflict pivoted on the idea of reform, several issues informed the strike such as the priorities of the United States to win the war, the maneuvers of PPD officials to become mediators of U.S. policies, and the effort of labor to introduce improvements at the workplace. Far from being immune to each other's concerns and pressures, these agents transformed colonial politics in Puerto Rico as well as themselves in the process.

THE STRIKE'S END AND OUTCOME

The shooting in Guayama convinced local and federal officials that the strike was spiraling out of control. Subsequent events confirmed the fears of the authorities. On February 2, workers from the town of Canóvanas overturned several train wagons of a sugar company. In the town of Arecibo, two employees of the Cambalache sugar mill suffered gunshot wounds after an agitated argument about the strike.[173] Two days later, an overseer of the Serrallés Co. in Ponce shot to death an alleged supporter of the strike.[174] The victim, Miguel Báez, worked in a construction project of military defense at Losey Field.[175] According to witnesses, Báez convinced his neighbors to abandon their work in the cane field and join the strike. As the labor stoppage grew more volatile, local and federal officials doubled their efforts to stop the agitation. Early in February, a rapid sequence of negotiations slowed down the conflict and eventually put an end to the strike.

First, Tugwell and the PPD had to deal with the FLT, APA, and the Coalition. Throughout the strike, but especially during its final days, these groups voiced their outrage about the conflict to federal agents in an attempt to win over their support or at least provoke a reaction. Resident commissioner Bolivar Pagán, who led the Coalition's lobbying efforts, notified President Roosevelt and the Secretary of the Interior Harold L. Ickes about his party's opposition to the strike.[176] Sugar producers cabled Secretary Ickes and the mainland press with the same aim. An anonymous letter to the *New York Sun* said that policemen on the island, who had no means of transportation, could do no other than walk and forget about law enforcement after Tugwell prohibited them to use company cars and horses.

Rivera Martínez tried a different tactic against Tugwell, the PPD, and CGT when he threatened to call a general strike by the FLT. With a touch of fatalism, Rivera Martínez said he was ready to "please in that way the government, which wants the strike to help the enemy win the war."[177] For the FLT, APA, and the Coalition nothing short of ousting Governor Tugwell would have been acceptable. Their attacks against the governor fed on Tugwell's controversial legacy as a reformer. The unorthodox views of Tugwell during the first days of the New Deal could still be recalled by the U.S. government and press. To make matters worse, the smear campaign on the island coincided with the opposition on the mainland. *Time* magazine accused Tugwell of being a "no impartial statesman." Also, *U.S. News and World Report* followed suit with a somber and unappealing article about the island's governor.[178]

To rebut these groups, Tugwell and the PPD informed federal officials about conditions in Puerto Rico. Muñoz expressed his support for Tugwell in cables to President Roosevelt, Secretary Ickes, Representative Vito Marcantonio, and the U.S. Senate. In his cable to Senator Tydings, Muñoz explained that the attacks of Bolivar Pagán provided "a basis for nazi propaganda in Latin America, which is already being used by the Berlin Radio."[179] The governor wrote to Roosevelt as the strike progressed. On January 29, he warned the president "that our sugar friends and the coalitionists have been hoping to stop the Puerto Rican New Deal with martial law."[180] Perhaps because he faced a hectic agenda, Tugwell scribbled a short note to Roosevelt about a "nasty sugar strike" two days after the Guayama shooting. Tugwell told the president that despite the pressure of sugar interests he did not use force, remembering that "you were proudest almost of anything that you came through without ever calling out the guard."[181] When the opposition to Tugwell and the PPD continued after the strike, the governor requested the help of the Federal Bureau of Investigation to find out about the "defamatory" statements of Republicans and to investigate "an unlimited drawing account" that had been put up for Pagán in Washington, D.C., by the APA.[182] The actions of Tugwell received the approval of President Roosevelt and Secretary Ickes.

Keeping the opposition at bay solved only part of the problem to end the strike. Besides averting the loss of confidence that the opposition could have caused among federal agents, Tugwell and the PPD had to offer a solution to the strike acceptable to the CGT. The same morning of the Guayama shooting, a meeting took place in San Juan between Haas, Boyd, Sáez Corales, Colón Gordiany, and Rivera Martínez.[183] CGT leaders said that a union assembly would consider ending the strike if Tugwell promised to form the Minimum Wage Board—Junta de Salario Mínimo (JSM). Several hours later, when the tragedy in Guayama became news, Tugwell and Haas agreed to establish the JSM and to immediately appoint the members of the agency.[184] Next day, after meeting with federal mediators and strike leaders, the governor reaffirmed his decision and asked the CGT to decree a truce for the sake of the war effort. CGT leaders responded to Tugwell's plea, announcing a convention of their union for February 2.[185] To reassure workers about Tugwell's decision, Muñoz wrote to the president of the CGT the same day of the convention. Muñoz's letter, which was read at the CGT assembly, told Colón Gordiany that the PPD would approve a project to make the sugar wage scale determined by the JSM "retroactive." That is, Muñoz promised to extend the wage scale coverage to the period ellapsed since the return to work of strikers.[186] This generous offer represented a last ditch effort of the government to secure the compliance of labor.

Except for the creation of a "Special Truce Committee," the CGT convention did not produce the results that Tugwell and the PPD desired. Workers expressed reluctance to accept Tugwell's offer without further guarantees. CGT leaders placed in the hands of Tugwell and Muñoz a message stating the conditions of the union's "Special Truce Committee." Workers demanded a joint meeting of the CGT and APA, wages above the FLT-APA contract, a retroactive wage scale as promised by Muñoz, protection from employers' reprisals, and the APA's recognition of the CGT.[187] The CGT's demands vexed Tugwell. He feared "to be back where we were, with a prospect of more violence." Tugwell also snapped at Muñoz: "I . . . told him that unless he gets the strikers to go to work and allow grievances to be settled, in an orderly way, I shall resign. I know that the agitation is kept up by his local leaders. If he has no discipline we may as well know it."[188]

After the CGT convention, Tugwell and the PPD had the opportunity to offer further reassurances to labor. On February 3, the PPD attended the annual hearings held by the Federal Department of Agriculture to determine wages and prices for the sugar industry. Governmental agents Teodoro Moscoso and Max Engloff attended the hearings as envoys of Muñoz to back labor's demands for better salaries.[189] That same day, Tugwell, Muñoz, and CGT leaders convened for two hours at the executive mansion to discuss the governor's new proposals. The CGT was asked to accept the wage determinations of the Department of Agriculture until further notice. In return, Tugwell and Muñoz voiced their support for retroactive wage scales, the inclusion of labor in the JSM's process to set wages, the reinstatement of strikers to work, and protection from unfair labor practices. Shortly after that meeting, the editors of *El Imparcial* wrote a piece for publication to express Muñoz's optimism about a strike truce.[190] Next day, Tugwell met with several representatives of sugar producers, and, after "a nasty exchange with a couple of their lawyers," the governor convinced them to abide by the JSM's decision over wages.[191]

The CGT announced another convention to consult with workers about the governor's proposals. Union leaders invited Muñoz to address the 339 delegates of the convention, but he could not assist due to health problems.[192] To the relief of Tugwell, on February 6 the CGT convention approved a truce to the strike. Communists favored the truce, arguing that the continuance of the conflict could benefit labor but at the expense "of providing a weapon to combat Tugwell."[193] The governor expressed to Ickes the toils to end the conflict: "by using ingenuity, bluff, and improvisation I succeeded in settling, for the time being, what I thought was going to be a general strike."[194] Although tensions ensued when the APA backpedaled its promise to comply with the JSM, the CGT truce held, and the strike was over.[195] According to Tugwell, "the CGT has evidently responded to Muñoz's appeal."[196] Besides Muñoz's intervention, the outcome also had to do with the reassurances of the governor. To allay any last-minute misgiving among workers, in the night of February 6, shortly after the CGT convention, Tugwell announced the appointment of two members of the CGT and another two of the FLT as part of the JSM.[197] During the next weeks, several meetings followed between labor and governmental officials to iron out the details and make final arrangements.

For Tugwell and the federal authorities, the strike's end meant resuming the tasks related to wartime priorities. The governor felt pleased to inform the Department of the Interior that conditions in Puerto Rico had returned to normal. Tugwell also reported to President Roosevelt that his demand for an increase in sugar production seemed possible to achieve.[198] Moreover, according to the governor, there were "programs well under way," and the legislature began to consider additional projects to improve local conditions. For Tugwell, the strike proved significant from an administrative point of view. The conflict underscored the need to have governmental agencies ready to deal with labor issues. The JSM represented an effective step, but the governor saw room for further action. As soon as the strike ended, Tugwell requested the U.S. secretary of labor, Frances Perkins, to send a permanent conciliator to Puerto Rico.[199] On the island, the commissioner of labor made several improvements to his department. It became official policy to cooperate with the organization of labor and to promote a "united front." In his annual report, the commissioner argued that "Puerto Rican labor cannot afford to have two or more organizations, less in time of war." According to the commissioner, "the mighty labor movement of the continental United States as represented by the AFL and the CIO, undivided in the war effort, aims at the final consolidation of forces, for one labor front in America. The Puerto Rican worker is in more want of that united front than his continental brother."[200] The Department of Labor also reorganized its services, initiated a training program for its personnel, and increased its budget.[201]

The CGT could claim the strike's end as a victory for workers. To comply with the promise made to labor, local authorities spent the rest of February working as quickly as possible to set up the JSM. CGT leaders were kept informed about the administration's efforts. On February 19, PPD leader Vicente Géigel Polanco notified Muñoz that Colón Gordiany had been consulted to know if the CGT found satisfactory the JSM legislation.[202] Colón Gordiany saw no problem with the project and informed the PPD that he would consult the rank and file. Although the JSM's pay-scale determination took several months to be handed down, it offered to labor substantial wage improvements. The JSM recommended a 33 1/3% increase over the wages that had been last paid in the sugar industry, coming close to Muñoz's proposal for a 36% hike of labor's salaries.[203] According to the JSM, its recommendation provided that "not less than $1.60 a day be paid to laborers engaged in cultivations and $1.90 to those engaged in harvesting operations."[204] In a separate decision, the JSM also recommended a pay scale for retroactive wages, a workday of eight hours, and double-time payment for excess hours of work. The JSM's pay scale fixed wages above the FLT-APA agreement. According to a report of the Anglo-American Caribbean Commission, the JSM's "most notable decision . . . awarded the workers an increase of about 20%, lifting them above the level of their union contract."[205]

Labor's victory was not just an economic one. Besides better wages, the JSM offered to include labor in decision making processes to determine not only pay rates but also hours of work and conditions of employment. Top officials of the CGT, such as Juan Sáez Corales, were soon invited to form part of the JSM.[206] Overall, the CGT could claim Tugwell and the PPD as their allies in the government.[207] CGT leaders tried to be careful about expressing political ties to any party. However, the CGT's closest ally, the PCP, had less reluctance to jump into the populist bandwagon of the PPD. Communist leader César Andreu Iglesias expressed it best when he released a party statement that included a resolution "to support the economical [sic] improvement and social justice program of Governor Tugwell and the Popular Party."[208] The statement reached the Department of the Interior in Washington, D.C. Besides CGT and PCP leaders, many workers openly expressed their appreciation toward Tugwell and the PPD. After the strike, the rank and file increasingly wrote to Muñoz to know about the progress of the JSM and other labor matters.[209]

For the PPD, the strike's end did not mean a return to normal conditions but an occasion to reflect on the meaning of the conflict and its importance as a political milestone. Few resources were spared to celebrate labor's victory and the government's swift response to workers. The PPD strove to shape the public's collective memory with constant follow ups of the strike in the pages of *El Imparcial*, *La Democracia*, and *El Batey*. A radio program initiated by the PPD in June also kept the strike alive in the mind of the population.[210] PPD officials insisted that the labor conflict confirmed the beginning of a new era for Puerto Rico. The strike, according to Muñoz's party, provided indisputable evidence that workers would no longer have to suffer humiliation, frustration, and shame. From that moment on, the PPD argued, labor could rightfully claim what had been denied to them so many times in the past. For Muñoz and his peers, moreover, the strike marked the rise of a political leadership willing to respect the demands of labor. The PPD presented Muñoz and his colleagues as leaders who listen, inform, and consult followers before making a decision.[211]

The strike provided the PPD an opportunity to formalize its relation to labor. Shortly after the conflict ended, the PPD welcomed the CGT as an organization that could solidify the party's institutional base. The PPD offered CGT leader Sáez Corales the position of sub-commissioner of labor.[212] Many other CGT leaders received invitations to occupy intermediate positions at town halls and governmental departments controlled by Muñoz's party.[213] For example, Sergio Kuilan Báez became an official of the Labor Department's Industrial Supervision Service.[214] The PPD also mobilized its forces to convert party officials into labor leaders. The effort to merge the PPD and CGT took a significant turn at the CGT's first annual congress in May. An attempt was made to amend the CGT's rule that banned union leaders from occupying governmental posts.[215] The amendment did not come through, but the PPD's setback was only momentary. A process of recomposition within the CGT was already under way and gained impetus after the strike. Since the appointment of Tugwell, according to Galvin, "the working class leaders who had spontaneously emerged during the dissolution of the FLT—CGT General Secretary Juan Sáez Corales was the prototype—began to see themselves supplanted by a corps of technocrats—lawyers, administrators, legislators, teachers—who were adept in representing workers before the new governmental bureaucracies."[216]

Besides trying to overlap the functions of CGT officials with those of the government, the PPD had another way to win over labor. Muñoz fomented a direct bond between himself and workers that cut across the CGT's organizational framework. Several times, the PPD reminded workers that Muñoz assisted the funeral of one of the victims of the Guayama massacre.[217] A remarkable example is a late event related to the strike. In September 1942, when the justice authorities exonerated Obén and his men for the Luce & Co.'s shooting, Muñoz went to Guayama to speak at a demonstration to protest the court's ruling. Representatives Samuel R. Quiñones and Ernesto Ramos Antonini also addressed the crowd. The leader of the PPD delivered a short, but dramatic, speech in which he spoke about the "equality of death and the injustice of life." According to Muñoz, he aimed his words at all the people who share labor's sufferings and "have the will to carry through the same fight to put an end to those sufferings."[218]

Muñoz told his audience that "through death, God Almighty tries to teach us how equality for all should be" and that "our ideal is to learn that lesson."[219] Hence, according to Muñoz, God's call for equality among living men cannot justify inequalities of wealth. The leader of the PPD warned the "powerful" that if the inequalities of wealth violate God's law, there is "only one remedy to guarantee the equality of human dignity. And that remedy would be to make also the wealth of men equal."[220] By toying with the idea of confronting the "powerful" to redistribute wealth, Muñoz probably conjured in the imagination of people the possibility of radical action. Although Muñoz grabbed his audience's attention with hints of retribution, he also entitled listeners to make demands of the PPD. Muñoz and his followers not only conceived social justice as the centerpiece of a new discourse on the island but also sealed a pact that would be tested before long. Beyond the immediate expectations of labor and Muñoz's party, their effort to shape a discourse of consent entailed obligations and avenues of action that could not be easily foreseen or brushed aside from the island's political arena.

NOTES

1. David Rock, "War and Postwar Intersections: Latin America and the United States," in David Rock, ed., *Latin America in the 1940s: War and Postwar Transitions* (Berkeley: University of California Press, 1994), pp. 15-40.

2. Fernando Henrique Cardoso and Enzo Faletto, *Dependencia y desarrollo en América Latina: Ensayo de interpretación sociológica* (Mexico, DF: Siglo Veintiuno, 1969), p. xiv.

3. Ernesto Laclau, *Emancipation(s)* (London: Verso Books, 1996), p. 44.

4. Ernesto Laclau and Chantal Mouffe, *Hegemony and Socialist Strategy: Toward a Radical Democratic Politics* (London: Verso Books, 1985), pp. 127-134; Ernesto Laclau, "Constructing Universality," in *Contingency, Hegemony, Universality* (London: Verso Books, 2000) pp. 281-307.

5. Jacob Torfing, *New Theories of Discourse: Laclau, Mouffe, and Žižek* (Oxford: Blackwell Publishers, 1999), pp. 101-119.

6. Ibid., p. 175.

7. *El Mundo*, January 23, 30, 1940.

8. *El Mundo*, May 3, 1940.

9. Ibid. Juan Angel Silén, *Apuntes para la historia del movimiento obrero puertorriqueño* (Río Piedras: Editorial Cultural, 1978), p. 106.

10. Ibid., p. 107.

11. *El Mundo*, March 30, April 7, 1940.

12. Silén, *Apuntes para la historia del movimiento obrero puertorriqueño*, pp. 107-110.

13. Ibid.

14. *El Mundo*, March 30, 1940.

15. *El Mundo*, August 16, 1940.

16. Angel G. Quintero Rivera, "Bases sociales de la transformación ideológica del Partido Popular en la década del '40," in Gerardo Navas Dávila, ed., *Cambio y desarrollo en Puerto Rico: La transformación ideológica del Partido Popular Democrático* (San Juan: Editorial de la Universidad de Puerto Rico, 1980), p. 113.

17. *La Democracia*, November 14, 1940.

18. Ibid. Quintero Rivera, "Bases sociales de la transformación ideológica del Partido Popular en la década del '40," p. 85.

19. See, for example, the petition of unemployed laborers to the legislature. *El Mundo*, March 1, 1940.

20. *El Mundo*, March 5, 27, 31, 1941.

21. *El Mundo*, March 21, 1941.

22. Miles Galvin, *The Organized Labor Movement in Puerto Rico* (London: Associated University Presses, 1979), p. 95.

23. Gervasio García and Angel Quintero Rivera, *Desafío y solidaridad: Breve historia del movimiento obrero puertorriqueño* (Río Piedras: Ediciones Huracán, 1986), p. 128.

24. *El Mundo*, November 20, 21, 22, 1940.

25. Galvin, *The Organized Labor Movement in Puerto Rico*, p. 95.

26. *El Mundo*, December 2, 14, 16, 27, 1940.

27. *El Mundo*, December 18, 1940, January 2, 1941.

28. *El Mundo*, December 14, 1940.

29. *El Mundo*, January 4, 17, February 3, 4, 1941.

30. *El Mundo*, January 21, 1941.

31. *La Democracia*, January 21, February 11, March 4, July 10, 1941. See also Mayra Rosario Urrutia, "'Mogollas, entendidos y malas mañas': La regeneración del partido político en el discurso muñocista, 1938-1948," in Fernando Picó, ed., *Luis Muñoz Marín: Ensayos del Centenario* (San Juan: Fundación Luis Muñoz Marín, 1999), pp. 209-232.

32. The PPD had a total of 214,857 votes in the 1940 election. The Coalition and the Puerto Rican Tripartite Unification almost had the rest of the 568,851 votes cast. Only 1,272 votes belonged to the short-lived Pure Agrarian Party. This party was an oddity of colonial politics. It was formed to cause confusion between its own insignia, the sketch of a *pava* (female turkey), and that of the PPD, which included *la pava* (a peasant's hat). Fernando Bayrón Toro, *Elecciones y partidos políticos de Puerto Rico, 1809-2000* (Mayagüez: Editorial Isla, 2000), p. 194; Luis Muñoz Marín, *Memorias, 1898-1940* (San Juan: Universidad Interamericana de Puerto Rico, 1982), p. 195. It should be noted that despite the slim margin of votes in favor of the PPD, the position of Muñoz's party in terms of mass support outmatched the first electoral run of other parties in the past. Juan Angel Silén, *Historia de Puerto Rico* (Santo Domingo: SUSAETA, 1993), p. 204.

33. *El Mundo*, January 8, February 11, April 25, August 21, 30, September 5, 1941.

34. Bayrón Toro, *Elecciones y partidos políticos de Puerto Rico*, pp. 195-196; Antonio Quiñones Calderón, *Trayectoria Política de Puerto Rico* (San Juan: Ediciones Nuevas de Puerto Rico, 1988), p. 51.

35. Silén, *Historia de Puerto Rico*, p. 204. Liberals within the Tripartite Unification, former colleagues of Muñoz, played a key role in steering their party in favor of the PPD.

36. *La Democracia*, April 15, 1941. The impasse ensued when the PPD opposed the nomination of Prudencio Rivera Martínez for commissioner of labor. The Tripartite representatives that initially gave their support to the PPD sided with the Coalition. Muñoz's party overcame the impasse when it secured the support of a Coalitionist. Silén, *Historia de Puerto Rico*, p. 204.

37. The first signs of political change came before the election of 1940. Governor Leahy shunned the Coalition after it opposed his initial policies. Jorge Rodríguez Beruff, "La Lija: la batalla contra la Coalición," *Fundamentos* 5-6 (1997-1998): 66-81.

38. Quintero Rivera, "Bases sociales de la transformación ideológica del Partido Popular en la década del '40," pp. 85-86.

39. Ibid., p. 86; García and Quintero Rivera, *Desafío y solidaridad*, p. 114; Juan Giusti Cordero, "La huelga cañera de 1942. Crónica de una huelga general," *Fundamentos* 5-6 (1997-1998): 83.

40. Letter from Rupert Emerson to Wallace M. Cohen, February 2, 1943, Commodity Files, Field Offices, Region IX, P.R., Price Department, Records of the Office of Price Administration (Record Group 188), National Archives and Records Administration of the Northeast Region. While addressing a shortage of newsprint in Puerto Rico, Emerson obtained the information that follows:

A curious situation has occurred in that Muñoz Marín personally has over 100 tons of newsprint. Muñoz Marín is the Director of *El Imparcial* but has claimed that he does not own it and has no connection with it. The authority for stating that Muñoz Marín is Director of *El Imparcial* is a notice to this effect published by *El Imparcial*. . . . I also have an Inspector in the staff here, a member of the Popular Party, who when he first was employed by the Insular Government, after the acquisition of power of the Popular Party, gave a month's salary as did practically all others for the acquisition of *El Imparcial* by Muñoz Marín. . . . Gordon Foote of the War Production Board and I have been discussing this problem from all angles. The obvious solution is to get shipping space for newsprint.

41. The first issues of *El Imparcial* under Muñoz offer a good source to grasp the discursive maneuvers of the PPD. In particular, see the publications of *El Imparcial* for the month of September 1941.

42. *El Imparcial*, September 20, 1941; *La Democracia*, September 20, 1941. According to Grace Tugwell, the wife of Governor Rexford G. Tugwell, "the inauguration went off beautifully—Luis worked up delegations of jíbaros from all over the island for ovation purposes and they say it was the largest attendance on record." Letter from Grace Tugwell to Ruby A. Black, September 22, 1941, Colección Ruby A. Black, Centro de Investigaciones Históricas, Universidad de Puerto Rico. Hereafter referred to as CRB, CIH/UPR.

43. Letter from Jesús T. Piñero to Ruby A. Black, October 23, 1941, CRB, CIH/UPR. Emphasis added.

44. Diario Hablado de *La Democracia* y *El Batey*, Fundación Luis Muñoz Marín, Archivo Luis Muñoz Marín, Sección IV, Serie 4 (Empresas Comerciales). Hereafter referred to as FLMM/ALMM, IV-4. According to the sources consulted, the PPD began to broadcast its radio program in June 1942. Interestingly, Muñoz placed much significance on the PPD's radio program. According to Muñoz, "this is until now the most important instrument of public information that the PPD has." Telegram, June 10, 1942, FLMM/ALMM, IV-4.

45. Ruth Berins Collier, "Combining Alternative Perspectives: Internal Trajectories versus External Influences as Explanations of Latin American Politics in the 1940s," *Comparative Politics* 26 (October 1993): 1-29.

46. Ruth Berins Collier and David Collier, *Shaping the Political Arena: Critical Junctures, the Labor Movement, and Regime Dynamics in Latin America* (Princeton: Princeton University Press, 1991).

47. Rexford G. Tugwell, *The Stricken Land: The Story of Puerto Rico* (New York: Doubleday, 1947), p. 70. See also pp. 3, 76-77.

48. Ibid., p. 71.

49. Jorge Rodríguez Beruff, ed., *Las memorias de Leahy: Los relatos del Admirante William D. Leahy sobre su gobernación de Puerto Rico, 1939-1940* (San Juan: Fundación Luis Muñoz Marín, 2002).

50. Swope worried about Communist influence within the PPD. Tugwell, *The Stricken Land*, p. 76. Leahy also had misgivings about the PPD. According to Leahy, the PPD "was radical or at least far leftist" and some of its legislators "were active in the Nationalist movement of two years ago." Leahy informed the Secretary of Interior that Ernesto Ramos Antonini, Luis Sánchez Franqueri, Vicente Géigel Polanco, Francisco M. Susoni,and José Soltero had been members of the Nationalist Party. Letters from William D. Leahy to Harold L. Ickes, November 6 and 9, 1940, File 9-8-82, Records of the Division of Territories and Insular Possessions, Department of the Interior (Record Group 126), National Archives and Records Administration. Hereafter referred to as DTIP, RG 126, NARA. Leahy also sent a list to the Department of the Interior in which he marked potential "trouble-makers" of the PPD who won seats in the legislature. Letter from William D. Leahy to the Director of the Department of Territories and Insular Possessions, November 12, 1940, File 9-8-82, DTIP, RG 126, NARA.

51. Bayrón Toro, *Elecciones y partidos políticos de Puerto Rico*, p. 199. Swope began his governorship in January and left the island at the end of July 1941. Despite the misgivings of Swope and his short governorship, the PPD approved key pieces of legislation during this period.

52. The United States took several steps to prepare Puerto Rico and the Caribbean for war. Jorge Rodríguez Beruff, *Política militar y dominación: Puerto Rico en el contexto latinoamericano* (Río Piedras: Ediciones Huracán, 1988), pp. 37-46.

53. Tugwell, *The Stricken Land*, p. 65.

54. The initiatives of Tugwell in Puerto Rico soon became the object of controversy. Tugwell got into complications when the PPD offered him the chancellorship of the University of Puerto Rico not long before his inauguration as governor of the island. Nereida Rodríguez, *Debate universitario y dominación colonial, 1941-1947* (San Juan: N. Rodríguez, 1996).

55. Tugwell, *The Striken Land*, p. 50-70.

56. Charles T. Goodsell, *Administration of a Revolution, Executive Reform in Puerto Rico under Governor Tugwell, 1941-1946* (Cambridge: Harvard University Press, 1965), pp. 15-20.

57. Ibid.

58. David F. Ross, *The Long Uphill Path: A Historical Study of Puerto Rico's Program of Economic Development* (San Juan: Talleres Gráficos Interamericanos, 1966), pp. 54-59.

59. Anthony Giddens, *The Nation-State and Violence* (Berkeley: University of California Press, 1987), p. 7.

60. Tugwell, *The Stricken Land*, pp. 79, 162.

61. Ibid., p. 161.

62. *El Mundo*, January 4, 1941.

63. Annual Report of the Commissioner of Labor, Govt. of P.R., 1941-1942, p. 85.

64. *El Mundo*, January 2, 4, 17, 1941.

65. *El Imparcial*, December 19, 24, 31, 1941, January 2, 1942.

66. *El Imparcial*, December 21, 1941.

67. *El Imparcial*, January 17, 1942.

68. Humberto García Muñiz, "El Caribe durante la Segunda Guerra Mundial: El Mediterráneo Americano," in Carmen Gautier Mayoral, Angel I. Rivera Ortiz, and Idsa E. Alegría Ortiz, eds., *Puerto Rico en las relaciones internacionales del Caribe* (Río Piedras: Ediciones Huracán, 1990), pp. 161-184.

69. Nelson Lichtenstein, *Labor's War at Home: The CIO in World War II* (New York: Cambridge University Press, 1982).

70. *El Mundo*, January 7, 1942.

71. Taller de Formación Política, *No estamos pidiendo el cielo: Huelga portuaria de 1938* (Río Piedras: Ediciones Huracán, 1988), pp. 126-132.

72. Tugwell, *The Stricken Land*, pp. 168-169.

73. *El Mundo*, April 9, 10, 22, 28, June 8, 14, July 6, 18, 25, September 21, 1941.

74. *El Mundo*, January 13, 1942.

75. *El Mundo*, January 10, 14, 17, 1942.

76. *El Imparcial*, January 14, 1942. Besides his experience as labor leader and lawyer, Colón Gordiany had been sub-secretary of the senate during the late-1930s.

77. *El Imparcial*, January 8, 1942; *El Mundo*, January 11, 1942.

78. Police Reports #1/1-304, January 20, 1942; #1/1-343, January 21, 1942, Caja #408, Colección La Fortaleza, Archivo General de Puerto Rico. Hereafter referred to as CLF #408, AGPR.

79. Police Report #1/1-343, January 23, 1942, CLF #408, AGPR.

80. Giusti, "La huelga cañera de 1942," p. 85.

81. *El Imparcial*, January 19, 1942.

82. Ibid.

83. Ibid.

84. *El Mundo*, January 20, 1942.

85. *El Imparcial*, January 22, 1942.

86. Telegram from Ernesto Carrasquillo to Muñoz Marín, January 20, 1942, Yabucoa, FLMM/ALMM, IV-7 (Pueblos). Telegram from Bruno Pimentel to Muñoz Marín, January 21, 1942, Luquillo; Telegram from Strike Committee to Muñoz Marín, January 27, 1942, Salinas, FLMM/ALMM IV-9 (Asuntos: Huelga azucarera). The Serie 7 (Pueblos) at the Luis Muñoz Marín Archive contains many other telegrams that express concerns about the police.

87. Tugwell, *The Stricken Land*, p. 193.

88. Ibid.

89. Giusti, "La huelga cañera de 1942," p. 90.

90. Circular #26 of the Insular Police of Puerto Rico, January 20, 1942, FLMM/ALMM, IV-9 (Asuntos: Huelga azucarera).

91. Telegram from Muñoz Marín to Pablo Suárez, January 21, 1942; Telegram from Muñoz Marín to José Vázquez Vélez, January 22, 1942; Telegram from Muñoz Marín to Aniceto Semidey, January 24, 1942; Telegram from Muñoz Marín to Luis Soto, January 24, 1942, FLMM/ALMM, IV-9 (Asuntos: Huelga azucarera).

92. *El Imparcial*, January 21, 1942.

93. See Chapter 2.

94. *La Democracia*, January 23, 1942.

95. Telegram from Pedro A. Cordero Pérez to Muñoz Marín, January 24, 1942, Salinas, FLMM/ALMM, IV-7 (Pueblos).

96. Letter from Amador Santos to Muñoz Marín, January 18, 1942, Fajardo, FLMM/ ALMM, IV-7 (Pueblos).

97. Telegram from Luis Soto to Muñoz Marín, February 10, 1942, Guayama, FLMM/ ALMM, IV-7 (Pueblos). See also telegram from Victor Vélez to Muñoz Marín, February 6, 1942, Juana Díaz, FLMM/ALMM, IV-9 (Asuntos: Huelga azucarera).

98. Telegram from José Vázquez Vélez to Muñoz Marín, January 22, 1942, Salinas, FLMM/ALMM, IV-9 (Asuntos: Huelga azucarera). The Serie 9 contains other telegrams that address similar issues.

99. Telegram from Muñoz Marín to Luis Ramirez Brau, January 24, 1942; Telegram from Muñoz Marín to Antonio R. Silva, January 24, 1942; Letter from Antonio R. Silva to Muñoz Marín, January 29, 1942, FLMM/ALMM, IV-9 (Asuntos: Huelga azucarera).

100. Telegram from Muñoz Marín to José A. Martínez, January 27, 1942, Yabucoa; Telegram from Muñoz Marín to Ernesto Carrasquillo, January 23, 1942, Yabucoa, FLMM /ALMM, IV-7 (Pueblos).

101. Consider the cables of PPD leaders published in *La Democracia*, *El Imparcial*, and *El Mundo* during the labor conflict.

102. Galvin, *The Organized Labor Movement in Puerto Rico*, p. 97.

103. *El Mundo*, January 19, 1942; *La Democracia*, January 23, 29, 1942.

104. Tugwell, *The Stricken Land*, p. 232.

105. *El Mundo*, January 24, 29, 31, 1942.

106. Giusti, "La huelga cañera de 1942," p. 86. Before long, federal authorities came to a similar conclusion. Surendra Bhana, *The United States and the Development of the Puerto Rican Status Question, 1936-1968* (Lawrence: University Press of Kansas, 1975), p. 54.

107. Tugwell, *The Stricken Land*, p. 221.

108. *El Mundo*, January 24, 26, 27, 29, 1942.

109. Ibid.

110. *El Mundo*, January 17, 22, 27, 1942.

111. *El Mundo*, January 24, 1942.

112. Giusti, "La huelga cañera de 1942," p. 84.

113. *El Imparcial*, January 30, 1942.

114. *El Mundo*, January 27, 28, 31, 1942.

115. *El Imparcial*, January 22, 1942; *El Mundo*, January 26, 27, 28, 1942.

116. *El Mundo*, January 29, 1942.

117. *El Imparcial*, January 31, 1942.

118. *La Democracia*, January 27, 1942.

119. *El Imparcial*, January 27, 1942.

120. *El Imparcial*, January 28, 1942.

121. Ibid.

122. *El Imparcial*, January 26, 1942.

123. Ibid.

124. *El Imparcial*, January 27, 1942.

125. Ibid.

126. *La Democracia*, January 24, 29, 30, 1942; *El Mundo*, January 26-31, 1942.

127. Ibid.

128. At the height of the conflict, President Roosevelt pressured Tugwell not only to resume sugar production but also to increase its allotment for the war effort by cultivating more land. Letter from President Franklin D. Roosevelt to Rexford G. Tugwell, February 3, 1942, Roosevelt's Secretary's Files, Series 48, Franklin D. Roosevelt Presidential Library. Hereafter referred to as RSF 48, FDRL.

129. *El Imparcial*, January 21, 1942. The Commission of Mediation and Conciliation visited the towns of Arecibo, Guayama, and Guayanilla to dialogue with strike leaders. No solution to the conflict was reached. Annual Report of the Commissioner of Labor, Govt. of P.R., 1942, pp. 85-86.

130. *El Imparcial*, January 20, 21, 22, 1942; *El Mundo*, January 22, 23, 1942.

131. *El Mundo*, January 17, 23, 25, 1942; *La Democracia*, January 25, 1942.

132. Letter from Teodoro Moscoso to William M. Leiserson (Chairman, NLRB), January 17, 1942, File 9-8-76, DTIP, RG 126, NARA.

133. Letter from Tugwell to Harold L. Ickes, February 9, 1942, File 9-8-76, DTIP, RG 126, NARA. Consider also Ickes's answer and Tugwell's response: Letter from Ickes to Tugwell, February 24, 1942 (ibid.); Letter from Tugwell to Ickes, February 26, 1942, CLF #386, AGPR.

134. Letter from Tugwell to Ickes, February 9, 1942, File 9-8-76, DTIP, RG 126, NARA. The governor had other concerns as well. Tugwell worried that "one of these situations is going to bring martial law down on my head some day and spoil everything we have been working for."

135. Giusti, "La huelga cañera de 1942," p. 90.

136. After his unsuccessful meeting with the CGT and FLT, Fernández García asked labor leaders to accompany him to request from Governor Tugwell the intervention of a federal conciliator. *El Mundo*, January 23, 1942. The PPD had optimism about Haas' visit to the island. *El Imparcial*, January 29, 1942; *La Democracia*, January 30, 1942.

137. *El Mundo*, January 28, 29, 30, 1942.

138. Police Reports #1/1-378, January 24, 1942; #1/1-395, January 26, 1942; #1/1-399, January 27, 1942; #1/1-428, January 28, 1942; #1/1-497, January 30, 1942; #1/1-511, January 31, 1942; #1/2-63, February 5, 1942; #1/2-95, February 7, 1942; #1/2-109, February 9, 1942, CLF #408, AGPR.

139. Colón Gordiany disputed the chief of police's final report about the strike. *El Mundo*, February 9, 1942. See also *La Democracia*, February 8, 1942.

140. *El Imarcial*, January 27, 1942.

141. *El Mundo*, January 23-31, 1942.

142. *El Mundo*, January 25, 28, 29, 1942; Giusti, "La huelga cañera de 1942," pp. 90-91.

143. Telegram from J. Serrallés to Tugwell, January 30, 1942, CLF #408, AGPR.

144. *El Mundo*, January 23-31, 1942.

145. *El Mundo*, January 25, 1942.

146. Police Reports #1/1-378, #1/1-395, #1/1-399, #1/1-428, #1/1-497, #1/1-511, #1/2-63, #1/2-95, #1/2-109, CLF #408, AGPR.

147. Ibid. Letter from F. A. Poets to Tugwell, January 30, 1942, CLF #408, AGPR.

148. Daniel James, "October 17th and 18th, 1945: Mass Protest, Peronism, and the Argentine Working Class," *Journal of Social History* 22 (Spring 1988): 441-461. See also Daniel James, *Resistance and Integration: Peronism and the Argentine Working Class, 1946-1976* (Cambridge: Cambridge University Press, 1988), p. 33.

149. *El Imparcial*, *La Democracia*, and *El Mundo*, January 19 - February 6, 1942.

150. Police Report #1/1-505-A, January 31, 1942; Letter from Luis R. Polo to George A. Malcolm, January 31, 1942; Summary Report from Pedro Santana, Jr. (Director of Legal Counsel and Assistant Service) to the Commissioner of Labor, February 5, 1942, CLF #408, AGPR.

151. Ibid. *El Imparcial*, February 3, 1942, *La Democracia*, February 3, 1942.

152. Letter from Luis R. Polo, January 31, 1942; Summary Report, February 5, 1942, CLF #408, AGPR.

153. Police Report #1/1-505-A; Giusti, "La huelga cañera de 1942," p. 91.

154. Telegrams from Marcelo J. Obén to Tugwell, January 30, 1942; Police Report #1/1-505-A; Telegram from Leo R. O'Neill to Tugwell, January 30, 1942, CLF #408, AGPR.

155. Telegram from Luis Soto to Muñoz Marín, January 30, 1942, Guayama, FLMM/ALMM, IV-7 (Pueblos).

156. Telegram from Muñoz Marín to Luis Soto, January 30, 1942, Guayama, FLMM/ALMM, IV-7 (Pueblos). Later, Muñoz asked Ernesto Ramos Antonini to provide legal assistance to the workers who had been hurt during the shooting. Memorandum from Muñoz Marín to Ramos Antonini, February 18, 1942, FLMM/ALMM, IV-2, Sub-Serie 54A.

157. La Democracia, February 1, 1942.

158. El Imparcial, February 2, 3, 1942; La Democracia, February 4, 1942.

159. El Imparcial, February 3, 1942.

160. Letter from Luis R. Polo, January 31, 1942; Summary Report, February 5, 1942, CLF #408, AGPR.

161. Letter from Luis R. Polo, January 31, 1942, CLF #408, AGPR.

162. El Mundo, January 31, Feburary 2, 1942.

163. El Imparcial, January 31, 1942.

164. Ibid.

165. Ibid.

166. Ibid.

167. El Mundo, January 31, 1942; El Imparcial, February 2, 1942.

168. El Imparcial, February 2, 1942.

169. La Democracia, February 1, 1942.

170. Ibid.

171. La Democracia, February 4, 1942.

172. Summary Report, February 5, 1942, CLF #408, AGPR.

173. El Mundo, February 4, 1942.

174. El Mundo, February 5, 1942.

175. Giusti, "La huelga cañera de 1942," pp. 92-93. This and other incidents had an impact on the U.S. military and their policies. According to Giusti, the situation in Puerto Rico was such that it warranted transferring the island's command directly to the navy and one of its high-ranking officials.

176. Telegram from Bolívar Pagán to Ickes, February 5, 1942; Letter from R. A. Kleindienst to Pagán, February 14, 1942; Telegram from the Fajardo Sugar Co. of Porto Rico and the Loíza Sugar Co. to Ickes, February 4, 1942; Letter from Guy J. Swope to the Fajardo Sugar Company of Puerto Rico and Loíza Sugar Company, February 12, 1942; Letter from E. K. Burlew to James M. Mead, February 14, 1942; Anonymous letter to the New York Sun, January 26, 1942; Anonymous letter to the New York Sun, January 29, 1942, File 9-8-76, DTIP, RG 126, NARA. Letter from Harold A. Medeiros to Senator Millard Tydings, February 3, 1942, Box #77A-F29 (298), Records of the Committee on Territories and Insular Affairs, U.S. Senate (Record Group 46), National Archives and Records Administration. Hereafter referred to as CTIA, RG 46, NARA. See also Bhana, The United States and the Development of the Puerto Rican Status Question, pp. 47-48.

177. El Mundo, February 6, 1942.

178. Giusti, "La huelga cañera de 1942," p. 94.

179. Telegram from Muñoz Marín to President Roosevelt, January 19, 1942, President's Official File, Series 400, Puerto Rico: Appointments, FDRL. Hereafter referred to as POF 400, FDRL. Letter from Muñoz Marín to Ickes, January 29, 1942, FLMM/ALMM, IV-1 (Gobierno Federal: Correspondencia General); Telegram from Muñoz Marín and Samuel R. Quiñones to Senator Millard Tydings, February 12, 1942, Box #77A-F29 (298), CTIA, RG 46, NARA; Telegram from Muñoz Marín to Vito Marcantonio, February 10, 1942; Letter

from Vito Marcantonio to Muñoz Marín, February 25, 1942, Colección Vito Marcantonio, Centro de Investigaciones Históricas, Universidad de Puerto Rico. Hereafter referred to as CVM, CIH/UPR.

180. Letter from Tugwell to President Roosevelt, January 29, 1942, POF 400, FDRL.

181. Letter from Tugwell to President Roosevelt, February 2, 1942, POF 400, FDRL.

182. Letter from Rexford G. Tugwell to Ickes, February 9, 1942; Letter from Ickes to Tugwell, February 24, 1942, File 9-8-76, DTIP, RG 126, NARA; Memorandum from Ickes to President Roosevelt, February 23, 1942, RSF 48, FDRL.

183. Giusti, "La huelga cañera de 1942," p. 93.

184. *El Mundo*, January 31, 1942.

185. *El Mundo*, February 1, 1942.

186. Letter from Muñoz Marín to Francisco Colón Gordiany, February 2, 1942, FLMM/ALMM, IV-9 (Asuntos: Huelga azucarera); *El Mundo*, February 3, 1942.

187. Resolution of the Special Truce Committee, February 2, 1942, FLMM/ALMM, IV-5 (Asociaciones No Comerciales); Letter from Juan Sáez Corales to Tugwell, February 3, 1942, and Resolution of the Special Truce Committee, February 2, 1942, CLF #408, AGPR. See also *El Mundo*, February 3, 1942; *El Imparcial*, February 3, 1942.

188. Tugwell, *The Stricken Land*, pp. 232, 233. The words of Tugwell make sense when one considers that several members of the Special Truce Committee belonged to the PPD or communicated with Muñoz during the conflict. Among them are Ernesto Carrasquillo, Severo Ramos, Luis Soto, and Aniceto Semidey.

189. *El Mundo*, February 4, 1942.

190. *El Mundo*, February 4, 1942; *El Imparcial*, February 4, 1942.

191. Tugwell, *The Stricken Land*, p. 233. This meeting and a previous one underscored the extent of sugar interests that were at work during the strike. On February 2, top officials of Olavarría & Co., a powerful sugar firm with offices in Cuba and New York, visited Tugwell. The meeting on February 4 included a well-known employer, Pedro Juan Serrallés, who soon became a member of the JSM. Giusti, "La huelga cañera de 1942," p. 94.

192. Giusti, "La huelga cañera de 1942," p. 95.

193. *El Mundo*, February 5, 1942; *El Imparcial*, February 5, 1942; Resolution of the CGT, February 6, 1942, FLMM/ALMM, IV-9 (Asuntos: Huelga azucarera).

194. Letter from Tugwell to Ickes, February 9, 1942, File 9-8-76, DTIP, RG 126, NARA. Muñoz explained to Haas the end of the strike. Letter from Muñoz Marín to Francis Haas, February 9, 1942, FLMM/ALMM, IV-9 (Asuntos: Huelga azucarera).

195. Although the labor strike came to an end, the employers did not let the matter rest. They banked upon lawyers and the judicial system to to defend their interests. For more than a year after the strike, the courts of law studied the allegations of the plaintiffs and defendants to hand down a decision. See *El Mundo* and *El Imparcial*.

196. Letter from Martínez Domínguez et al., to Tugwell, February 9, 1942, CLF #408, FDRL. Tugwell, *The Stricken Land*, p. 234.

197. Giusti, "La huelga cañera de 1942," p. 95. A useful summary of the events after the strike can be found in Letter from James R. Watson to Oscar S. Smith, June 23, 1944, "Recapitulation of Sugar Situation in Puerto Rico," National Labor Relations Board, File 9-8-76, DTIP, RG 126, NARA. Also, the sugar strike came up a number of times during the hearings that federal authorities held on the island in late 1942 and 1943. See U.S., Congress, Senate, Subcommittee of the Committee on Territories and Insular Affairs, Dennis Chavez of New Mexico, Chairman, Hearings, *Economic and Social Conditions in Puerto Rico*, 77th Cong., 2nd. Sess., 1942; 78th Cong., 1st. Sess., 1943; U.S., Congress, House, Subcommittee of the Committee on Insular Affairs, C. Jasper Bell of Missouri, Chairman, Hearings, *Investigation of Political, Economical, and Social Conditions in Puerto Rico*, 78th

Cong., 1st. Sess., 1943, parts 1-14; 78th Cong., 2nd. Sess., 1944, parts 15-19.

198.Telegram from Tugwell to Guy J. Swope, February 12, 1942, File 9-8-76, DTIP, RG 126, NARA; Letter from Tugwell to President Roosevelt, February 11, 1942, RSF 48, FDRL. Not all sectors of the federal bureaucracy had reasons to celebrate the end of the labor conflict. Although the strike came to a conclusion, shortly thereafter labor unrest flared up again in the construction projects of military defense. This new protest of workers lasted almost a month and required another round of negotiations. Giusti, "La huelga cañera de 1942," pp. 95-96.

199. Letter from E.K. Burlew to Frances Perkins, February 10, 1942; Letter from Ickes to Tugwell, February 24, 1942, File 9-8-76, DTIP, RG 126, NARA. The U.S. Conciliation Services of the Department of Labor designated Charles A. Goldsmith as federal conciliator for Puerto Rico.

200. Annual Report of the Commissioner of Labor, Govt. of P.R., 1941-1942, p. 13; Annual Report of the Commissioner of Labor, Govt. of P.R., 1942-1943, pp. 6-7.

201. Ibid.

202. Letter from Vicente Géigel Polanco to Muñoz Marín, February 19, 1942, FLMM/ALMM, IV-3 (Individuos: Vicente Géigel Polanco). See also *El Imparcial*, February 9-27, 1942, editorials.

203. Annual Report of the Minimum Wage Board, Fiscal Year 1942-1943, p. 6, File 9-8-88, DTIP, RG 126, NARA; *El Imparcial*, October 3, 31, 1942.

204. Annual Report of the Minimum Wage Board, 1942-1943, p. 6.

205. Paul Blanshard, "The Labor Position in United States Territory in the Caribbean," United States Section, Anglo-American Caribbean Commission, November 27, 1944, p. 13, File 9-8, "Confidential" Central Classified Files, DTIP, RG 126, NARA. According to the Caribbean Commission:

Even more important than national labor laws has been the 1942 Insular Minimum Wage Law which created in the Department of Labor a Minimum Wage Board of 9 members (4 employers, 4 labor leaders, and a paid impartial chairman) with sweeping powers to establish minimum wage rates, maximum hour schedules, and general labor standards for all industries in Puerto Rico. . . . Puerto Rico has a general 8-hour day law passed, in 1935, but it has been largely superseded by the rulings of the Minimum Wage Board.

206. Silén, *Apuntes para la historia del movimiento obrero puertorriqueño*, p. 110.

207. Making common cause with the PPD seemed as an appropriate move at that time. In February, the CIO rejected the CGT's request for affiliation. The CIO found it improper to accept as a member a union that had broken U.S. labor's wartime antistrike pledge. *El Mundo*, February 6, 1942. For further details about the impasse between the CGT and CIO, see Giusti, "La huelga cañera de 1942," p. 95.

208. César Andreu Iglesias, Organization and Propaganda Secretary of the Communist Party, "Communists Back the Governor" (From *El Mundo*, March 17, 1942), March 23, 1942, File 9-8-76, DTIP, RG 126, NARA.

209. FLMM/ALMM, IV-7 (Pueblos) and IV-2, Sub-Serie 33 (Junta de Salario Mínimo).

210. After the strike, the PPD emphasized Muñoz's participation. Two examples are *El Batey*, March 14, 1942; "Message to the People," Radio Program "El Diario Hablado de *La Democracia y El Batey*," June 22, 1942, FLMM/ALMM, IV-4 (Empresas Comerciales).

211. See, especially, *La Democracia* and *El Imparcial* up to the fall of 1942.

212. Sáez Corales rejected this offer. Juan Sáez Corales, "Twenty-Five Years of Struggle—My Reply to Persecution" (1955), in Angel Quintero Rivera, ed., *Workers' Struggle in Puerto Rico: A Documentary History* (New York: Monthly Review Press, 1976), p. 156; Juan Sáez Corales, "25 años de lucha es mi respuesta a la persecusión" (1955), in Angel G. Quintero Rivera, ed., *Lucha obrera en Puerto Rico: Antología de grandes*

documentos en la historia obrera puertorriqueña (San Juan: CEREP, 1971), p. 131.

213. Ibid. Luis A. López Rojas, *Luis Muñoz Marín y Las Estrategias del Poder, 1936-1946* (San Juan: Isla Negra, 1998), p. 121.

214. Annual Report of the Commissioner of Labor, Govt. of P.R., 1942, p. 3.

215. Silén, *Apuntes para la historia del movimiento obrero puertorriqueño*, pp. 110-111.

216. Galvin, *The Organized Labor Movement in Puerto Rico*, p. 95.

217. *El Imparcial*, February 2, 1942; *El Batey*, March 14, 1942; *El Imparcial*, September 21, 1942. See also FLMM/ALMM, IV-7 (Pueblos) and IV-2, Sub-Serie 33 (Junta de Salario Mínimo).

218. *El Imparcial*, September 21, 1942; Muñoz Marín, Luis, "La igualdad de la muerte y la injusticia de la vida," FLMM/ALMM, IV-11, Cart. 22, Doc. 1 (Mensajes y Discursos). See also Fernando Picó, ed., *Luis Muñoz Marín: Discursos, 1934-1948*, vol. 1 (San Juan: Fundación Luis Muñoz Marín, 1999), pp. 179-180. Muñoz's message to the workers of Guayama gained renown in years to come. As late as 1948, when Muñoz became governor of Puerto Rico, the PPD press reprinted Muñoz's words about death and life. *Diario de Puerto Rico*, November 6, 1948.

219. Muñoz Marín, "La igualdad de la muerte y la injusticia de la vida," FLMM/ALMM, IV-11.

220. Ibid.

However obvious this political process might seem at hindsight, an array of options and views to secure reforms counterweighed the leanings of PPD leaders after the sugar strike of 1942. As an episode that marked a shift of political forces in Puerto Rico, the sugar strike made evident the inception of a "historical bloc" able to accommodate the interests of the PPD and many other groups. After the labor conflict, the mass movement in Puerto Rico entered a new phase of growth and transformation. The misgivings that people may have had during the formative years of the movement gave way to formal ties between them and the PPD. The discourse of consent meant, above all, an advocacy for reform to overcome the worst socioeconomic and political grievances of Puerto Ricans. It also entailed the incorporation of popular groups as part of the island's political arena and a degree of accountability from political leaders. Other than that, the discourse of consent had few boundaries in terms of the meanings given to reform by the agents of Puerto Rico's mass movement. The same assertion applies to how party supporters viewed their relationship to the PPD. Before long, the groups that joined forces with the PPD to support the New Deal began to articulate provocative views about the aim of social justice, their relationship to Muñoz, and the future of Puerto Rico.

This chapter examines different groups and perceptions to understand the transformation of the island's mass movement. By focusing on labor, Communists, dissident Socialists, independentists, technocrats, and other groups that felt entitled to voice their views about reform and their relationship to the PPD, I shed light on a multifaceted political reality underlying the common ground that led toward a discourse of consent. The chapter's main concern is what I call visions of consent, perceptions that had in common an expressed need for comradeship and change but gave a different spin to political action and reform. My analysis of how different groups nurtured their relationship to the PPD with visions and initiatives unlike those of Muñoz's party serves to highlight the elastic quality that characterized the discourse of consent. Since the disposition of party supporters to imagine a better future bordered at times on enthusiasm, their visions of consent parallel the "agency" that Marshall Berman finds in people's lives in contemporary society: "modern men and women asserting their dignity in the present—even a wretched and oppressive present—and their right to control their future; striving to make a place for themselves in the modern world, a place where they can feel at home."[1] Berman's words relate well to the perceptions and actions examined here not only because of the yearnings expressed by different agents but also because of their many efforts to transform Puerto Rico into a modern society to their liking.

To emphasize the elasticity of the discourse of consent is not to say that the island's mass movement could shift and turn without producing political tensions and contradictions. If the sugar strike of 1942 marked a turning point for colonial politics overall, the visions of consent that became evident after the labor conflict represented a political crossroad for the island's mass movement itself. While the discourse of consent remapped the island's political scene without being yet a hegemonic worldview or imaginary, political tensions rippled through the mass movement headed by the PPD without emerging fully fledged or as open challenges to the party. Although the discourse of consent had just a foothold on its claim to hegemony, it faced a challenge well defined by Anna Marie Smith: "when a hegemonic project attempts to articulate more and more symbols and demands, it quickly comes up against the following problem: many of these elements stand in antagonistic relations against each other."[2] With the potential for a hegemonic outcome but lacking any guarantees about its future, the island's "historical bloc" maintained its momentum as it approached a political threshold: the ever-increasing demand for social justice and reform produced visions as well as "antagonistic relations" within the mass movement that promised to rearticulate, reorient, or break up the common ground underlying the discourse of consent.

The emerging political logic in Puerto Rico not only was flexible enough to usher in amiable relations into the island's political scene but also made way for new sorts of tension. Despite sharing a common ground of articulation, the visions of consent competed and attempted to prevail over the others as they deployed what I call the tactics of political displacement. PPD leaders, labor, independentists, and other groups tried to rearrange the terms of their coexistence by pushing to the sidelines alternative visions. Since these agents tapped unevenly the resources of political power in Puerto Rico and the mainland, the discourse of consent gradually centered on the precepts of Muñoz's party. Even after this shift became evident, the discourse of consent kept legitimating different and often conflictive courses of action, making the attempt of multiple groups to shape the future of Puerto Rico far from a harmonious process.

This reality demands a careful attention of two disparate processes that worked in tandem. On the one hand, focusing on the factors that enabled the mobilization of agents for a common cause can help explain the ligatures that connected different visions of consent to each other. On the other hand, besides the discourse of consent's common ground, it is important to consider the process by which different groups struggled to present their own vision over that of others. In this sense, the nascent discourse of consent had to do with visions that eventually were pushed aside, the mechanisms that made this possible, and questions about "what could have been." Since the discourse of consent already had the potential to become a hegemonic imaginary, much more was at stake on the island than the fate of the mass movement headed by the PPD. What could be glimpsed to be at hand during the mid-1940s can be summed up as follows: whether the island's "historical bloc" would bring to the fore an "expansive hegemony"[3]—meaning a social formation that would allow the genuine participation of people in decision making and further linkages between progressive demands for reform—or an "authoritative hegemony"—meaning a social formation that "manages difference through the deployment of assimilatory, disciplinary, and exclusionary strategies."[4]

THE CGT, PPD, AND THEIR PARTNERSHIP'S FATE

The sugar strike of 1942 forced the CGT to rethink its relationship to politics. Through their actions and words, leaders and followers of the CGT produced new expectations about the priorities of their union. For CGT officials, it was no longer an issue of distancing labor from political parties in an effort to avoid the mistakes of the past. Although the CGT met this challenge with a degree of apprehension, the union welcomed the possibility of exploring new grounds of labor organization. The PPD's embrace of labor's cause also provided food for thought to Muñoz and his peers. As a party that advocated social justice and joined forces with labor during the sugar strike of 1942, the PPD owed much more than promises to workers. That is, the time came for serious consideration of how to accommodate the demands of labor. Both the CGT and PPD soon took issue with the concerns of labor for the future.

Shortly after the sugar strike, labor met at the first congress of the United Railroad Workers of Puerto Rico. The congress enabled the main participants to affirm the ties between labor, the PPD, and Tugwell. Labor leaders and PPD officials stated as the basis for a common understanding the need for labor's unity, further reform, and adequate political leadership. Despite the enthusiasm shared by labor and the PPD, the main ideas of their messages set them apart. Dr. José A. Lanauze Rolón, a U.S.-trained physician and a leader of the PCP, emphasized labor's long history to achieve unity. According to Lanauze, since Europe first heard the shout "Workers of the World, Unite!," labor grasped that their emancipation lay in their own hands. Although Lanauze regretted labor's weakness and the lack of "one great confederation" in Puerto Rico, he trusted that labor would play a key role in bringing about better days. With a strong union, Lanauze argued, labor could help to win the war, safeguard democracy, and ensure "social justice." Lanauze warned workers: "Do not expect anything from anyone and trust only yourself, your strength, your work and your justice."[5]

In his "words of orientation" to the congress, labor and PPD leader Ramón Barreto Pérez commended the call to unite workers but for different reasons than for Lanauze. In a subtle way, Barreto Pérez downplayed labor's initiatives so as to focus on what he alleged to be the demands of workers for "authentic leadership"[6]—that is, leaders who had not sold out as in the past. Barreto Pérez's solution was to keep labor away from political parties but not from leaders who had proven to be loyal. In this way, Barreto Pérez placed the PPD in the spotlight without mentioning his party's name. At the same time, Barreto Pérez presented workers as "victims" who had suffered years of indignity at the hands of bad leaders. By paying little attention to the past victories of labor and its role as an agent, Barreto Pérez placed all hope for "victimized workers" on the PPD.

The statements of Lanauze and Barreto Pérez exemplified embryonic perceptions of the CGT-PPD partnership. Gradually, labor and the PPD further developed their own views about the nature of their ties. The same is true of how the CGT and PPD worked out their partnership in actual practice. When the CGT's first congress met in the summer of 1942, the role of PPD officials within the union became an issue. The PPD presented a motion to be included as part of the CGT's leadership.[7] Although the PPD's motion did not come through, the petition of the party could not be dismissed. In the long run, the status of PPD leaders within the CGT depended less on petitions and paperwork than on actual events. While the CGT pondered about the inclusion of PPD leaders as part of its organization, day-to-day exchanges between the union and the party set the tone of their relationship. What enabled PPD leaders to join the CGT was not the result of an oversight or inaction of union officials. Much to the contrary, as the organizational drive of the CGT gathered momentum, the potential and expectations about what the union could achieve emboldened labor and political leaders to grasp the opportunity at hand.

Besides tackling immediate issues such as reform and union growth, CGT and PPD leaders made room for ambitious plans. An initiative that stood out early in 1943 is their effort to explore new grounds of labor support in the mainland. Whether union leaders traveled to Latin America or the United States to address their peers, the CGT delegation often included officials of the PPD as well as their own rank. On one occasion, PPD officials Ernesto Ramos Antonini and Ramón Barreto Pérez joined union leader Juan Sáez Corales as part of a delegation to a labor congress in Cuba.[8] On another occasion, Barreto Pérez accompanied Francisco Colón Gordiany to address the CIO in the United States.[9] As they addressed labor organizations abroad, CGT and PPD officials touched upon issues not limited to labor such as the island's political status and federal legislation. The discussion of issues beyond the scope of labor's main concerns helped to merge the initiatives of the CGT and PPD. It comes as no surprise that the union allowed PPD officials into its top leadership during the CGT's second annual congress in 1943.[10] Although the decision was no free from tensions and antagonism, the CGT and PPD not only formalized the ties between them but also showed an avid disposition to elaborate further their perceptions about each other.

In this context of labor activity the CGT and PPD began to articulate their visions of consent. Particularly useful to identify these visions is a book titled *Organización obrera*,[11] which labor advocate René Jiménez Malaret published in 1943. It consists of several speeches he delivered at local assemblies of the CGT during the previous year. Jiménez did not belong to the CGT's top leadership. However, since Jiménez was a CGT affiliate and employee of the Department of Labor, the union had a stake at having his ideas circulated among workers. From the outset, Jiménez provided his understanding of labor's role in society. Like Lanauze, he left no doubt about the need of workers to organize themselves. Through unity, Jiménez argued, workers can ensure not only a better livelihood but also their incorporation as major participants in society's decision-making processes. Jiménez had no qualms about labor's higher call: "A union of workers must be also a cultural vanguard to prepare workers for when the time comes to direct the politics of the country, for when the time comes for the exploited workers to decide the fate of the exploitative employers."[12] Far from being a capricious statement, these words are consistent with the author's main argument. With a strong labor movement capable of defending the rights of people, workers could ensure a just distribution of political power and wealth in Puerto Rico. In short, Jiménez envisioned a future that labor was entitled to control.

Jiménez's vision of consent presented the PPD not as the axis of the island's populist movement but as a political variable that workers had to consider to achieve their goals. That is, the PPD could be lauded for being "the only progressive party"[13] in Puerto Rico, but labor could trust it only as long as reform became a reality. This meant policies initiated under the New Deal such as wage increases, social security, and pensions for the old. For Jiménez, then, workers' effort to make a place for themselves in a better society entailed a particular definition of the PPD. Puerto Rico's political spectrum could offer the PPD as a worthy partner but only under conditions set by labor.[14] With such an emphasis on the rights of workers to shape key policies on the island, Jiménez's perspective not only introduced great expectations about the PPD but also portrayed the party as a close ally. His view about the PPD welcomed speculations about further inroads of workers within the party and shifting its program even more in favor of labor.

According to Jiménez, workers did not have to narrow down their aspirations for the future. He envisioned a postwar era in which all the people of Puerto Rico could feel at home, meaning a place where individuals could transcend their fear of economic destitution, injustice, and inequality. A community where "comfort" and "dignity" rules over "prejudices" and "misery" should be within the reach of everyone. For Jiménez, the mobilization of labor and its moral and cultural preparation were a step toward a society in which people could have their say about policies affecting their lives.[15] In this sense, consent would not mean passive acquiescence toward a party but dialogue and consultation between agents in search of an agreement. Jiménez's final analysis employed Karl Marx's vision of a classless society to imagine a better future for Puerto Rico. The homeland would be defined by those who work, and democracy would allow people to meet eye to eye. For Jiménez, democracy meant:

a government in which a class cannot exploit any other class; in which everybody possesses material security and in which all adults have a voice in the manner in which economic affairs are handled; it means equality of cultural opportunities so that all can share equally the fruits of culture; it means equality of sexes in which legally, as in any other appropriate ways, women keep themselves in the same plane as men; it means, in short, racial equality in that all racial groups are at the same social level.[16]

While the CGT argued for a better society, the PPD offered its own version of the CGT-PPD partnership. Two speeches of PPD representative Cruz Ortiz Stella sum up well the party's point of view. He delivered one speech at the *público* drivers' congress early in 1943 and the other at a CGT meeting later that year.[17] Although Ortiz viewed reform as a basis for common action, he saw workers as subordinates of the PPD. Ortiz presented a rigid split between an old epoch in which labor was a "resigned and patient victim" suffering atrocities and self-perceptions of inferiority and a new epoch of "redemption" that labor welcomed under the aegis of the PPD.[18] Ortiz recognized grievances among workers, an issue with which the CGT could sympathize, but by displaying labor as a helpless victim and the PPD as a selfless benefactor, he took away from workers the agency that the CGT so insistently assigned to them. The way Ortiz's words cleansed labor of initiatives shows how the PPD accommodated workers' demands without making major compromises. The PPD reversed the agency of the CGT-PPD partnership: far from being a participant in a mutual pact, the CGT was a beneficiary of a party that came to the rescue of labor. To define the proper place of labor, Ortiz stressed that workers are "a small part in a great totality, . . . a small wheel united to many other small wheels that together endow movement to the total machinery."[19] With a vision of society as a mechanical whole immune from human variables—choices, perceptions, uncertainties, and doubt—the PPD assigned a role to labor and ascertained its fate.[20]

Ortiz did not omit the discursive style of labor from his speeches but appropriated it as part of his own. Ortiz's tactic illustrates how the PPD blurred the line between labor and political leaders from outside the ranks of workers. By wrapping themselves in the mantle of labor advocacy, PPD leaders not only pleaded for acceptance among workers but also strove to alter the meaning of their vision. Ortiz, for example, made sure to place workers up front as a major force to contend with on the island.[21] However, he argued that as a force recently awakened from a dormant state, labor remained unaware of its power. Under these circumstances, the PPD supplied the spark of life that labor lacked. On the one hand, Ortiz sided with labor by acknowledging its presence. On the other hand, labor appeared in Ortiz's speech as an empty shell, a body without soul or mind to act on its own. In short, the PPD absorbed and mirrored back to workers their own discourse but with a key element transfigured: labor's vision of consent. The approval that workers expressed toward their own version of the CGT-PPD partnership was displayed by PPD officials as proof of labor's unconditional acquiescence toward Muñoz's party.

The perceptions of the CGT and PPD about their partnership formed the backdrop of the union's second congress in 1943.[22] Labor and party officials met again to address issues on which they could agree, such as social reform and the improvement of the island's economy. Despite a common agenda, the CGT and PPD visualized differently the plans for the future. For example, the CGT favored industrialization as a policy that could include labor's input to devise the best way to end unemployment and avoid exploitation.[23] This proposal, however, did not elicit a response from the PPD, and the party remained mute about workers' role in its plan for industrial development. Besides stressing the importance of labor to increase production, the CGT assigned workers a key function in the management of the economy and the administration of relief programs. To leave no doubt about its concern for the political welfare of Puerto Rico, the CGT impugned the island's colonial situation, petitioned the release from prison of Nationalist leader Pedro Albizu Campos, and lent an ear to the advocates of independence.[24] Again, the PPD did not warm up to the proposals of the CGT and refrained from offering words of approval. Despite the lethargy of the party, the CGT promised bold action and inspired favorable assessments about the potential of its own resources. For example, Pascual Sáez Corales, brother of Juan Sáez Corales, believed that "within a year the CGT will have such a great number of affiliated workers that it will be in a condition to decide the political status of this country at any moment."[25]

By mid-1943, tensions existed between the CGT and PPD, but neither side showed a disposition to end their partnership. To be sure, too many interests were at stake with a union desiring further reform and a party vying for power. The CGT and PPD probably hoped to reach some sort of compromise, or perhaps they believed in their own devices to steer the partnership as they wished. In either case, the decision that CGT officials reached after the PPD demanded again to be part of the union's leadership was symptomatic of this situation. Labor and PPD representatives would alternate for periods of six months in the presidency and vice-presidency of the union.[26] This would take place after an interim of three months in which Colón Gordiany and Barreto Pérez would jointly direct the CGT. That this arrangement produced a tense situation became evident during intervals of unfriendly exchanges and sour rhetoric within the CGT.[27] Before long, the union's joint leadership proved to be a failure. When union leaders made official their irreconcilable differences, an assembly of the CGT's Sugar Workers' Union—Sindicato Azucarero de la CGT—witnessed the first cracks in the CGT-PPD partnership in mid-1944.[28] Conflict between labor and Muñoz's party steadily grew during the following years.

Some authors argue that the CGT-PPD partnership deteriorated due to the irreconcilable class interests of these organizations.[29] That is, as a party of the elite, the PPD manipulated the CGT for its own gains. According to labor historian Juan Angel Silén, the CGT succumbed to PPD's schemes after being infiltrated by party officials.[30] Although there is no doubt that PPD leaders used the CGT for their own benefit, placing too much emphasis on manipulation raises certain problems. For one, it is hard to answer why the CGT backed the PPD under such unfavorable circumstances. In the worst case, workers may be viewed as passive subjects at the disposal of populist leaders. Besides the issue of agency, binding the CGT and PPD too rigidly to class interests obscures the conditions that sustained the CGT-PPD partnership. That is, no room is left to grasp an ambiguous zone of action and the elasticity of meaning that nurtured the discourse of consent. At the heart of the matter lie not just the particular interests and aims contained within the island's mass movement but also the overlap of loyalties, mixed feelings, and emotions of its participants. To grasp the impasse between the CGT and PPD, it is vital to focus on that space of interaction where lines and boundaries cannot be easily drawn. This can help us to understand the difficult choice faced by people torn between their loyalty to the union and their sympathy for the party.

A close look at the history of the CGT and PPD reveals a complex reality. Far from being a passive subject, labor emerges as a key agent that shaped the island's mass movement and colonial politics. By focusing on the CGT's motives and perceptions, it is possible to see the logic of the union's actions and the assurance with which the CGT presented a vision of consent.[31] As noted, the CGT viewed the PPD as a reliable ally as long as it did not spoil the policies of reform. Although the PPD did not welcome the CGT's broader plans, the union found it compatible to support the party and still express its own views. A key event that sheds light on this issue took place in February 1944. Dissidents from the island's political parties such as Socialists, Liberals, Republicans, and Laborists met in Caguas under the name of Social Left Movement—Movimiento de Izquierdas Sociales (MIS). The CGT helped organize the MIS and joined its assembly, which had as a goal to align the new organization with the PPD.[32]

The MIS produced a *Manifiesto* that mirrored the vision of consent of the CGT. A specific party program of political action did not motivate the organization. According to the MIS, support of the PPD did not compromise the organization's existence as a separate entity or its members' political beliefs. Reform, above all else, brought into being the MIS.[33] With their urgent and unequivocal call for "SOCIAL JUSTICE," the MIS produced yet another vision of consent in Puerto Rico. The MIS' *Manifiesto* emphasized the fact that many reforms of the PPD had already been proposed by other political parties but without success. In this sense, dissident politicians highlighted their own initiatives toward reform during the past as a basis to join forces with the PPD. Overall, the MIS assembly made evident that the island's populist movement was not what the PPD made it to be: a totality of groups that gracefully accepted the gift of leadership that the PPD bestowed on them. Joining forces with the PPD in the form of the MIS enabled political dissidents to back social justice and economic improvement with themselves as agents of Puerto Rico's transformation. That is, people joined forces with the PPD on their own volition and under certain conditions.

The CGT's and MIS' support toward the PPD is not unusual compared to the stance adopted by Communists early in 1944. When Earl Browder gave full support to Roosevelt's wartime policies by disbanding the Communist Party in the United States, local Communists followed suit when they announced the dissolution of the PCP to join forces with the PPD. The PCP's decision stands at a distance from the position assumed by Communists before 1944. As noted in Chapter 2, the PCP backed away at least publicly from Muñoz's party when the PPD rejected the support of Communists during the electoral campaign of 1940.[34] Since the start of World War II, local conditions combined with international events to reshape the relationship between the CGT, PPD, and Communists. Above all, the German invasion of the U.S.S.R. in 1941 not only put an end to the Nazi-Soviet Non-aggression Pact but also convinced Communists to join the Allies against Hitler.

Juan Santos Rivera, president of the PCP, explained his party's motives in a publication titled *Puerto Rico: Ayer, hoy y mañana*.[35] His words help us grasp how the PCP, as a close ally of the CGT, enriched the union's vision of consent. For Santos, war demanded that people contribute to the conflict's outcome by performing a leading role as agents of world politics. Otherwise, the benefits of reform, economic improvement, and democracy would be lost.[36] Santos shifted Jiménez's emphasis on labor organization to the war effort to assert people's right to control their future. To shape postwar events that could affect their lives, people had to include themselves as participants of policy-making processes beyond the local level. Communists in the mainland had taken this step. By joining the democratic forces under the leadership of Roosevelt, Communists did not relinquish their own goals but hoped to crush fascist and reactionary regimes.

Communists in Puerto Rico pursued a similar goal but adapted their views to suit local conditions. Supporting the PPD did not mean blind adherence to the party or seeing it as a homogeneous entity. For Communists, the PPD's cooperation with reform had proven to be "anti-colonial" despite the party's "bourgeois leaders."[37] Like the CGT and MIS, the PCP considered the continuance of social justice as the basis for joining forces with the PPD. The way Communists saw the PPD added to the efforts of the CGT and MIS to make a place for themselves in a better society. Instead of defining the PPD as a harmonious whole, Santos viewed the party as a mix of contradictory interests.[38] He credited many groups for shaping the PPD. Overall, the PCP's vision of consent shows that acquiescence toward the PPD was not the response of subordinates but of agents well aware of their reality. Because of their sense of self, the people who informed the island's mass movement felt entitled to make demands of the PPD and to claim rights from party leaders who said otherwise. At this juncture of the PPD's short political life, the mobilization of people promised to steer reform in new directions, rearrange the island's political forces, and sweep Muñoz's party with its momentum. In short, the meanings given to consent spilled beyond the bounds of the party's discourse and authority.

Like the CGT, Communists envisioned the postwar era as a time of prosperity for Puerto Ricans. Santos mentioned as a priority the safeguarding of labor's independence of action and opinion to ensure a more inclusive society.[39] The PCP went a step further when it imagined a future in which Puerto Rico as a country could feel welcomed by the international community. Santos praised the island for the guarantees it could offer as a democratic republic. For example, according to Santos, Puerto Rico featured modern means to communicate with the world, experience with democratic institutions, and a well-organized labor movement. To these features, Santos added several future projects, among which industrial development stood out. All these aspects informed the PCP's long-term plans "to provide abundance to all." Santos envisioned a republic that would manage most of the economy "in the interest of workers and all the people." He called it a "popular republic of the people and for the people."[40] As in the case of CGT officials, Communists closed ranks with the advocates of independence to imagine the best future for Puerto Rico. Instead of limiting their concerns to the problems of labor, CGT and PCP leaders pondered the merits of sovereignty and, in doing so, established a link between their own goals and those of independentists.

By reinforcing the CGT's vision of consent with their own views, Communists pulled the CGT-PPD partnership in a direction that the PPD did not like. The PCP's grasp of the island's mass movement downplayed the grandiloquent self-perception of the PPD. This could only heighten the PPD's reluctance to accept a notion of consent that sidestepped the party's lofty call for its own enthronement. For some time, the affinities that sustained the CGT-PPD partnership outweighed the discrepancies between the union and the party. While reform and social justice remained a matter of debate, a basis for common action existed. When reform gained greater precision as part of the visions of consent of different groups, this base of agreement eroded. For organizations such as the CGT, MIS, and PCP social justice was more than the PPD made it to be. It meant people's inclusion as agents of decision-making processes. It also entailed a definition of the PPD that conventionalized the role of party leaders. This posed a threat to the PPD's aspiration for power. When party leaders saw the PPD being defined as something beyond their scope—as an entity capable of incorporating leftist groups and fully open to radical demands for reform—they resorted to more than persuasion to articulate their discourse of consent.

By mid-1944, the CGT and PPD had stretched to the limit the bounds of their mutual understanding. The jolt that unhinged the CGT-PPD partnership was the successful maneuver of PPD leader Ernesto Ramos Antonini to become legal adviser of the CGT's Sugar Workers' Union. Ramos Antonini secured the post at an unsanctioned assembly of union officials that took place at the headquarters of the island's legislature.[41] This incident infuriated a group of CGT leaders who claimed that Ramos Antonini did not consult them. Only after extensive debate did the CGT avert a full-blown confrontation with the PPD.[42] Although labor leaders defused a tense situation, the admittance of Ramos Antonini into the CGT augured badly for the union and its relationship with the PPD. Ramos Antonini's role as representative of sugar workers added momentum to the formation of two factions within the CGT. One faction coalesced around Ramos Antonini and Barreto Pérez's attempt to bring the CGT closer to the PPD. The other faction heeded Francisco Colón Gordiany's call to safeguard the autonomy of the union.[43]

There were factors that counterbalanced the volatile state of the CGT-PPD partnership. On the one hand, Colón Gordiany knew he could not cut ties with the PPD without doing irreparable damage to the CGT. The mixed loyalties of workers toward the CGT and PPD made clear that distancing the union from the party could tear the CGT apart. On the other hand, Ramos Antonini and Barreto Pérez realized that if their hold on labor split the CGT, the PPD could lose a good source of support for the next election. Despite the threads that held the CGT and PPD together, the boundaries of the CGT-PPD partnership had been redrawn. Reform as a basis for common action gave way to the narrow objectives of the union and the party. For six months before the 1944 election, the CGT and PPD held to the remnants of their mutual understanding.

The effort of Colón Gordiany and his group to pull the CGT in their direction recognized the limits of tolerance of the CGT-PPD bond. To reduce the PPD's influence within the CGT without alienating the party, CGT leaders loyal to Colón Gordiany made it a policy to divorce their union from all political affairs.[44] The CGT prohibited its affiliates from using the union's name to support any of the island's parties. In addition, the CGT made an earnest call to unite all labor organizations in Puerto Rico.[45] The CGT's call for unity had been voiced before, but hardly ever had the union made such an overt invitation to workers. Since breaking with the PPD could imperil the union's cohesion, CGT leaders hoped for a broad realignment of labor forces to strengthen their hold on the CGT and minimize the union's ties to the PPD. With this aim in mind, the CGT scheduled a reunion open to all labor groups.[46]

The plan of the CGT to unite labor did not fulfill the expectations of union leaders. To the disappointment of Colón Gordiany, the CGT's reunion to bring labor together failed to produce a majority. The FLT, to which the CGT primarily aimed its call for unity, declined the invitation.[47] Besides its failure to mobilize labor, the CGT's reunion was not a smooth operation. According to the CGT's treasurer, "a machinery of division" spoiled the event. In a similar vein, the president of the *público* drivers' union stated that the CGT's project "failed at birth."[48] While the CGT saw its plan collapse, the FLT countered the former's call for unity with its own offer. Socialists proposed a "pact of honor" to unite the FLT and CGT without risk to either's autonomy.[49] Although the CGT joined the FLT to discuss the pact, it soon became evident that the FLT's offer entailed a plan to introduce changes in the sugar industry.[50] Another obstacle against the pact was the interference of Ramos Antonini. He called off the pact saying it was against labor's best interests.[51]

The PPD's landslide victory at the election of 1944 intensified the party's inclination to act unilaterally toward the CGT. Left with no other options, the CGT attacked the PPD at the end of the year. Juan Sáez Corales, for example, accused Ramos Antonini of wanting to divide the CGT.[52] For workers, the conflict between the CGT and PPD entailed much confusion.[53] This sorry state of affairs spelled the demise of the CGT-PPD partnership. At the core of the conflict lay an inescapable reality: consent, as labor understood it, was not consent as the PPD desired it. Instead of making room for the CGT's vision of consent, the PPD pushed it aside. The discourse and actions of the party informed the process of displacement. PPD leaders praised workers as party followers while undermining labor's ability for autonomous action. They also hindered the CGT's plan to strengthen the union or safeguard its independence. The PPD's unwillingness to compromise with the CGT decided the fate of a partnership that had proven crucial to secure ample reforms.

THE CPI AND PPD: A COMPROMISE UNDONE

Unlike other supporters of the PPD, advocates of independence for Puerto Rico joined the party under special circumstances. While the PPD went out of its way to publicize the benefits it could offer to all sorts of groups, the party avoided overt statements about the island's sovereignty. This was not a fortuitous occurrence but the result of an informal compromise between Muñoz and PPD leaders who favored independence.[54] Independentists agreed to hold back their call for sovereignty in exchange for the PPD's commitment to address the status issue in the future. That the PPD committed itself in favor of sovereignty became clear in the party's campaign pamphlet *The People's Catechism—Catecismo del Pueblo*—which detailed the advantages of independence as a political alternative.[55] The compromise between the PPD and independentists informed the PPD's departure from the constant debate about the status that dominated political life in Puerto Rico. The

PPD formally stated that social justice, not the status question, would receive the party's full attention. Although the PPD did not dismiss the colonial situation as unimportant, the party's emphasis on reform eclipsed the status issue as a source of political mobilization.

Initially, Muñoz found it easy to justify the compromise he reached with PPD leaders and followers who favored independence. World War II gave Muñoz a reason to postpone the status issue. According to Muñoz, the PPD would do best not to embarrass the United States with unsuitable claims at a time of national emergency.[56] Besides the war, Muñoz said that the economic situation demanded focus on problems other than the island's political status. Despite Muñoz's insistence, there were factors that made the Puerto Rican status question unavoidable. The PPD's postponement of the status issue faced a significant challenge when President Franklin D. Roosevelt and British prime minister Winston S. Churchill produced the eight-point statement of war aims known as the Atlantic Charter in August 1941.[57] With its emphasis on national self-determination, this statement not only broadened the scope of wartime cooperation but also enlisted the support of many countries for the Allied cause. The anti-colonial affirmation of the Atlantic Charter bolstered the concern about Puerto Rico's sovereignty. It also enabled Puerto Ricans to frame the status issue as part of an international agenda. On January 1, 1942, twenty-six countries signed the Declaration of the United Nations, which pledged cooperation in achieving the aims of the Atlantic Charter.[58]

Further impetus for the discussion of the political status came from the Anglo-American Caribbean Commission. Although British and American agents organized the commission to deal mainly with the emergency problems and socioeconomic needs of the Caribbean, it offered a forum to debate colonial issues.[59] Since the commission recruited officials of Caribbean countries as members, Puerto Ricans had the opportunity to discuss their political concerns with their neighbors. Finally, Governor Tugwell saw the need to address the island's status to appease the opposition to his administration.[60] As a representative of Roosevelt's wartime policies and a member of the Caribbean Commission, Tugwell urged the president about the need to revamp U.S. policies and introduce political changes on the island. Due to the significance of national self-determination in world politics, in the mainland, and in Puerto Rico, the status question could do no other than gather momentum early in 1943. In this context Puerto Ricans witnessed a rare case of cooperation among political leaders. All leading parties and legislators signed a concurrent resolution to demand self-determination for the island.[61]

Under these circumstances, independentists seized the opportunity to organize themselves in April 1943. A few days after Senator Millard S. Tydings introduced a bill in Congress for Puerto Rico's sovereignty, a group of independentists formed what came to be known as the Pro Independence Congress—Congreso Pro Independencia (CPI).[62] This organization hoped not only to mobilize support for the Tydings bill but also to uphold the longtime goals of independentists such as securing a republican form of government, self-sustained economic growth, protection of the island's cultural identity, and international recognition. Although the CPI welcomed advocates of independence regardless of party affiliation, the organization grouped an absolute majority of PPD leaders and followers.[63] Since the CPI was both a group with strong ties to the PPD and an organization with an agenda of its own, it had to negotiate a difficult situation. The compromise that Muñoz secured from independentists to keep the status issue on hold forced the CPI to walk a thin line between being loyal to the PPD and advocating independence for the island. To quell any uneasiness of Muñoz about the CPI, independentists insisted that they posed no threat to the PPD. The CPI defined itself as a nonpartisan organization. As such, the CPI hoped to reassure Muñoz as well as to give free rein to its vociferous call for independence.[64]

Despite the CPI's hasty rise, the organization did not enter the island's political arena empty-handed. An important precedent had been established a decade earlier when a group of independentists under the leadership of Dr. Juan Augusto Perea and his brother Salvador Perea formed the Independentist Party in the town of Mayagüez.[65] After its unsuccessful run in the 1936 election, the party became a nonpartisan organization called the Puerto Rican Patriotic Group—Agrupación Patriótica Puertorriqueña. Many leaders and followers of the Patriotic Group joined the effort to form the CPI. Moreover, the organizers of the CPI included well-known individuals such as poet Luis Lloréns Torres, Nationalist leader Juan Antonio Corretjer,[66] the editor of El Imparcial Antonio Ayuso Valdivieso, and the journalists José S. Alegría and Antonio Pacheco Padró.[67]

Besides grouping many advocates of independence, the CPI received the support of Communist and labor activists, including Juan Santos Rivera, José A. Lanauze Rolón, Juan Sáez Corales, and César Andreu Iglesias.[68] The PCP's president, Santos Rivera, endorsed the CPI's resolutions, and Lanauze spoke at the initial assembly of the organization. CGT leaders Sáez Corales and Barreto Pérez also joined the activities of the CPI.[69] Finally, the CPI had its share of support in Latin America, the United States, and Europe. An important ally was Congressman Vito Marcantonio, who several times in the past sided with workers and independentists.[70] Expressions of solidarity came from the American Communist Party, the CIO, and many labor and civic organizations abroad.[71] Puerto Rican independentists in the mainland also had their say through CPI delegates such as Corretjer and Professor María Teresa Babín.[72]

In its effort to secure ample representation, the CPI grouped perceptions about independence as varied as its base of support. This fact, however, was not entirely evident due to the overwhelming presence of PPD leaders within the CPI. Consequently, even after welcoming different groups and views, the CPI became the abode of a particular perspective about independence. For example, the sort of independence that Communist leaders called for—one that would allow fundamental changes in society and the removal of class differences—did not surface in the CPI's rhetoric or sway the organization.[73] Instead, the CPI greatly benefited from the perceptions of PPD leaders who made sovereignty indispensable for the mobilization of people and the implementation of reform. With a version of sovereignty that was not entirely all-inclusive but that outmatched alternative views, the CPI articulated a vision of consent that upheld political aims as its core values. To grasp this vision of consent centered on sovereignty, it is useful to focus on the writings of attorney Vicente Géigel Polanco, who was a prominent leader of both the PPD and CPI. As a senator and former employee of the Department of Labor, Géigel dealt with issues mostly related to the island's status question and social legislation.[74] Above all, Géigel's work offers a vision of consent that inextricably intertwined his veneration of the PPD and his belief in independence.

Among the best-known publications of Géigel is *El despertar de un pueblo*, a collection of essays that he compiled one year before the formation of the CPI.[75] This book gave cohesion to the PPD's populist discourse. It also brought the PPD's perceptions to a different plane by focusing on independence. Like PPD leaders who addressed labor, Géigel drew a rigid line between a terrible past and a great new era. The title of his book, "the awakening of a people," refers to the moment of transition between these two periods. Géigel described Puerto Ricans of the past as "passive," "dormant," "anesthetized," "unconscious," "insensible," "indifferent," "lazy," and "tired."[76] Instead of "a people," Géigel saw "a multitude" suffering the effects of "suicidal disregard."[77] The new era brought joy to Géigel because Puerto Ricans became "a people" well aware of how to overcome exploitation. According to Géigel, the "awakening of the people" was possible because the PPD provided "the will" that the masses lacked to be more than victims.[78]

The words of Géigel are significant as much for what they say as for what they leave out. Despite the passion of his claims, Géigel did not explain who exactly "the people" are and their specific interests and aims. If by "the people" Géigel meant different sectors of labor in Puerto Rico, he gave few thoughts to the strong conviction of many workers about the benefits of statehood. As scholars Gervasio García and Angel G. Quintero Rivera point out, "proletarian annexionism" upheld the belief about a greater likelihood of socioeconomic improvement and unionization under U.S. sovereignty.[79] To make clear their misgivings about independence, many workers condemned the sort of nationalism and homeland advocated by the elite—sovereignty under the rule of national capital—a regime that would likely strengthen class divisions and exploitation. Géigel as well as other PPD leaders in favor of independence not only left unanswered these concerns of labor but also contributed to a familiar bias of the island's nationalist thought. By visualizing Puerto Ricans as "passive" and "dormant," Géigel made an argument that has often served to oversimplify the shortcomings of the independence movement: the "alienation," "confusion," or "indifference" of the masses are to blame for independence's lack of mass appeal.[80] This is one of the key features of *El despertar de un pueblo* and the discourse of certain CPI leaders.

Géigel's vision of consent shows how the PPD constructed a notion of Puerto Ricans beneficial to the party. By acknowledging "the people" as an alert newcomer never far from the center stage of politics, the party sought legitimacy as representative of broad sectors of society. To make further claims and define itself as the catalyst of change, the PPD constantly perceived "the people" as an idle subject that overcame its "lethargy" thanks to the actions of the party. The PPD's perception of "the people" as an all-encompassing abstraction amplified the scope of the party's leadership. PPD officials stressed that since their party embodied "the people's will," Puerto Rico could do no better than to embrace its tutelage. When Géigel stressed the need for new political leadership to guide "the people," he did not act according to a whim or last-minute strategy to justify his party. Instead, Géigel's words are consistent with his past statements and exemplify the self-perception of his peers—a generation of leaders who had called for reform even before the formation of the PPD. This self-perception is well stated in *El despertar de un pueblo*, which includes several articles that Géigel wrote in the 1930s. In one of them, Géigel stated: "It is urgent to form a new governing class linked to the legitimate interest of the people, capable of arousing in our multitudes the sense of self-worth and conducting them rightfully to the achievement of their collective destiny."[81] By visualizing the "destiny" of "the people" as a "collective" affair of leaders and followers, Géigel championed a vision of consent that made sovereignty the most significant goal on the island.

For Géigel, "the awakening of the people" demanded applause not only because it made Puerto Ricans aware of their reality but also because it brought the island closer to independence. No doubt existed in Géigel's mind that independence entailed all the unconditional imperatives of a religion. For Géigel, sovereignty meant "redemption," leaders embodied the "apostles" of emancipation, and the fight for independence was nothing short of a "crusade."[82] He relentlessly insisted that political freedom demanded higher "moral virtues" such as "sacrifice," "abnega- tion," "sincerity," and "apostolic devotion."[83] Above all, it was clear to Géigel that certain leaders had the blessing to stand above a bygone wasteland of political mediocrity. Géigel's genealogy of liberators, who included Simón Bolívar, Ramón E. Betances, and Eugenio M. de Hostos, made obvious that Muñoz was next in line. As a book that opens with a dedication to Muñoz and closes by quoting the PPD's maximum leader, *El despertar de un pueblo* celebrated the coming of a new emancipator.[84]

It is not by chance that a spiritual force seems to underlie Géigel's genealogy of liberators. It is also no accident that Géigel saw Muñoz as "the second apparition of Hostos."[85] Géigel visualized independence as a theological manifestation of utmost significance in an effort to narrow the basis of legitimate political action in Puerto Rico. For Géigel, leaders who revered independence acted within the bounds of legitimacy, while those with less high-minded ideals did not deserve respect. The implication was clear: failure to worship independence meant an act of heresy. Géigel's notion of independence offers an example of how independentists tried to steer the PPD and Muñoz their way. By conceiving independence as the most important source of legitimate action, Géigel wanted to ensure that the PPD did not wander far from that goal. Géigel assigned to Muñoz a moral obligation of great weight. The only role that Muñoz could play in Géigel's vision was that of a liberator. Géigel created expectations about Muñoz that made it hard to imagine any reluctance on his part to favor sovereignty.

In Géigel's vision of consent, people can make a place for themselves in a better society only under independence. Géigel imagined a terrible future for Puerto Rico as a consequence of Americanization. The perpetuation of U.S. colonialism meant for Géigel not only the decline of all aspects of life but also the loss of the cultural values that define Puerto Ricans as "a people."[86] Géigel hoped for a future in which Puerto Ricans could live in comfort without the influence of Americans. Independence, for Géigel, could not only ensure the full expression of the Puerto Rican culture but also improve the island's economic and political life.[87] According to Géigel, only an "either/or" approach could solve what he saw as the main source of confusion: "The disorientation springs from postulating at one tribune the urgency to yankeesize our soul and in another, to conserve and enrich our historical values. Statehood, independence, and colonialism require antagonistic inculcations. Either we affirm our self or we propitiate our dissolution."[88]

Géigel, like many other independentists, made inseparable the plans to address the island's socioeconomic situation, its cultural identity, and its colonial regime. For the advocates of independence, the struggle to improve the quality of life inevitably demanded a defense of cultural values and a debate about the status question. This might have been the result of the overwhelming impact that U.S. colonialism had on all aspects of life in Puerto Rico. However, even after taking into consideration the brunt of colonialism during the first decades of U.S. rule—meaning its worst aspects such as the policies of Americanization, the abuses of absentee corporations, the pauperization of the labor force, and the reduction of the elite's economic and political power—certain sectors in Puerto Rico did acknowledge that socioeconomic improvement, national culture, and the status issue have a complex relationship and do not always go hand in hand. One case already mentioned is that of labor. The prostatehood tendency of the working class cannot be taken as an example of groups that had been brainwashed by assimilation. Labor groups in favor of statehood did not wish the demise of cultural values but wished to facilitate the extension of mainland benefits to Puerto Rico. As Ramón Grosfoguel explains, "the Puerto Rican people's strategy has been pragmatic rather than utopian; that is, they are not struggling to be freed from imperialist oppression . . . but are instead attempting to struggle for a milder version of this oppression."[89] This has given way to a "strategy of *subversive complicity* with the system" and "feelings of nationhood" that do not necessarily entail the formation of a nation-state.[90]

Independentists elicited a lukewarm response from Muñoz and his supporters. The gradual detachment of the PPD from the ideal of independence has been the object of study. Authors such as Carmelo Rosario Natal and Carlos Zapata Oliveras view Muñoz and other PPD leaders as committed individuals who realized the impossibility of independence.[91] According to these authors, Muñoz abandoned independence in favor of autonomy only after reaching a critical point against unsurmountable odds during the 1940s. Adverse data about the economic consequences of sovereignty and the relentless opposition of U.S. interests left no other option to PPD leaders. Other authors argue that the PPD went through a process of ideological transformation that left independence and other goals out of the party's agenda.[92] For example, Gerardo Navas Dávila explains the adjustment and accommodation of the PPD's program to a new international order with an interpretation that is partly based on dependency theory.[93] That is, the structural shift of the world economy caused the transformation of the party's ideology. It has also been argued that Muñoz and the PPD's commitment toward independence was either ambiguous, moderate, or nearly nonexistent.[94] Instead of focusing on Muñoz's state of mind or the PPD's response to global developments, there are interpretations that stress the economic interests, discursive practices, or short-term priorities that made the party's commitment toward independence highly inconsistent. Thus, due to certain factors, sovereignty became a distant aim of the PPD.

Despite the merits of recent approaches, a difficulty still haunts the efforts to understand the political nature of the PPD. The problem to grasp the PPD is one of degrees. Too many times the PPD has been seen as a well-defined entity—a party acting as the extension of a boss—that debated by itself the benefits or shortcomings of independence. Less attention has been paid to the exchanges between the PPD and other groups that allowed for the temporary coexistence of different agendas within the party. By seeing the PPD as a party not entirely immune to the sway of multiple agents, one can grasp independentists and their ideals as one of several interests that competed and informed the PPD before their displacement. This approach stresses the fluid ground of contestation between the PPD and other groups that made possible different visions of consent. Common aims between agents such as reform and social justice brought the PPD and other groups together along with their divergent perceptions and courses of actions. Not only social justice produced close ties between the PPD and other sectors. Officials of the PPD and independentists such as Géigel shared a particular interest besides reform. They had visions of consent that subordinated people to the whims of the party. That is, party officials and advocates of independence saw the PPD as the motivational drive of a mass population that had lain "dormant" for too long. Despite having a similar discourse, the PPD and CPI conceived their respective visions of consent as a means toward different ends. The former focused on social justice, while the latter insisted on independence.

Muñoz, the PPD, and party members that formed the CPI articulated a similar perception about "the people." The discourse of the PPD constantly featured a notion of Puerto Ricans as "passive," "dormant," or "dozing" victims of terrible atrocities from the past. In this sense, Muñoz and independentists such as Géigel could meet eye to eye. The leader of the PPD could agree with ideologues who saw the party as the rescuer of all the "defenseless people" of the island. Muñoz not only banked upon the perceptions of PPD spokesmen but also added his own spin to the party's discourse. He envisioned for himself a prerogative that was not to be invoked by any other PPD official or political leader: a direct and completely unmediated relationship to "the people" that cut across party lines and governmental institutions.[95] For Muñoz, he and "the people" formed an inseparable nexus around which everything else revolved. By conceiving his link to "the people" as an earnest rapport irreducible to narrow interests, the leader of the PPD nurtured his image as a larger-than-life figure. Muñoz's self-proclaimed role as the "agitator of God" corresponded with his so-called "communion" with the "the people."[96]

The "Muñoz-people" nexus enabled the leader of the PPD to argue against visions of consent that he did not like. By presenting himself as the "savior" for whom Puerto Ricans had been waiting, Muñoz sought to avoid challenges to his notion about the "people" or unrestrained views that did not place him in the spotlight. When faced with perceptions or demands that constrained the PPD, Muñoz displaced them by making reference to what he saw as the all-important pledge to uphold the needs of "the people." Muñoz used this tactic to deal with the claims that independentists made about the PPD.[97] According to Muñoz, any moral obligation that independentists placed on the PPD could not compare to the party's obligation to help "the people." Although the expectations that the CPI had about the PPD weighed heavily on Muñoz, it was most difficult to influence the aims and thoughts of a leader who claimed extraordinary virtues as a defender of all Puerto Ricans. Since Muñoz constantly insisted he was one with the "the people," independentists could not present themselves as a majority within the PPD. To refute the CPI, Muñoz spoke as if he embodied the voice of "the people."[98]

PPD leaders used a twofold strategy to deal with the demand for independence of the CPI. Muñoz and his followers tried to forestall the mobilization of the CPI without alienating the support of independentists toward the party. To achieve this goal, Muñoz took the lead in reminding PPD members within the CPI about the compromise between the party and independentists.[99] He stressed that social justice, not the political status, constituted the basis of the PPD's pledge toward "the people." According to this compromise, the status issue would be addressed at a later date. Muñoz mobilized several PPD leaders to add support to his arguments. Besides the points raised by Muñoz, party officials such as Samuel R. Quiñones, Ernesto Ramos Antonini, Benjamín Ortiz, Pablo Defendini, and Blas Oliveras offered other reasons to postpone the status issue.[100] PPD officials argued that the status issue could interfere with the war effort.[101] They also thought it futile to address the status issue when U.S. authorities had their attention elsewhere. Puerto Rico, according to the PPD, could count on Roosevelt's commitment to solve the island's political problems. Besides the war, PPD officials insisted that the island's social and economic maladies had to be addressed first to make independence viable.[102] Once Puerto Rico became a self-sustaining territory, the PPD would advocate the principle of national self-determination. PPD leaders also argued that the opposition could use the status issue as leverage to ruin social justice.[103]

While the PPD publicized many arguments to persuade independentists to drop the status issue, Muñoz and his followers engaged U.S. officials to make political changes in Puerto Rico. In March 1943, a month before the introduction of the Tydings bill and the formation of the CPI, President Roosevelt sent a message to the U.S. Congress recommending the expansion of self-government on the island and to permit Puerto Ricans to elect their governor.[104] Roosevelt also announced the appointment of local and mainland advisers—a group often referred to as the

President's Committee or Presidential Commission—to examine and inform the U.S. executive branch about possible changes to the island's Organic Act. With a different aim and strategy from those of the Tydings bill, the President's Committee not only set in motion a simultaneous process of consultation but also enabled Muñoz and his peers to engage U.S. authorities. Although Muñoz criticized the goals of the President's Committee as being too narrow, he accepted his appointment and became a member of the advisory board.[105] For many months, while CPI leaders fought an uphill struggle to have the Tydings bill approved by Congress, PPD officials tried against the odds to broaden the scope of the President's Committee. In mid-1943, for example, Miguel Guerra Mondragón and Teodoro Moscoso complied with Muñoz's instruction to submit an ample proposal of self-government to federal authorities.[106] Instead of sovereignty, as the PPD's compromise with independentists called for, the party began to show a preference for autonomy.

Meanwhile, the CPI organized its first mass demonstration on the island, which proved to be more successful than the organization's lobbying efforts in Washington, D.C.[107] The PPD did not stay idle when the CPI announced a congress open to all independentists for August 1943. CPI delegates who belonged to the PPD became the targets of a careful plan to remind them about the party's priorities.[108] Several days before the CPI congress, PPD agents such as Raúl Gandara, Yldefonso Solá Morales, and Jorge Font Saldaña visited local committees throughout the island to evaluate the leaning of party officials.[109] After their inspection tours, each one of these agents prepared a full report. The top leadership of the PPD met three days before the CPI congress to discuss the implications of the event.[110] A meeting of sixty local committees of the PPD also took place before the CPI congress.[111] While many steps were taken to draw a line between the PPD and CPI, Muñoz made sure to avoid issues that could alienate independentists. The leader of the PPD employed a double tactic. He steered clear from any public statement compromising him with the CPI but showed a sympathetic disposition toward the congress.

Muñoz mentioned that to assist the congress would be an honor if he were not bound by a pledge to avoid using people's votes as support for any political status.[112] Just before the CPI met, Muñoz announced his effort to help the organization by requesting the federal authorities to ease the wartime restrictions on transportation.[113] He also welcomed any declaration of the CPI that did not affect the PPD.[114] To leave no doubt about his goodwill toward independentists, Muñoz sent a message of support to be read at the assembly of the CPI.[115] After stressing the reasons that did not permit him to accept the CPI's invitation, Muñoz wished the congress success in expressing the "ideals that undeniably are those of a great number of Puerto Ricans."[116] Despite Muñoz's message of support, he did not ease his party's policies toward the CPI. After the congress, the leader of the PPD put pressure again on party members to honor their pledge to "the people." He also reemphasized the difference between the PPD and CPI.[117] According to Muñoz, the PPD stood by its pledge to postpone the status issue while the CPI stood for independence with the support of party leaders who acted only as private citizens.

The CPI had a double tactic of its own. Independentists tried to ease the misgivings of Muñoz and the PPD without silencing their demand for sovereignty. Delegates of the CPI saw their islandwide congress as an event free of political consequences. Géigel assured the PPD that independentists had no intention to form a party.[118] He insisted that the only aim of the CPI was "to keep alive" the island's demand for sovereignty. Antonio Pacheco Padró, another leader of the CPI and PPD, stated that the meeting of the CPI was not a "political act."[119] For him, the event lacked the features of partisan politics. After all was said and done to organize the CPI congress, independentists made a resounding call for the sovereignty of Puerto Rico. Around 1,800 delegates oversaw an assembly of more than 15,000 people at the Sixto Escobar ballpark in San Juan.[120] Juan Augusto Perea presided over the event. For several hours the public heard the speeches of CPI advocates such as Géigel, Ayuso Valdivieso, Rafael Soltero Peralta, María Libertad Gómez, Felisa Rincón de Gautier, Benjamín Ortiz, Rafael Arjona Siaca, and Ernesto Juan Fonfrías.[121] These speakers had close ties to the PPD either as leaders or as sympathizers of the party.

Besides the prominent participation of PPD officials, the CPI congress welcomed representatives of labor, Communists, and Nationalists.[122] Sáez Corales, the CGT's general secretary, spoke about the contributions of workers to the independence movement. PCP official Lanauze Rolón professed his belief in sovereignty. Santos Rivera, the PCP's president, ended his speech promising unconditional support toward independence and raising up high the name of Nationalist leader Pedro Albizu Campos.[123] Rather than the exception, Santos Rivera' hurrah for Albizu was one of many enthusiastic expressions in favor of Nationalists. Rafael Rivera Matos assisted the CPI congress as spokesperson of the Nationalist Party. He delivered a message of Pedro Pérez Pagán, the party's interim president. According to Pérez Pagán, the war for democracy in the world would not end until the recognition of the island's independence. With the unanimous approval of attendees, the CPI offered greetings to Albizu, Corretjer, and other Puerto Ricans who had been jailed for attacking colonialism and defending sovereignty. Independentists at the assembly also passed a resolution to request from President Roosevelt the release of Albizu and other Nationalists still behind bars.[124] In addition to the statements of independentists, the CPI read the words of encouragement sent by Congressman Vito Marcantionio.

During the congress, CPI advocates visualized broad consent among Puerto Ricans toward their political ideal. Independentists stressed the need for common action and impugned many colonial abuses such as the island's political subordination, the exploitation of labor by U.S. capital, the absentee ownership of land, and restrictive tariff laws. In particular, Géigel's speech called for the solidarity of workers, rural laborers, and the poor in an effort to secure the only political status that could guarantee social justice.[125] The CPI congress summed up its aims in the Pro Independence Declaration of Puerto Rico, which was sent to U.S. officials, Latin American neighbors, European governments, and the countries constituting the United Nations.[126] Independentists improved the CPI with the creation of several committees. Géigel accepted his appointment as CPI vicepresident, and Gilberto Concepción de Gracia became the organization's legal adviser.[127] Plans were made to send a lobbying group to Washington, D.C., under the name of Permanent Diplomatic Mission. The CPI also decided to form "permanent delegations" throughout the island as part of its orientation campaign to diffuse the ideal of independence.[128]

Not long after the congress, several CPI leaders became impatient with the PPD. They found unsustainable Muñoz's double standard of distancing the PPD from the status issue while lobbying for changes to the colonial system through the President's Committee. Delegates of the CPI affiliated with the PPD began to doubt the party's commitment to the ideal of sovereignty. For example, lawyer and university professor Rafael Soltero Peralta censured the PPD for supporting the U.S. initiatives to redefine the functions and power of the island's government.[129] According to Peralta, the federal plan to introduce political reform could only reinforce the U.S. colonial regime to the detriment of independence.

Engineer and hotel owner Félix Benítez Rexach, who ran unsuccessfully for mayor of San Juan under the PPD ticket, also made an aggressive accusation in November 1943. He vituperated the "popular leader, the prophet of demagogy" for promising things larger than nature and for dragging his people toward "total destruction."[130] On another occasion, Benítez said that "while Muñoz maintains his party without political status he would be contributing to the exploitation of Puerto Rico."[131] Benítez believed that the status issue had to be tackled first to solve the island's economic maladies. For him, only sovereignty could offer the protection needed to launch the PPD's program of industrial development. Moreover, according to Benítez, Muñoz cannot help the working class by wrecking the island's economy with the federal project of political reform. Benítez accused Muñoz of using a "smoke screen" and for retreating from independence as "the Devil from the Cross."[132]

Benítez did more than reproach the leader of the PPD. He countered Muñoz's effort to distance the PPD from independentists and their demand for sovereignty. In the local press, Benítez predicted that the PPD would triumph in the next election because the party aimed directly at the ideal of independence, the only status guaranteeing the happiness and well-being of Puerto Ricans.[133] Before a congressional committee, Benítez and his colleague, Sergio S. Peña, stated that a great majority of PPD members wanted independence for Puerto Rico. According to Benítez, "the truth is, the fact is, that 80 percent of the Popular Party are staunch advocates of independence, and have been so for many, many years."[134] Benítez presented his case most strongly to Senator Tydings, who was the main contact of the CPI in the U.S. Congress. In one of his many letters to the senator, Benítez wrote that "it can be assured that 95% of those who voted for the Popular Party are outright independentists."[135] Similarly, Peña stated to U.S. authorities that "95 percent of all the members of the Popular Party have the independence feeling."[136] Apparently, quoting the percentage of PPD supporters in favor of sovereignty became a common strategy among CPI advocates. A similar statement to that of

Benítez and Peña came from Benjamín Cole, who placed the strength of independentists within the PPD at 85 percent.[137]

Although the constant repetition of their claims promised results, CPI leaders conceived other ways to make their case. Besides his own statements, Benítez overwhelmed Tydings with press clippings about the independence of Puerto Rico. For example, many articles of poet and independentist leader Luis Lloréns Torres reached the hands of the senator.[138] According to the articles of Lloréns, colonialism entailed maladies such as poverty, the military draft, and cultural dislocation, while sovereignty offered advantages such as protective tariff laws, control over local resources, industrial development, and social reform. Another political tactic of Benítez was his insistence that Muñoz stood for sovereignty. He informed Tydings and other congressmen about Muñoz's vote for independence in a status poll held by *El Imparcial* in December 1943.[139] Benítez said to the senator: "As you will see Muñoz Marín voted for Independence and in explaining his vote he stated: 'In peace and friendship with the people of the United States, Independence is the permanent guaranty of social justice for our people.'"[140] The fuzziness of colonial politics is obvious at this point. On the one hand, Muñoz abstained from making comments about his vote, even though the front page of *Claridad* made public a copy of his ballot, which included his signature and a hand-written statement.[141] On the other hand, Benítez mirrored Muñoz's duplicity with a questionable tactic of his own. Benítez did not seem to mind that a month ago he condemned Muñoz and called him "the prophet of demagogy."[142] Without hesitation, Benítez now took over Muñoz's name and employed it as an asset in his efforts in favor of independence. Evidently, he and other CPI leaders had run out of patience.

A group of independentists could not accept the PPD's disregard of their demand any longer. The president of the CPI, Juan Augusto Perea, and other independentists saw the need for further action. In March 1944, Perea, Benítez, and several of their colleagues proposed the formation of an independentist party at an assembly of the CPI.[143] For them, the CPI no longer served its purpose, and the time had come to disband the organization. It soon became evident that the proposal lacked support. The majority of CPI leaders opted to maintain their compromise with the PPD.[144] That is, they decided to respect the party's neutrality on the status issue while advocating independence as part of the CPI. Despite being in the minority, Perea and his group went ahead with their plan. They resigned their positions and walked out of the organization. Géigel took over the CPI's presidency. Among the reasons that were offered to create a party, Perea emphasized his belief that the CPI had become an "outlet" of the PPD.[145] He criticized the CPI's intention to postpone independence as well as to place a "colonial political party" above the goals of the organization. Perea and his group wrote a manifesto to affirm their party's urgent call for sovereignty.[146] They praised independence as an ideal that stood above any other issue.

Although Perea's party had little impact, its existence is significant from a political point of view. The creation of the Independentist Party illustrates the reluctance of certain sectors to relinquish the status issue as a source of political mobilization. The Independentist Party's agenda ran against the grain. While social justice kept gathering momentum as the basis of consent, Perea and his supporters embraced independence as the best option for common action. This was as much an effort at political competition as an attempt to safeguard the aspirations of independentists. Perea's party was the reaction of CPI leaders not content to see their aims and ideals being displaced by the PPD. As was the case with other groups and their visions of consent, the perceptions of independentists stressed the need for comradeship and change but gave a different spin to political action and reform. Since Muñoz kept postponing the status issue in the name of social justice, several independentists questioned not only their compromise with the PPD but also reform as the main basis to address the island's problems. For Perea and his group, the PPD's version of social justice became unattractive and hopeless.

Most members of the CPI avoided cutting ties with the PPD. Although many CPI leaders objected to the PPD's handling of the status issue, they felt it untimely to withdraw support from the party. Delegates of the CPI such as PPD official Antonio Pacheco Padró and Communist leader Juan Santos Rivera argued that the PPD would need the assistance of all independentists to defeat the opposition in the next election.[147] As president of the PCP, Santos Rivera made a statement commending the CPI and hoped for "a party of all the people to rescue our national sovereignty."[148] During the campaign months of 1944, the CPI found it compatible to support the PPD and defend the ideal of independence. By this time, the CPI felt little obligation to uphold its compromise with Muñoz to postpone the status issue.

Even though Muñoz and independentists visualized people's consent toward the party in different ways, CPI leaders blurred the line between themselves and the PPD. For example, Soltero Peralta, who was said to be a PPD affiliate, publicized for several weeks the interviews he had with U.S. congressmen to discuss the island's sovereignty.[149] In the same vein, the new president of the CPI, Gilberto Concepción de Gracia, announced he would vote for the PPD because it promised to facilitate independence.[150] The willingness of these independentists to act simultaneously as CPI members and PPD supporters sheds light on their perception of the party. Advocates of independence saw the PPD as the core of a mass movement in favor of sovereignty. Comradeship and change in their vision of consent did not lead to Muñoz's social justice but to the demise of U.S. colonial rule in Puerto Rico.

As in the case of labor, the PPD's overwhelming electoral victory of 1944 intensified the party's intransigence toward the CPI. To make matters worse, the PPD's campaign and the celebration of its success coincided with the CPI's preparations of its second congress, which had been scheduled for early December. Under these circumstances, the CPI congress had unreconcilable consequences. On the one hand, the event proceeded as planned and proved to be a success for independentists. On the other hand, the congress spelled further tensions between the CPI and PPD. Concepción de Gracia presided over 1,600 delegates during the activity.[151] PPD leaders joined the event such as Géigel, Pacheco Padró, Samuel R. Quiñones, Rafael Arjona Siaca, Ernesto Juan Fonfrías, and Felisa Rincón de

Gautier. Again, the CPI welcomed the support of labor, Communists, and Nationalists. Santos Rivera attended the assembly, even though the PCP had been dissolved. Sáez Corales participated as CGT representative, and Rafael Rivera Matos headed the Nationalist Party's delegation. The resolutions of CPI delegates prioritized the mobilization of people, their lobbying efforts in the United States, and the initiation of proceedings by the end of 1945 to solve the status issue.[152]

While the congress enabled the CPI to vaunt its organizational and numerical force, independentists could not avoid the ever-growing gap between themselves and the PPD. The preparations for the assembly and the event itself produced an exchange between the CPI and Muñoz unlike the one of 1943. Before the congress, the CPI and PPD voiced their own precautions. Concepción de Gracia insisted that the CPI did not constitute a political party, nor did it favor violence to achieve independence.[153] After stating that his organization welcomed independentists of all social and political groups, Concepción rejected the existence of ties between the CPI and any of the islands' political parties. According to Concepción, the CPI mainly aimed its words at that 80% of the island's population, the "rural and working class masses."[154] Meanwhile, Muñoz allowed PPD members to attend the congress as "citizens" but not as party affiliates, meaning that they had to avoid advocating any status "in the name of the people."[155] This instruction of Muñoz was the corollary of an argument he repeatedly made in the previous months: only by consulting "the will of the people" can the island decide its "final liberty."[156]

The CPI's second congress did not proceed as smoothly as the first one. Apparently, contrary to the previous year, fewer PPD officials attended the event or offered ardent discourses. Albizu's name did not come up as often, and the Nationalist Party's spokesperson left the congress without delivering a speech.[157] Before long, CPI delegates faced the criticism of Perea, the Independentist Party's president, who believed that the first congress already attested to the island's preference for sovereignty.[158] Moreover, the differences between Muñoz and independentists stood out during and after the CPI congress. Although the CPI acknowledged the need to consult the status issue with "the people," leaders such as Concepción and Géigel implied in their speeches that the PPD's electoral victory was a triumph for sovereignty.[159] For Géigel, the PPD's commitment toward social justice included "the mandate of the people" to end colonialism. Instead, Muñoz sent a letter to the congress saying that "the people, directly, without intermediaries of any kind" should decide the island's political status.[160] After the congress, Muñoz warned that he would be in a state of "constant alert" to preempt any "maneuver" of the CPI to form a party "behind the people's back."[161] For him, the CPI's "permanent delegations" throughout the island already composed the basis of a new political party. Concepción repudiated Muñoz's distrust of the CPI with the same vehemence by saying that he, too, would be "alert" against the "enemies" not merely of "social justice" but of "political justice" as well.[162]

The unfriendly exchange between Muñoz and the CPI came as no surprise. Muñoz hammered, relentlessly, before and after the election that the political status was not an issue for the PPD. He excised from the PPD's campaign literature the original compromise to defend independence. According to *The People's Catechism—Catecismo del Pueblo*—Muñoz would set the date for a status plebiscite because he "more than anyone else, is responsible before the whole people to act wisely in the name of the people and for their greatest justice and welfare."[163] The unique marriage that Muñoz claimed to cherish with "the people" was invoked in full force by the leader of the PPD to displace the CPI. Muñoz had a better chance to shape public opinion during a plebiscite to consult Puerto Ricans directly about the political status. A poll of that nature could offer the best stage for Muñoz to act his part as the benefactor of "the people." Although the events during December 1944 made imminent a major showdown between the CPI and Muñoz, the moment of confrontation remained latent, and tensions dragged on for several months. While the CPI and Muñoz postponed taking drastic action, the PPD's fate swiveled between two different visions of consent. That is, while Muñoz defined the PPD as a party of "the people" with him at its core, the CPI defined the PPD as an independentist party in spite of the political leanings of its main leader.

By the end of 1944, Muñoz constantly used his notion of "the people" as a trump card to call off demands for sovereignty. Even when the CPI made independence the most important goal of the party, Muñoz gradually tilted the balance in favor of a definition that reinforced his authority. By presenting himself, the PPD, and "the people" as spokes of the same axis, Muñoz sought to legitimate his own course of action: to decide without interference the island's future. As in the case of labor, the CPI's vision of consent did not correspond with the PPD's agenda. This disparity remained dormant while there was enough of a common ground to sustain the CPI-PPD compromise. The polarization between the CPI and PPD grew when Muñoz and his adherents failed to keep their pledge for sovereignty. Besides steering the PPD away from independence, the party's intransigence alienated key supporters who provided strength to the island's mass movement as well as encouragement to demand ample reforms from U.S. authorities.

MUÑOZ AND HIS VISION OF CONSENT

The political thought of Muñoz evolved vis-á-vis his interest in economic development to remodel Puerto Rico. At an early stage of his political career, Muñoz gave much thought to projects that promised the benefits of modern life to Puerto Ricans. For instance, he visualized the impact that air transportation could have on the island's culture as follows: "Puerto Rico, with fast means of communication, would no longer be a country to become a great city of one and a half million inhabitants, Mayagüez being in as close proximity to Humacao by air as 125th Street is to Wall Street by subway."[164] Muñoz heralded the potential of development projects to transform Puerto Rico. He also pictured with clarity the extent of the transformation. Muñoz's experience in the United States enabled him to imagine the entire island as a city comparable to New York. According to Muñoz, economic development promised to improve the livelihood of Puerto Ricans and to reshape the island's culture.

Muñoz's disposition toward economic development did not find an appropriate context until the start of the New Deal. The reconstruction plan of federal authorities coincided with Muñoz's interest in "modernizing" Puerto Rico. As noted in previous chapters, to join the local New Deal, Muñoz and his colleagues presented themselves to U.S. officials as "a generation educated in the United States ... sympathetic with the best in American life."[165] Despite the potential of the New Deal, the program did not live up to its promise. The failure of the PRERA and PRRA hit Muñoz most severely. After savoring the possibility of economic development, Muñoz saw the New Deal crumble along with his vision of transforming Puerto Rico into a modern society.

Far from relinquishing his goal, Muñoz faced the challenge shared by many other groups in favor of reform. If Muñoz wished for his vision to have an impact on the island's society, his goal demanded negotiations and compromises with other agents aiming for social justice. The mobilization of mass support for the PPD demonstrated the potential of collective action and the futility of single-handed efforts to introduce reforms. As a party that grew, thanks to a myriad of interests, the PPD not only revived for Muñoz the promise of the New Deal but also offered a platform to enhance the appeal of economic development. While many supporters formulated their views and appealed to PPD leaders, Muñoz discussed, debated, and nurtured the compromises that best suited the aims of his party. To be sure, all agents placed their views at the mercy of other people's acquiescence but they did not share this burden evenly. The aims of Muñoz thrived with an advantage not accessible, for example, to labor and independentists: his own acquiescence. What made Muñoz's approval so predominant had largely, but not exclusively, to do with the expectations of people at the time. Tired of the sterile politics of the depression era, Puerto Ricans made clear their thirst for earnest leadership. Muñoz stepped into the fray of politics, pledged to uphold those expectations, and steered the standards of leadership into unforeseen realms. With a degree of compliance to the demands of people as well as a disposition for political manipulation, Muñoz fashioned himself as a leader above and beyond petty interests.

Instead of relying entirely on the logic of his arguments or the orginality of his proposals, Muñoz based his political legitimacy on claiming qualities unavailable to any other leader. Unsurprisingly, Muñoz's political style is often compared with the manifestation of hidden powers or special abilities that defy logic. While Edgardo Rodríguez Juliá describes Muñoz as an "old Merlin" or "magician" performing an act imbued with "creole surrealism," Carlos Gil views him as a "shaman" or "priest-prophet" often undergoing "trances" and "rituals" to reveal occult messages to his people.[166] Similarly, Arcadio Díaz Quiñones portrays Muñoz as a "poet-politician-translator" and his disposition to "deal with" problems as part of a "poetics of action."[167] By stressing the elusive character of Muñoz's leadership, these authors shed light on a key feature of populism. The intense rapport between the leaders and followers of populist movements does not depend simply on a party's program, electoral campaigns, governmental policies, or the doling out of relief. Too strong an emphasis on those aspects would fail to acknowledge the full experience of agents or the irreducible ambiguousness of the movement. From a perspective that focuses on the plurality of agents and their discourses, the bond between PPD leaders and followers largely depended on their constant effort to negotiate a basis for reform and reshape, accordingly, their visions of consent.

By acting as a "shaman" or "prophet" ready to expedite the most urgent "dreams" of Puerto Ricans, Muñoz did much more than foster his role as main leader of the island's mass movement. The special qualities he claimed as leader remained vague enough to converge with a vast array of demands and interests. Bound by the need to negotiate his way to power, Muñoz made his leadership available to other groups with words and actions that left room for interpretation. As they threaded a fluid ground of interaction, PPD leaders and followers shaped the discourse of consent as much with their compromises as with the uneven relationship of power between them. While the agents of mass politics heightened the importance of common action and sustained the elastic meaning of consent, Muñoz and the PPD used their resources to steer the mass movement in a certain direction. As noted, through the articulation of traditional values such as those of rural people, the PPD blurred the gap between its own interests in economic development and the demand for reform of other groups. To secure the acceptance of projects to "modernize" the island, the PPD packaged and delivered its pleas for change using common features of people's everyday life. Only after a prolonged interim in which the PPD coalesced with many advocates of reform, Muñoz and his adherents managed to resume the New Deal policies of economic development.

As sociologist Emilio Pantojas García indicates, the Chardón Plan of the 1930s informed the PPD's socioeconomic program of the 1940s.[168] During the first two years of Tugwell's administration, the PPD enacted its main projects. Agrarian reform such as the application of the 500-acre law and the redistribution of land came with the creation of the Land Authority—Autoridad de Tierras—in 1941. With Carlos Chardón as its first director, the Land Authority intervened with corporations that had land in excess of the 500-acre limit. Besides breaking up corporate land, the key policies of the Land Authority included the proportional profit farms, the individual farms program, and the distribution of small plots of land.[169] Despite introducing benefits in the lives of Puerto Ricans, according to James L. Dietz, "the attack on the absentee sugar corporations never went beyond what was necessary to reorganize the industry and was little more than symbolic reform necessary for the consolidation of the PPD's power."[170]

The program of industrial development began in 1942 with the enactment of the "Compañía de Fomento," also known as the Puerto Rico Industrial Development Company (PRIDCO). Teodoro Moscoso became the general manager of PRIDCO. The agency acquired first a cement factory of the PRRA.[171] This publicly owned enterprise offered a good example by operating successfully even when faced with shortages during the war. With the cement factory as a model and many other projects on the drawing board, Moscoso and his team set as their goal to build light industries dependent on local raw materials and oriented toward the local market. PRIDCO soon started the construction of plants to manufacture several products such as glass, cardboard, shoes, and ceramic items.[172] These state-based factories, PRIDCO argued, did not aim to displace private capital or U.S. interests but to serve as pilot projects in a program of import-substitution during the war period. According to Dietz, "to avoid political and economic crises that might have driven the PPD from power, it was necessary to respect the constraints of what was regarded as acceptable capitalist and colonial behavior."[173]

The plan of the PPD to develop the island informed the backdrop of Muñoz's vision of consent. During the interval between the PPD's first legislative session in 1941 and the next one in 1942, when the party approved most of its program, Muñoz produced an interpretation of contemporary events in Puerto Rico. As was the case with the authors of *Organización obrera* and *El despertar de un pueblo*, Muñoz understood that a book-length publication could best portray the island's situation during the early 1940s. He wrote a manuscript that was published many years later as *La Historia del Partido Popular Democrático*.[174] This book offers an unusual glimpse of Muñoz's outlook at the start of the PPD's political endeavors. Although the book's scope is broad and delves into the island's past, Muñoz elaborated further many tenets of the PPD's campaign propaganda. He did not miss the opportunity to make a familiar claim. Muñoz envisioned himself, his party, and "the people" as interchangeable entities. In Muñoz's version of events, to speak about him or his party is to speak about all Puerto Ricans. Muñoz made clear his claim: "we were all part of a spiritual organism in rapid development."[175] By presenting himself, his party, and "the people" as a single being, Muñoz concocted a vision of consent that could be grasped without looking beyond his own utterances. Although never stated in terms that are too obvious, Muñoz's account leaves little room to the imagination when it leads the reader to believe that he was not just a spokesman of Puerto Ricans but Puerto Rico itself voicing its aspirations.

The implications of Muñoz's vision of consent should not be underestimated. Except for his imprecise description of the upper and lower echelons of Puerto Rican society, Muñoz left unanswered in his book who exactly the people are. After noting that "habits and concepts" are the main "frontier" dividing society in two sectors, Muñoz made no reference to specific party supporters. Absent from his text are the negotiations, compromises, and plurality of interests that informed the PPD as well as the possibility to grasp the party as a "decentered" site of interaction. Muñoz rendered invisible the groups that had joined the PPD in accordance with a mutual understanding between themselves and the party. Indeed, Muñoz's book is the first installment of a historiography that gave no credit to groups such as the UPD, CGT, PCP, MIS, and CPI that informed the rise of the PPD.[176] Other groups such as peasants, farmers, teachers, and women suffered similar consequences. Muñoz credited these agents only after cleansing them of their own perceptions and reducing them to offshoots of his vague, barren, and docile notion of "the people."

Muñoz did much more than render the history of PPD supporters invisible. Besides glossing over the interests of many groups, Muñoz filled the gaps in his account with his own uncompromising views about people's aspirations. By speaking as the embodiment of Puerto Rico, Muñoz presented his life experiences and outlook as those of the entire island. Muñoz not only acknowledged himself to be the product of the Puerto Rican and American culture but also saw his cultural background as applicable to Puerto Rico:

The people and the historical process, searching blindly for servants, found one free of group solidarities, attentive to the immemorial significance of the people—the people: creator under God of history, idioms, justices, gods—, cured from birth of any fright or seduction of posts, glory, social or personal importance; being his spirit in conjunction with two wide cultures that unite themselves in this island and will coordinate and understand themselves in this hemisphere.[177]

As "one free of group solidarities" and with a" spirit in conjunction" with Puerto Rican and U.S. culture, Muñoz aimed for the trust of his people and what he saw as the best future for the island. Contrary to Géigel, Muñoz believed that Puerto Ricans could make a place for themselves in the modern world under the influence of the United States. Far from seeing the U.S. and local culture as incompatible, Muñoz viewed the blend of both heritages as most beneficial. He said that the culture of "our people" comes from Spain and is influenced by the United States.[178] The island's Spanish heritage, Muñoz argued, could use the attributes of American traditions. According to Muñoz, the rich virtues that Puerto Rico acquired from Spain such as religious devotion and human dignity went along with flaws, meaning a deficient grasp of collective needs and organization.[179] Muñoz stressed that U.S. values could fix the problem. For Muñoz, a cultural merger promised the best future for Puerto Rico and Latin America:

What is being fused in Puerto Rico are the emotive and spiritual factors of Spanish democracy with the dynamic and organizational ones of American democracy—the profound Spanish respect for men and the genuine American respect for the citizen; the Spanish sense of human equality, the American genius to organize the citizen's equality. Possibly here, the democratic forces of Hispanic tradition will finally encounter the manner to organize themselves permanently in government, in collectivity, in order, in creation, after acquiring those virtues of American democracy. It seems dignified to note what is sighted for the future of Hispanic democracy in all America under the light ignited by Puerto Rican democracy.[180]

Muñoz imagined a society in which Puerto Ricans could feel at ease despite the infusion of American values. He envisioned a future that depended on the capacities of the United States. According to Muñoz, garnering the attributes of American traditions was less an option than a historical necessity. The leader of the PPD praised the U.S. heritage because it could offer what the island's culture did not receive from Spain. Muñoz argued that American individualism had proven to facilitate "action," "collective achievements," and "physical creation."[181] On the one hand, according to Muñoz, the U.S. culture stood for entrepreneurs such as Henry Ford, who used "initiative," "capacity," and "organizational individualism" for the benefit of production. On the other hand, Muñoz argued, the U.S. culture stood for leaders such as Franklin D. Roosevelt, who counterbalanced with rules and protections the worst excesses of American capacity for economic development.[182]

Muñoz believed that Puerto Rican and American customs translated, correspondingly, into emotional and rational essences. By stereotyping the U.S. culture with facile assumptions about its rational attributes, Muñoz sought to equate the United States with economic development. According to Muñoz, American pragmatism corresponded to the logic of production. This meant for Muñoz that the United States could lead the way to overcome stagnation in Puerto Rico. Muñoz's argument is unusual in the sense that it does not rely on raw numerical data to portray as essential the PPD's plan for economic development. Agencies such as PRIDCO shouldered the effort to justify the colonial policies of production with a vast array of quantitative measurements.[183] As a politician worried about the mood swings of the public, Muñoz's tools of the trade consisted of symbols, values, and meanings to render understandable the policies that colonial authorities saw as best for Puerto Rico. Besides offering insights about his concerns as a politician, the cultural assumptions of Muñoz exemplify the context of political action confronted by PPD leaders. Faced with the difficulty of catering to local and mainland interests, Muñoz and his peers defined culture as a realm of constructive exchanges.

Muñoz enjoyed the benefits of leadership but remained bound to an array of groups acting collectively to introduce reforms. His tactics and rhetoric did not escape the challenge faced by other agents of the island's mass movement. Since so much was at stake with a movement that could act forcefully to demand improvements, the leaders and followers of the PPD did more than voice their concerns and vigorously defend their interests. Beyond the safety of narrow opinions, people offered visions of consent that neither foreclosed the common interest in reform nor guaranteed a compatibility of agendas. This assertion applies to Muñoz, a leader who shared with other agents an interest in U.S. policies of reform but offered a different approach to secure them. Muñoz's cosmetic references about American cultural values reveal his interest in the regulatory functions of the New Deal.[184] Without fully acknowledging it, Muñoz particularly marveled at the innovations of the federal government to save the capitalist economy. Muñoz thought that the role played by President Roosevelt in the United States could be extended to Puerto Rico.[185] The leader of the PPD appointed himself as an impartial agent, as "one free of group solidarities," to provide the safeguards needed for proper economic management.[186] No doubt existed in Muñoz's mind that the New Deal of Roosevelt could be adapted to local conditions. However, Muñoz's elaborate vision about a cultural blend illustrates that such an adaptation demanded a broad reinterpretation of the island's colonial reality.

The cultural influence of the United States in Puerto Rico had for Muñoz a political counterpart. Although the assertions of Muñoz about the status issue are ambiguous in his book, he mentioned the need to consider "a new sense of sovereignty."[187] Muñoz's perception of "a world in a state of transition" focused on what is best known today as "globalization" to rethink the island's political future.[188] According to Muñoz, as the world became smaller due to such factors as faster means of transportation and communication, countries faced a greater need for understanding and cooperation between them. The leader of the PPD presented a view of international affairs that minimized the value of sovereignty. Muñoz tacitly narrowed the status choices for Puerto Rico to autonomy, an option that corresponded with his notion of global interdependency. The effort of Muñoz to find a political middle ground for the island mirrored his role as an intermediary for U.S. colonialism. Muñoz favored a status option that would leave untouched the "brokerage" of the PPD between Puerto Rico and the United States.

Muñoz's interest in economic development and autonomy as expressed, incipiently, in his vision of consent left no room for reform or sovereignty as demanded by the CGT and CPI. Muñoz's vision of consent and the displacement of groups such as the CGT and CPI are two sides of the same coin. The leader of the PPD wanted to preempt any challenge to economic interests that became more evident each day. Muñoz and the PPD procured without delay the transition from social justice to the policies of industrial production. The PPD's discourse articulated the reorientation of priorities. Soon after the creation of PRIDCO, Muñoz sent a letter to Moscoso inviting him to write a piece for *La Democracia*.[189] Moscoso welcomed the opportunity with an article about the potential of PRIDCO to avert the near "catastrophe" posed by all sorts of maladies in Puerto Rico. According to Moscoso, the island's problems manifested themselves in the form of "extreme poverty, chronic unemployment, illiteracy, malnutrition, city slums, and social irresponsibility."[190] This situation, Moscoso said, ensued from resources that were scarce, mismanaged, and badly distributed. He placed aside the discussion of political and social aspects.

For the general manager of PRIDCO, the extreme problems of the island demanded extreme solutions. Emigration and birth control, Moscoso argued, were "desirable" measures but did not work as fast as industrialization. PRIDCO was one of many drastic policies that meant for Moscoso the adaptation of the New Deal to Puerto Rico.[191] The logic of Moscoso's argument depended on how well different policies met his expectations. Missing from his approval or dismissal of different options is any consideration about the people to be affected by his proposals. Moscoso placed aside emigration and birth control because they are "impractical and slow" not because of discussions about who would leave the island or undergo policies to limit childbirths. Moreover, instead of invalidating emigration and birth control, Moscoso simply left them on the drawing board. In this respect, an aspect that demands attention is what Alex W. Maldonado calls "Moscoso's unshakable tenet."[192] According to Maldonado, Moscoso believed "that the most fundamental long-range solution was to lower the island's birth rate dramatically through widespread birth control programs."[193] The fact that Moscoso had such an inclination for drastic measures and "was so single-minded in his effort to industrialize Puerto Rico" should not be taken simply as the idiosyncrasies of one individual. Moscoso's position on key issues mirrored the PPD's tendency to rely less on dialogue and consultation as it steered the island's mass movement into a new direction. While Moscoso vaunted the benefits of industrial development, the

PPD backed PRIDCO with writings that focused less on reform and more on economic issues.[194]

The displacement of groups and perceptions alien to PPD's interests eased the transition from social justice to industrial production. The arguments of PPD leaders to legitimate their own actions and vision also helped to reorient political priorities. Muñoz played a key role in this process. His message to gather mass support was as important as how he delivered that message. The leader of the PPD conceived for himself an image that laid an aura on his actions and words. He bore the nickname of "el Vate"—the Poet—a title bestowed by Muñoz's colleagues to denote his easygoing character and trustworthiness.[195] The emphasis given to Muñoz's colloquial disposition implied that his claims could mean only the best for Puerto Rico. Muñoz also made sure that the beneficiaries of reform credited him with the improvements in their lives. That was the case when Muñoz took part in the first distribution of small plots of the Land Authority to make a speech.[196] Muñoz's cameo appearances at ground zero of reform served as tokens to beef up his notion of a special nexus between himself and "the people."

A good example of Muñoz's effort to build an image is his self-assigned role as a purveyor of welfare between 1943 and 1944. The exchange of letters that the PPD encouraged between Muñoz and his audience enabled the party to conceive its leader as an unofficial intermediary of relief agencies such as the Works Projects Administration.[197] Muñoz answered the public's request for aid with reassurances, referrals, or statements about policies. By drafting letters to answer a wide range of requests, Muñoz presented himself as an indispensable agent for the distribution of relief. As an informal avenue of communication, the exchange of letters between Muñoz and his audience nurtured a sense of complicity that reinforced Muñoz's image as a worthy ally.

Under these circumstances, it is not difficult to grasp how Muñoz informed the reorientation of policies of the PPD. The aura that Muñoz claimed for himself as a special breed of leader enabled him to bridge social justice and industrial production despite the contrasts between these measures. By stressing Muñoz's trustworthiness and his zeal for "the people," the PPD displayed its leader as the best guarantor of the benefits of different policies. Several press releases of Muñoz explained the transition from reform to economic development.[198] According to Muñoz, measures to increase production such as PRIDCO constituted the second phase of the PPD's program. Increasing production, Muñoz argued, overlapped with the PPD's first set of policies, which called for a fair distribution of resources. Muñoz's words paralleled the activities of local and federal agents concerned with industrial development. Consider, for example, the meeting of the Anglo-American Caribbean Commission of 1944. Several functionaries such as Moscoso, Rafael Picó, Antonio Fernós Isern, and Charles W. Taussig underscored not the U.S. policies of reform in Puerto Rico but the economic needs that made indispensable the industrialization of the island.[199]

By the end of 1944, the PPD had several reasons to celebrate. Besides cheering its landslide electoral victory, the PPD reveled in seeing the initiatives of PRIDCO in full swing. In December, PRIDCO completed its bottle factory, the Puerto Rico Glass Corporation (PRGC).[200] Many problems tested the resolve of PRIDCO such as the slow delivery of machinery, the plant's faulty design, high operation costs, delays in production, and the low quality of the plant's first bottles.[201] PRIDCO officials, however, did not lose faith in their project. As the first major endeavor of Moscoso's agency, the construction and inauguration of the PRGC received much attention. Conferences and press releases highlighted the technological prowess of the factory.[202] According to Moscoso and his team, even by U.S. standards, the PRGC's capacity was nothing short of a marvel. The bottle factory, PRIDCO announced, could supply the whole Puerto Rican market and still export to the rest of the Caribbean.[203]

Great expectations surrounded the start of operations of the PRGC as well as its sister plants already under construction. Maldonado describes well the impression caused by the initial activities of PRIDCO's industrial complex near the capital: "The sheer physical impact of what [Moscoso] called 'little Pittsburgh' across San Juan Bay—the factory buildings, the line of tall stacks, the congested traffic, the movement of goods, plus the noise—were all dramatic proof that Puerto Rico was being industrialized."[204] During the final days of 1944, Muñoz and his party could feel certain about the future. While the main elements of Muñoz's vision of consent seemed ever more present, the agents that challenged it steadily became for the PPD a woeful remnant of the past.

NOTES

1. Marshall Berman, *All That Is Solid Melts into Air: The Experience of Modernity* (New York: Penguin Books, 1988), p. 11.

2. Anna Marie Smith, *Laclau and Mouffe: The Radical Democratic Imaginary* (London: Routledge, 1998), p. 174.

3. Jacob Torfing, *New Theories of Discourse: Laclau, Mouffe, and Žižek* (Oxford: Blackwell Publishers, 1999), pp. 111-113.

4. Smith, *Laclau and Mouffe*, pp. 177-181.

5. Obreros Unidos de las Ferrovías de Puerto Rico, *Primer Congreso* (San Juan: Baldrich, 1942), p. 5, Colección Puertorriqueña, Biblioteca José M. Lázaro, Universidad de Puerto Rico. Hereafter referred to as CPR/UPR. The congress was held in Ponce, February 22, 1942.

6. Ibid., pp. 9-10.

7. Juan Angel Silén, *Apuntes para la historia del movimiento obrero puertorriqueño* (Río Piedras: Editorial Cultural, 1978), pp. 110-111.

8. *El Mundo*, January 2, 1943.

9. *El Mundo*, October 29 and November 6, 1943. The CGT's lobbying efforts abroad exemplified its militancy. According to Miles Galvin, "the CGT from the outset had a clearly left-of-center thrust. Its international affiliation, for example, was with the *Confederación de Trabajadores de America Latina* (CTAL), the western hemispheric branch of the leftist World Federation of Trade Unions (WFTU), from which the AFL had split because of Communist domination." Miles Galvin, *The Organized Labor Movement in Puerto Rico* (London: Associated University Presses, 1979), p. 100.

10. *El Mundo*, June 28, 1943.

11. René Jiménez Malaret, *Organización obrera: Discursos en torno al movimiento obrero de Puerto Rico* (San Juan: Editorial Esther, 1943). CPR/UPR.

12. Ibid., p. 5. See also p. 25.

13. Ibid., p. 71.

14. Ibid., pp. 14, 22-26, 71-73, 87.

15. Ibid., pp. 6, 37, 52.

16. Ibid., p. 56.

17. *La Democracia*, February 4, September 9, 1943.

18. *La Democracia*, February 4, 1943.

19. Ibid.

20. Ortiz's perception comes close to the notion of corporatism. Philippe Schmitter and Gerhard Lehmbruch, eds., *Trends toward Corporatist Intermediation* (Beverly Hills: Sage Publications, 1982); Wyn Grant, ed., *The Political Economy of Corporatism* (New York: Cambridge University Press, 1983).

21. *La Democracia*, September 9, 1943.

22. *El Mundo*, June 28, 1943.

23. *La Democracia*, July 7, 8, 1943.

24. *El Mundo*, June 28, 1943. The CGT also saluted Stalin, the CIO, and joined CTAL.

25. War Department, "Prospective Political Plans of the General Confederation of Laborers (CGT) in Latin America," February 13, 1943, File 9-8, "Confidential" Central Classified Files, Division of Territories and Insular Possessions, Department of the Interior (Record Group 126), National Archives and Records Administration. Hereafter referred to as File 9-8-C, DTIP, RG 126, NARA. This document offers a rare glimpse of the CGT's potential to sway the island's politics. Early in 1943, an informant of the War Department interviewed Pascual Sáez Corales, brother of Juan Sáez Corales, secretary of the CGT in Puerto Rico. According to the findings of the War Department, "Pascual Sáez Corales stated that the 'Union System' of the working classes is being gradually infiltrated into the people's conscience. In Puerto Rico the fact that the working class movements are holding an important position in the political evolution and economical [*sic*] development of the island, has been overlooked." In addition, according to the War Department,

Pascual Sáez Corales stated, "We have [in Puerto Rico] the Tugwell case. Who is supporting Tugwell? It is the working class organizations affiliated to the CGT. Should we cease backing Tugwell, he would be immediately removed. In this case the Popular Party would lose a great deal. We are getting, in exchange, a good return, i.e., laws passed by the Popular Party, which controls the Legislature, approved by Tugwell, that are in harmony with the ideology of the CGT. Among these laws are 'The Minimum Wage Law,' which is applied to past transactions (retroactive); right of the Public Service Commission to intervene in the sugar factories; and other of the same nature which have so favorably affected the workers that they find themselves each day more closely attached to the CGT, thus making the organization more powerful every day."

26. *El Mundo*, June 29, 1943. Silén, *Apuntes para la historia del movimiento obrero puertorriqueño*, pp. 112-113.

27. *El Mundo*, April 8, 10, 19, 21, May 4, 8, 15, 1944.

28. *El Mundo*, May 8, 15, 1944.

29. Gervasio L. García and Angel G. Quintero Rivera, *Desafío y solidaridad: Breve historia del movimiento obrero puertorriqueño* (Río Piedras: Ediciones Huracán, 1986); Emilio González Díaz, "La Lucha de Clases y la Política en el Puerto Rico de la Década 40: El ascenso del PPD," *Revista de Ciencias Sociales* 22, no. 1-2 (March-June 1980): 37-69; Emilio González Díaz, "Class Struggle and Politics in Puerto Rico During the Decade of the 40's: The Rise of PDP," *Two Thirds* 2, no. 1 (1979): pp. 46-57; Silén, *Apuntes para la historia del movimiento obrero puertorriqueño*; Angel G. Quintero Rivera, *Conflictos de clase y Política en Puerto Rico* (Río Piedras: Ediciones Huracán, 1977).

30. Silén, *Apuntes para la historia del movimiento obrero puertorriqueño*, pp. 112-113.

31. Of course, in hindsight, the CGT's approach to politics can be seen as folly. Many years after the division of the union, Sáez Corales concluded that "ingenuousness and lack of political vision contributed" to the CGT's downfall. Despite this shortcoming, the CGT managed to articulate a bold discourse about its consent toward reform and social justice in the 1940s. Juan Sáez Corales, "Twenty-Five Years of Struggle—My Reply to Persecution" (1955), in Angel Quintero Rivera, ed., *Workers' Struggle in Puerto Rico: A Documentary History* (New York: Monthly Review Press, 1976), pp. 156-157.

32. *El Mundo*, December 29, 1943, February 3, 1944.

33. Concentración de Izquierdas Sociales, *Manifiesto a todos los hombres y mujeres de Puerto Rico que quieren la JUSTICIA SOCIAL* (San Juan: El Imparcial, 1942), Fundación Luis Muñoz Marín, Archivo Luis Muñoz Marín, Sección IV, Fotocopias. Hereafter referred to as FLMM/ALMM, IV-FC. The MIS organized itself and produced its "Manifesto" several months before its meeting of 1944. The assembly of the MIS, however, formalized the stance of these political dissidents. Historian Juan Angel Silén mentions the early initiative of the MIS. Juan Angel Silén, *Historia de Puerto Rico* (Santo Domingo: SUSAETA, 1993), p. 207; Juan Angel Silén, *Historia de la nación puertorriqueña* (Río Piedras: Editorial Edil, 1973), p. 240. Although it seems that the MIS was mostly the initiative of Socialists, later on, individuals with other political affiliations joined the organization. *El Mundo*, December 29, 1943, February 3, 1944. Additional information about the MIS can be found in: Angel G. Quintero Rivera, "Bases sociales de la transformación ideológica del Partido Popular en la década del '40," in Gerardo Navas Dávila, ed., *Cambio y desarrollo en Puerto Rico: La transformación ideológica del Partido Popular Democrático* (San Juan: Editorial de la Universidad de Puerto Rico, 1980), pp. 86-87.

34. Early in 1943—a year before the PCP's decision to disband their party— the relationship between the CGT, PPD, and Communists remained ambiguous at best. Consider the statements of Pascual Sáez Corales to an informant of the War Department. The War Department summarized its findings as follows:

Pascual Sáez Corales stated that there exists a complete understanding between the CGT and the Popular Party. . . . The Popular Party, whose ideology is purely Communistic, has the unconditional support and cooperation of the CGT because their ideals are quite similar. Pascual Sáez Corales stated that there are many enemies of Communism in Puerto Rico and thus the CGT can not as yet give the open impression of being frankly fighting for this ideal . The Popular Party, in the public opinion, is openly pro-Communistic. Pascual Sáez Corales stated that the CGT is not in a condition to declare itself working in conjunction with the Popular Party. However, the CGT is working wisely to infiltrate into the masses the reformatory tendencies and political reformations of the Popular Party. . . . Sáez Corales stated that on February 5, 1943, his brother (Juan) called for a meeting of the CGT at the cock-fighting area of Senator's Dávila's house, Manatí, P.R. (Senator Dávila is a Popular Party leader). At the same time, a meeting of the Popular Party leaders was announced to take place in Manatí. According to Pascual Sáez Corales both meetings were to be held in the same place. (War Department, "Prospective Political Plans of the General Confederation of Laborers (CGT) in Latin America," February 13, 1943, File 9-8-C, DTIP, RG 126, NARA).

35. Juan Santos Rivera, *Puerto Rico: Ayer, hoy y mañana* (San Juan: Editorial Moderna, 1944). This is the chairman's report of the PCP's Central Committee. See also *El Mundo*, February 1, 3, 1944.

36. Santos, *Puerto Rico*, pp. 14-15, 23-24.

37. Ibid., pp. 21, 33.

38. Ibid., pp. 28-30.

39. Ibid., pp. 29-31.

40. Ibid., pp. 16-18. See also Wilfredo Mattos Cintrón, *La política y lo político en Puerto Rico* (México, DF: Ediciones ERA, 1980), pp. 121-123, 201-203 n.157.

41. *El Mundo*, May 8, 15, 1944. Francisco Colón Gordiany was out of Puerto Rico when Ramos Antonini made his move. *El Mundo*, May 7, 1943; Higinio Feliciano Avilés, "Origen, desarrollo y división de la Confederacion General de Trabajadores de Puerto Rico" (M.A. diss., University of Puerto Rico, 1976).

42. *El Mundo*, May 17, 18, 23, 24, 1944. The CGT had expressed its misgivings about Ramos Antonini before this incident took place. *El Mundo*, April 8, 10, 21, 1944.

43. Silén, *Apuntes para la historia del movimiento obrero puertorriqueño*, pp. 115-116. See also Kenneth Lugo, "Dos documentos perdidos de nuestra historia laboral," *Homines* 11, no. 1-2 (1987-1988): 164-177; Kenneth Lugo, "Un Peculiar Manifiesto Obrero Puertorriqueño - Epoca Confederación General de Trabajadores," *Homines* 13, no. 1 (February-July 1989): 226-235.

44. *El Mundo*, August 11, 1944; *La Democracia*, September 22, 1944; *El Mundo*, September 25, 1944.

45. *El Mundo*, July 30, August 10, 1944.

46. *El Mundo*, July 30, August 30, 1944.

47. *El Mundo*, July 31, August 14, 30, 31, 1944.

48. *El Mundo*, September 5, 22, 1944.

49. *El Mundo*, October 7, 9, 11, 1944.

50. At the same time that the FLT called for a "pact of honor," the union initiated a "round table" to discuss labor issues in the sugar industry. *El Mundo*, September 27, October 9, 10, 1944.

51. *El Mundo*, October 27, 1944.

52. *El Mundo*, December 7, November 30, 1944.

53. *El Mundo*, December 15, 1944. Labor sectors sympathetic to Ramos Antonini and the PPD, such as *público* drivers and dockyard workers, expressed their discontent with the CGT. *El Mundo*, December 5, 10, 1944.

54. Robert W. Anderson, *Party Politics in Puerto Rico* (Stanford, CA: Stanford University Press, 1965), pp. 52-55.

55. Ibid., p. 54.

56. Luis Muñoz Marín, *La Historia del Partido Popular Democrático* (San Juan: Editorial El Batey, 1984), p. 68. Although published in 1984, Muñoz wrote most of this book between 1941 and 1942.

57. Thomas G. Paterson, J. Garry Clifford, and Kenneth J. Hagan, eds., *American Foreign Relations: A History* (Lexington, MA: D. C. Heath and Company, 1995), pp. 206-209.

58. Ibid., p. 209.

59. María del Pilar Argüelles, *Morality and Power: The U.S. Colonial Experience in Puerto Rico from 1898 to 1948* (Lanham, MD: University Press of America, 1996), p. 122.

60. Surendra Bhana, *The United States and the Development of the Puerto Rican Status Question, 1936-1968* (Lawrence: University Press of Kansas, 1975), pp. 57-58.

61. Ibid., p. 59.

62. Argüelles, *Morality and Power*, p. 142.

63. Several authors agree on this point. Amalia Alsina Orozco, *Los Congresos Pro-Independencia* (San Juan: Editora Corripio, 1994), pp. 22-24, 31; Anderson, *Party Politics in Puerto Rico*, p. 56; Argüelles, *Morality and Power*, p. 143; Bhana, *The United States*, p. 74; Carmelo Rosario Natal, *Luis Muñoz Marín y la Indedependencia de Puerto Rico (1907-1946)* (San Juan: Producciones Históricas, 1994), p. 177.

64. *El Mundo*, April 8, 9, 10, 12, 1943.

65. Alsina Orozco, *Los Congresos Pro-Independencia*, pp. 30-31.

66. *El Mundo*, July 12, 1943.

67. *El Mundo*, April 8, 9, 1943.

68. Alsina Orozco, *Los Congresos Pro-Independencia*, pp. 31, 37, 39, 41; *El Mundo*, April 11, 1943.

69. Alsina Orozco, *Los Congresos Pro-Independencia*, pp. 31, 41.

70. Félix Ojeda Reyes, *Vito Marcantonio y Puerto Rico: Por los trabajadores y por la nación* (Río Piedras: Ediciones Huracán, 1978); *El Mundo*, June 15, 18, 19, 1943.

71. *El Mundo*, June 25, July 12, August 2, 1943.

72. *El Mundo*, July 12, 1943; Alsina Orozco, *Los Congresos Pro-Independencia*, p. 32.

73. A provocative discussion about the relationship between independentists and Communists can be found in Arcadio Díaz Quiñones, *Conversación con José Luis González* (Río Piedras: Editorial Huracán, 1976), pp. 96-106.

74. Consider, for example, Vicente Géigel Polanco, *Legislación social de Puerto Rico* (San Juan: Negociado de Materiales, Imprenta y Transporte, 1936).

75. Vicente Géigel Polanco, *El despertar de un pueblo* (San Juan: Biblioteca de Autores Puertorriqueños, 1942). CPR/UPR.

76. Ibid., pp. 8-9, 33-35, 82, 91-99, 115-116.

77. Ibid., pp. 51-59. Géigel said: "We confess the sad truth that we still have not been able to bring our people together. This multitude . . . are merely a bunch of poor devils that are willing to carry their anguish under the banners of political parties." Ibid., p. 51.

78. Ibid., pp. 12-13, 119-131. Although a haphazard process informed the articulation of the PPD's discourse, party leaders constantly focused on key ideas such as the notion of "the people." Literary critics highlight the threads that underlay the discursive practices and political rhetoric of writers of Géigel's generation. Arcadio Díaz Quiñones, "Recordando el Futuro Imaginario: La Escritura Histórica en la Década del Treinta," *Sin Nombre* 14, no. 3 (1984): 21-35; Arcadio Díaz Quiñones, *La Memoria Rota* (Río Piedras: Ediciones Huracán, 1993); Juan G. Gelpí, *Literatura y paternalismo en Puerto Rico* (Río Piedras: Editorial de la Universidad de Puerto Rico, 1993).

79. García and Quintero Rivera, *Desafío y solidaridad*, pp. 33-34. Of course, not all calls for independence caused apprehension among workers. A sector of labor identified with the CGT's working-class nationalism, which was different to that of Géigel and his peers. For the CGT's view about the status issue, see "Third CGT Congress Report by Secretary General Juan Sáez Corales" (1945), in Quintero Rivera, *Workers' Struggle in Puerto Rico*, pp. 144-146.

80. For a discussion about the shortcomings of nationalist discourses in Puerto Rico, see: Ramón Grosfoguel, "The Divorce of Nationalist Discourses from the Puerto Rican People: A Sociohistorical Perspective," in Frances Negrón-Muntaner and Ramón Grosfoguel, eds., *Puerto Rican Jam: Essays on Culture and Politics* (Minneapolis: University of Minnesota Press, 1997), pp. 57-76.

81. Géigel, *El despertar de un pueblo*, p. 56.

82. Ibid., pp. 41, 66-69, 84, 87, 89, 102-115.

83. Ibid.

84. Carlos Gil offer an analysis of *El despertar de un pueblo* in Carlos Gil, *El orden del tiempo: Ensayos sobre el robo del presente en la utopia puertorriqueña* (San Juan: Editorial Posdata, 1994), pp. 80-100.

85. Géigel, *El despertar de un pueblo*, p. 103.

86. Ibid., pp. 42-47.

87. Ibid., p. 48.

88. Ibid., pp. 45-46.

89. Grosfoguel, "The Divorce of Nationalist Discourses from the Puerto Rican People," p. 68.

90. Ibid., pp. 68, 74. In a similar vein, Arcadio Díaz Quiñones' notion of *arte de bregar* (literally, the "art of dealing with") stresses how Puerto Ricans solve difficulties on the island or the mainland opting for subtle tactics other than a direct confrontation. Arcadio Díaz Quiñones, *El arte de bregar: Ensayos* (San Juan: Ediciones Callejón, 2000).

91. Rosario Natal, *Luis Muñoz Marín y la Indedependencia de Puerto Rico*; Alex W. Maldonado, *Teodoro Moscoso and Puerto Rico's Operation Bootstrap* (Gainesville: University of Florida Press, 1997); Carlos R. Zapata Oliveras, *"Nuevos Caminos hacia Viejos Objetivos": Estados Unvidos y el Establecimiento del Estado Libre Asociado de Puerto Rico (1945-1953)* (Río Piedras: Editorial Edil, 1991); Carlos R. Zapata Oliveras, *De independentista a autonomista: La transformación del pensamiento político de Luis Muñoz Marín (1931-1949)* (San Juan: Fundación Luis Muñoz Marín, 2003). Zapata Oliveras and Maldonado go as far as to pinpoint the threshold of Muñoz's shift toward autonomy. According to these authors, Muñoz cried and opted for autonomy after he read a report of economist Ben Dorfman that confirmed to him the impossibility of independence. Zapata Oliveras, *"Nuevos Caminos hacia Viejos Objetivos,"* p. 178; Maldonado, *Teodoro Moscoso and Puerto Rico's Operation Bootstrap*, pp. 50-51. The problem with this perspective is that it presents the transformation of Muñoz's political thought as a seamless process above and beyond a power struggle within his party. For example, in Zapata's *De independentista a autonomista*, little attention is paid to the bitter conflict that ensued between Muñoz and the independentists, which climaxed with the expulsion of the latter from the PPD in 1946. Muñoz reacted against independentists and certain labor activists in his party as he came closer to political power.

92. Emilio González Díaz, "El Populismo en Puerto Rico: 1938-1952" (Ph.D. diss., UNAM, 1977); Emilio González Díaz, "Muñoz, el populismo y el ELA," *Claridad*, July 25-31, 1980, pp. 2-3; Gerardo Navas Dávila, ed., *Cambio y desarrollo en Puerto Rico: La transformación ideológica del Partido Popular Democrático* (San Juan: Editorial Universitaria, 1980).

93. Gerardo Navas Dávila, *La Dialéctica del Desarrollo Nacional: El Caso de Puerto Rico* (Río Piedras: Editorial de la Universidad de Puerto Rico, 1978).

94. Rafael Alberto Bernabe and Emilio Pantojas García question interpretations that portray Muñoz and his party as advocates of nationalist values. Rafael Alberto Bernabe, "Prehistory of the 'Partido Popular Democrático': Muñoz Marín, the Partido Liberal and the Crisis of Sugar in Puerto Rico, 1930-1935" (Ph.D. diss., State University of New York at Binghamton, 1989); Emilio Pantojas Garcia, "Puerto Rican Populism Revisited: The PPD during the 1940s," *Journal of Latin American Studies* 21 (October 1989): 522-557; Emilio Pantojas García, *Development Strategies as Ideology: Puerto Rico's Export-Led Industrialization Experience* (Boulder, CO: Lynne Rienner Publishers. Río Piedras: Editorial de la Universidad de Puerto Rico, 1990). José J. Rodríguez Vázquez sees Muñoz as representing a moderate form of nationalism. José J. Rodríguez Vázquez, "El Sueño que no cesa: La nación deseada en el debate intelectual y político puertorriqueño, 1920-1940" (Ph.D. diss, University of Puerto Rico, 1998). A different approach comes from authors that focus on World War II to understand the reorientation of Muñoz's political convictions about the status issue. Silvia Alvarez Curbelo, "Las lecciones de la guerra: Luis Muñoz Marín y la Segunda Guerra Mundial, 1943-1946" and Jorge Rodríguez Beruff, "La pugna entre dos grandes sistemas: la guerra en el discurso político de Luis Muñoz Marín hasta Pearl Harbor," in Fernando Picó, ed., *Luis Muñoz Marín: Ensayos del Centenario, ed. Fernando Picó* (San Juan: Fundación Luis Muñoz Marín, 1999), pp. 31-59, 127-152. Yet, other authors emphasize Muñoz's cultural nationalism vis-à-vis the PPD's disassociation from independence. Juan M. García Passalacqua, ed., *Vate, de la cuna a la cripta: El nacionalismo cultural de Luis Muñoz Marín*, (San Juan: Editorial LEA, 1998).

95. The special bond that Muñoz perceived between himself and "the people" is a key feature of his book *La Historia del Partido Popular Democrático*. One can find a provocative perspective about the relationship between Muñoz and his followers in Edgardo Rodríguez Juliá, *Las tribulaciones de Jonás* (Río Piedras: Ediciones Huracán: 1981). At one point, Rodríguez focuses on the absence of a state in a colonial context to explain the unmediated bond that existed between Muñoz and his followers. See also Edgardo Rodríguez Juliá, "Las tribulaciones de Jonás (Veinte años después)," in Fernando Picó, ed., *Luis Muñoz Marín: Perfiles de su gobernación, 1948-1964* (San Juan: Fundación Luis Muñoz Marín, 2003), pp. 137-143. For a critical overview of Rodríguez Juliá's work, see Juan Gelpí, "Las tribulaciones de Jonás ante el paternalismo literario," in Juan Duchesne Winter et al., *Las tribulaciones de Juliá* (San Juan: Instituto de Cultura Puertorriqueña, 1992), pp. 95-115.

96. Luis Muñoz Marín, *Memorias, 1898-1940* (San Juan: Universidad Interamericana de Puerto Rico, 1982), pp. 178, 221.

97. Repeatedly, Muñoz referred to his compromise with "the people" when faced with issues contrary to his interests. In the case of independence, Muñoz compelled his colleagues to abide by that compromise. *El Mundo*, July 18, September 9, 13, December 8, 1944.

98. Muñoz Marín, *La Historia del Partido Popular Democrático*, pp. 86, 111-113.

99. *El Mundo*, July 2, 1943, August 14, 17, 19, 1943, September 19, 1943.

100. *El Mundo*, April 6, July 29, August 4, 12, 23, 1943; *La Democracia*, October 1, 1943; *El Mundo*, November 26, 28, 1943.

101. Ibid.

102. Ibid.

103. Ibid.

104. Bhana, *The United States*, p. 59. It should be noted that resident commissioner Bolívar Pagán introduced a bill to provide for an elective governor in 1942.

105. Argüelles, *Morality and Power*, pp. 128-29; Zapata Oliveras, *De independentista a autonomista*, pp. 121-123.

106. Ibid., p. 144; *El Mundo*, July 20, 1943. Unfortunately, even the modest proposals of political reform did not find much support in Congress. Specially, Democrats Dennis Chávez and C. Jasper Bell—the chairmen of the House and Senate Committees on Territories and Insular Affairs—decided the fate of key proposals. Chávez showed reluctance in granting ample autonomy. Bell's hostility proved fatal to any form of political change on the island. He offered a bleak perspective of local politics during the hearings he held between 1943 and 1944 to investigate conditions in Puerto Rico. Zapata Oliveras, *"Nuevos caminos hacia viejos objetivos,"* pp. 63-64.

107. José Augusto Perea and Félix Benítez Rexach took charge of the initial lobbying efforts of the CPI. *El Mundo*, April 28, June 3, 4, 1943.

108. Rosario Natal, *Luis Muñoz Marín y la Indedependencia de Puerto Rico*, p. 179.

109. Ibid., p. 180.

110. *El Mundo*, August 12, 1943.

111. Rosario Natal, *Luis Muñoz Marín y la Independencia de Puerto Rico*, p. 180.

112. *El Mundo*, August 13, 1943.

113. *El Mundo*, August 14, 1943.

114. Rosario Natal, *Luis Muñoz Marín y la Independencia de Puerto Rico*, p. 180.

115. *El Mundo*, August 16, 1943.

116. Ibid.

117. *El Mundo*, August 17, 1943; *La Democracia*, August 19, 1943.

118. *El Mundo*, August 11, 14, 1943.

119. *El Mundo*, August 14, 17, 1943.

120. Alsina Orozco, *Los Congresos Pro-Independencia*, pp. 37-42; *El Mundo*, August 16, 1943.

121. Alsina Orozco, *Los Congresos Pro-Independencia*, p. 37.

122. *El Mundo*, August 16, 1943.

123. Ibid.

124. Ibid.

125. Ibid.

126. Ibid.

127. Alsina Orozco, *Los Congresos Pro-Independencia*, p. 42.

128. Ibid. *El Mundo*, August 16, 21, 27, 1943.

129. *El Mundo*, October 31, 1943.

130. *El Imparcial*, November 29, 1943. Félix Benítez Rexach was owner of the Hotel Normandie in San Juan.

131. *El Mundo*, December 17, 1943.

132. Ibid.

133. *El Mundo*, January 13, 1944.

134. U.S. Congress, Senate, Subcommittee of the Committee on Territories and Insular Affairs. "A Bill to Amend the Organic Act of Puerto Rico," S. 1407, 78th Congress, 1st. Sess., November 16 - December 1, 1943, p. 175.

135. Letter from Félix Benítez Rexach to Senator Millard E. Tydings, January 19, 1944, Records of the Committee on Territories and Insular Affairs, United States Senate, Record Group 46, National Archives and Records Administration. Hereafter referred to as CTIA, RG 46, NARA.

136. "A Bill to Amend the Organic Act of Puerto Rico," p. 198.

137. Alsina Orozco, *Los Congresos Pro-Independencia*, p. 48.

138. *El Imparcial*, December 16, 1943, January 26, February 9, 18, 29, 1944; *Puerto Rico World Journal*, Feburary 2, 1944.

139. Letter from Félix Benítez Rexach to Senator Milliard E. Tydings, December 28, 1943; Letter from Benítez to Senator Homer T. Bone, January 7, 1944; Letter from Benítez to SenatorAllen J. Ellender, February 21, 1944, CTIA, RG 46, NARA.

140. Letter from Benítez to Tydings, December 28, 1943, CTIA, RG 46, NARA.

141. *Claridad*, December 18, 1943. The status poll of *El Imparcial* included two options: sovereignty and statehood.

142. *El Imparcial*, November 29, 1943.

143. Alsina Orozco, *Los Congresos Pro-Independencia*, pp. 51-61.

144. *El Mundo*, March 7, 10, 15, 1944.

145. *El Mundo*, March 16, 17, 1944.

146. Alsina Orozco, *Los Congresos Pro-Independencia*, pp. 52-53.

147. *El Mundo*, March 7, 1944.

148. Ibid.

149. *El Mundo* from July 8 to August 19, 1944. According to Bhana, Soltero Peralta also publicized the interviews he had with U.S. congressmen in *La Prensa*. Bhana, *The United States and the Development of the Puerto Rican Status Question*, pp. 75-76, 244-245. While the CPI carried out its campaign with greater vigor, the tensions within the PPD became evident during its convention on August 19, 1944, to nominate party candidates for the next election. After a long and heated debate, Muñoz turned down the assembly's request to nominate independentist Rafael Arjona Siaca for the position of resident commissioner. Muñoz preferred the nomination of Jesús T. Piñero. See Mary Frances Gallart, "Conversaciones con el pueblo," in Fernando Picó, ed., *Luis Muñoz Marín: Perfiles de su gobernación, 1948-1964* (San Juan: Fundación Luis Muñoz Marín, 2003), pp. 290-294.

150. *El Mundo*, November 6, 1944.

151. Alsina Orozco, *Los Congresos Pro-Independencia*, p. 70. *El Mundo*, December 11, 1944.

152. Ibid.

153. *El Mundo*, December 1, 1944.

154. Ibid.

155. *El Mundo*, December 8, 1944. Reece B. Bothwell, ed., *Puerto Rico: Cien años de lucha política* (Río Piedras: Editorial de la Universidad de Puerto Rico, 1979), vol. 4, pp. 419-420.

156. *El Mundo*, July 18, 1944.

157. *El Mundo*, December 11, 1944.

158. *El Mundo*, December 22, 1944.

159. Alsina Orozco, *Los Congresos Pro-Independencia*, pp. 70-72; *El Mundo*, December 11, 1944.

160. Bothwell, *Puerto Rico*, vol. 4, pp. 421-422; *El Mundo*, December 11, 1944.

161. *El Mundo*, December 13, 15, 1944.

162. *El Mundo*, December 14, 16, 1944.

163. PPD, *Catecismo del Pueblo*, 1944, p. 5, FLMM/ALMM, IV-FC; *El Mundo*, November 2, 1944. Equally overbearing were the words that Muñoz used to instruct a party official: "I do not wish . . . that any public explanation reaches the people if it is not directly through my voice." Alsina Orozco, "Deslinde e Incompatibilidad: Luis Muñoz Marín y los Congresos Pro-Independencia" in García Passalacqua, *Vate, de la cuna a la cripta*, p. 218.

164. Luis Muñoz Marín, "Informe preliminar no. 1 a la Comisión Económica de la Legislatura de PR de su representante en los Estados Unidos," 1927, Comisión Económica de la Cámara de Puerto Rico (Luis Muñoz Marín Papers, New York Library), Centro de Investigaciones Históricas, Universidad de Puerto Rico. An early statement of Muñoz in favor of economic development appears in a letter he sent to John Crone:

Puerto Rico, the southern doorstep of the U.S., is clamoring for American capital to go down there to turn it into "the workshop of the Caribbean." The American regime has proved of great material benefit to the island, multiplying its volume of trade by twelve from 1898 to 1927. A wonderful road system has been developed and schools have been placed within reach of eight times the number of children that had access to them during the last years of the former sovereignty. But, nevertheless, we must industrialize if we are to take proper care of our 1,500,000 American citizens. (Letter of October 20, 1927, Comisión Económica, CIH/UPR).

165. Copy to Ruby A. Black of a letter sent by Luis Muñoz Marín to Eleanor Roosevelt, December 8, 1933, Colección Ruby A. Black, CIH/UPR.

166. Carlos Gil, "'Yo no me voy, yo regreso.' Luis Muñoz Marín y el montaje del leviatán," in Picó, *Luis Muñoz Marín*, pp. 209-232; Rodríguez Juliá, *Las tribulaciones de Jonás*, pp. 35, 100. Calling Muñoz a "shaman" or "prophet" comes close to Max Weber's notion of charisma. The concept is useful as long as charisma is not simply seen as a gift of personality that, through an enigmatic process, is bestowed upon society and becomes the fundamental and all encompassing basis of a political system. A provocative interpretation of charisma is Clifford Geertz, "Centers, Kings, and Charisma: Reflections on the Symbolics of Power," in Sean Wilentz, ed., *Rites of Power: Symbolism, Ritual, and Politics since the Middle Ages* (Philadelphia: University of Pennsylvania Press,1984), pp. 13-38.

167. Díaz Quiñones, *El arte de bregar*, p. 64.

168. Pantojas García, *Development Strategies as Ideology*, p. 41.

169. Ibid., pp. 42-43; James L. Dietz, *Economic History of Puerto Rico* (Princeton: Princeton University Press, 1986), pp. 194-201.

170. Dietz, *Economic History of Puerto Rico*, p. 220.

171. Annual Report of PRIDCO, 1943, pp. 35, 82.

172. Dietz, *Economic History of Puerto Rico*, pp. 189-194.

173. Ibid., p. 219.

174. Muñoz Marín, *La Historia del Partido Popular Democrático*.

175. Ibid., p. 113.

176. I am referring to a series of books written by PPD functionaries, members, and sympathizers that reproduce or at least resemble the official discourse of Muñoz and his party. R. Elfrén Bernier, *Luis Muñoz Marín: Líder y Maestro, Anecdotario Mumarino I* (San Juan: Ramallo Bros. Printing, 1988); R. Elfrén Bernier, *Luis Muñoz Marín: Anecdotario Mumarino II* (San Juan: Fundación Luis Muñoz Marín, 1999); R. Elfrén Bernier, *Anecdotario Mumarino III (y el asunto de las carpetas)* (San Juan: Fundación Luis Muñoz Marín, 2002); Enrique Bird Piñero, *Don Luis Muñoz Marín: El poder de la excelencia* (San Juan: Fundación Luis Munoz Marín, 1991); Lieban Córdova, *Luis Muñoz Marín y sus campañas políticas: Memorias de su secretario - taquígrafo personal* (Río Piedras: Editorial de la Universidad de Puerto Rico, 1983); Lieban Córdova, *7 años con Muñoz Marín, 1938-1945* (Arecibo: Editora Corripio, 1988; orig. 1945); Lieban Córdova, *¿Cómo era Muñoz Marín?*, 2 vols. (Arecibo: First Book Publishing of Puerto Rico, 1996); Antonio Fernós Isern, "From Colony to Commonwealth," *The Annals of the American Academy of Political and Social Studies* (January 1953); Antonio Fernós Isern, *El Estado Libre Asociado de Puerto Rico: Antecedentes, creación, y desarrollo hasta la época presente* (Río Piedras: Editorial Universitaria, 1973); Ernesto Juan Fonfrías, *Historia de mi vida política en la fundación del Partido Popular Democrático* (Río Piedras: Imprenta ESMACO, 1986); Manuel de Heredia, *Luis Muñoz Marín: Biografía abierta* (Río Piedras: Ediciones Puerto Rico, 1973); Arturo Morales Carrion, *Historia del pueblo de Puerto Rico* (San Juan: Editorial del Departamento de Instrucción Pública, 1968); Carmelo Rosario Natal, "Prólogo," in Carmelo Rosario Natal, ed., *Luis Muñoz Marín: Juicios sobre su significado histórico* (San Juan: Fundación Luis Muñoz Marín, 1990), pp. 10-18; Carmelo Rosario Natal, "Prólogo del editor," in Carmelo Rosario Natal, ed., *Luis Muñoz Marín: Servidor Público y Humanista (Cartas)* (San Juan: Producciones Históricas, 1998), pp. 7-13; José Trías Monge, *Historia constitucional de Puerto Rico* (Río Piedras: Editorial Universitaria, 1980). The memoirs that Muñoz wrote after retiring from politics reinforced the official history of the PPD. It is no surprise, for example, that several decades after the PPD's first electoral campaign, Muñoz presented Communists of that era as a nuance outside the scope of the party's history and legacy (see Muñoz Marín, *Memorias, 1898-1940*, p. 206). The books mentioned above are the most obvious cases that mirror the PPD's discourse. Many other works suffered the effects of the PPD's political hegemony after World War II. According to Francisco A. Scarano, there was a supposition that uniformly permeated most of the postwar historiography. He explains that many works incorporated notions about "social peace," "homogeneity," and "abstractions" such as "the people of Puerto Rico." Francisco A. Scarano, "La historia heredada: Cauces y corrientes de la historiografía puertorriqueña, 1880-1970," *Exégesis* 6, no. 17 (1993): 40-52.

177. Muñoz Marín, *La Historia del Partido Popular Democrático*, p. 86.

178. Ibid., p. 29.

179. Ibid., pp. 30-31.

180. Ibid., p. 33.

181. Ibid., p. 31.

182. Ibid., p. 32.

183. Arjun Appadurai, "Numbers in the Colonial Imagination," Chapter. 6 in *Modernity at Large: Cultural Dimensions of Globalization* (Minneapolis: University of Minnesota Press, 1996); David Ludden, "India's Development Regime," in Nicholas B. Dirks, ed.,

Colonialism and Culture (Ann Arbor: University of Michigan Press, 1992), pp. 247-287.

184. Consider the economic regulations of the New Deal in Alan Brinkley, "The New Deal and the Idea of the State," in Steve Fraser and Gary Gerstle, eds., *The Rise and Fall of the New Deal Order, 1930-1980* (Princeton: Princeton University Press, 1989), pp. 85-121.

185. Consider a similar case to the discourse articulated by Muñoz: Laura Ruíz Jiménez, "Peronism and Anti-imperialism in the Argentine Press: 'Braden or Perón' Was Also 'Perón Is Roosevelt,'" *Journal of Latin American Studies* 30 (October 1998): 551-571.

186. Muñoz Marín, *La Historia del Partido Popular Democrático*, p. 86.

187. Ibid., p. 70.

188. Alvarez Curbelo, "Las lecciones de la guerra: Luis Muñoz Marín y la Segunda Guerra Mundial, 1943-1946," pp. 31-59.

189. Letter from Muñoz Marín to Teodoro Moscoso, July 16, 1942; Letter from Teodoro Moscoso to Muñoz Marín, July 23, 1942, FLMM/ALMM, IV-4 (Empresas Comerciales: *La Democracia*). Moscoso's article appeared in *La Democracia*, July 25, 1942.

190. *La Democracia*, July 25, 1942.

191. Although Moscoso did not describe himself as a New Dealer, he aligned PRIDCO with the ideas of John Maynard Keynes, a prominent economist who influenced the New Deal. *La Democracia*, July 25, 1942. Keynesianism and the New Deal is studied in Fraser and Gerstle, eds., *The Rise and Fall of the New Deal Order, 1930-1980*.

192. Maldonado, *Teodoro Moscoso and Puerto Rico's Operation Bootstrap*, p. 53.

193. Ibid., pp. 53-54.

194. Muñoz stressed the importance of PRIDCO. *El Mundo*, March 24, 1943, July 7, 1944. Wilfredo Braschi of *La Democracia* also wrote about PRIDCO and economic development. *La Democracia*, February 25, March 3, September 30, 1944.

195. See writings such as Bernier, *Luis Muñoz Marín: Líder y Maestro, Anecdotario Mumarino I*; Bird Piñero, *Don Luis Muñoz Marín: El poder de la excelencia*; Córdova, *Luis Muñoz Marín y sus campañas políticas*.

196. Luis Muñoz Marín, "Discurso del señor Luis Muñoz Marín a los campesinos objeto de la primera distribución de tierras bajo la Autoridad de Tierras en Sábana Seca, del municipio de Toa Baja," FLMM/ALMM, IV-FC.

197. The Serie 7 (Pueblos) at the FLMM/ALMM contains an extensive number of letters that were exchanged between Muñoz and his followers.

198. Muñoz explained the economic objectives of the PPD in *El Mundo*, March 24, 1943. Although shorter, other press releases stated the aims of Muñoz and his party. *El Mundo*, June 26, December 13, 16, 1943, July 7, 8, 1944.

199. *El Mundo* gave ample coverage to the Caribbean Commission's conference of 1944. *El Mundo*, March 13 - April 3, 1944.

200. Maldonado, *Teodoro Moscoso and Puerto Rico's Operation Bootstrap*, pp. 37-45.

201. Ibid., pp. 42-43.

202. Besides the detailed presentation given by Moscoso about the PRGC (Maldonado, *Teodoro Moscoso*, p. 37), consider the conference that R. Fernández García, the technical director of PRIDCO, delivered at the Annual Assembly of Engineers in September 1943 (found at the Library of the Economic Development Administration). Among the press releases that marked the inauguration of PRIDCO, see *El Mundo*, December 19, 23, 1944, January 11, 1945.

203. See the Annual Reports of PRIDCO, 1943-1949. CPR/UPR.

204. Maldonado, *Teodoro Moscoso and Puerto Rico's Operation Bootstrap*, p. 48.

5

CONFRONTING VICTORY: ELECTORAL AFTERMATH AND THE ASCENDANT DISCOURSE OF CONSENT

Puerto Rico must play its role in history and it must be free to look ahead toward posterity.

—Pedro Albizu Campos

Without economic security there is no liberty.

—Ernesto Ramos Antonini

After testing the potential of collective action during the early 1940s, leaders and supporters of the PPD approached the next elections with more than a foothold in colonial politics. The island's mass movement moved ahead to face not only the odds beyond its control but also the conditions informed by its own transformation. As an ensemble of political forces with different visions of consent, the constituency headed by the PPD confronted in the mid-1940s many tensions and contradictions. Although the political disagreement between the PPD and certain groups showed signs of resolving itself in favor of the former, these agents still had room for negotiation during the last days of World War II and the immediate postwar era. The fate of the mass movement pivoted between further cooperation among its main participants and the vanquishment of its multivocal and all-inclusive drive.

As people prepared themselves for the election of 1944, the support that the PPD received during its campaign hardly seemed a cause for concern but a reason for celebration. The people who had joined forces with the PPD used the political campaign as an opportunity to express their satisfaction with reform, the possibility of additional improvements for the island, and their continued inclusion in colonial politics. Besides the enthusiastic acclaims for governmental programs such as land reform, labor legislation, public housing, and industrial development, many agents of the island's mass movement expressed ambitious goals, including an equitable access to material resources and a meaningful participation in social, economic, and political decision making. Whether people referred to social justice, industrialization, or political change, they made clear the need for their inclusion and consultation in the management of policies. The opportunity that people had in the mid-1940s to envision all sorts of improvements is not a rare exception applicable to the island's history but a situation comparable with historical developments in Latin America and other regions. In their comparative analysis of the "postwar conjuncture" in Latin America, Leslie Bethell and Ian Roxborough offer as part of their conclusion the words that follow:

At the end of the Second World War, and to a large extent because of the Second World War, not only was there in Latin America a forward march by democracy, the Left, and labor, but there was also a shift in the nature of political discourse and ideology. There were expectations in Latin America, as elsewhere in the world, that a new era of democratic government was about to commence. And democracy was seen by many to imply a commitment to popular, more particularly working-class participation in politics, and social and economic improvements for the poorer sections of the population. Democracy increasingly became identified with development and welfare.[1]

As in other regions of the world, the promise for broad reform soon faded in Puerto Rico due to local conditions and international pressures. After Muñoz defeated the opposition with a resounding majority of votes in the election of 1944, the island began the postwar era under the political dominance of his party.[2] PPD officials no longer faced the precarious position of their first term in office. This reality set the stage for different kinds of political practices on the island. While the PPD still competed against political rivals to win over supporters, Muñoz and his peers used their unmatched position to shift the party's orientation and exclude "undesirable" elements from its ranks. Just as the PPD unequivocally confirmed itself as the representative of the island's mass movement, the party shed the precepts that brought many agents together. PPD officials not only forfeited the support of groups that saw the party's policies as unacceptable but also took action to marginalize highly vocal detractors—a reference in this chapter to the censure and exclusion of Communists, independentists, Nationalists, and the most militant elements within the labor movement. This turn of events robbed the PPD of agents who had done much to invigorate the island's mass movement and maintain a healthy balance of forces within the party. Steadily, the PPD's emphasis on reform and social justice gave way to policies that focused almost exclusively on industrial development and the party's call for the "battle of production."

The trajectory of colonial politics combined with the international conflict known as the Cold War to produce a backlash against the remnants of New Deal policies in Puerto Rico. Local and world events also boosted the PPD's program of industrialization. As the United States and the Soviet Union failed to maintain their cooperation after World War II and embarked head-on into Cold War politics, the international order suffered the effects of a bipolar alignment of forces.[3] Soviet-American rivalry divided the world into alliances that heeded equally uncompromising objectives. Many countries faced a difficult choice: to follow the liberal-capitalist policies of Washington, D.C., or the Communist ones of Moscow. Caught within the "sphere of influence"[4] of the United States, Puerto Rico partook in the effort of Washington, D.C., to fashion a postwar international order according to its aims. The authorities in Puerto Rico not only made the containment of Communism one of their highest priorities[5] but also complied with the needs of U.S. entrepreneurs for the investment of capital in the postwar era.[6] While the end of the war effort unleashed a wave of mainland capital that found its way to Puerto Rico, the island moved further along a path that left little room for broad reform. By the end of the 1940s, Puerto Rico suffered a fate similar to that of other countries. As Bethell and Roxborough indicate, "an opportunity, however limited, for significant political and social change, as well as for the first steps perhaps toward a Latin American version of social democracy, was lost."[7]

Understood as a period that marked the end of ambitious reform, the immediate postwar era is examined in this chapter to grasp the unrest of PPD supporters, the affirmation of new priorities by party leaders, and the steady reorientation of colonial politics. Although the Cold War introduced unforeseen events that had an impact on local affairs, the trajectory of political change in Puerto Rico had been set before the postwar era and displayed a logic of its own. After many years of exchanges between PPD leaders and other groups, a movement came into being that could act forcefully to demand social justice. Not only did people benefit from the initial policies of reform in the early 1940s, but they could also hope for additional improvements in the years to come. Puerto Ricans had a stake in the PPD and many expectations about the future of reform when the postwar era arrived. While the call for social justice did not wane, the fate of the mass movement remained in the hands of competing agents and visions. Leaders and supporters of the PPD shaped further the discourse of consent but soon met at a crossroad that gave the advantage to the former. Despite the resonance of visions based on reform, the call for social justice lost its momentum. PPD officials redefined their policies just when the party approached the zenith of its popularity and Cold War politics took hold of Puerto Rico. Before long, the discourse of consent privileged party leaders to the detriment of followers but without limiting its potential as a "surface of inscription" or a "space of representation" for a wide range of demands.[8]

This does not mean that the discourse of consent lost its capacity for the inclusion of people in the late 1940s. It means that the incorporation of different views into that "space of representation" ultimately mirrored a new political logic on the island: the ascendance of a hegemonic discourse under the "moral-intellectual leadership" of the PPD. For a time, the situation on the island pivoted between an "expansive hegemony"[9]—meaning an outcome allowing genuine participation in decision making and ample reform—and an "authoritative hegemony"[10]—meaning an outcome overrun with disciplinary measures and modest improvements. Ultimately, the direction of colonial politics under the PPD came closer to the latter. On the one hand, the PPD became the axis of a hegemony that made indispensable the industrialization of Puerto Rico even if it meant the subordination of particular groups. On the other hand, the hegemonic outcome not only limited the extent of reform but also restrained the dialogue, negotiations, and compromises that had characterized the island's mass movement during its formative years. Collaboration with the PPD became increasingly difficult for those groups that demanded more than modest improvements.

This chapter studies two different, but closely related, aspects that informed the discourse of consent in the postwar era. At one end of the political spectrum lie supporters of the PPD who confronted the aftermath of Muñoz's electoral victory. Left with few options to have their say about policies, groups such as labor, Communists, independentists, and Nationalists expressed their discontent and recalled the PPD's pledge in favor of social justice. My analysis focuses on the conflict that ensued between the CGT and PPD. Although this conflict was not limited to a single issue or context, the CGT faced the worst consequences. After examining the insertion of PPD officials into the CGT's Sugar Workers' Union early in 1945, I study the estrangement between the party and labor during the strikes that shut down the factories of the Puerto Rico Industrial Development Company (PRIDCO). These circumstances informed the split of the CGT. Unwilling to abide by PPD policies with which they disagreed, a significant sector of CGT workers questioned Muñoz and his party. The PPD responded in kind with harsh measures.

Despite being a minority, the groups that challenged the dominance of PPD leaders deserve attention because they unbalanced the discourse of consent and unveiled its limits. As Anna Marie Smith points out, "the work of a hegemonic discourse is never finished; it remains endlessly troubled by alienation—a condition that can become acute even among its most fervent followers—dysfunctional incitements, and resistances inspired by 'outsider' discourse."[11] The PPD's reaction to the "incitements" and "resistances" of former supporters sheds light on a different facet of colonial politics from that discussed in the first chapters. Besides people's incorporation into the island's mass movement, the discourse of consent took form through a process of exclusion. In this sense, the exchanges between agents of colonial politics did not veer away from a corollary of Gramscian analysis: the means of persuasion increasingly converge with the deployment of coercion when the effectiveness of the former is put into question.

If at one end of the political spectrum lie supporters who were excluded from the PPD, at the other end are party leaders who eased the shift of policies in Puerto Rico. Partha Chatterjee's theoretical framework can be useful in this respect.[12] In his analysis of nationalist thought in a colonial context, Chatterjee refers to the culmination of the elite's political discourse as the "moment of arrival." At this point, political leaders articulated "a discourse of order, of the rational organization of power . . . not only conducted in a single, consistent, unambiguous voice, [but also] glossing over all earlier contradictions, divergences and differences."[13] Muñoz and his peers produced in Puerto Rico a discourse of such a nature. PPD leaders constructed a seamless and homogeneous version of events that belied the past. They also imagined a future that suited the ascendancy of the party. The PPD's rhetoric cannot be well grasped if it is seen only as the elocution of a party in power. The hegemonic outcome that PPD leaders appraised with their expressions was inseparable from the process of subordination, marginalization, and exclusion of people who had informed the discourse of consent. To saturate and monopolize public dialogue and debate with its own political precepts became a "built-in" trait of the PPD. Since Muñoz's party formed the core of the island's "historical bloc," the future of the PPD would be inextricably linked to its discourse of consent and its continued hegemony.

LABOR UNREST AND THE LIMITS OF CONSENT

Although the PPD initiated its second term in office unchallenged by the political opposition, electoral support for the party did not translate into the unconditional form of consent that Muñoz and his adherents desired from their followers. The reluctance of the CGT to be an extension of the PPD tinged the electoral victory of the party. CGT leaders and PPD officials began the year 1945 on terms that left little room for negotiation. While the CGT demanded better conditions for labor, the PPD prioritized the program of industrial development.[14] The PPD was no longer a political newcomer in search of allies but a party with vested interests and unwilling to compromise. Muñoz's party fixed its attention on launching successfully the projects of PRIDCO.

Although the defeat of the political opposition augured well for the PPD, it had a double implication for the CGT. First, the absence of any real threat from Socialists, Republicans, and other political groups removed an element unifying the CGT and PPD. The lack of political opposition not only lessened the basis of common action between the CGT and PPD but also made the union confront a party with few restraints to its power. Second, unlike the PPD, the CGT had to face the remnants of the Socialist Party and the still-strong FLT at the labor front. The challenge of withstanding two rivals at once, the PPD and the FLT, faced the CGT in early 1945. Undaunted by the odds stacked against the union, the CGT furthered plans of labor organization that did not sit well with the FLT and PPD. On the one hand, the CGT demanded elections in the sugar industry to decide which union had the right to sign a collective agreement.[15] On the other hand, the CGT began to organize workers in the factories of PRIDCO.

Labor conflicts ensued on both of these fronts. Early in 1945, the strike of sugar workers coincided with the clash that took place between the CGT and the Puerto Rico Glass Corporation, the first factory constructed by PRIDCO. Both strikes marked a beginning and an end in the trajectory of the island's economy and labor relations. The protest of rural workers highlighted the steady decline of the sugar industry and confirmed the rise of PPD officials within the ranks of the CGT. At the factories of PRIDCO, the strikes of workers evidenced the inflexibility of the PPD's initial steps toward industrialization as well as the policies that gradually put an end to labor's autonomy. As Pedro A. Cabán explains, "the prevailing developmental ethos called upon workers to forsake union militancy and to exercise moderation at the negotiating table in order to preserve a favourable investment climate."[16] This does not mean that the PPD hoped to demobilize labor by hindering the possibility of unionization. Instead, the PPD favored the formation of trade unions but balanced that policy with its effort to "affect directly their internal operations and relations with employers." That is, according to Cabán, "although unions were officially recognized as assisting in the process of industrialization, the PPD challenged those that attempted to build an independent political base."[17]

The CGT's Sugar Workers' Union and the PPD

In 1945 a situation climaxed that had been brewing in the sugar industry during the past two years.[18] Mainly because of the war effort, the CGT complied with the authorities and temporarily toned down its demands after the sugar strike of 1942. Despite the gains of labor after this conflict, the CGT had claims that had not been met to its satisfaction, particularly, the union's request for the representation of workers in the sugar industry. Just before the harvest season of 1944, the CGT raised again its call for representation to the APA and secured from local officials their commitment to address the problem. To decide whether the CGT or FLT represented a majority of sugar workers and had the right to sign a collective agreement with the APA, the Insular Labor Relations Board—Junta Insular de Relaciones del Trabajo (JIRT)—promised to hold an election but only after the political election of 1944 to avoid any kind of conflict.[19] The denouement of World War II in 1945 enabled CGT leaders to forcefully demand a collective contract with APA. Moreover, the final days of the war facilitated an appropriate context for the election in the sugar industry. However, shortly after entering negotiations in January, the CGT's Sugar Workers' Union and APA reached an impasse. Sugar producers opposed a collective agreement recognizing the CGT as the exclusive bargaining representative of all workers.[20]

Nicolás Nogueras Rivera, the FLT's general secretary, added his voice of protest to that of the APA.[21] He accused the legal adviser of the CGT's Sugar Workers' Union, PPD leader Ernesto Ramos Antonini, of following "undemocratic procedures" in the negotiations between labor and employers. Nogueras complained that no determination had been made about wages and the legitimate union to sign a contract. When the FLT brought these issues to the attention of workers at an assembly in San Juan on January 14, the CGT had already done so the day before in Ponce.[22] The Sugar Workers' Union considered a course of action that promised results but at a price. On the one hand, sugar workers had the support of intermediaries such as federal mediator Charles A. Goldsmith, conciliation commissioner Fernando Sierra Berdecía, and Representative Ramos Antonini. At their assembly in Ponce, which included the participation of PPD mayor Andrés Grillasca, CGT workers and their intermediaries agreed to wait until the election in the sugar industry before taking further action. Goldsmith went as far as to say that "he would offer his blessing and tell workers to go on strike" if their conditions were not met after winning the election.[23] On the other hand, the Sugar Workers' Union faced the disapproval of CGT leaders who had previously condemned the interference of PPD officials in the affairs of labor. Despite joining the assembly in Ponce, neither Francisco Colón Gordiany nor Juan Sáez Corales spoke to the audience. Also, rumors circulated that Sáez Corales was not invited to the assembly.[24]

Upheld as the first of its kind in U.S. territory, the election in the sugar industry proceeded under the supervision of the JIRT and the assistance of the National Labor Relations Board (NLRB).[25] The representatives of these agencies, correspondingly, Fernando Sierra Berdecía and James R. Watson, worked along with the Departments of Labor, the Police, and Education to ensure a fair process. On January 30, APA associates hosted the election at thirty-one sugar mills throughout the island. The election took place without major incidents, thanks in part to the help of school principals, superintendents, and teachers. With so much riding on this election, CGT observers also kept a close watch on procedures. PPD leaders participated in the event as functionaries of the CGT. Particularly important was the role of PPD senator Ramón Barreto Pérez, who served as the CGT's "general supervisor of the election."[26] Contrary to the CGT and PPD, FLT officials distanced themselves from the event. Besides depriving the electoral centers of FLT observers, union officials demanded from the rank and file to boycott the election. FLT leaders offered few words on January 29 and 30. Nogueras Rivera, for example, made only a short comment to praise the FLT's boycott and to portray the election as a sham.

Over 25,000 workers cast their votes in the election. After placing aside blank and invalid ballots, the JIRT certified 20,180 votes for the CGT, 320 for the FLT, and 180 for "none."[27] Considering that the sugar industry had more than 120,000 employees,[28] the electoral turnout fell far short of the total number of sugar workers in Puerto Rico. Also, it did not come close to the 41,600 names in the JIRT's inscription list.[29] Consequently, the electoral outcome left room for interpretation, even if it had proven decisive enough to shape future policies. Nogueras Rivera ridiculed the initiative of the government and insisted that the FLT's boycott had been effective. Barreto Pérez and Ramos Antonini interpreted the election as a triumph for the CGT. For them, several factors hindered a higher turnout such as seasonal employment, relocations of workers, distance to the electoral centers, and the shortage of ballots. Ramos Antonini also mentioned the "sabotage" and "coercion" of employers.[30] The JIRT added the fact that employees who did not work for APA associates could not vote. Although the election contributed to the insertion of PPD officials into the Sugar Workers' Union, Sáez Corales offered words of support to labor in the sugar industry. Besides calling the election a "glorious victory" and "another page in the indestructible history of the CGT," Sáez Corales perceived it as an episode in a long struggle that harked back to the sugar strike of 1942.[31]

On January 31, Ramos Antonini recalled the CGT's decision of granting employers a grace period of ten days after the election to sign a collective agreement with them.[32] Otherwise, the senator warned, the CGT would declare a "total strike" in Puerto Rico. A day later, the JIRT mirrored the firm stance of Ramos Antonini when it certified the CGT as the exclusive representative of labor in the industries of APA associates.[33] Although APA complied with the JIRT's decision before the week's end, the negotiations between the CGT and sugar producers broke down over an issue of salaries.[34] Sugar producers placed the burden on federal and local policies for their inability to offer a raise above the minimum wage. According to APA, the U.S. secretary of agriculture and the island's JSM placed caps on wages. The Sugar Workers' Union did not buy the argument and left the negotiating table. Labor responded to the intransigence of sugar producers with a strike.

The sugar strike of 1945 confirmed the militancy of CGT workers but under circumstances that hardly resembled their past victories. Although the numerical strength and commitment of workers represented a major challenge, their protest fell short of being a repetition of the sugar strike of 1942. The strike of the Sugar Workers' Union was not as fast paced and intense as the former one, nor did it received the same degree of publicity. Moreover, labor unrest in 1945 did not require the sort of urgent response that was indispensable at the height of the war. To the relief of local and federal authorities, the last months of World War II eased the need of uninterrupted production at the home front.[35] Most of all, besides taking place in a different context, the sugar strike of 1945 evidenced a decisive shift in the leadership of the CGT's Sugar Workers' Union. Not only did the protest fail to proceed under the sole leadership of the CGT, but it also allowed PPD officials to overshadow labor representatives such as Sáez Corales and Colón Gordiany. CGT leaders participated in the protest, but the coordination of the strike was mostly the affair of PPD officials such as Ramos Antonini and Barreto Pérez. This situation spelled disaster for labor, according to Sáez Corales, Colón Gordiany, and other CGT leaders.[36] Although subsequent events would prove them right, the shift of leadership during the strike did not hamper the militancy of workers just yet.

In contrast to their previous involvement in the labor movement, PPD leaders maintained a degree of formality and tempered their expressions of solidarity during the sugar strike of 1945. Also, Muñoz did not go out of his way to support the protest. Nevertheless, despite the difficulty of representing the PPD and CGT simultaneously, party leaders did not shy away from the conflict. Shortly after the spontaneous walkout of workers in Humacao and Yabucoa, Ramos Antonini legitimated their initiative and confirmed that the strike had begun ahead of schedule.[37] When the strike spread to the rest of the island, Ramos Antonini and Barreto Pérez occupied the public limelight with their visits to the zones of conflict.[38] Labor leaders such as Sergio Kuilan Báez and Alberto E. Sánchez worked alongside PPD officials. Meanwhile, Sáez Corales, the CGT's general secretary, could hardly counterbalance the central role of party leaders when he encouraged labor with public statements that recalled the union's past victories.[39] In particular, Ramos Antonini made headlines with accusations that antagonized sugar producers. After Ramos Antonini blamed APA for "coldly" provoking the strike and for what he called a "patronal stoppage," sugar producers accused the PPD official of using the strike to emerge as a labor leader in spite of his rivals within the CGT.[40] Surely, Sáez Corales and his supporters could not have missed the irony of seeing their quandary so well stated by APA, their main contender in the strike.

PPD officials combined their assertive actions to lead the strike with their effort to find a quick solution. Ramos Antonini and his team had to solve the conflict not only to avoid any challenge from CGT leaders but also to cut short the maneuvers of the FLT. When the CGT declared the strike, FLT officials announced their union's decision to join the conflict.[41] According to Nogueras Rivera, the FLT decided to support the strike out of solidarity toward its fellow workers. PPD officials as well as CGT leaders questioned the FLT's intention and steeled their resolve to solve the conflict. Two proposals stood above the rest and competed during the strike to address the problems of labor. Governor Tugwell proposed the appointment of a "federal administrator" to take charge of the sugar industries in Puerto Rico.[42] This alternative met the outright rejection of APA and elicited an ambivalent response from CGT leaders. Labor feared that federal authorities might overturn the decisions of JIRT in favor of their union. Instead of approving the plan of Tugwell, the Sugar Workers' Union sent a cable to Congress requesting an investigation of Puerto Rico's high living expenses and work conditions.[43] Despite lacking support, Tugwell's proposal lingered until the last days of the strike.

A second proposal took shape before the strike started, but it became the object of sporadic discussions during the labor conflict. This alternative called upon the Commodity Credit Corporation to increase the subsidies that the agency had been handing out to the sugar industry to ease production difficulties during the war.[44] The increase of federal subsidies would be accompanied by a policy to equitably assign the funds between workers and sugar producers. Although less radical than Tugwell's proposal, this alternative did not satisfy the APA. Sugar producers said the subsidies would not be enough to cover the costs of increasing wages. They also stated that the subsidies had to come first before a wage raise could take effect. The PPD and CGT insisted that sugar producers could better justify a increase of federal subsidies after scaling up production costs with a wage raise.[45]

While the previous proposals stirred debate and gained public attention, Muñoz pondered yet another option in conversations with PPD leader Jesús T. Piñero. Muñoz's position became clear in a letter he wrote to his colleague on February 20: "my personal inclination is to believe that [wages] can be raised, but possibly not to the point requested by workers."[46] Muñoz also believed that workers would accept a lower raise than the one they requested. He told Piñero that sugar producers simply rejected negotiating with workers and were adamant in their refusal to raise wages. Instead of revealing to Piñero a full-fledged solution, Muñoz offered his thoughts about the ongoing discussion of policymakers aimed at increasing the price of sugar. In his effort to provide a course of action for the PPD, Muñoz pitched for a balance between the island's economy and the demands of workers. Contrary to his actions in the past, Muñoz wrote words to Piñero that did more to unveil his uncertainties than to confirm his solidarity with labor:

Concerning the strike situation and the price of sugar, our position, it seems to me, should be as follows: we are in favor of increasing its price and should petition this increase in the most vigorous way possible. This increase will be beneficial for the general economy of Puerto Rico, including industrialists, farmers, and workers. What we should not admit or deny—simply because we do not have sufficient means of information for that—is that an increase in prices is necessary to raise wages. We should not put workers in that situation. It is very possible that wages could be raised to a certain point, even without increasing the price. If the price is increased, the wage raise could be even better. But we do not know to what point wages can be raised nor if it is true that they cannot be raised.[47]

At the height of public debate about the strike, the PPD made an important move to bring the conflict to an end. Ramos Antonini left the island on March 12 and stayed in Washington, D.C., for a week to consult federal authorities.[48] He publicized his activities and kept in touch with the coordinators of the strike with frequent press releases. After probing different proposals at the U.S. capital, Ramos Antonini returned to Puerto Rico and announced the result of his lobbying efforts without delay.[49] Of all the proposals to solve the strike, the alternative that called for an increase of federal subsidies for the sugar industry came out on top. U.S. officials approved a grant that, according to Ramos Antonini, represented for workers an additional benefit of $4 million.[50]

With that piece of information at hand, PPD officials felt confident enough to put pressure on sugar producers and labor. Ramos Antonini played on the fears of APA, saying that if the subsidies did not come through, the only alternative would be to seize the sugar industry and place it under the supervision of a federal administrator.[51] Meanwhile, Muñoz made a short statement in *La Democracia* about the availability of a solution "satisfactory to all."[52] The PPD's main leader saw no need to continue the strike of the CGT. That same day, another newspaper added an ominous note when it mentioned Muñoz's plan to introduce legislation to control labor disputes.[53] According to the press, the legislation would reorganize the JIRT and establish guidelines to regulate "how, when, and why" a strike is declared. This measure, said the press, resembled the War Labor Disputes (Smith-Connally) Act aimed at the CIO after the strike of coal miners in 1943. Congress passed the Smith-Connally Act to curtail the outbreak of strikes that hindered production during the war.[54] Evidently, PPD leaders felt that in Puerto Rico, as in the mainland, labor unrest had gone too far. Some party followers understood the concerns of their leaders about the unabated protests of workers. For example, one day after Muñoz made his statements to the press, Ramón Sánchez Justiniano wrote him a provocative letter of support. Sánchez offered these words:

I extend my sincere felicitation for your intelligent declaration about the stoppage in the sugar industry. Those that desired and expected another attitude on your part—so as to accuse you of being an enemy of the strike or, better said, a strikebreaker—have met with disappointment! Those responsible for everything should shoulder their guilt and get out as they can from the mire! . . . I will permit myself to suggest that you serenely examine the different factors involved in the current "epidemic" of strikes before adopting any coercive measure. Now, on the one hand, while employers and their agents say "even Muñoz Marín has become aware that strikes must end in Puerto Rico," on the other, the partisans of a certain labor leader of new lineage and the enemies of the PPD that belong to certain labor organizations proclaim that Muñoz Marín wants to snatch away the right (to strike) of workers. Don Luis, you know that this is a very delicate matter. I dare advise you not to touch this even with a long stick; do not worry; everything will calm down in time.[55]

While PPD officials worried about the excessive protests of labor, party followers pondered the merits of Muñoz's plan to control strikes. Notwithstanding the apprehension that many workers may have felt after hearing Muñoz's plan, a deep-seated trust existed between followers and the PPD's main leader that could be the result only of several years of dialogue and consultation between them. Due in large measure to this trust, Sánchez found it possible to write his open letter to Muñoz and level with his leader on an argumentative plane that was right on target and promised results. Instead of lashing out against labor unrest with coercive measures, Sánchez suggested patience as an alternative but only after demonstrating that he understood Muñoz's difficulties vis-à-vis the bold accusations of opponents. By offering a view that contrasted with the one at the higher levels of policy-making processes, Sánchez shed light on the experience of PPD followers, a realm that could be sound and reasonable to reach decisions.

Sánchez made an argument about how best to avoid political complications as well as to address the problems of labor. To leave no doubt in Muñoz's mind about his grasp of the problem, Sánchez further explained that "those embryonic strikes are the logical and inevitable result of the awakening of the masses after being submerged for decades in tyranny and exploitation."[56] Vladimir Lenin had called this predicament, said Sánchez, the "infantile sickness of emancipatory social struggles." Once he made clear his critique about the "epidemic" of strikes, Sánchez emphasized that the "principal strength of the Party is the support that the lax and thin shoulders of the working and rural masses offer." Also, he warned Muñoz about "the advice that comes from the lips of persons who, if they did not exploit the workers, always stayed indifferent to the exploitation of workers."[57] According to the final words of Sánchez, "I share the idea of Dr. Susoni . . . to undertake a campaign of working-class education" and "a program of acculturation of the masses, including principles of social morals directed at creating a big idea of life." Sánchez believed that "the misery of our people is as much of the stomach as of the mind," and to demand only bread "would be to construct on air."[58] Although party followers such as Sánchez offered arguments against rash measures and discussed the alternatives, Muñoz and the PPD would soon choose a course of action that left little room for negotiation. Muñoz's effort to stop the sugar strike and introduce labor-control legislation offered a glimpse of the PPD's change of policies.

The sugar strike's denouement followed Muñoz's statements to the press. After Ramos Antonini met with the Sugar Workers' Union and explained the terms of the federal offer on March 14, negotiations began in earnest next morning between the CGT and APA.[59] Several days of meetings took place under the supervision of Sierra Berdecía, the conciliation commissioner, and PPD leader Antonio Fernós Isern, who acted as provisional governor at the time. A major challenge was to determine the distribution of the federal subsidies. Once they completed that task, the CGT and APA began the negotiations to sign a collective agreement. The long awaited announcement putting an end to the strike came on March 19.[60] Fernós Isern confirmed the declarations of labor and sugar producers with his own public statement. He highlighted the fact that semi-independent farmers,[61] or *colonos*, also approved the collective agreement between the CGT and APA. The most congratulatory remark came from *La Democracia*, which announced that the final negotiations in the sugar industry in fact produced a total benefit of $5 million for workers.[62] The immediate result of the sugar strike of 1945 definitely represented a great success. In the long run, however, labor paid a high price. Workers reaped the benefits that PPD officials had to offer, but what good would that bring when the unity of the CGT had been compromised by leaders mostly loyal to their party? That is a question that can be best answered in the next part of the chapter, which brings us to the labor strike at the glass factory of PRIDCO.

The CGT, PPD, and PRGC Strike

Despite taking place at the same time, there is a marked contrast between the labor conflict that engulfed the sugar industry and the one that occurred in the Puerto Rico Glass Corporation (PRGC). While the former saw the intervention of PPD leaders who had influence within the CGT, the latter was directed by CGT officials who stood at a distance from the party. Due to their close ties with labor in the sugar industry, Ernesto Ramos Antonini and other party officials negotiated on behalf of rural workers, a situation that did not take place in the strike of PRGC workers.[63] The labor conflict at the glass factory of PRIDCO struck at the heart of the PPD's agenda for the future, which placed much hope on the success of industrial development. As the locus of acute political tensions, the PRGC strike defied the swift reorientation of priorities desired by the PPD. Moreover, the labor conflict made unavoidable the political crossroad that cornered the PPD and brought to the forefront the limits of consent. As a party that depended on labor support, the PPD had to decide between workers and its own plan of industrialization.

Notwithstanding the deterioration of the CGT-PPD relationship, there were few indications that a labor strike would take place in the PRGC. Labor difficulties in the cement factory of PRIDCO had been quickly solved the previous year.[64] Moreover, the PRGC was a new industry that had just started operations in January.[65] Expectations ran high among governmental circles about the potential of the PRGC.[66] The managers of PRIDCO counted on the cooperation of labor to launch their pet project.[67] When workers of the glass factory informed the PRGC that they had several demands, it seemed to be a routine labor petition. The points raised by workers were hardly out of the ordinary and could do little to hinder the operation of the new factory. The management of the PRGC thought otherwise. For PRIDCO, the demands of labor could not be understood as cooperation.[68]

What at first appeared to be an unremarkable affair sowed the seeds of a major conflict. On January 12, workers informed Rafael Ríos, the PRGC's general manager, of their decision to form a union and their request for a collective agreement.[69] The Employees' Union of PRIDCO and its Annexes—Sindicato de Empleados de Fomento y Ramas Anexas (SEFRA)—took the initiative to organize PRGC workers into the Employees' Union of the Glass Industry—Unión de Empleados de la Industria de Cristal (UEIC). Félix Morales, head of SEFRA and president of the Cement Workers' Union, wrote again to Ríos on January 15 when he failed to receive an answer to his first letter.[70] In his second letter to Ríos, Morales expressed concern about the lack of a response from the PRGC. He stated workers' intention to "start well, in complete harmony and to make an agreement . . . satisfactory as much to employees as to the industry; on which depends the bread of all in general and the progress of our country."[71] Workers made clear to PRIDCO that they valued industrial development but not at the expense of labor.

Morales' second letter was met with silence. Instead, on January 17, Ríos passed along the message of Morales to PRIDCO's general manager, Teodoro Moscoso, and to CGT leaders Juan Sáez Corales and Alberto E. Sánchez.[72] Ríos' decision to involve PRIDCO and the CGT not only escalated the labor concerns of the glass factory but also diminished the possibilities for a quick solution. Workers did not wait for an answer from Ríos. According to Morales, "since so little attention was paid to my communications, I decided to call for an extraordinary assembly . . . to let workers themselves . . . discuss the problem of your silence."[73] Glassworkers met on January 19 to iron out the last details to organize the UEIC. They elected the directors of the new union. Besides the organization of the UEIC, labor discussed the recent decision of the PRGC to fire several workers. The UEIC demanded their reinstatement. Morales wrote a letter to Ríos about the results of the meeting.[74] Shortly thereafter, SEFRA circulated a leaflet to announce the first assembly of the UEIC for January 21.[75]

The managers of the PRGC and PRIDCO reacted to the steps taken by labor. At last, Ríos responded to the demands of workers. In his letter of January 20, Ríos explained to Félix Morales that the labor issue of the glass factory had been referred to Moscoso, Sáez Corales, and Sánchez.[76] Ríos also stated that several workers "were fired for ineptitude or for not being necessary for the functioning of this factory."[77] On January 23, Moscoso wrote to Muñoz about the conflict.[78] As a follow-up to his previous conversations with Sáez Corales and Sánchez, Moscoso informed Muñoz that, according to the "opinion" of these labor leaders, "the CGT's Executive would act to avoid having only one union controlling all of the factories of the Fomento Company."[79] Moscoso worried about the lack of communication between the CGT and Morales, who kept organizing workers at the bottle factory, the Division of Transportation of PRIDCO, and the Puerto Rico Pulp and Paper Corporation. According to Moscoso, Morales stressed in his daily letters to PRIDCO that he represented the majority of workers and that the unions he had organized should be given recognition.

The general manager of PRIDCO also told Muñoz that labor at the PRGC threatened to stop production "without justification."[80] With words that conveyed mixed feelings of urgency, vexation, and hope, Moscoso explained that the lack of skilled personnel to operate "a completely new industry in Puerto Rico" demanded the training of 150 workers, "most of them young men." The Wage and Hour Division of the U.S. Department of Labor granted the contract to initiate the training of workers. Apprentices showing a lack of aptitude for learning, Moscoso said, were soon replaced. The substitution of apprentices, according to Moscoso, did not concern Morales and his union, which was "absolutely uninformed about the fabrication of glass." For Moscoso, since the training of glass bottle makers was in the hand of U.S. technicians, workers mastering the craft could not have a say in the dismissal of apprentices. The general manager of PRIDCO lamented the time lost on "quarrels of little importance with those elements whom precisely we are trying to benefit with our labor."[81] Besides downplaying labor's claims with a highhanded attitude, Moscoso included an obscure comment in his letter. He said to Muñoz that mainland technicians unsatisfied with labor might leave Puerto Rico, forcing PRIDCO to close the glass factory.

On January 26, an assembly of workers considered the reluctance of the PRGC to negotiate with the UEIC.[82] Labor enacted a resolution demanding the recognition of their union and the reinstatement of fired workers. The UEIC also condemned the formation of a "company union" under the leadership of "administrative employees" such as Isabelo Orta and Agustín Vélez. Labor concluded their resolution with an ultimatum, giving the PRGC forty-eight hours either to comply with the union's demands or to face a strike. On January 27, Ríos wrote a long and detailed memorandum to Muñoz summarizing the exchanges that had taken place since the first weeks of the month.[83] The next day, he sent a letter to Sáez Corales saying that Charles A. Goldsmith, the federal labor mediator for Puerto Rico, planned to intervene in the conflict.[84] Meanwhile, Fernando Sierra Berdecía, the insular mediator, sent a telegram to Morales informing him about Goldsmith's intervention.[85] On January 29, Morales wrote to Ríos that the UEIC accepted the call for a truce.[86] The PRGC and UEIC met the next day with Goldsmith.[87] Unfortunately, this meeting and other ones in early February were in vain. Not even the intervention of James R. Watson, the regional director of the NLRB , offered a solution.[88] On the one hand, in a statement to the press, Ríos said he was untroubled by the labor conflict and boasted of his experience: "I had John L. Lewis in my hair when I was in the coal business in New York."[89] On the other hand, Morales saw more reasons for protest when he found out about PRGC employees working against the unionization drive of the UEIC.[90]

The failure of governmental agencies to solve the conflict prompted workers to appeal directly to Muñoz. On February 19, Héctor J. Cifredo Bravo, secretary of the UEIC, wrote to Muñoz explaining the grievances of PRGC workers.[91] Cifredo's message highlighted the sort of response that labor had come to expect from Muñoz, the PPD, and the government. Underlying the UEIC's petition for help was workers' conviction that Muñoz and his party would intervene on their behalf. This comes as no surprise since the PPD relentlessly hammered the party's availability to address the needs of "the people." Moreover, less than a year earlier, Muñoz directly intervened in a labor dispute at the Communication Authority.[92] Cifredo's words to Muñoz appealed as much to his role as a "political arbiter" as to his party's constant reminders of its sense of duty. The secretary of the UEIC told Muñoz that labor's "faith in you is unmovable" and that "we know that the government we have is good." Cifredo said that trouble came from a few "reactionaries" in government. "That should not be allowed," said Cifredo, "and wherever they are, we will denounce them so that the government knows who they are."[93]

According to Cifredo, an effort to solve the problem might not come due to "fear of public opinion" or because it might make the government look "guilty." He added that since the government directly managed the factories, the "spontaneous reaction of the masses is to believe that the government is aware of those troubles and that it tolerates them indifferently."[94] Notwithstanding these concerns, the secretary of the UEIC believed there was no excuse for inaction. Denouncing those "reactionaries," Cifredo concluded, would not belittle the government but could help "to demonstrate once more to the people that it knows how to do justice."[95] It is not surprising that Cifredo circumvented direct references to Ríos, Moscoso, or PRIDCO employees forming a "company union" when one considers that the PPD press constantly used abstractions to refer to its rivals. The UEIC secretary employed a "language" already familiar to PPD leaders. Despite Cifredo's insistence and his attempt to level with the PPD on a common discursive ground, no evidence exists that the main leader of the party offered an answer.

The apparent silence of Muñoz did not discourage the factory workers of PRIDCO. They still had hope and once again appealed to the PPD's main leader. After a UEIC assembly met to discuss further reverses at the glass factory, labor sent another letter to Muñoz on February 24.[96] Workers placed in Muñoz's hands the resolution they approved during the assembly. The worsening of the conflict at the PRGC made the UEIC expand its list of demands. Workers asked for the recognition of their union, a collective agreement, the reinstatement of fired workers, wages as paid before the introduction of cutbacks, and the dismissal of two employees hostile to labor. The UEIC's resolution stressed that, according to what was stated at the "grandstands"—meaning the campaign propaganda of the PPD—"the people are called to make their own justice."[97] If PRIDCO did not meet the demands of labor, the UEIC would go on strike on February 27. Workers warned that "this time there would be no truce."[98]

No answer came from Muñoz, even after he received two cables during the ensuing days. A third telegram from Morales stated this fact and lamented that labor did not receive a reply. Morales cabled his message on February 28, just one day after the strike broke out, to inform Muñoz about the labor protest and stress, once again, the factory manager's abuses.[99] According to Morales, Ríos suspended twenty-two members of the UEIC, reduced the wages of labor leaders, and pushed for a "company union." Morales explained to Muñoz that workers stayed in the factory to protect the bottle-making machinery and other equipment. At odds with this initiative, Morales said, the PRGC manager countered labor's goodwill by making the mistake of turning off the plant's furnaces. Melted glass would solidify and, according to Morales, cause "damages to the government and the people of

Puerto Rico."[100] Morales told Muñoz that "we await your intervention as the representative of the people to get the truth known."[101] Despite the insistence of PRGC workers, Muñoz failed to hear their case and to offer a reply to their pleas for help.

Compared to the sugar strike of 1942, the labor dispute at the PRGC turned out to be a quite different affair. Many factors shaped the course of the conflict such as the enclosure of the glass plant, the concentration of labor on one site, and the novelty of a factory not yet essential for the island's economy. Moreover, the few workers involved in production and the limited possibilities to expand the labor protest determined the nature of the conflict. All of these factors not only isolated the strike from public view but made the event a less immediate concern for the people of the island. According to a police report of March 2, the number of workers on strike totaled 531.[102] Not all workers on strike came from the PRGC. The protesters benefited from the support of labor from a nearby factory of PRIDCO still under construction, the Puerto Rico Paper and Pulp Corporation. Construction workers and other employees of the paper factory of PRIDCO joined the labor conflict.[103]

The intricacies that made the PRGC labor dispute unlike the sugar strike of 1942 partly account for its relevance. While the sugar strike of 1942 was an event that led to the incorporation of workers, the PRGC strike contributed to the disarticulation of the labor movement. Although the conflict at the glass factory lacked the conditions to be a major strike, the PPD made sure to render the event invisible. A party that had been so outspoken about the needs of labor not long ago remained silent during the strike of PRIDCO's factory workers. If it had been in the PPD's best interest, the party would have transformed the strike into an episode of utmost consequence. As it was, the PPD steered clear of a situation that posed a threat to its political aims. Despite its modest size, the PRGC strike is significant because for once the interests of the PPD stood unveiled, without rhetorical subtleties. The factory workers of PRIDCO brought the PPD into an arena of conflict that demanded from the party an immediate choice between labor and industry. Contrary to the past, no amount of rhetoric would save the PPD from the challenge at hand.

Although the PRGC strike remained small in size, it loomed large in symbolic value. The factory workers of PRIDCO made clear the issues at stake in a leaflet that the UEIC distributed several days before the strike.[104] Teodoro Morales Luchessi and Cifredo Bravo, the union's president and secretary, undersigned the document. Labor protested against the wage increases of several administrators of the glass factory. Workers found appalling the fact that agents such as Rafael Ríos and Raúl García began to receive better wages with the start of production, while labor had to face many perils at the glass factory. Workers stressed dangers such as exposure to the extreme heat of furnaces, tasks that could maim the arm of operators or puncture the eye of workers handling broken glass. Labor said that certain PRGC managers had "feudal ideas, retrogressive ideas of 25 years ago, when workers were assassinated in the canefield."[105] According to labor, by employing bad managers, "the actual government would dig its own grave in the heart of workers, who were the ones who brought it to power."[106] Besides the issue of wages, the UEIC stressed the problem of administrators who "humiliated" workers and treated them with "disrespect." The UEIC leaflet also stated:

We want to remind glassworkers that the majority of them gave their votes to implement a decent government, saturated with good faith and that would know how to defend the rights of workers that are the ones that form the suffering part of the country, a government that spoke to us about social justice and we expect that this government does not defraud the hope we have placed on it.

It is good that this government, so that it might accomplish that program, brings into the direction of Fomento's industries, men of capacity, equable, capable of understanding the pain of the suffering masses and then this government would have complied with that program of social justice.

Companions be alert, because you are the majority and therefore the most strong. It is enough to think that the 250 men that work there are 1,000 of family that claim "social justice."[107]

For labor, the issues at stake in the PRGC strike went beyond the specific demands of their union. Workers made a powerful statement with their reference to "social justice," a recent past that the PPD could not easily dismiss. A major concern of the UEIC had to do with the commitment toward "the people" that the PPD assigned to itself. As part of that commitment, the PPD's call for "social justice" could not be taken lightly by workers. Instead, labor held the PPD accountable to the precepts that the party relentlessly preached throughout Puerto Rico. The factory workers of PRIDCO reminded the PPD that they fulfilled the political pleas of the party with their votes. If the PPD had asked for consent to run the government, the party received it in the last election. During the PRGC strike came the time for the PPD to answer back and fulfill its part in exchange for labor's consent to intervene on behalf of workers in the name of "social justice." For workers, it seemed only fair to receive the support of a party that owed much of its history to the actions of labor and other groups. The PPD's insistence that it embodied "the people" entitled its followers to make legitimate claims of Muñoz and his party. Only after fulfilling their part as "men of capacity" in favor of "social justice" could PPD leaders expect the full support of labor.

Not all workers shared the perspective of the UEIC. The PRGC strike mirrored the higher-level conflict within the CGT. Just as PPD leaders such as Ramos Antonini fought for control of the CGT against union leaders such as Sáez Corales, the workers of the glass factory did not express their concerns as a single voice. Several times, the UEIC denounced certain individuals for hindering its unionization efforts with the creation of a "company union." Before the start of the strike, according to UEIC leaders, the members of the "company union" improperly approached employees during working hours and pressured them to join the organization.[108] Morales Luchessi, the UEIC president, specifically criticized the entry of "unknown persons" to the factory. Meanwhile, those workers being accused by the UEIC refused to accept blame and presented an argument about their opposition to the strike. They said that labor's legitimate representative was not the UEIC but the Glass Workers' Union—Unión de Trabajadores de la Industria de Vidrio—a name hardly distinguishable from the former and seldom heard during the strike.[109] This union summed up its position as follows: (1) to accept the apprentice status that PRIDCO assigned to workers, (2) to avoid "sabotages" against the company's program, and (3) to request from the CGT's Executive Committee an investigation of the strike.

Despite never becoming a union with a majority of workers or a strong contender during the strike, the Glass Workers' Union made bold claims that shed light on the overall conflict within the CGT. The opponents of the strike relied on their union's president, Hilaro Castro Maysonet, to present their case. Castro undersigned and apparently wrote a leaflet that circulated among glassworkers on March 4, six days after the strike began. According to Castro, UEIC leaders did not declare the labor strike "to demand a wage raise," "to end the outrages of an unjust and exploitative employer," or "to protest the undemocratic endeavors of an irresponsible government such as the one faced by the people of Puerto Rico 6 years ago."[110] Other motives, said Castro, led UEIC leaders to stop work at the "beautiful factory." He avowed that the strike was "the desire of brazen gentlemen, hurt doves, for whom it has cost nothing, no effort, the structuring of this Government of today, which guarantees the right of workers, the enjoyment of a better livelihood." Moreover, Castro blasted away against UEIC leaders with the words that made clear his annoyance:

If these gentlemen have so much interest in defending workers, why do they not go to fight in the canefield against the Sugar Producers' Association? Or, why do they not go to struggle against the owners of Ponce Cement, who are paying miserable wages to their workers? Why do they not do it? No, they do not do it, workers, friends, because what they are interested in is to destroy the Glass Factory as they have done it; sabotaging the Fomento Company.

To end for today, companions, I am going to tell you that you are being fooled; you are being told that the CGT is backing this embarrassing sabotage. The CGT is not backing this movement. Sáez Corales, Víctor Bosch, Félix Morales, are not the CGT. The CGT are hundreds of unions represented by their Executive Committee and this body has not said a single word about this matter.[111]

Even without declaring it, Castro and his followers squarely identified themselves with that part of the CGT headed by Ramos Antonini, Barreto Pérez, and other PPD leaders. By mentioning the "fight in the canefield" against APA, Castro contrasted what he saw as the legitimate initiative of the CGT and the invalid action of glassworkers. In this way, the opponents of the strike offered credentials about their commitment toward labor despite the UEIC's accusation of being a "company union." They also countered the prostrike arguments of UEIC leaders with the same resourcefulness. As in the case of the UEIC's leaflet, the opponents of the strike not only addressed bread-and-butter issues but also focused on broad concerns. They placed aside the arguments of strike organizers about the government's wavering pledges, its mishandling of policies, and the unfulfilled expectations of labor. According to Castro and his followers, far from letting slide its compromise toward social justice, the government made possible a reality that bore no resemblance to the past. Strike opponents highlighted the improvements in their lives to confirm that the basis of consent between labor and the PPD remained intact. They marveled at the "gigantic machinery" and "beautiful factory" that gave employment to over "300 workers."[112] More important, strike opponents credited the government for improving and guaranteeing labor rights and living standards. Thus, they rejected the UEIC and CGT supporters of the strike.

Although Castro and his followers made a strong case, the fact remains that Sáez Corales, Morales, and other labor leaders could not be summarily dismissed as individuals alien to the CGT. To be sure, strike opponents had a basis to make their claim. After the CGT experienced a transformation due to its close ties to the PPD, no group of leaders could single-handedly represent all the interests within the union. Like other agents who welcomed common action to secure social justice, CGT workers joined forces with the PPD, informed the policies of reform, and, in doing so, suffered changes along the way. In short, the agents of the island's mass movement shared an understanding and expressed it through a discourse of consent but always in tandem with their own transformation. This argument, however, cannot be taken to the extreme. The CGT's transformation should not lead to the conclusion that the union simply lost its orientation and could no longer be identified with its original founders such as Sáez Corales and Colón Gordiany. The truth lies somewhere in the middle. While agents negotiated the basis of reform and shaped the discourse of consent in Puerto Rico, they engaged in a hegemonic process that neither left their identities untouched nor caused a total transformation. In this sense, the CGT was still the union of its founders, but also an organization closely bound to the PPD. A similar assertion applies to the PPD, a party ruled by Muñoz and his peers but largely owing its origin to labor and other agents.

What made so bitter the infighting of labor during the PRGC strike is that workers shouldered a history of unsuccessful negotiations. Supporters and opponents of the UEIC had a chance to address their grievances in early February. Sierra Berdecía, Goldsmith, and Watson tried to mend the differences between glassworkers by arranging an assembly to choose a "new board of directors" for their union.[113] After that plan was carried out and failed, Watson made one final attempt to find a solution when he met alone with the UEIC on February 26, one day before the strike. The NLRB's regional director promised to investigate which group of workers had a majority and the right to sign a collective agreement. Watson's pledge came short of convincing labor, and the strike proceeded as planned.[114]

The NLRB's failure to address the discrepancy between workers and stop the strike made PRIDCO less willing to consider negotiations with labor. The challenge posed by PRIDCO's position became imminent. On March 5, the officials of PRIDCO explained in a press release why they found unacceptable the demands of labor.[115] For the managers of industrialization, the problem at the glass factory had little to do with social justice. That is, PRIDCO rejected the issue raised by the

UEIC about the government's vague commitment toward labor. At best, PRIDCO officials saw the problem as Moscoso did, as "quarrels of little importance" that hindered the agency's effort to offer benefits.[116] Instead of social justice, PRIDCO emphasized the technical aspects of production at the glass factory. Workers' demands had to be placed on hold, according to PRIDCO, until the completion of their training several months later. Only after becoming skilled and permanent workers, PRIDCO added, could they expect negotiations with the agency to address their demands. For company officials, the bottom line of their argument was the status of workers as apprentices and the fact that they remained on probation. With that explanation, PRIDCO rejected, across the board, the demands of labor. PRIDCO conceded only the creation of a committee to address grievances.

The officials of PRIDCO echoed the argument that Moscoso presented to Muñoz in January. Workers could not have a say in the administration of the PRGC because they lacked the knowledge needed for production. According to PRIDCO, this knowledge remained in the hands of U.S. technicians. While the technical assistance of the U.S. experts remained necessary, labor would have to remain mute.[117] Although crudely, PRIDCO's argument articulated early on an aspect that became part of the PPD's discourse about industrial development. PRIDCO presented the process of production as an exclusive area of knowledge. Not only did the public have to accept production "as it is," but it would need to trust almost unconditionally the decisions of certain experts. PRIDCO's technical know-how demanded sacrifices by conceiving production as an esoteric activity beyond the grasp of average people. The assurances of PRIDCO that to leave matters to technicians was the right decision assumed the infallibility of their expertise. For PRIDCO, technicians brandished indisputable knowledge that was not to be questioned by workers. That is, objective conditions and incontrovertible facts made no room for the demands of labor. In years to come, Puerto Ricans would have to relinquish their particular interests at the technological altar of PRIDCO. Intolerance would become irrefutable as well as justifiable in the name of industrial production.

As the PRGC strike progressed, it drew attention from different quarters except the PPD. The commissioner of labor, Manuel A. Pérez, wrote to Governor Tugwell about the efforts of federal authorities to solve the conflict.[118] He reported the lack of progress, notwithstanding the help of Goldsmith, Watson, and the NLRB. A group of teachers and students cabled the governor to urge his intervention in the labor strikes of the PRGC and the sugar industry.[119] When the CGT requested the legislature to investigate the PRGC strike, a group of labor unions cabled Muñoz to express their support.[120] An editorial of *El Mundo* criticized labor's accusations against Ríos but voiced its support for an investigation.[121] Meanwhile, the UEIC repudiated PRIDCO's attempt to dismiss the claims of workers with arguments about their status as apprentices.[122] According to Morales and Cifredo, only twenty to twenty-five apprentices formed the PRGC's labor force of approximately 200 workers. They said the UEIC "demonstrated its desire to solve the problem in an amiable fashion" at four consecutive meetings in which the union yielded and postponed its claims. Also, UEIC leaders stressed that workers "have participated in the formation of our government" but lamented that PRIDCO's Board of Directors did not include a representative of labor. Morales and Cifredo believed that "the industrialization of Puerto Rico should develop giving organized labor the administrative participation that corresponds to it."[123] For them, consent to the PPD did not mean passive support but full engagement in defining governmental policies.

Although the strike raised many concerns, the PPD had little to say about the situation. On March 15, two weeks after the strike started, the PPD made a flash and peremptory comment about the labor conflict during the transmission of its radio program, "El Diario Hablado de *La Democracia* y *El Batey*."[124] The radio broadcast of the PPD must have been a bitter affront to PRGC workers. According to the commentator of the PPD, the party did not find enough justification for the labor strike. The broadcast asked workers for a "restful pause," "deep thought," and "serene reflection." According to the PPD, the fact that PRIDCO was a new agency demanded from labor "a spirit of conciliation."[125] A hint of empathy softened the PPD's patronizing message: "We understand that workers—for reasons that do not escape our perception—must make pertinent claims and aspire to the most reasonable wages, more so when living expenses . . . are rising."[126] After this digression, the PPD renewed its argument. The radio commentator said that in the government's "new industry" the position of workers should be of "a very especial order."

To persuade workers about the need to reconsider their position, the PPD not only stressed the vulnerability of the glass factory but also identified labor with the interests of the PRPC. As a "fountain of life" for Puerto Ricans, new industries required both the acquiescence of workers as well as their best effort to ensure production. "Without harming themselves or making sacrifices," said the PPD, workers should "struggle to avoid wasting the glass factory."[127] Despite the tact and subtlety of the radio broadcast, the PPD bowed to the arguments of PRIDCO. The summons of Muñoz's party to immobilize labor corresponded with PRIDCO's claims that technical experts reached decisions beyond the grasp of laypeople to deliver the benefits of industrialization. The PPD made clear its choice between workers and industry when the party distanced itself from the strike. Muñoz's party also demarcated the limits of consent: workers who did not accept the policies of PRIDCO could not expect in return the sympathy or support of the PPD.

As if the party's remarks about the PRGC strike were not enough, that same week Ramos Antonini and his team took decisive steps to bring the conflict in the sugar industry to an end. An astounding contrast existed between the successful outcome of the sugar strike and the utter frustration of PRGC workers to win the PPD's support. While the sugar strike converged with the PPD's interest to steer the labor movement, the protest at the glass plant challenged the party's policies of industrial development. This contradiction did not stop the PPD. Party officials offered words of approval to sugar workers but summarily dismissed with their statements the PRGC strike. They gave an answer to why a section of the CGT had, according to them, an excessive militancy. PPD officials blamed what they saw as elements from outside the ranks of labor such as Communists and Nationalists.[128] With arguments of this sort, Muñoz's party silenced the history of common action not only between Communists, Nationalists, and labor, but also between those groups and the PPD. Moreover, the PPD turned the tables on the argument that Colón Gordiany and Sáez Corales expressed during the sugar strike. For PPD officials, all but their party were outsiders alien to labor's best interests.

Swift action accompanied the words of the PPD. In the midst of labor troubles at PRIDCO and the sugar industry, the CGT met to celebrate its third annual congress at the end of March.[129] As before, the PPD sent Barreto Pérez to the congress as its most trusted delegate. Barreto Pérez received instructions from Muñoz to read a telegram he sent to the labor assembly.[130] At face value, Muñoz's cable meant no more than a display of sympathy. Muñoz told workers to expect "the stimulation, sympathy, and cooperation of the government created in the elections of November 7."[131] As a political maneuver, the words of Muñoz came down like a sledgehammer. They made perfectly clear Muñoz's intention to tighten the PPD's grip within the CGT. The third congress of the CGT was an unsettling event and a turning point for the union. At the worst point of the meeting, the delegates resorted to physical aggression. A skirmish ensued when Félix Morales, the leader of the PRGC strike, interrupted the proceedings to address the audience at the assembly.[132] This episode made more than evident the division of the CGT.[133] Workers paid the ultimate price when the ties between pro-PPD forces and pro-CGT forces within the union snapped shortly after the congress. Labor leaders such as Sáez Corales and Colón Gordiany tried mending the split and salvaging the CGT but to no avail. Their union came to be known as the "CGT 'Auténtica'" (CGT-A), while the union loyal to the PPD received the name of "CGT 'Gubernamental'" (CGT-G). The leaders of both unions fought over which represented the original CGT.

After the CGT congress and its debacle, negotiations began to end the strike at the glass factory. On April 2, a meeting took place between workers and managers of PRIDCO.[134] Along with Moscoso, company officials met with a broad line up of labor leaders, including Sáez Corales, Colón Gordiany, and Morales. Several UEIC representatives joined the negotiations such as union president Morales Luchessi, secretary Cifredo, and legal adviser Víctor M. Bosch. Goldsmith, the mediator of the U.S. Labor Department, also intervened in the conference. Despite the assistance of high-level officials, no solution was reached on that day. The negotiations dragged on for several more weeks. On behalf of PRGC workers, the CGT-A announced its plan in mid-April to inform Governor Tugwell and the legislature about conditions in the glass factory.[135] According to Colón Gordiany, the CGT-A would send a "memorandum" detailing the "history" of past and present difficulties of PRGC workers. While making this announcement, Colón Gordiany summed up labor's demands, which by now entailed the recognition of their union and the creation of a committee to address grievances.

The UEIC, Colón Gordiany said, would not take further action until the authorities gave an answer to the "memorandum." Glassworkers demonstrated their firm decision to wait with preparations for a long-term struggle. According to the latest UEIC resolution, workers committed themselves to a "two-year strike" plan. The union also instructed labor to concentrate on two tasks. Some workers would remain on the picket lines, while others took jobs in other parts of the island. No major news was heard about the PRGC strike until May 15, when a labor assembly agreed to end the conflict after accepting a new offer of PRIDCO.[136] Several gains came as a relief to workers such as the recognition of their union, a bargain agreement to be discussed in 1946, and their inclusion in a committee to address grievances.[137] This committee consisted of two labor representatives, two company officials, and, in the case of an impasse, the regional director of the NLRB. Although far from a resounding victory, the PRGC strike was not in vain. Glassworkers achieved some of their original demands and could expect improvements at the factory. Overall, however, the PRGC strike loomed as a gloomy precedent for labor. It made clear the PPD's reluctance to negotiate with workers at the expense of industry. Social justice had been displaced to the background of colonial politics in Puerto Rico.

POLITICAL EXCLUSION AND ITS EFFECTS

If the PRGC strike and the division of the CGT left any doubt about the PPD's political intentions, another event of consequence dispelled all questions about the aims of Muñoz and his adherents. In February 1946, the PPD made a deliberate show of force when it met in Arecibo to expel the CPI and the CGT-A from the ranks of the party. No particular event seemed to have triggered the decision of the PPD. Instead, all evidence indicates that Muñoz planned the "ukase" most carefully.[138] Before the expulsion of the CGT-A from the PPD, labor made several unsuccessful attempts to reconcile the two factions of the CGT.[139] Colón Gordiany and Barreto Pérez extended many offers and counteroffers to each other to reunite the union.[140] Despite the initiatives taken by both sides, CGT-A leaders expressed mistrust of the CGT-G's assurances, deeming them lame at best.[141] Meanwhile, independentists within the CPI continued their campaign for sovereignty. The president of the CPI, Concepción de Gracia, stepped up his critique of Muñoz and his party's stance on the status issue.[142]

The leader of the PPD planned the Arecibo Assembly to produce maximum effect. Muñoz's political maneuver entailed a series of articles he published one after another for four days before the meeting of the PPD.[143] His articles not only set the stage for the event but also attempted to imprint into the collective memory of Puerto Ricans the political reorientation of the PPD. To make his point, Muñoz focused little on the past history of the PPD such as the party's pledge toward labor and independentists. Instead, Muñoz stressed what he called a matter of "life or death": the economic situation of Puerto Rico.[144] In his first article, Muñoz spelled out his main concerns such as the rate of deaths, overpopulation, poverty, and the few resources of the island. Muñoz's distress was such that he worried about "a catastrophe more tragic than a lost war" if the island did not augment production to solve its problems.[145] Failure to improve the economy, Muñoz argued, could mean only that "Puerto Rico is lost."[146] According to the leader of the PPD, "the people of Puerto Rico, in their civilization, would disappear as a luminous and brief flare that turned into smoke in the great gloom of time."[147]

In his next articles, Muñoz noted that the increase of production "must be a common interest of all Puerto Ricans."[148] On the one hand, Muñoz saw no need for "discrepancy" because "maximum production" was for the "general benefit." On the other hand, Muñoz argued that economic improvement demanded "intangible forces of spiritual vigor and honesty of understanding; and tangible forces of maximum effectivity in the economic process of production."[149] The CPI and CGT-A did not fit Muñoz's call for higher values and the utmost effort to solve the problems of the island. According to Muñoz, instead of showing earnest concern for the urgent needs of Puerto Rico, the CPI and CGT-A acted as "saboteurs" against the program of the PPD.[150] Muñoz vilified both organizations by stressing what he saw as "conspiratorial subterfuges" and "maneuvers to infiltrate" the PPD. For Muñoz, Puerto Rico faced a "New Coalition," a "snake" under the "disguise" of the CPI and CGT-A.[151]

Muñoz's articles paid no attention to the fact that labor and independentists were the ones being assaulted by a party that once profited from their support. Far from being the targets of a biased attack, labor and independentists appeared as villains against the PPD in the articles of Muñoz. The leader of the PPD tried to legitimate with his arguments a course of action that did not correspond with the basis for consent of party followers. For many PPD supporters, consent meant dialogue, consultation, and room for their own demands. CGT-A workers, for example, insisted on an inclusive policy-making process. The unilateral decisions of Muñoz's party fell outside the scope of a flexible and inclusive form of consent. It was not enough for the PPD to expel the most dynamic organizations from its ranks. The PPD also began to redraw the basis of consent. Muñoz's accusations against the CGT-A and CPI left no room for ambiguities. By viewing the economic situation as a matter of "life or death," Muñoz sanctioned reprimands against agents with different aims from those of the PPD. Muñoz's notion of "maximum production" served the PPD in demanding conformity from Puerto Ricans.

The process of political exclusion that began with Muñoz's articles climaxed on February 10 at the Arecibo Assembly. No doubt could have existed among PPD members about the gravity of the meeting. An event that brought together the Founders Council, central committee, and legislators of the PPD had few precedents.[152] After the Arecibo Assembly, it was open season on the CGT-A and CPI. The PPD informed its members about the expulsion of both groups from the party. To identify dissidents, Muñoz and his closest aides coordinated their efforts to check out the statements of party members in the press and other sources. On February 18, Muñoz specifically instructed the PPD's general secretary, Yldefonso Solá Morales, to go over the letters published in *El Mundo* and *El Imparcial* since the assembly.[153] Once Solá found out about "the under signers of letters backing those that have been left outside the party," he had to write to all of them in "friendly but firm terms" about the PPD's position and inquire if they "insist in their attitude." Muñoz said to Solá, "take note of all persons as they answer. Check what position they occupy in the Party and in the Government." What Muñoz had in mind became clear in a letter he sent to the mayor of Corozal.[154] Not even municipal positions related to the PPD could be held by those deemed disloyal to the party.

Frequently, Muñoz indicated the proper course of action in dealing with dissidents. For example, Muñoz's brief memorandum to House speaker Francisco M. Susoni informed that, due to the manifestations of "Mr. Quiñones Elías, to the effect that he would not retire from the [CPI], that compatriot no longer is a Popular and, consequently, should not be summoned" to the party's meetings.[155] On another occasion, when Muñoz asked Solá to address the cases of María Luisa Quiñones and Severo Ramos, he insisted that party officials "had to maintain themselves serene in the expression but absolutely clear, definitive, and firm in the strict compliance of the Arecibo accords."[156] Certain phrases never failed to repeat themselves in the correspondence that Muñoz sent directly to party followers. For him, the activities of political rivals were "sabotages" and their organizations equaled "disguised parties" within the PPD. On February 15, just five days after the PPD's resolution, Muñoz made official the expulsion from the party of Senator William Córdova Chirino, Representative José Luis Feliú Pesquera, Representative Baltazar Quiñones Elías, and Aguadilla's mayor Fernando Milán.[157]

Muñoz orchestrated the Arecibo Assembly not only to cleanse the PPD of dissidents but also to keep party members in line. Without delay, PPD followers pledged loyalty toward Muñoz with words that matched their leader's zeal against dissidents. For Leandro Cabranes, the mayor of Corozal, "Muñoz is the only ship that can conduct the people of Puerto Rico to a safe port without risking their happiness with patriotic impulsiveness."[158] In a similar vein, other supporters of Muñoz viewed him as the "only man that will liberate us from hunger, misery, and slavery" and as "a beacon of salvation in this stormy night of Puerto Rican politics."[159] Religious motifs abounded in some messages of PPD followers, such as the cable of Justo A. Casablanca, who praised Muñoz's "gospel," his "versicles," and the "light illuminating the path toward the future."[160] Besides the messages that commended Muñoz for his "brilliant" and "patriotic" decisions, many correspondents offered proof that they no longer belonged to the CPI or CGT-A. For example, after sending letters of resignation to Concepción de Gracia, the CPI president, individuals forwarded a copy of the document to Muñoz. Often, people professed their belief in independence even if they agreed to abandon the CPI.

PPD followers did not shy away from taking an aggressive stance against dissidents. In their letters to Concepción and his aides, some people vilified the CPI by calling it, for example, a "little group," the "enemy," and an organization with a "fatal deviation" of goals.[161] In a cable to Muñoz, a group of workers was said to be "killing the snake," an epithet that the PPD used against the CPI and CGT-A.[162] A similar case is the letter of Manuel Torres Reyes, who wrote to Muñoz that most of the CPI consisted of "veiled enemies of the PPD and, above all, personal enemies of yours."[163] He added that "each [CPI] Committee is a cave of conspirators that speaks of killing, of overthrowing the Popular Party and fantastic revolutions." To explain why he delayed his decision to abandon his position in the CPI, Torres said that Solá, the PPD's secretary, "recommended me not to renounce so I may render a good intelligence service to the party" and "learn about anything being forged by the 'revolutionaries' of the CPI."[164] Recruiting spies was not off-limits for the PPD. Party officials not only distanced themselves from dissidents and snooped their activities, but also accused members of the CPI and CGT-A. For example, Ismael Cruz Nieves denounced to Muñoz the mayor of Toa Baja, his secretary, and the school director as members of the CGT-A.[165] A similar charge came from Elías Martínez, who said that a "gang of saboteurs" in his town enjoyed the best wages and privileges.[166]

The expulsion of CGT-A and CPI members from the PPD caused confusion among the ranks of the party. Many PPD officials asked Muñoz for advice. The PPD committee of Aguadilla asked Muñoz what to do with their mayor, who was an active member of the CPI.[167] In the towns of Añasco and Toa Baja, conflicts ensued between supporters and opponents of the Arecibo Assembly resolution. PPD officials of both towns worried about hasty sanctions against "good Populars" or those "without political experience."[168] Meanwhile, Miguel Rosado, the mayor of Toa Baja, solemnly asked Muñoz if his noncompliance with the party's resolution would led to the exclusion of his town from the benefits of government agencies. In reply to the apparently tongue-in-cheek letter of Rosado, Muñoz wrote back simply saying that his question could be best answered by other mayors "who, like you, are not Populars."[169] In some cases, the PPD initiated investigations such as the one carried out in Ponce by Barreto Pérez to verify the loyalty of a PPD official.[170] Although the PPD expelled several members without opposition, the CGT-A and CPI did not remain passive. For example, Héctor Graciani, the secretary of the CGT-A, visited a group of workers in Río Piedras to obtain declarations for a radio program.[171] Similarly, CPI leader Baltazar Quiñones Elías toured several towns to secure signatures for his cause.[172] Fernando Milán, the mayor of Aguadilla, and Abelardo Ceide, a member of the municipal assembly, accompanied Quiñones as representatives of the CPI to the towns of Aguada, Rincón, and Añasco.[173]

Whether they leaned in favor of, or against the PPD's resolution, independentists and workers expressed varying degrees of uncertainty to Muñoz. According to Pedro Almodóvar, secretary of the PPD committee in Guánica, "I continue being an independentist, I shelter that ideal in my heart, and I will sustain it always, though outside the CPI."[174] Rubén Gaztambide, president of the PPD committee in Río Piedras, asked Muñoz if he wanted written statements from CPI members who "were not attacking us" and represented a local branch "without strength." Gaztambide informed that, "although the immense majority of us Populars are independentists," he would take care of the situation in his town. Pedro Rodríguez Díaz, the treasurer and school director of Hormigueros, informed Muñoz that he would comply with the PPD by renouncing his position as local president of the CPI. Having said that, Rodríguez highlighted the inconsistency of the party for failing to include statehooders in its latest resolution. According to Rodríguez, many

PPD members belonging to the so-called Pro Statehood Congress deserved the sort of response that the party aimed only against the CPI. Statehooders within the PPD, said Rodríguez, "pitilessly attacked" Muñoz and the party, leading many followers to comment why the collectivity had not taken action.[175]

Some workers voiced to Muñoz their displeasure about the PPD's reorientation before and after the Arecibo Assembly took place. According to a letter from workers of Mayagüez, Muñoz relied in a "partial way" on representatives of the CGT-G and FLT. Workers said that CGT-G officials "had done nothing for their organization" and that the FLT was "reactionary to social justice."[176] Muñoz, said labor, did not extend an invitation either to the CGT-A, "which truly represents the majority of workers in this suffering colony," or to the CPI, "which is giving everything to solve the political status of P.R. according to the true cause, which is sovereignty." Workers concluded by saying, "Don Luis, we lament very much to tell you that it seems that you are only interested . . . in men that take big causes for personal ends, and those that fight for true causes and for the good of the people" are not wanted.[177] A similar critique is the strong letter that Muñoz received from workers of the beer and soft drink industry. After reminding Muñoz that his political endeavors "opened the eyes of all workers," labor asked him: "is it the case that you want to close them now, converting us into slaves of the employer?"[178]

Several months after the Arecibo Assembly, Pablo L. Molina, union treasurer of sugar workers in Toa Baja, wrote to Muñoz about his misgivings.[179] Molina introduced himself as "a conscious, responsible, and honest worker" who joined the PPD in 1942. He did so under the conviction that "this party is the best instrument in the struggle of the working masses and rural people." Molina's "ardor, enthusiasm, and courage" during the 1944 election led him to spread the PPD's message among workers. After presenting his credentials as a genuine supporter of the party and labor, Molina conveyed to Muñoz his feelings about the PPD's reorientation. Molina explained that "today, I do not know if I am morally authorized to call myself a Popular." He found "hurtful" the dilemma of being at the same time a "politician" and a "worker." Molina said to Muñoz: "As a politician, I am squared and on the level with the party. As a worker . . . I am squared and on the level with my union, I am a worker! That is to say, I consider myself loyal and faithful to my labor union." Molina concluded by saying, "like me, in an identical position, are thousands and thousands of humble and suffering workers . . . that believe in you and trust you, not knowing if we are in or out of the party. What is our position? You have the word, Don Luis."[180]

Like Molina, many other workers in Puerto Rico wondered about the discrepancy between the PPD's actions in the past and its sudden change of policies. What was possible some years ago, to work alongside the party in favor of reform, had given way to a different sort of relationship. By the late 1940s, labor could expect help from the PPD only after accepting a passive role. A portion of the rank and file could not find a good explanation for the latest decisions of Muñoz's party. Many workers had a notion of consent that did not correspond with the tactics of PPD officials. For labor groups such as the CGT-A, consent meant that its support toward the party demanded obligations from Muñoz and his adherents in return. Since the PPD imagined itself as the champion of "the people" in an era that outshone the past, workers saw all the more reason for PPD leaders to honor their obligation toward labor. Many workers expected the PPD to reciprocate their acquiescence toward the party with a range of policies such as support for labor protests, commitment to social reform, and their inclusion in decisionmaking. Muñoz's unilateral measures must have come as a shock to many workers. The Arecibo Assembly veered far from the demands for dialogue and consultation that informed the notion of consent of certain labor groups.

For CGT-A leaders, the Arecibo Assembly lacked any justification. Colón Gordiany asked Muñoz to prove when, where, and how labor perpetrated the sabotage.[181] According to Colón Gordiany, the unfounded accusations of Muñoz, a leader who knew and spoke so much of democracy, could only mean an act of bad faith. The president of the CGT-A said that "the working people" demanded an explanation from Muñoz. Colón Gordiany felt it unnecessary to express once again his union's support for the industrial and economic program that "the people" approved on 1940. Long before that year, Colón Gordiany argued, CGT workers had been striving for "a new order of economic justice."[182] When Muñoz failed to respond to the CGT-A, Colón Gordiany reiterated his words.[183] Union leaders of the CGT-A added their voice of protest to that of Colón Gordiany with a manifesto against the PPD's "political claw."[184] Despite the affirmations of the CGT-A, the union faced a well-entrenched foe. The PPD used *La Democracia, El Batey*, and its radio program to launch a barrage against the CGT-A.[185] Muñoz's party pictured the CGT-A as an unruly minority in an effort to undermine a strong advocate of labor not docile to the PPD.

The consequences of the Arecibo Assembly were felt before long. On the one hand, Muñoz and his party gave full support to the policies of PRIDCO. On the other hand, the CGT-A faced adversity as a union no longer under the auspices of the PPD. This became evident in mid-1946, when PRIDCO completed the construction of its second factory, the Puerto Rico Paper and Pulp Corporation (PRPPC). As a final touch before production began, the JIRT initiated an election to determine which one of two unions had the right to sign a collective agreement with the PRPPC.[186] The election pitted the Union of the Paper Industry of the CGT-A—Unión de la Industria del Papel (UIP)—against the Brotherhood of Workers of the CGT-G—Hermandad de Trabajadores (HT). From the very start, trouble tinged the vote at the PRPPC factory. Friction between the UIP and HT impaired the proceedings of the JIRT.

The JIRT held two elections that failed to determine the union with a majority.[187] Both unions of the paper factory questioned the alleged advantage of their opponent. After some debate, workers cast their vote a third time in an election that the JIRT announced as final.[188] Instead of solving the labor situation at the PRPPC, the electoral outcome as proclaimed by the JIRT made matters worse. Shortly after declaring the victory of the UIP, the JIRT reversed its decision in favor of the HT.[189] Although the UIP did not wait to make its protest heard, it took several weeks for the JIRT to reconsider its position. To the disappointment of the UIP, the government made clear its stance in favor of the CGT-G. The CGT-A received a letter from the PRPPC stating the exclusive right of the HT to negotiate with the factory.[190] On November 1, Moscoso wrote to Muñoz about the situation at the PRPPC.[191] One day later, the JIRT made public its decision to affirm once more the electoral victory of the HT.[192]

The CGT-A did not accept the determination of the government without protest. UIP workers requested again that JIRT reconsider their case.[193] The CGT-A appealed to the newly appointed governor of Puerto Rico, PPD leader Jesús T. Piñero.[194] Workers had a chance to meet with the governor to present their case in late November 1946. Colón Gordiany and other labor leaders expressed their concern about their union's lack of representation in the factories of PRIDCO. CGT-A officials also worried about the formation of company unions. Although Piñero listened to labor's concern, it was clear that the CGT-A lacked the clout it once had to make itself heard. As a union that opposed the unfriendly labor policies of PRIDCO, the CGT-A faced the PPD's reluctance to deal with agents at the fringes of its rigid notion of consent. After the Arecibo Assembly, the PPD viewed consent toward the party as unconditional support for the program of industrial production. Nothing short of faith, devotion, and loyalty for PRIDCO sufficed for Muñoz and his aides. When the patronage of Muñoz became off-limits for the CGT-A, the PPD stigmatized the union so as to make workers think twice before following in the steps of Colón Gordiany and his supporters.

Despite the CGT-A's precarious position, the union declared a strike at the paper factory on December 5.[195] During the next five days, the UIP felt the extent of the opposition against the PRPPC strike. PRIDCO simply ignored the demands of strikers and began to negotiate with the HT.[196] The general secretary of the CGT-G, Armando Rivero, recalled the HT's victory at the labor election sponsored by the JIRT.[197] As if to back Rivero, Fernando Sierra Berdecía, the president of the JIRT, argued that before reviewing the election, the agency would have to prove the CGT-A's claims against the HT.[198] According to Colón Gordiany, the HT was a company union that dissolved itself in late November. The controversy at the paper factory reached the legislature but to no avail. Ramos Antonini voiced the decision to dismiss the demands for an investigation of the PRPPC strike.[199] Despite the broad opposition to the strike, the UIP had a strong case against the HT. *El Mundo* stated it well in an editorial.[200] The fact that far more men were on strike than at work disproved the HT's claims as the union with a majority. Moreover, the UIP's petition for another election did not seem unreasonable, considering that the JIRT had as a function to help labor.

Although the PPD avoided any comment about the PRPPC strike, the position of the party toward workers became more than clear by mid-December. The PPD pushed ahead legislation to control labor strikes in the government.[201] Muñoz presented the project of the PPD as necessary. Puerto Rico, Muñoz argued, had to protect democracy from the pointless actions of "minorities." According to Muñoz, allowing strikes against the government "is to open the road toward fascism, that is the disorder and terrorism of any transitory minority that exercises practices of coercion."[202] The words of Muñoz ended all possibilities for the CGT-A to recall the PPD's pledge toward social justice. Since the PPD stressed industrial production above any other concern, even the modest demands of the CGT-A seemed out of place. Besides having little chance to outmatch the PPD's relentless call for industrialization, CGT-A workers could no longer include themselves in the definition of consent of Muñoz's party. The CGT-A had to endure beyond the boundaries of consent of the PPD as one of the party's so-called minorities. By redrawing the lines of consent to comply with the needs of industrial production, the PPD excluded from its plans agents with interests, claims, and ideals of their own.

At first, the effort of the government to solve the PRPPC strike had little effect. Although Piñero named Judge Arcilio Alvarado as labor mediator, the policies of the JIRT, PRIDCO, and legislature eclipsed the initiative of the governor.[203] Too many agencies had their say about the strike, making it hard to find an appropriate course of action. The deficiency of the government in coping with labor unrest not only worried Piñero's administration but also prompted a better response toward the PRPPC strike. On December 11, 1946, James W. Balano sent a confidential memorandum to Piñero about the lack of an agency to investigate labor unrest, the JIRT's policy of addressing disputes after they started, and the need to promote agreements between industry and labor.[204] Balano feared that "sugar and dock strikes are imminent." He also stressed that "the Paper Factory strike has set a bad precedent to the detriment of the Insular Labor Relations Board."[205] The lost of credibility and prestige of the government prompted the PPD into action. Although the PPD prioritized industrial production above all else, the party could not push its policies too far. Muñoz's party faced the fact that its political legitimacy depended on a certain degree of accountability toward followers.

Three days after Balano delivered his memorandum to Piñero, the JIRT decided to intervene in the PRPPC strike. Sierra Berdecía offered to hold a new election in exchange for the UIP's return to work.[206] Before the end of the year, workers of the paper factory called off the strike. The conclusion of the PRPPC strike seemed a victory for labor. Workers secured a new election and a temporary mediator to address grievances before the negotiation of a collective agreement. Subsequent events, however, overshadowed the partial success of the UIP. The factory workers of PRIDCO faced another challenge when the PPD reevaluated the policies of industrial development. For several months after the PRPPC strike, constant news reached the public about the financial difficulties of PRIDCO's factories and the company's attempts to cut losses. In 1948, PRIDCO made final its decision to sell all its factories and invite U.S. capital to industrialize the island.[207]

Despite PRIDCO's failure in 1944 and its partial success in 1947 to get approval for industrial incentive laws, the company achieved its goal the third time around with the Industrial Tax Exemption Act. According to Alex W. Maldonado, "on May 13, 1948, the legislature approved Act No. 184 granting full tax exemption—income, property, excise, and municipal taxes—to new industries for a period of ten years, with an additional three years of partial exemption."[208] The introduction of this policy—the core of PRIDCO's "Operación Manos a la Obra" (Operation Bootstrap) and its program of "industrialization by invitation"—highlighted the PPD's decision to shed its contradictory role as labor representative and employer. By doing away with the ambiguous double bind of the PPD, Muñoz and his aides improved their chances to build consent for industrial development without the need for major compromises with labor.

After the factory strikes of PRIDCO workers, the gap between the CGT-A and PPD forced these organizations into very different paths. Workers who no longer had access to the patronage of Muñoz faced a dismal reality. During the early months of 1947, leaders of the CGT-A made an effort to form a "united labor front."[209] From the start, however, conflict within the CGT-A marred the initiatives of the union. The foremost leaders of the CGT-A, Colón Gordiany and Sáez Corales, could not agree on many points to unite the labor movement.[210] To make matters worse, the attitude of CGT-G leaders ranged from noncooperation to opposition.[211] The final blow against the labor movement came with the extension of the Taft-Hartley Act to Puerto Rico.[212] At that point, the CGT-A abandoned its efforts to form a "united front." Instead, the "Pro Unity Committee" of the CGT-A decided to create a new labor organization under the name of General Union of Workers—Unidad General de Trabajadores (UGT).[213] Far from offering a measure of unity, the UGT represented another episode in the division and fragmentation of the labor movement. At a later date, Sáez Corales concluded that the formation of the UGT was a "bad mistake."[214] Even so, according to Sáez Corales, the UGT proved its mettle in two strikes against the Taft-Hartley Act before succumbing to the law and facing an "employers' paradise" in Puerto Rico.

While the CGT-A's plan to unite labor collapsed, the PPD fully embraced the policies of industrial development. It is telling, for example, that Ramos Antonini, an official of the CGT-G, delivered a speech at the opening of a PRIDCO factory in early 1947.[215] He emphasized the benefits of greater production for labor and industry. Equally noteworthy was Moscoso's assistance to the fifth congress of the CGT-A to make a speech.[216] He foresaw a great future for industry. While the PPD and PRIDCO tried to endear themselves to labor, state officials introduced policies of few benefits for workers. A case that demands attention is a measure that decided the fate of labor for years to come. Moscoso stated it well in a letter he sent to Muñoz, Piñero, and Fernós after the landslide victory of Harry S. Truman and the Democratic Party in the election of 1948.[217] The general manager of PRIDCO stressed the need to exclude the island's workers from the federal laws of minimum wage. Considering that Moscoso's argument would have a vital impact on the future policies of PPD officials, it is appropriate to quote his letter at length:

Everyone here at PRIDCO is as same as you very happy for the victory of President Truman . . . . However, it should not be overlooked the fact that the program of industrialization can end up *totally destroyed* if Puerto Rico is not permitted to continue enjoying the privilege that it now has to establish minimum wages through industrial committees according to the Federal Labor Standards Act. Without any doubt, Truman and the Congress owe their victory to the backing that was given by the labor unions. I do not believe that anyone doubts that the federal minimum wage will be raised. . . . You should not have the slightest doubt either that due to the protests that you already know, there will be an attempt to fully include Puerto Rico in the federal law. If this takes place, it would terminate in a *fulminating way* the program of industrialization.

It is lamentable that our government, which has given so much backing to the labor movement and to the rights of workers, sees itself compelled to solicit its exemption from the federal law of Minimum Wage, but frankly I see no other way to keep afoot our program of industrialization.

If we want the program of industrialization to keep apace *we have to sit down and discuss the means that we will utilize to confront and vanquish the pressure that labor unions will exercise to frustrate our program.* (emphasis added)[218]

At the expense of labor, the PPD raised once again the specter of economic doom to ensure the relentless march to increase production. With a flair for dramatic language and apocalyptic imagery, Moscoso visualized the worst scenario possible for the program of PRIDCO. According to Moscoso, industrial development could face a catastrophe—it could be "totally destroyed" or "terminate in a fulminating way"—if Puerto Rico did not vaunt a "cheap" labor force to attract U.S. capital. The general manager of PRIDCO argued that "only the hope of obtaining a cheaper labor force than the one on the mainland" induced the relocation of entrepreneurs to the island. Compared to tax exemption, according to Moscoso, the low cost of labor in Puerto Rico was a "non-artificial factor" that did more to attract capital than the former.[219] Moreover, Moscoso succinctly spelled out his request for joint action between the PPD and PRIDCO to neutralize the island's labor movement. Besides delegitimating the protests of workers, Moscoso placed the blame on labor for trying "to frustrate" the program of PRIDCO. For Moscoso, far from having a stake in industrial development, the adverse intentions of workers warranted PRIDCO's scheme to keep the demands of labor at bay.

The letter of Moscoso is troubling even if we place aside the merits or flaws of his argument—the need to exclude Puerto Rico from minimum wage laws—and his assertion about the PPD's prolabor credentials—a government that "has given so much backing to the labor movement and to the rights of workers." Both issues could have well led to debate between PPD leaders and followers, being even possible for the party to have its claims fully endorsed by its constituency or at least carefully appraised after a suitable round of negotiations. The problem is that Moscoso did not acknowledge at all the possibility of dialogue and consultation with PPD supporters. He and the PPD triumvirate—Muñoz, Piñero, and Fernós—would "sit down and discuss" labor policies without giving a second thought to the position of workers. In this way, Moscoso informed the process that led PPD leaders to choose unilateral policy-making as a course of action.

To some degree, Moscoso's letter confirmed what Muñoz had already told labor. Miles Galvin says that "Muñoz Marín, according to César Andreu Iglesias, a CGT activist at the time, warned the CGT leadership that unless 'we cooperated we would be crushed like cockroaches.' 'We didn't and he did,' Andreu Iglesias went on to remark."[220] When the PPD asked labor to cooperate "responsibly" with

PRIDCO, the party in fact demanded from workers a passive role. The PPD's position in the late 1940s made clear that social justice was no longer the basis of consent. On the one hand, the party portrayed the consent of its followers as hardly more than blind adherence and total devotion to industrial development. On the other hand, people still gave their consent to the PPD for a myriad of reasons, even though their words might have been drowned by the party's discourse. That is, although the island's mass movement did not fail to encompass a multiplicity of interests and aims in the late 1940s, it shifted away from the sort of interaction between agents that brought forth social justice, made possible ample demands for reform, and gave free rein to alternative visions of consent. Tolerance was one of many casualties at the end of the decade.

THE PPD'S "MOMENT OF ARRIVAL"

The years between 1946 and 1948 encompassed the initial stage of the PPD's "moment of arrival." During this period, which climaxed with Muñoz's electoral victory as governor of Puerto Rico, the PPD produced what Chatterjee calls "a discourse of order, of the rational organization of power."[221] With the exclusion of the CGT-A and CPI from the party, the PPD eliminated the need for broad compromises with labor and advocates of independence. The Arecibo Assembly left the ground open for the reorientation of priorities of the party. Without the challenge of political rivals, PPD officials articulated their "moment of arrival" as Chatterjee describes it, "in a single, consistent, unambiguous voice . . . glossing over all earlier contradictions, divergences and differences."[222] Moreover, the discourse of PPD officials, which professed economic rationales to justify the political interests of the party, mirrored the rhetorical maneuvers of the colonial elite studied by Chatterjee. In their effort to define consent mainly as support for industrialization, PPD officials geared the island's nationalist thought into concerns of little consequence for their own political aspirations. That is, the PPD used its policies of industrial development to demand the compliance or noninterference of sectors championing independence as the best way to end colonialism.

Muñoz delivered two vital messages to reorient the PPD in the summer of 1946. Although not meant as sequels, these pieces share similar ideas. One cannot overestimate their relevance, since both messages shaped the rhetoric of the PPD for years to come. The first case is the "invitation" of Muñoz to the "battle of production."[223] Muñoz delivered this message to commemorate his father's birth date, an annual ritual that had served many times before to loudly voice the objectives of the PPD. Although Muñoz visited his hometown to honor the past, he pronounced a speech that focused entirely on the future. Political concerns about the status question served Muñoz as a springboard to address economic matters. Muñoz reworked the topic of colonialism to avoid references to divisive concerns such as different status options. The economic maladies of Puerto Rico informed Muñoz's rationale for common action. He argued that economic improvement demanded the cooperation of all people because it affected all on the island. The "battle of production," as proclaimed by Muñoz, was meant as a populist cry to secure the consent of all society in favor of industrial development.

To some extent, the call for a "battle of production" was less an effort to introduce a new policy than to provide an unambiguous and seamless definition of consent. Piecemeal remarks of PPD officials had already identified the party with modern life. The PPD press and radio program presented the party as the embodiment of factories, dams, electricity, technology, concrete houses, roads, planes, and airports.[224] As a slogan, the "battle of production" summed up the appeal of PPD officials to the imagination of people to transform Puerto Rico into a modern society. Increasing production, Muñoz argued, promised political emancipation, economic freedom, and a better livelihood. As a miracle solution to all problems, the "battle of production" stood far apart from the previous claims of the PPD. Muñoz's party portrayed the economy as an apolitical realm that welcomed the concerted action of Puerto Ricans. According to the PPD, all people could consent to industrial development because it represented an infallible force for the benefit of the entire island. The "battle of production" as proclaimed by Muñoz proved most advantageous to the PPD since it made the economy inhopitable to dialogue and debate. By presenting industrial development as an esoteric activity not open to questions, the party required blind faith from its followers.

With the "battle of production," consent became a unidirectional affair for the PPD. It is not far-fetched to visualize the cry for "battle" of Muñoz as the order of a commander in chief during a war. People engaged in the "battle of production" were not expected to ponder or probe the policies handed down from above by Muñoz. Indeed, the "battle of production" entailed many of the implications of armed conflict. Let us recall that when Muñoz expelled the CGT-A and CPI from the PPD, he made industrial development a matter of "life or death."[225] With a similar emphasis on mortal consequences, Moscoso warned his peers that the program of PRIDCO could be "totally destroyed" or "terminate in a fulminating way" if the federal laws of minimum wage were extended to Puerto Rico. It just took a small stretch of the imagination to carry the analogy of death, destruction, battle, and war further. The PPD did so when it voiced the need for "good soldiers" to watch out for "enemies" and denounce any sort of "sabotage."[226] For example, after examining the contrast between the "battle of production" and war, a columnist of *La Democracia* saw the former as most important and as the duty of all Puerto Ricans.[227]

The PPD's policies of industrial development demanded great sacrifices from the people. No doubt existed among PPD leaders that Puerto Ricans had to give their best in the name of production. Despite many sacrifices, the PPD argued that it was worth fighting the "battle of production." To make industrial development appealing, Muñoz highlighted the advantage of basic utilities such as roads, schools, houses, telephones, water, and electricity as well as the prospect of a better life.[228] The gadgets of modernity glittered in the discourse of the PPD, because Muñoz's party depicted such an unattractive image of the past.[229] In contrast to the PPD's squalid sketch of the years before 1940, the promise of industrialization seemed nothing short of a technopastoral paradise. Although the PPD cherished old traditions as part of its discourse, few concerns for cultural values from the past slowed down the party's rampage to increase production.

The second piece that Muñoz delivered to reorient the PPD was an article called "New Roads toward Old Objectives."[230] This article offered a grandiose vision of what Muñoz considered to be the facts of modern life. The setting for Muñoz's discussion of the status issue is not Puerto Rico but the world. Readers are drawn into a cosmopolitan society enthralled by fast-paced change and mobility. "New Roads toward Old Objectives" mirrored the "battle of production" in that it saw as best for Puerto Rico the innovative and dynamic qualities that Muñoz attributed to modern life. However, while the latter focused on the role of people to achieve liberty through production, the former assessed the consequences of global modernity for Puerto Rico. With greater sophistication than before, Muñoz raised again his idea of a world becoming interconnected due to modern techniques of communication and transportation. According to Muñoz, Puerto Rico belonged to a small global community that had just entered the atomic age. Muñoz argued that the swiftness of cars, airplanes, atomic energy, and world wars made political interdependency around the earth inevitable.[231]

By overwhelming the reader with what we call today "globalization," Muñoz sought to render obsolete notions of political freedom based on national sovereignty.[232] In his effort "to modernize" the status issue and the concept of liberty, Muñoz stressed that the international community as a "single world" no longer faced clearly defined political, territorial, and cultural boundaries. This meant for Puerto Rico that U.S. dominance amounted to no more than "silly imperialism."[233] Muñoz argued further that the aggressive U.S. economy in an interdependent world made it advantageous for Puerto Rico to secure ties with Americans through a status option such as autonomy. Muñoz argued that autonomy promised the fast pace of development that Puerto Rico needed to avoid a "collapse" of "civilization" and "life."[234]

The fancy argument of Muñoz sought to build consent for the continuance of U.S. colonial rule in Puerto Rico. Far from advancing the familiar appreciation of colonialism as a source of shame, Muñoz presented the island's political reality as an arrangement most attractive to Puerto Ricans. The island's colonial situation, as presented by Muñoz, shed its stigma as a political quagmire and acquired a legitimate name with autonomy. It followed from Muñoz' article that Puerto Ricans could feel good about the benefit of a political status that stood at the vanguard of modern life. As the perfect counterpart of Muñoz's interdependent world, colonialism under the guise of autonomy offered few reasons to Puerto Ricans for the denial of consent. Opposing colonialism soon became for the PPD an illogical reaction against the historical forces that Muñoz described in his article. By masking colonialism with references to modern interdependency, Muñoz made it hard to argue against the political policies of the PPD.

The ideas of Muñoz soon acquired the status of a dogma among PPD officials. Leaders of the party incorporated into their discourse Muñoz's notions about political and economic policies. That was the case to a greater extent after the PPD achieved a major political victory with the appointment of the first Puerto Rican governor, Jesús T. Piñero, in mid-1946. This event not only strengthened the PPD's resolve in favor of industrialization and autonomy but also enhanced the party's discourse. A good example is a speech that Antonio Fernós Isern, the resident commissioner of the PPD, delivered at the Club de las Américas in Washington, D.C., early in 1947.[235] Like Muñoz, Fernós made reference to historical forces that determined Puerto Rico's fate in the international community. In his quick review of the past, Fernós presented as inevitable the separation of the island from Spain. Despite this break, Fernós argued, Puerto Rico remained part of "western civilization" under the aegis of the United States. Fernós lauded Puerto Rico from a cultural standpoint as follows: "Let us look at the map of America. Where is Puerto Rico? It is on the main highway of American transit. It is a point on which air navigation converges, an obligatory stop for those traveling from North to South and South to North. The two languages of America live in Puerto Rico. The two cultures of America fuse and are fused in Puerto Rico. The races of America meet and become brothers in Puerto Rico."[236]

The speech of Fernós informed the PPD's effort to build consent for self-government under the U.S. flag. As in the messages of Muñoz, the economic needs of Puerto Rico stood at the forefront of Fernós' argument. However, the resident commissioner of the PPD gave a different spin to the modern demands of the economy. Instead of focusing on global interdependency, Fernós highlighted the need for Puerto Rico to overcome its isolation. Although Fernós pictured life in Puerto Rico as "hard, swift, energetic, dynamic," qualities that the PPD saw as modern, he believed in greater change to make the island a participant in the world economy. By presenting as unquestionable the global conditions of economic production, Fernós made home rule under U.S. tutelage a matter of common sense. Consent toward autonomy, according to Fernós, corresponded well with a simple fact of modern life: an interdependent world that required rapid economic development to keep up with modern changes. Fernós, like Muñoz, had played with these ideas before. A case to consider is what Fernós said in an earlier speech: "We are now at the beginning of the atomic age, we call it so because of the invention of the atomic bomb. But we do not mean that an era of atomization of the world is begun. We mean precisely the opposite. The mastering of the secrets of nature should lead to the maximum integration of mankind into one spiritual world of understanding and concerted peaceful effort."[237]

By referring to the "integration of mankind" and "one spiritual world," Fernós replayed the PPD's theme about the compatibility between the island's autonomy and global interdependency. Like Muñoz, Fernós used economic and technological rationales to legitimate U.S. colonialism. In Puerto Rico, as in other colonial contexts, the interplay of assumptions about modern life and the nation served the interests of local leaders. According to Chatterjee, the economic policies to "modernize" society informed the construction of nationalist thought in India. As a "new theoretical framework," the economy enabled the political elite of India to justify many sorts of demands in the name of the nation.[238] In Puerto Rico, too, economic policies shaped nationalism. In their effort to build consent for industrialization and autonomy, PPD leaders steered nationalist thought into concerns that posed few threats to the continuance of U.S. colonial rule in Puerto Rico. By conceiving nationalism as a cultural issue of no consequence to economic policies and political decisions, the PPD sought to secure its role as intermediary of U.S. interests on the island.[239] The PPD made Puerto Rican nationalism a bedfellow of U.S. colonialism. Muñoz's party made claims about the possibility of fulfilling nationalist aspirations with political autonomy under U.S. tutelage.

After the PPD's electoral victory of 1948, when Muñoz became the first Puerto Rican to be elected as governor, the party gave full endorsement to the articulation of a seamless and unambiguous discourse. The PPD's celebration of its victory and Muñoz's inauguration as governor marked the beginning of ample self-praise for the policies of the party. Leaders of the PPD voiced most strongly their views in a newly acquired press, *El Diario de Puerto Rico*.[240] Muñoz's party also made forceful claims in the mainland after it won the attention of U.S. publishers such as *Time, Newsweek, Life,* and several newspapers.[241] While the PPD basked in the attention of local and mainland audiences, the concerns of party officials about political status and industrial development saturated the media.[242]

Muñoz's inauguration speech of 1948 reinforced the connection that the PPD saw between modern conditions and the political future of Puerto Rico. According to Muñoz, "neither socialism, capitalism, communism or nationalism are forces comparable to the tremendous and ineluctable one of atomic energy."[243] All of those "-isms," Muñoz argued, could not compete with historical conditions that compelled Puerto Ricans to rethink the island's economic and political situation. With atomic energy, technology, science, and production at his side, Muñoz presented a dynamic and interdependent world that made room only for fast industrialization and autonomy in Puerto Rico. Instead of being a constraint, the atomic age represented for Muñoz a time of great potential to secure all those improvements already under way such as roads, schools, houses, electricity, airports, and other amenities. The rhetoric of Muñoz was not an isolated case but a variation of a theme that became dominant in the United States in the mid- and late 1940s. In a sense, Muñoz's words resembled mainland visions about the best and worst consequences of atomic energy. According to Paul Boyer, along with their fears, Americans concocted "fantasies of a techno-atomic utopia" and came up with implausible ideas such as "atomic cars" and "cancer-curing isotopes."[244] Although Muñoz's notion of the atomic age did not go that far, he devised his own "utopia" about the benefits of production and a future full of plenty for Puerto Ricans.

Besides Muñoz's inauguration speech of 1948, other messages demonstrated the single-mindedness of the party's technopastoral discourse. Of all the postelection statements of the PPD, two remarkable examples appeared in *Norte*, a magazine published in New York. Both pieces are valuable because they brought to a different plane Muñoz's speech about the "battle of production" and "New Roads toward Old Objectives." The first message is an article of Muñoz titled "A New State."[245] In this piece, the leader of the PPD summarily stated his view about the island's political status. Instead of examining, as before, the effects of modern life on Puerto Rico, Muñoz asserted as a matter of fact the creation of a "new state" as a result of major "historical forces." According to Muñoz, the "new state" owed its origin to "the creative dynamic of a modern policy" and not to "juridical" or "theoretical" premises.[246] This assertion led Muñoz to conclude that Puerto Rico did not constitute a colony. Muñoz argued that industrialization enabled Puerto Rico, unlike a colony, to produce more than raw material for exportation. Muñoz also stressed the island's political rights despite its exemption from federal taxes and representation. Although not equal to a U.S. state, Muñoz said that the island's association with the United States made it part of a "greater independence."

Muñoz's article exemplifies the discourse that gained ground as the mainstay of the PPD's "moment of arrival." As a statement of the PPD's political aims, the discourse of the party became dispassionate, uncomplicated, and straightforward. PPD leaders had already in mind the political formula that eventually produced the Commonwealth of Puerto Rico. As an effort to build consent toward that goal, the discourse of the PPD suffered a subtle, yet obvious, shift after the party's third electoral victory. A monologue supplanted the sense of dialogue that the PPD once tried to produce between the party and its audience. The discourse of the PPD not only became unambiguous but made no reference to previous contradictions of the island's populist movement.[247] The multifaceted political reality that underlay the common ground for consent received no acknowledgment from the PPD. Muñoz's party either glossed over or effaced the reasons for support of followers. PPD leaders assumed that consent toward the party came without divergences, uncertainties, hesitancy, indecision, doubt, or reluctance. This is best understood when one considers that the PPD no longer debated the merits of Puerto Rico's political situation but simply concluded that the island was no longer a colony.

On the one hand, the exclusion of agents who pressured the PPD to open up to them enabled the party to redefine consent. It was not just the exclusion of groups such as the CGT-A and CPI that informed the reorientation of consent but also the PPD's effort to appropriate as its own the concerns of former followers of the party. Consider, for example, how the PPD articulated a nationalist discourse despite the maneuvers of the party to accommodate itself to an enhanced version of colonial rule. On the other hand, consent acquired the meaning that best suited the PPD when the party embraced the economy as a key source of political legitimacy. The PPD never moved far from its urgent call to address economic problems above all other issues. This is well illustrated in an article of Salvador Tió titled "Industry or Death."[248] As a public relations official of PRIDCO, Tió focused on the economic aspects of Muñoz's "new state."

Although "Industry or Death" built upon the ideas about the "battle of production," Tió offered an extreme outlook of the island's economic grievances. The spokesman of PRIDCO presented the agricultural economy as a dead end.

According to Tió, the limits of agriculture to increase production and the inexorable rise of population constituted the main elements of an untenable situation. Economic conditions in Puerto Rico, Tío argued, demanded drastic measures. Since Tió saw emigration, education, and birth control as insufficient, he regarded "industry or death" as the most immediate challenge that beset the island. If industrial development did not work, Tió saw no other options than to disperse the people to the coasts of America, implement sterilization, or face death.

By viewing industrial development as a matter of life and death, Tió heightened the warlike implications of the "battle of production." The island's economic problems, which seemed akin to those of a war-torn country according to Tió's standards, demanded the ultimate sacrifice from Puerto Ricans to uphold the higher call of the PPD. Muñoz's party stressed that the "battle of production" was not to be taken lightly. Through the press and radio, the PPD highlighted the relevance of all aspects of life to ensure industrial development. The PPD argued, for example, that Puerto Ricans had to be healthy to fight with efficiency the "battle of production."[249] Having people well acquainted with machines was also a concern of the PPD. According to Muñoz, the education of Puerto Ricans about the devices of modern life had to start with children's toys.[250] PRIDCO focused on another concern when it asked local communities to open their clubs and civic centers to make foreign industrialists feel at home.[251] All these policies and many others demanded that Puerto Ricans had to perceive themselves, and behave, like modern individuals, as defined by the PPD.

Tió's "Industry or Death" highlighted the unambiguous character of the PPD's "moment of arrival." It followed from the article of Tió that consent toward the PPD's plan of industrial development meant an embrace of life. Inversely, Tió's article led one to believe that a lack of consent toward the plan of the PPD was equivalent to "death." These alternatives made clear to Puerto Ricans what they could expect from Muñoz's party. Advocates of industrial development could hope for the PPD's promise of better material and spiritual conditions. Opponents of industrialization faced the PPD's stigma as the one on a path of fatal consequences. Since the PPD pictured the economy as a truth well above and beyond the slightest doubt, the party shunned any questions about the choice between "industry or death." The PPD's approach to industrialization made the process of political exclusion complete. As the PPD's alternative to industrial production, "death" became the realm of dissidents. Consent as the political counterpart of economic development and modern life became the legacy of a dubious future.

NOTES

1. Leslie Bethell and Ian Roxborough, "The Postwar Conjuncture in Latin America and Its Consequences," in Bethell and Roxborough, eds., *Latin America between the Second World War and the Cold War, 1944-1948* (Cambridge: Cambridge University Press, 1992), pp. 327-328.

2. The number of people who cast their votes in the 1944 election came up to 591,978. The PPD won the election with a total of 383,280 votes. A total of 208,516 votes belonged to the opposition, which included the the Progressive Republican Union Party (with 101,779 votes), the Socialist Party (with 68,107 votes), and the Liberal Party (with 38,630 votes). In short, the PPD won by a margin of 174,764 votes over its main rivals. The PPD took control of the Legislature, except for four seats that belonged to the opposition. The party also elected resident commissioner Jesús T. Piñero. Two oddities in this election were the Authentic Party, which obtained 159 votes, and the Proletarian Party, which obtained 23 votes. Fernando Bayrón Toro, *Elecciones y partidos políticos de Puerto Rico 1809-2000* (Mayagüez: Editorial Isla, 2000), pp. 202-206.

3. Thomas G. Paterson, J. Garry Clifford, Kenneth J. Hagan, *American Foreign Relations: A History since 1895*, vol. 2, (Lexington, MA: D. C. Heath and Company, 1995), pp. 265-313.

4. Ibid., pp. 272-282.

5. Ivonne Acosta, *La Mordaza: Puerto Rico, 1948-1957* (Río Piedras: Editorial Edil, 1987), pp. 19-59; Georg Fromm, *César Andreu Iglesias: Aproximación a su vida y obra* (Río Piedras: Ediciones Huracán, 1977), pp. 46-48.

6. Emilio Pantojas García, *Development Strategies as Ideology: Puerto Rico's Export-Led Industrialization Experience* (Río Piedras: Editorial de la Universidad de Puerto Rico, 1990), pp. 61-99.

7. Bethell and Roxborough, *Latin America*, p. 1. U.S. politics suffered a similar fate. Nelson Lichtenstein, "From Corporatism to Collective Bargaining: Organized Labor and the Eclipse of Social Democracy in the Postwar Era," in Steve Fraser and Gary Gerstle, eds., *The Rise and Fall of the New Deal Order, 1930-1980* (Princeton: Princeton University Press, 1989), pp. 122-152.

8. Ernesto Laclau, *New Reflexions on the Revolution of Our Time* (London: Verso Books, 1991), p. 61; Ernesto Laclau, *Emancipation(s)* (London: Verso Books, 1996), p. 45.

9. Jacob Torfing, *New Theories of Discourse: Laclau, Mouffe, and Žižek* (Oxford: Blackwell Publishers, 1999), pp. 111-113.

10. Anna Marie Smith, *Laclau and Mouffe: The Radical Democratic Imaginary* (London: Routledge, 1998), pp. 177-181.

11. Ibid., p. 173. This relates to the effects of hegemony overall. According to Raymond Williams,

a lived hegemony is always a process. It is not, except analytically, a system or a structure. It is a realized complex of experiences, relationships, and activities, with specific and changing pressures and limits. In practice, that is, hegemony can never be singular. Its internal structures are highly complex, as can readily be seen in any concrete analysis. Moreover (and this is crucial, reminding us of the necessary thrust of the concept), it does not just passively exist as a form of dominance. It has continually to be renewed, recreated, defended, and modified. It is also continually resisted, limited, altered, challenged by pressures not at all its own. We have then to add to the concept of hegemony the concepts of counter-hegemony and alternative hegemony, which are real and persistent elements of practice. (Raymond Williams, *Marxism and Literature* (Oxford: Oxford University Press, 1977), pp. 112-113)

12. Partha Chatterjee, *Nationalist Thought and the Colonial World: A Derivative Discourse* (Minneapolis: University of Minnesota Press, 1986).

13. Ibid., p. 51.

14. *El Mundo*, January 13, 1945; *La Democracia*, January 14, February 10, 1945.

15. *El Mundo*, January 11, 13, 15, 31, 1945.

16. Pedro A. Cabán, "Industrial Transformation and Labour Relations in Puerto Rico: From 'Operation Bootstrap' to the 1970s," *Journal of Latin American Studies* 21 (October 1989): 559-591.

17. Ibid., pp. 560, 562-563.

18. Letter from James R. Watson to Oscar S. Smith, June 23, 1944, "Recapitulation of Sugar Situation in Puerto Rico," National Labor Relations Board, File 9-8-76, Records of the Division of Territories and Insular Possessions, Department of the Interior (Record Group 126), National Archives and Records Administration. Hereafter referred to as DTIP, RG 126, NARA. The situation was complicated. According to Watson, the regional director of the NLRB,

in December 1943, the CGT requested, in substance, that the [Sugar Producers'] Association recognize it as the exclusive bargaining representative of all the employees, both agricultural and industrial, of the Association's members. The Association refused on the ground that its contract with the FLT prevented it from so doing. The CGT then passed a strike vote, setting a deadline of February 9, 1944. The CGT demanded a collective contract with the Association and an increase in wages. A series of conferences with the various parties to the dispute was held in the latter part of 1943 and the early part of 1944 by Charles A. Goldsmith, U.S. Commissioner of Conciliation. No agreement could be reached. The FLT threatened to call a strike of the dock workers and sugar workers if the Association signed a contract with the CGT; the CGT threatened to strike in the sugar and other industries if the Association did not. . . . Finally, the strike threat of the CGT was averted in February by a promise by the Governor that the Insular Labor Relations Board . . . would be activated and assume jurisdiction of the representation dispute. Provision for the ILRB had been made by the Insular Labor Relations Act, which was passed in 1938. No board had ever been appointed, however, nor had any other action been taken pursuant to said Act, which is virtually identical with the NLRA except that it covers agricultural workers in addition to other employees.

19. Ibid.

20. *El Mundo*, January 11, 1945.

21. *El Mundo*, January 13, 1945.

22. Ibid.

23. *El Mundo*, January 15, 1945.

24. *El Mundo*, January 13, 1945.

25. *El Mundo*, January 31, 1945.

26. Ibid. Nevertheless, the election had its glitches. In a letter to the PPD, Rodolfo Ramírez Celaya criticized the JIRT and the election, saying that "I have never observed more poverty and misbehavior in acts of this sort as yesterday, January 30." Ramírez explained the improper action of individuals that claimed to represent the CGT and JIRT. They managed, according to Ramírez, to hinder the electoral process. Ramírez concluded with a favorable comment: "all the public stayed there protesting the injustices being perpetrated because all knew from well-authorized sources that [Muñoz and Ramos Antonini] warned the working-class people in the sugar industry that not even one of them should fail to vote on January 30, because it would implement the true justice for the men in the canefield and the factory. Close to a thousand men stayed without voting." Letter from Rodolfo Ramírez Celaya to Muñoz Marín, January 31, 1945, Mayagüez, FLMM/ALMM, IV-7 (Pueblos).

27. *El Mundo*, February 1, 1945. According to the press, the JIRT nullified 4,410 ballots. A total of 91 ballots were blank. The high number of invalid ballots raised questions about the impartiality and procedures of the electoral process. The same can be said about the overwhelming number of votes for the CGT. FLT leaders highlighted these concerns to downplay the electoral outcome.

28. Letter from Watson to Smith, June 23, 1944, "Recapitulation of Sugar Situation in Puerto Rico," File 9-8-76, DTIP, RG 126, NARA.

29. *El Mundo*, February 1, 1945.

30. Ibid.; *La Democracia*, February 1, 1945.

31. *El Mundo*, February 2, 1945.

32. *El Mundo*, February 1, 1945; *La Democracia*, February 1, 1945.

33. *El Mundo*, February 2, 1945.

34. *El Mundo*, February 6, 9, 1945.

35. Mary Berth Norton et al., *A People and a Nation: A History of the United States*, vol. 2 (Boston: Houghton Mifflin Co., 1994), pp. 852-855.

36. Juan Angel Silén, *Apuntes para la historia del movimiento obrero puertorriqueño* (Río Piedras: Editorial Cultural, 1978), pp. 114-116.

37. *El Mundo*, February 9, 1945.

38. *El Mundo*, February 12, 23, 1945; *La Democracia*, February 16, 1945.

39. *El Mundo*, February 13, 1945.

40. *La Democracia*, March 10, 1945; *El Mundo*, March 12, 1945.

41. Ibid. Besides Nogueras Rivera, workers explained the position of the FLT. For example, Alejandro Silva disagreed with the election in the sugar industry and stated the union's reasons to join the strike. Silva wrote to Muñoz "in the name of over 15,000 unemployed workers affected by the strike." Silva made his case as follows:

you are the only person capacitated and authorized to fix this labor conflict affecting all of P.R. . . . I ask you to solve this malady that is harming thousands of families in our Island. Hunger and misery is atrocious and each day will be worse if this is not addressed as it should. If this continues I believe that you will not let die of hunger that many thousands of children and elders that live off this industry. . . The FLT joined this strike, which is vicious, more than anything else, to avoid personal mishaps and to be recognized as the bargaining identity in the collective agreement, which is the work of the FLT. And for having the majority in the boycott. In P.R., over 150,000 work in the sugar industry and the CGT only obtained 20,000 [votes]. 130,000 joined the boycott. All these people get hungry, whatever is their party, religion, or union. If you with all your power cannot solve this, I am sure that a revolution of hunger will rise. (Letter from Alejandro Silva to Muñoz Marín, February 19, 1945, Corozal, FLMM/ALMM, IV-7 (Pueblos)). In the 1930s, Silva was president of the National Council of the Unemployed. Letter from Alejandro Silva to Ernest Gruening, August 19, 1935, File 9-8-76, DTIP, RG 126, NARA.

42. *El Mundo*, February 21, 1945.

43. *El Mundo*, February 23, 1945.

44. *El Mundo*, February 9, 1945; *La Democracia*, March 10, 1945; Harvey S. Perloff, *Puerto Rico's Economic Future, a Study in Planned Development* (Chicago: University of Chicago Press, 1950), pp. 73, 116.

45. *El Mundo*, February 9, March 13, 1945.

46. Letter from Muñoz Marín to Jesús T. Piñero, February 20, 1945, Fundación Luis Muñoz Marín, Archivo Luis Muñoz Marín, Sección IV, Serie 3 (Individuos). Hereafter referred to as FLMM/ALMM, IV-3.

47. Ibid.

48. *La Democracia*, March 5, 1945.

49. *El Mundo*, March 13, 1945; *La Democracia*, March 13, 1945.

50. Ibid.

51. *El Mundo*, March 12, 1945.

52. *La Democracia*, March 15, 1945.

53. *El Imparcial*, March 15, 1945.

54. Norton et al., *A People and a Nation*, pp. 829-830.

55. Letter from Ramón Sánchez Justiniano to Muñoz Marín, March 16, 1945, Mayagüez, FLMM/ALMM, IV-7 (Pueblos). A question that comes to mind is to what extent workers exhibited a momentum of their own beyond the control of union and political leaders in the 1940s. Labor militancy has led to political backlashes not uncommon in the history of Latin America. Ruth Berins Collier and David Collier, *Shaping the Political Arena: Critical Junctures, the Labor Movement, and Regime Dynamics in Latin America* (Princeton: Princeton University Press, 1991). An extreme case about the dynamics and contradictions of working-class mobilization is addressed in the groundbreaking book of Peter Winn,

Weavers of Revolution: The Yarur Workers and Chile's Road to Socialism (New York: Oxford University Press, 1986). The Puerto Rican labor movement deserves further study to shed light on how the militancy of workers informed the island's political transformation.

56. Letter from Ramón Sánchez Justiniano to Muñoz Marín, March 16, 1945, Mayagüez, FLMM/ALMM, IV-7 (Pueblos).

57. Ibid.

58. Ibid.

59. *La Democracia*, March 14, 16, 17, 1945.

60. *La Democracia*, March 19, 20, 1945.

61. James Dietz, *Economic History of Puerto Rico: Institutional Change and Capitalist Development* (Princeton: Princeton University Press, 1986), p. 107.

62. *La Democracia*, March 20, 1945.

63. *El Mundo*, February 1, 1945.

64. *El Mundo*, December 13, 1944.

65. *El Mundo*, January 11, 1945.

66. *El Mundo*, December 23, 19, 1944, January 11, 1945.

67. See the Annual Reports of PRIDCO for 1944 and 1945, CPR/UPR.

68. Ibid. p. 13.

69. Letter from Félix Morales to Rafael Ríos, January 12, 1945, FLMM/ALMM, IV-2-23.

70. Letter from Félix Morales to Rafael Ríos, January 15, 1945, FLMM/ALMM, IV-2-23.

71. Ibid.

72. Letters from Rafael Ríos to Teodoro Moscoso, Alberto Sánchez, and Juan Sáez Corales, January 17, 1945, FLMM/ALMM, IV-2-23.

73. Letter from Félix Morales to Rafael Ríos, January 19, 1945, FLMM/ALMM, IV-2-23.

74. Ibid.

75. Leaflet of SEFRA, "Primera Asamblea," FLMM/ALMM, IV-2-23.

76. Letter from Rafael Ríos to Félix Morales, January 20, 1945, FLMM/ALMM, IV-2-23.

77. Ibid.

78. Letter from Teodoro Moscoso to Muñoz Marín, January 23, 1945, FLMM/ALMM, IV-2-23.

79. Ibid.

80. Ibid.

81. Ibid. PRIDCO confronted other problems as well. According to Alex W. Maldonado, American technicians also went on strike; they had come lured by Moscoso's claims that they would be working in "Puerto Rico, U.S.A." But despite the presence of the American flag, they felt they were in a foreign country. They found little in San Juan that reminded them of the mainland. "It was terrible," recalled Ramírez. The American families had to be housed in the Normandie Hotel, which was outfitted with a communal kitchen. "Some of the men," he added, "became so stressed that they fled from their screaming wives and took local mistresses." (Alex. W. Maldonado, *Teodoro Moscoso and Puerto Rico's Operation Bootstrap* (Gainesville: University Press of Florida), pp. 43-44)

82. Letter from Héctor J. Cifredo Bravo to Rafael Ríos and Resolution of the UEIC, January 26, 1945, FLMM/ALMM, IV-2-23.

83. Letter from Rafael Ríos to Muñoz Marín, January 27, 1945, FLMM/ALMM, IV-2-23. See also the Statement of Rafael Ríos, General Manager, Puerto Rico Glass Corporation, January 30, 1945, FLMM/ALMM, IV-2-23.

84. Letter from Rafael Ríos to Juan Sáez Corales, January 28, 1945, FLMM/ALMM, IV-2-23.

85. Letter from Félix Morales to Rafael Ríos, January 29, 1945, FLMM/ALMM, IV-2-23.

86. Ibid.

87. Letter from Rafael Ríos to Muñoz Marín, February 1, 1945, FLMM/ALMM, IV-2-23.

88. Memorandum from Commissioner of Labor Manuel A. Pérez to Governor Rexford G. Tugwell, March 5, 1945, Caja #408, Colección "La Fortaleza," Archivo General de Puerto Rico. Hereafter referred to as CLF #408, AGPR.

89. *Puerto Rico World Journal*, February 3, 1945.

90. Letter from Félix Morales to Rafael Ríos, February 7, 1945, and attachment of written declarations of factory workers, FLMM/ALMM, IV-2-23. Ríos referred the matter to Charles A. Goldsmith. Letter from Rafael Ríos to Charles A. Goldsmith, February 8, 1945, FLMM/ALMM, IV-2-23.

91. Letter from Héctor J. Cifredo Bravo to Muñoz Marín, February 19, 1945, FLMM/ALMM, IV-2-23.

92. *El Mundo*, September 9, 15, 1944. Although events demonstrated that Muñoz could not possibly exert direct control over all conflicts, increasingly, the perception was that he did. The words of Miles Galvin apply well to this situation: "The image of Muñoz Marín . . . as champion of the underdog and ultimate authority in all controversies, grew rapidly and eventually became pervasive as all other leadership and institutions became tacitly subordinate." Miles Galvin, *The Organized Labor Movement in Puerto Rico* (London: Associated University Presses, 1979), p. 97.

93. Letter from Cifredo to Muñoz Marín, February 19, 1945, FLMM/ALMM, IV-2-23.

94. Ibid.

95. Ibid.

96. Letter from Héctor J. Cifredo Bravo to Muñoz Marín and Resolution of the UEIC, February 24, 1945, FLMM/ALMM, IV-2-23.

97. Ibid.

98. Ibid.

99. Telegram from Félix Morales to Muñoz Marín, February 28, 1945, FLMM/ALMM, IV-2-23.

100. Ibid.

101. Ibid.

102. Police Report #1/3-114, March 2, 1945, CLF #408, AGPR.

103. Ibid.

104. Although the leaflet does not have a date, it preceded the labor strike at the glass factory. Workers titled the leaflet "Siguen Los Atropellos en la Fábrica de Cristal" and sent it to Muñoz along with a letter of Cifredo Bravo. Letter from Héctor J. Cifredo Bravo to Muñoz Marín, February 19, 1945, FLMM/ALMM, IV-2-23.

105. Ibid.

106. Ibid.

107. Ibid. CGT workers not only raised their voice against grievances in the factories of PRIDCO but also protested against major labor policies of the PPD. After the island's legislature passed the Puerto Rico Labor Relations Act of 1945—which was based on the National Labor Relations Act of 1935 (Wagner Act)—the CGT produced a statement with similar words to that issued during the PRGC strike. This was the case, even though the local law was broader than the national one, "in that it guaranteed the right of collective bargaining to agricultural workers and employees of public corporations as well as to all other workers." Dietz, *Economic History of Puerto Rico*, p. 223. According to the unfavorable statement of the CGT,

the Puerto Rico Labor Relations Act is an instrument which serves the interests of the employers and neutralizes the hard-won democratic gains of Puerto Rican labor of the past quarter century, gains which are part and parcel of the democratic progress of the Puerto Rican people as a whole. We are surprised that it should have been enacted by a Legislature to which we gave our votes in November and that it should have been signed by a Governor whom we have regarded as a friend of the working man. [...] The General Confederation of Workers of Puerto Rico opposes the Puerto Rico Labor Relations Act as being defective, anti-labor, and undemocratic –because it constitutes a positive threat to labor's fundamental right to freely choose its representatives, conduct its own internal affairs, be protected against employer provocation, and when necessary, to strike to defend its rights and accomplishments. (Executive Committee of the General Confederation of Workers of Puerto Rico, Statement on the Puerto Rico Labor Relations Act, Act 130 of 1945, June 29, 1945, Records of the Committee on Territories and Insular Affairs, United States Senate, Record Group 46, National Archives and Records Administration. Hereafter referred to as CIA, RG 46, NARA)

108. Letter from Félix Morales to Rafael Ríos, February 7, 1945, and attachment of written declarations of factory workers, FLMM/ALMM, IV-2-23; Letter from Rafael Ríos to Charles A. Goldsmith, February 8, 1945, FLMM/ALMM, IV-2-23.

109. Telegram from Félix Morales to Muñoz Marín, February 28, 1945, and attachment, "A todos los trabajadores de la Fábrica de Vidrio," Presidente Hilaro Castro Maysonet, Unión de Trabajadores de la Industria de Vidrio, FLMM/ALMM, IV-2-23.

110. Ibid.

111. Ibid.

112. Ibid.

113. Memorandum from Commissioner of Labor Manuel A. Pérez to Governor Rexford G. Tugwell, March 5, 1945, CLF #408, AGPR.

114. Ibid.

115. The statements of PRIDCO appear in an editorial of *El Mundo*, March 14, 1945.

116. Letter from Teodoro Moscoso to Muñoz Marín, January 23, 1945, FLMM/ALMM, IV-2-23.

117. Ibid.

118. Memorandum from Commissioner of Labor Manuel A. Pérez to Governor Rexford G. Tugwell, March 5, 1945. CLF #408, AGPR.

119. Telegram from Manrique F. Cabrer et al., to Governor Rexford G. Tugwell, March 1, 1945. CLF #408, AGPR.

120. Telegram from Miguel Sánchez León to Muñoz Marín, March 3, 1945. FLMM/ALMM, IV-2-23.

121. *El Mundo*, March 14, 1945.

122. *El Mundo*, March 15, 1945.

123. Ibid.

124. Radio message of March 15, 1945, FLMM/ALMM, IV-4 (Empresas Comerciales: El Diario Hablado de *La Democracia* y *El Batey*).

125. Ibid.

126. Ibid.

127. Ibid. The PPD developed further the notion of industries as "fountains of life" in *La Democracia*, March 27, 1945.

128. *La Democracia*, March 31, 1945.

129. *El Mundo*, March 24, 1945.

130. *El Mundo*, March 24, 26, 1945; Silén, *Apuntes para la historia del movimiento obrero puertorriqueño*, pp. 115-116; Higinio Feliciano Avilés, "Origen, desarrollo y división de la Confederación General de Trabajadores de Puerto Rico" (M.A. diss., University of Puerto Rico, 1976).

131. Ibid.

132. *El Mundo*, March 24, 1945.

133. *El Mundo*, March 26, 1945.

134. *El Mundo*, April 3, 1945.

135. *El Mundo*, April 14, 1945.

136. *El Mundo*, May 16, 1945.

137. Ibid.

138. During the late months of 1945, the PPD distanced itself further from the CGT-A and CPI. PPD officials made obvious their reluctance to tolerate groups beyond the scope of Muñoz's authority. The discourse of the PPD left no room for doubt. See, for example, *La Democracia*, August 29, September 8, 1945; *El Imparcial*, September 15, 1945; *El Batey*, January, 1946. Also, Robert W. Anderson, *Party Politics in Puerto Rico* (Stanford, CA: Stanford University Press, 1965), p. 161.

139. *El Mundo*, April 13, May 9, October 1, November 10, December 7, 1945.

140. Ibid.

141. *El Mundo*, November 26, December 4, 5, 12, 1945.

142. *El Mundo*, September 10, 17, October 15, 27, November 16, 1945; Anderson, *Party Politics in Puerto Rico*, p. 59.

143. *El Mundo*, February 7, 8, 9, 10, 1946.

144. *El Mundo*, February 7, 1946.

145. Ibid.

146. Ibid.

147. Ibid.

148. *El Mundo*, February 8, 1946.

149. Ibid.

150. *El Mundo*, February 9, 10, 1946.

151. Ibid.

152. *El Mundo*, February 11, 1946.

153. Memorandum from Muñoz Marín to Yldefonso Solá Morales, February 18, 1946, FLMM/ALMM, IV-2.

154. Letter from Muñoz Marín to Leandro Cabranes, February 23, 1946, Corozal, FLMM/ALMM, IV-7 (Pueblos).

155. Memorandum from Muñoz Marín to Francisco M. Susoni, February 13, 1946, FLMM/ALMM, IV-2.

156. Memorandum from Muñoz Marín to Yldefonso Solá Morales, February 13, 1946, FLMM/ALMM, IV-2.

157. Letter from Muñoz Marín, February 15, 1946, FLMM/ALMM, IV-2.

158. Letter from Leandro Cabranes to Gilberto Concepción de Gracia, February 13, 1946, Corozal, FLMM/ALMM, IV-7 (Pueblos).

159. Letter from Ismael Cruz Nieves to Muñoz Marín, February 11, 1946, Toa Baja; Letter from Manuel Torres Reyes to Muñoz Marín, February 23, 1946, San Juan, FLMM/ALMM, IV-7 (Pueblos).

160. Cable from Justo A. Casablanca to Muñoz Marín, February 16, 1946, San Juan, FLMM/ALMM, IV-7 (Pueblos).

161. Letter from Guillermo Cruz to Gilberto Concepción de Gracia, February 11, 1946, Comerio; Letter of Gonzalo Salas to Carmelo Rios February 25, 1946, Toa Baja, FLMM/ALMM, IV-7 (Pueblos).

162. Cable of Gumersindo Ramón Osorio et al., to Muñoz Marín, February 15, 1946, Bayamón, FLMM/ALMM, IV-7 (Pueblos).

163. Letter from Manuel Torres Reyes to Muñoz Marín, February 23, 1946, San Juan, FLMM/ALMM, IV-7 (Pueblos).

164. Ibid.

165. Letter from Ismael Cruz Nieves to Muñoz Marín, February 11, 1946, Toa Baja, FLMM/ALMM, IV-7 (Pueblos).

166. Letter from Elías Martínez to Muñoz Marín, March 5, 1946, Aguadilla, FLMM/ALMM, IV-7 (Pueblos).

167. Letter from Juan Acevedo Mendez and Arturo Ramos Hidalgo to Muñoz Marín, February 18, 1946, Aguadilla, FLMM/ALMM, IV-7 (Pueblos).

168. Letter from M. Figueroa del Rosario to Muñoz Marín, February 16, 1946, Añasco; Letter from Heraclio H. Rivera Colón to Muñoz Marín, June 18, 1947, Toa Baja, FLMM/ALMM, IV-7 (Pueblos).

169. Letter from Miguel Rosado to Muñoz Marín, February 28, 1946, Toa Baja; Letter from Muñoz to Rosado, March 1, 1946, Toa Baja, FLMM/ALMM, IV-7 (Pueblos).

170. Letter from Ramón Barreto Pérez to Muñoz Marín, October 8, 1946, Ponce, FLMM/ALMM, IV-7 (Pueblos).

171. Sworn statement of Juan Náter, February 14, 1946, Río Piedras, FLMM/ALMM, IV-7 (Pueblos).

172. Letter from Andrés Bonilla to Muñoz Marín, February 14, 1946, Añasco, FLMM/ALMM, IV-7 (Pueblos).

173. Letter from Juan Acevedo Mendez and Arturo Ramos Hidalgo to Muñoz Marín, February 18, 1946, Aguadilla, FLMM/ALMM, IV-7 (Pueblos).

174. Letter of Pedro Almodóvar Figueroa to Muñoz Marín, February 14, 1946, Guánica, FLMM/ALMM, IV-7 (Pueblos).

175. Telegram from Rubén Gaztambide Arrillaga to Muñoz Marín, February 12, 1946, Río Piedras; Letter from Pedro Rodríguez Díaz to Muñoz Marín, February 13, 1946, Hormigueros, FLMM/ALMM, IV-7 (Pueblos). The Pro Statehood Congress organized itself early in 1943. *El Mundo*, April 19, 1943. Interestingly, PPD supporters in favor of statehood also raised questions about their party's political orientation and the status issue. For example, several months before the Arecibo Assembly, statehooders from Mayagüez wrote to Muñoz, asking him to clarify with a statement the PPD's view about the island's political status. Letter from Andrés Cámara, Presidente de la Asociación Puertorriqueña Pro Estadidad, to Muñoz Marín, August 31, 1945, Mayagüez, FLMM/ALMM, IV-7 (Pueblos).

176. Letter from Virgilio Román Alvarez et al., to Muñoz Marín, December 31, 1945, Mayagüez, FLMM/ALMM, IV-7 (Pueblos).

177. Ibid.

178. Letter from the Guillermo Morales et al., to Muñoz Marín, February 15, 1946, Santurce, FLMM/ALMM, IV-7 (Pueblos).

179. Letter from Pablo L. Molina to Muñoz Marín, August 16, 1947, Toa Baja, FLMM/ALMM, IV-7 (Pueblos).

180. Ibid.

181. *El Mundo*, February 12, 1946.

182. Ibid.

183. *El Mundo*, February 13, 1946.

184. *El Mundo*, March 18, 1946.

185. See, for example, radio message of February 16, 1946. FLMM/ALMM, IV-4 (Empresas Comerciales: El Diario Hablado de *La Democracia* y *El Batey*); *El Mundo*, February 18, 1946; *El Batey*, March 1946; *La Democracia*, March 4, 1946.

186. *El Mundo*, February 7, 1946.

187. *El Mundo*, November 2, 1946.

188. Ibid.

189. Ibid.

190. Letter from M.C. Stinson, General Manager of the PRPPC, to Francisco Colón Gordiany, October 31, 1946, FLMM/ALMM, IV-2-23.

191. Letter from Teodoro Moscoso to Muñoz Marín, November 1, 1946. FLMM/ALMM, IV-2-23.

192. *El Mundo*, November 2, 1946.

193. *El Mundo*, December 5, 1946.

194. *El Mundo*, November 23, 1946.

195. *El Mundo*, December 5, 1946.

196. *El Mundo*, December 6, 1946. Long before the strike, PRIDCO had shown reluctance to negotiate with the CGT-A. Functionaries of PRIDCO condemned the actions of the CGT-A as politically motivated. According to a confidential memorandum of PRIDCO, Colón Gordiany "manifested on recent occasions that he has the industrial plants of the government in his grip." PRIDCO concluded that instead of honoring the union's collective agreement with the company, Colón Gordiany promoted disobedience. Confidential memorandum from David S. Ramírez and Mariano H. Ramírez to Teodoro Moscoso. September 27, 1946, CLF #356, AGPR.

197. *El Mundo*, December 7, 1946.

198. Ibid.

199. *El Mundo*, December 9, 1946.

200. *El Mundo*, December 6, 1946.

201. *El Mundo*, December 12, 16, 17, 1946; *La Democracia*, December 18, 1946.

202. *El Mundo*, December 17, 1946. Although this measure preceded the PPD's so-called *ley de la mordaza*—literally, " gag law"—it made evident the sort of rhetoric and intolerance that came in full force with the former. Historian Ivonne Acosta has studied in detail the introduction and effects of this law. Acosta, *La Mordaza: Puerto Rico, 1948-1957*.

203. *El Mundo*, December 7, 1946; *La Democracia*, December 11, 1946.

204. Confidential memorandum from James W. Balano to Jesús T. Piñero, December 11, 1946, CLF #408, AGPR.

205. Ibid.

206. *El Mundo*, December 10, 14, 1946.

207. *El Mundo*, November 11, 1948.

208. Maldonado, *Teodoro Moscoso and Puerto Rico's Operation Bootstrap*, pp. 57-58.

209. *El Mundo*, May 19, June 5, 9, 1947.

210. *El Mundo*, May 18, June 23, June 28, 1947.

211. *La Democracia*, May 23, 1947; *El Mundo*, June 24, 26, July 8, 1947.

212. *El Mundo*, July 4, 1947.

213. *El Mundo*, August 24, 1947.

214. Juan Sáez Corales, "Twenty-Five Years of Struggle—My Reply to Persecution" (1955), in Angel Quintero Rivera, ed., *Workers' Struggle in Puerto Rico: A Documentary History* (New York: Monthly Review Press, 1976), pp. 158-160.

215. *La Democracia*, January 29, 1947.

216. *El Mundo*, December 15, 1947.

217. Letter from Teodoro Moscoso to Muñoz Marín, Antonio Fernós Isern, and Jesús T. Piñero, November 9, 1948, CLF #356, AGPR. Also at FLMM/ALMM, IV-2-23.

218. Ibid.

219. Calling "cheap" labor a "non-artificial factor" of the island's economy is to miss entirely the inequalities that capitalism imposes between social classes and between developed and underdeveloped countries. If low wages are to be understood as a natural phenomenon, then hardly could there be expectations for social justice and improvements. These issues have been the object of exhaustive research among dependency theorists, who introduced an effective model to grasp Latin America's economic reality. André Gunder Frank, *Capitalism and Underdevelopment in Latin America* (New York: Monthly Review Press, 1967); Fernando Henrique Cardoso and Enzo Faletto, *Dependency and Development in Latin America* (Berkeley: University of California Press, 1979); Tulio Halperín-Donghi, "Symposium: 'Dependency Theory' and Latin American Historiography," *Latin American Research Review* 17, no. 1 (1982): 115-130; Joseph L. Love, "The Origins of Dependency Analysis," *Journal of Latin American Studies* 22 (Feb. 1990): 143-168; Sing C. Chew and Rober A. Denemark, *The Underdevelopment of Development: Essays in Honor of Andre Gunder Frank* (Thousand Oaks: Sage Publications, 1996).

220. Galvin, *The Organized Labor Movement in Puerto Rico*, p. 101.

221. Chatterjee, *Nationalist Thought and the Colonial World*, p. 51.

222. Ibid.

223. *La Democracia*, June 18, 1946; *El Mundo*, July 12, 1946. For a later version of Muñoz's "battle of production" message, see FLMM/ALMM, IV-11, Cart. 3, Doc. 1 (Mensajes y Discursos); Fernando Picó, ed., *Luis Muñoz Marín: Discursos, 1934-1948*, vol. 1 (San Juan: Fundación Luis Muñoz Marín, 1999), pp. 301-305.

224. Consider, especially, the radio messages of the PPD. FLMM/ALMM, IV-4 (Empresas Comerciales: El Diario Hablado de *La Democracia* y *El Batey*).

225. *El Mundo*, February 7, 1946.

226. *El Mundo*, February 9, 1946; *La Democracia*, October 4, 1946; *El Batey*, November, 1946; *La Democracia*, May 19, 1947.

227. *La Democracia*, October 4, 1946.

228. *La Democracia*, October 5, 1946.

229. See, for example, *El Batey*, August, 1947, June 15, 1948.

230. *El Mundo*, June 28, June 29, 1946.

231. Ibid.

232. Silvia Alvarez Curbelo offers provocative ideas to grasp this aspect of Muñoz's discourse. Silvia Alvarez Curbelo, "Los Ejes de la Carreta: Emigración y Populismo," Conference Paper, 5th Annual Meeting, Puerto Rican Association of Historians, Inter-American University, Arecibo, October 3-4, 1997, p. 3; Silvia Alvarez Curbelo, "Las lecciones de la guerra: Luis Muñoz Marín y la Segunda Guerra Mundial, 1943-1946," in Fernando Picó, ed., *Luis Muñoz Marín: Ensayos del Centenario* (San Juan: Fundación Luis Muñoz Marín, 1999), pp. 31-59.

233. Ibid.

234. Ibid.

235. Antonio Fernós Isern, "Political, Intellectual, and Social Aspects of Puerto Rico," Address delivered before the Club de las Américas, Washington, D.C., February 1947. FLMM/ALMM, IV-11 (Mensajes y Discursos).

236. Ibid., p. 27.

237. Statement of Antonio Fernós Isern at the 2nd. Session of the West Indian Conference, March 12, 1946. CLF #424, AGPR.

238. Chatterjee, *Nationalist Thought and the Colonial World*, p. 140.

239. If the island's nationalist discourses today offer little more than a trivial play on words—compared, for example, to Pedro Albizu Campos' rhetoric and actions—it largely has to do with the consequences of the PPD's political and economic policies. For a critique of current trends of nationalist thought, see Carlos Pabón, *Nación Postmortem: Ensayos sobre los tiempos de insoportable ambigüedad* (San Juan: Ediciones Callejón, 2002). Instead of clinging to sterile views of the nation, Pabón's analysis leaves the way open for alternative lines of thought to grasp the challenges faced by Puerto Rico today.

240. *El Diario de Puerto Rico* began to be published not long before the election of 1948. Muñoz began to consider the publication of a new newspaper at the beginning of the year. FLMM/ALMM, IV-4 (Empresas Comerciales).

241. After the election of 1948, the press of the United States and other countries paid close attention to the endeavors of the PPD. *El Mundo*, November 24, 25, 28, December 10, 1948, January 10, 17, 1949.

242. The period that elapsed between Muñoz's electoral victory and his inauguration as governor saw an astounding amount of press releases from the PPD. See *El Diario de Puerto Rico*, *El Mundo*, and *El Imparcial*.

243. *El Diario de Puerto Rico*, January 3, 1949.

244. Paul Boyer, *By the Bomb's Early Light: American Thought and Culture at the Dawn of the Atomic Age* (Chapel Hill: University of North Carolina Press, 1994), pp. 107-121.

245. Luis Muñoz Marín, "Un Nuevo Estado," *Norte* 9, no. 9 (October 1949): 15-16.

246. Ibid., p. 16.

247. It should be noted that by this time the so-called gag law was in effect. Acosta, *La Mordaza.*

248. Salvador Tió, "Industria o muerte," *Norte* 9, no. 9 (October 1949): 20-22, 70-71.

249. Radio message of March 7, 1947; Radio message, May 8, 1948, FLMM/ALMM, IV-4 (Empresas Comerciales: El Diario Hablado de *La Democracia* y *El Batey*).

250. Arcadio Díaz Quiñones, *La Memoria Rota: Ensayos sobre cultura y política* (Río Piedras: Ediciones Huracán, 1993), pp. 42-43.

251. *El Diario de Puerto Rico*, May 11, 1949.

6

THE CHALLENGE OF A NEW
POLITICAL LOGIC

When for any reason one stops fearing the punishment beyond the grave or the
verdict of general opinion, these lose their efficacy.

—Juan B. Soto

Participants of mass movements in Latin America often stepped into an uncertain
ground of political interaction when the time came to negotiate the best option for
addressing their socioeconomic needs. While agents sometimes faced a difficult
choice between collaboration and resistance, they also had the opportunity to shift
the terms of political negotiation. The path that led to mutual cooperation between
different sectors of society entailed political constraints as well as avenues for
people to shape the outcome of events and advance their own perceptions about the
past. In this sense, the effort of people to reach an agreement about policies of
reform in Puerto Rico produced an uneasy relationship between followers, leaders,
political parties, and governmental authorities. Far from prescribing an adverse
outcome or a promising future, the discourse of consent gave free rein not only to
the best intentions of people desiring the general welfare of society but also to
socioeconomic disparities and an unequal access to political power. On the one
hand, as these forces played themselves out in the island's political arena, they
benefited political leaders willing to step over their peers and subordinates just to
get ahead and achieve their ends. On the other hand, the initial urge of multiple
agents to approach, negotiate, and agree with each other made it possible for people
to effectively shape political events and the colonial policies of reform.

Thus, political practices in Puerto Rico were not just about who did what to
whom. Although social injustices and abuses of power certainly informed the
mobilization of people on the island, these aspects offer only a partial view of the
events. Colonial politics entailed more than a sharp divide between agents fully in

favor of reform and those adamantly opposed to it. To be specific, the discourse of consent did not necessarily force a choice between collaboration and contestation among agents favoring reform but meant a fluid ground of interaction that left open to dialogue and debate the basis of common action. As bearers of a new discourse, political leaders and supporters in favor of reform did not always act unilaterally according to their particular interests but traversed an unmapped crossroad of political negotiation. The events in Puerto Rico during the 1930s and 1940s demonstrate that the discourse of consent hardly confined political practices to a hierarchical order and entailed instead a "decentered" site of engagement—a reference to a multifaceted and multivocal political reality.

Far from just being a factor of political change in the 1930s, the onset of the Great Depression represented for the island an "organic crisis": a pervasive form of dislocation that not only weakened the capacity of institutions and practices to define people's place in the colonial order but also allowed agents to imagine new possibilities for the articulation of a different political logic. Puerto Rico already faced many difficulties when the Great Depression took place. The first decades of U.S. rule plagued the island with the worst effects of economic and political subordination. When the Great Depression aggravated the island's problems, the grievances of people reached an extreme point, but so did the possibility to envision a different reality. While the "organic crisis" steadily eroded the colonial order and caused new forms of antagonism, conditions in Puerto Rico became sufficiently unhinged for the emergence of discourses offering alternatives to the island's plight. Not long after the first unsavory experiences of the Great Depression, several sectors on the island took initiatives to address urgent socioeconomic difficulties. Left to their own devices, people opened their imagination, proved their capacity for innovation, and offered solutions to address specific needs. This reality became clear during the sugar strike of 1934, which not only saw the participation of workers but also drew the attention of dissident Socialists, Nationalists, and Communists.

While pressure "from below" made clear the need for reform, political exchanges "from above" between PPD leaders and U.S. authorities facilitated the introduction of the New Deal to Puerto Rico. Local demands for social justice and U.S. policies of reform intersected each other in the early 1940s to produce the first expressions that can be ascribed to the discourse of consent. In its early form, the discourse of consent allowed a rapport between agents but did not lead yet to a formal agreement. At the most, different groups simultaneously employed a number of "nodal points"[1]—privileged discursive elements that produce partial fixations of meaning—such as *pueblo* (the people), *jíbaro* (subsistence farmer), "social justice," and "popular democratic." People used these terms in a haphazard and often contradictory fashion. A good example is the use of the slogan "Bread, Land, and Liberty" by both the PPD and Communists. Although the expressions shared by many groups did not efface the differences between them, they helped form a new "political language" on the island. Hence, the discourse of consent owes much to how agents articulated according to their needs many ideas that were not exclusively their own.

Multiple agents informed the discourse of consent in Puerto Rico. Besides the political exchange that took place between PPD leaders and U.S. officials to introduce the New Deal to Puerto Rico, the PPD engaged several sectors of the island in favor of reform. Without the reinforcement that came from different quarters of society, the initiatives of party leaders and federal officials would have laid only a partial basis for articulating the discourse of consent in Puerto Rico. Indeed, several groups such as urban workers, rural laborers, the unemployed, religious groups, women, Communists, independentists, technocrats, and dissidents from other political parties not only influenced the program of PPD officials but they also shaped the nascent discourse of consent.

Labor groups formed organizations that made strong demands to address socioeconomic needs. For instance, the ACPR and UPD mobilized workers who suffered many grievances, including poor political representation. Besides organizing assemblies, marches, demonstrations, and other forms of protests, *público* drivers and unemployed laborers not only grabbed the attention of PPD leaders but also helped form a "chain of equivalences"[2]—a linkage between the demands for reform of different groups. Despite their specific goals, people overcame their isolation and informed the discourse of consent with notions of mutual cooperation and solidarity. After the formation of the CGT, workers from many industries secured a significant avenue of action to make themselves heard in the island's political arena. Besides *público* drivers and unemployed laborers, the CGT included workers from the dockyards, needlework industry, liquor industry, restaurants, commerce, and agriculture. Communists lent an important hand in this process as they steered the relationship between labor and politics toward new directions.

In addition to labor, other groups had their say about the discourse of consent in Puerto Rico. Although practically excluded from the higher echelons of Muñoz's party, women ran as PPD candidates, contributed in spreading the PPD's message, and expressed many of their concerns. Independentists added a significant voice to that of PPD leaders as they strongly stated their demand for the island's sovereignty. Whether or not the rural population expressed its thoughts in letters to *La Democracia, El Batey*, or Muñoz, this sector heeded the calls for reform and supported the island's mass movement in the best way possible. While a range of groups helped shape the discourse of consent, Muñoz and his peers began to act not only as mediators between local and mainland interests but also as the "moral-intellectual leadership" of an emerging "historical bloc." Before long, the discourse of consent meant an advocacy for reform to overcome the worst socioeconomic and political grievances of Puerto Ricans. It also entailed the incorporation of popular groups as part of the island's political arena and a degree of accountability from political leaders.

The interaction between U.S. officials, PPD leaders, and their supporters tells us much about colonial politics and the discourse of consent. As the sugar strike of

1942 demonstrates, the rise of a new discourse in a colonial context entailed more than formal and discrete forms of contact between dominant and subordinate subjects. That is, the discourse of consent spilled beyond the tussles of individuals imprisoned within the boundaries of colonial institutions. Instead of exclusively producing a repressive order against local interests, the island's colonial situation introduced an ambiguous site of political engagement between Puerto Ricans and U.S. authorities. A degree of cultural permeability and diffusion not only allowed agents to step beyond the metropole-colonial nexus but also enabled them to find within many blurred areas of political interaction a basis for common action.

Besides what it can tell us about the "agency" of people, the sugar strike of 1942 sheds light on the relationship between PPD leaders, party followers, and U.S. authorities. The labor conflict informed the growth of the island's mass movement and marked a turning point for colonial politics. While different groups operated as a "collective will" under the spell of social justice, Muñoz and his peers came closer to becoming the "moral-intellectual leadership" of people in favor of reform. Since the sugar strike of 1942 faced off a new alignment of forces—CGT workers, Communists, PPD officials, and mainland New Dealers—against a rival combination of forces—FLT workers, Socialists, sugar producers, and their mainland allies—the labor conflict stepped beyond immediate issues and informed the rise of a "historical bloc" under the direction of PPD leaders. It should be clear that far from being a process that any one agent determined single-handedly, the transformation of colonial politics entailed the collective action of people and their effort to shape the discourse of consent. As participants of a hegemonic process, a myriad of agents contributed to expand the discourse of consent and convert it into "a dominant horizon of social orientation and action."[3] This is the case, even though the struggle for hegemony on the island meant relations of power that gave an advantage to PPD leaders—meaning the conditions that enabled party officials to escape their narrow interests, become the "moral-intellectual leadership" of a broad movement, and conceive their designs as part of "universal aims."[4]

Without shedding particular goals and ideals, many agents joined forces with the PPD to support the call for reform in Puerto Rico. The discourse of consent permeated the island's mass movement with a double bind. A tug of war existed between the concerns that bound together the bearers of that discourse and the forces that threatened to tear apart their common understanding. On the one hand, reform and social justice became the locus of colonial politics and tenets deeply embedded in the discourse of consent. On the other hand, the common aspiration of agents for socioeconomic improvement did not preclude different courses of action and perceptions. Workers and Communists, for example, conceived a vision of consent that highlighted their disposition to support Muñoz's party but without undermining the capacity of the CGT and PCP to make claims of their own and shape the outcome of events. Similarly, independentists did not subordinate their voice to the whims of Muñoz and his peers but sought to identify the PPD with their call for the island's sovereignty.

While different groups contributed with their visions to transform the discourse of consent into a hegemonic imaginary, the island's "historical bloc" became unstable with its steady incorporation of conflicting demands. What began as a haphazard call of multiple agents for reform soon produced a coexistence of agendas that rarely rose above many tensions and contradictions. Different groups in favor of social justice nurtured their relationship to the PPD with visions and initiatives unlike those of Muñoz's party. Without abandoning their initial demands for socioeconomic improvement, many advocates of reform made room in their plans of action and discourse for their newly gained allies—the PPD, Rexford G. Tugwell, and their mainland supporters. For instance, workers, Communists, independentists, and political dissidents—groups that did not take lightly the PPD's relentless avowals to introduce reform—conceived a future amiable to their most ambitious demands. Meanwhile, PPD leaders increasingly followed a path in a different direction. Although they were not the only ones hoping to sway public dialogue and debate in their favor, Muñoz and his aides made the most successful attempts to rearrange the discourse of consent by displacing to the sidelines any vision incompatible with their own.

At the final stage of the hegemonic process in Puerto Rico, a sequence of events cleansed the island's "historical bloc" of its most obvious contradictions. Although the discourse of consent allowed multiple agents to stake high claims, it also enabled PPD officials to reorient the island's mass movement. As political power became for PPD leaders more a reality than a distant hope, Muñoz's party searched for a vision of consent best attuned to its own aims. The possibility for a swift change of priorities ensued after the landslide victory of the PPD in the election of 1944. As if that had not been enough, political conditions in Puerto Rico combined with the Cold War to speed up the demise of social justice and ensure the policies of industrialization. On the one hand, Communists, independentists, Nationalists, and certain sectors of labor became "pariahs" on the island. On the other hand, PPD leaders abandoned the state-based industries and welcomed a flood of mainland capital to Puerto Rico.

The political tensions that the island's mass movement inherited from the past reached their climax under the specter of the Cold War era. Workers' unrest in the sugar industry evidenced the insertion of PPD leaders into the labor movement. The conflict between PPD leaders and supporters in favor of different visions of consent exploded during the strikes that took place in the glass and paper factories of PRIDCO. At this point, a process of exclusion informed the discourse of consent. With the harsh measures taken by the PPD to expel the CGT and CPI from the party, the means of persuasion converged with the deployment of coercion. Notwithstanding the conflict that ensued between entrepreneurial interests and labor, the discourse of consent remained elastic enough to allow the PPD a fast reorientation of policies. By maneuvering within the interstices of a fluid ground of political interaction, PPD leaders did more than exclude "undesirable" groups from their ranks. The partnership between the PPD and other agents became the domain of Muñoz's call for the "battle of production." As the labor strikes in the factories of PRIDCO demonstrate, the PPD displaced the concerns of labor in favor of its own program of industrial development.

By the end of the 1940s, people faced the challenge of a new political logic in Puerto Rico: the ascendance of a hegemonic discourse under the "moral-intellectual leadership" of the PPD. As a dominant imaginary that owed as much to the collective action of people as to the unequal relations of power between them, the discourse of consent articulated innumerable demands but could not avoid a representational order that favored PPD leaders at the expense of subordinate groups. After easing the worst tensions between party leaders and followers, PPD officials produced a homogeneous discourse with their relentless quest to modernize Puerto Rico. Their discourse glossed over previous contradictions that characterized the island's mass movement. With Muñoz's call for the "battle of production" as one of its central tenets, the discourse of consent meant at this point all forms of sacrifices to implement without delay the PPD's program of industrial development. Instead of advocating the meaningful participation of agents in decision making and ample reform as its agenda for the future, the ascendant discourse of consent assigned a subordinate role to the followers of Muñoz and modest improvements for the island.

Despite the effort of PPD leaders to portray their supporters as docile and completely loyal to Muñoz's party, the initial pattern that informed the discourse of consent haunted the PPD for many years to come. That is, the need to negotiate with followers a basis of common action led to compromises that delimited the clout of PPD officials in spite of their persistent discourse to the contrary. Many years later, when the discourse of consent unraveled and offset the remnants of a "historical bloc" that once advocated social justice, the rebirth of political pluralism in Puerto Rico confirmed the frailty of Muñoz's party as it unsuccessfully strove to keep together a range of disparate interests. Underneath the PPD's discourse of consent but not far from the surface level of open dissent, multiple agents coexisted as part of Muñoz's party after the 1940s. The fate of the PPD after flaunting an unrivaled political legacy during most of the Cold War era lies somewhere between futile remembrances of the past and a future that it can no longer claim as its own. It is yet to be seen how the collective effort of people may tackle once again but with a greater degree of success the colonial grievances that are still rampant in Puerto Rico today.

NOTES

1. Ernesto Laclau and Chantal Mouffe, *Hegemony and Socialist Strategy: Toward a Radical Democratic Politics* (London: Verso Books, 1985), p. 112.

2. Ibid., pp. 127-134; Ernesto Laclau, "Constructing Universality," in Judith Butler, Ernesto Laclau, and Slavoj Žižek, *Contingency, Hegemony, Universality* (London: Verso Books, 2000), pp. 281-307.

3. Jacob Torfing, *New Theories of Discourse: Laclau, Mouffe, and Žižek* (Oxford: Blackwell Publishers, 1999), p. 101.

4. Ernesto Laclau, "Identity and Hegemony: The Role of Universality in the Constitution of Political Logics," in *Contingency, Hegemony, Universality*, pp. 281-307. See also Judith Butler, "Restaging the Universal: Hegemony and the Limits of Formalism," in *Contingency, Hegemony, Universality*, pp. 11-43.

SELECTED BIBLIOGRAPHY

Acosta, Ivonne. *La Mordaza: Puerto Rico, 1948-1957*. Río Piedras: Editorial Edil, 1987.
———. *La palabra como delito: Los discursos por los que condenaron a Pedro Albizu Campos, 1948-1950*. San Juan: Editorial Cultural, 1993.
Acosta Belén, Edna, ed. *La mujer en la sociedad puertorriqueña*. Río Piedras: Ediciones Huracán, 1980.
Acosta Belén, Edna, et al. *"Adiós, Borinquen querida": La diásporapuertorriqueña, su historia y sus aportaciones*. Albany: CELAC, 2000.
Adelman, Jeremy. *Colonial Legacies: The Problem of Persistence in Latin American History*. New York: Routledge, 1999.
Agosto Cintrón, Nélida. *Religión y cambio social en Puerto Rico, 1898-1940*. Río Piedras: Ediciones Huracán, 1996.
———. "Género y discurso religioso en dos movimientos carismáticos en Puerto Rico," *Fundamentos* 5-6 (1997-1998): 97-124.
Alegría, Ricardo, ed. *Temas de la Historia de Puerto Rico*. San Juan: Centro de Estudios Avanzados de Puerto Rico y el Caribe, 1988.
Alegría, Ricardo, and Eladio Rivera Quiñones, eds. *Historia y cultura de Puerto Rico: Desde la época pre-colombina hasta nuestros días*. San Juan: Fundación Francisco Carvajal, 1999.
Alonso, María Mercedes. *Muñoz Marín vs. the Bishops: An Approach to Church and State*. Hato Rey: Publicaciones Puertorriqueñas, 1998.
Alsina Orozco, Amalia. *Los Congresos Pro-Independencia*. San Juan: Editora Corripio, 1994.
Althusser, Louis. *Lenin and Philosophy*. London: New Left Books, 1971.
———. *For Marx*. London: New Left Books, 1977.
Althusser, Louis, and Etienne Balibar. *Para leer "El Capital."* México, DF: SigloVeintiuno, 1969.
Alvarez Curbelo, Silvia. "La Casa de Cristal: El Ejercicio Senatorial de Luis Muñoz Marín, 1932-36." In Fernando Picó, Silvia Alvarez Curbelo, and Carmen Raffucci, eds., *Senado de Puerto Rico, 1917-1992: Ensayos de historia institucional*, pp. 105-135. San Juan: Senado de Puerto Rico, 1992.

———. "La conflictividad en el discurso político de Luis Muñoz Marín: 1926-1936." In Silvia Alvarez Curbelo and María Elena Rodríguez, eds., *Del Nacionalismo al Populismo: Cultura y Política en Puerto Rico*, pp. 13-35. Río Piedras: Ediciones Huracán, 1993.

———. "Populismo y autoritarismo: reflexiones a partir de la experiencia muñocista." In Irma Rivera Nieves and Carlos Gil, eds., *Polifonía Salvaje: Ensayos de cultura y política en la postmodernidad*, pp. 319-327. San Juan: Editorial Postdata, 1995.

———. "La década del '40 y el movimiento populista." In Carlos Di Núbila and Carmen Rodríguez Cortés, eds. *Puerto Rico: Sociedad, cultura y educación*, pp. 91-104. San Juan: Editorial Isla Negra, 1997.

———. "Los Ejes de la Carreta: Emigración y Populismo." Conference Paper, 5th Annual Meeting, Puerto Rican Association of Historians, Inter-American University, Arecibo, October 3-4, 1997.

———. "Las lecciones de la guerra: Luis Muñoz Marín y la Segunda Guerra Mundial, 1943-1946." In Fernando Picó, ed., *Luis Muñoz Marín: Ensayos del Centenario*, pp. 31-59. San Juan: Fundación Luis Muñoz Marín, 1999.

Alvarez Junco, José, ed. *Populismo, Caudillaje y Discurso Demagógico*. Madrid: Siglo Veintiuno, 1987.

———, ed. *El Populismo en España y América*. Madrid: Editorial Catriel, 1994.

Anderson, Benedict. *Imagined Communities: Reflections on the Origin and Spread of Nationalism*. London: Verso Books, 1983.

Anderson, Perry. *The Origins of Postmodernity*. London: Verso Books, 1998.

Anderson, Robert W. *Party Politics in Puerto Rico*. Stanford, CA: Stanford University Press, 1965.

———. "El papel de Puerto Rico en el Caribe." In Carmen Gautier Mayoral, Angel I. Rivera Ortiz, and Idsa Alegría Ortega, eds., *Puerto Rico en el Caribe hoy*, pp. 9-25. Buenos Aires: CLACSO, 1987.

———. "Luis Muñoz Marín." In Carmelo Rosario Natal, ed., *Luis Muñoz Marín: Juicios sobre su significado histórico*, pp. 19-23. San Juan: Fundación Luis Muñoz Marín, 1990.

———. "Puerto Rico since 1940." In Leslie Bethell, eds., *Cambridge History of Latin America*, vol. 7, pp. 579-599. Cambridge: Cambridge University Press, 1995.

———. "Politics and Government." In Lynn Darrell Bender, ed., *The American Presence in Puerto Rico*, pp. 30-70. San Juan: USA Centennial Commission, 1998.

———. "Las elecciones y la política." In Robert W. Anderson, ed., *Política electoral en Puerto Rico*, pp. 13-82. San Juan: Editorial Plaza Mayor, 1998.

Andreu Iglesias, César. *Luis Muñoz Marín, un hombre acorralado por la historia*. Río Piedras: Editorial Puerto Rico, 1972.

Appadurai, Arjun. "Numbers in the Colonial Imagination." In Appadurai, *Modernity at Large: Cultural Dimensions of Globalization*, Chapter 6. Minneapolis: University of Minnesota Press, 1996.

Appleby, Joyce, Lynn Hunt, and Margaret Jacob. *Telling the Truth about History*. New York: W. W. Norton, 1994.

Argüelles, María del Pilar. *Morality and Power: The U.S. Colonial Experience in Puerto Rico from 1898 to 1948*. Lanham, MD: University Press of America, 1996.

Arselay Santiago, Carmen Lydia. "La política de la enseñanza de la historia de Puerto Rico: 1950-1960." Ph.D. diss., University of Puerto Rico, 1992.

Ashcroft, Bill, Gareth Griffiths, and Helen Tiffin, eds. *The Postcolonial Studies Reader*. London: Routledge, 1995.

Azize Vargas, Yamila. *La mujer en la lucha*. San Juan: Editorial Cultural, 1985.

————, ed. *La mujer en Puerto Rico: Ensayos de investigación.* San Juan: Ediciones Huracán, 1987.

Baczko, Bronislaw. "Stalin: Fabricación de un carisma." In Baczko, *Los Imaginarios sociales: Memorias y esperanzas colectivas,* pp. 137-152. Buenos Aires: Ediciones Nueva Visión, 1984.

Badillo, Américo. "Fin del autonomismo: El PPD y la alianza populista." *Pensamiento Crítico* 4, no. 25 (August-September 1981): 7-12.

Baerga, María del Carmen, ed. *Género y trabajo: La industria de la aguja en Puerto Rico y el Caribe Hispánico.* San Juan: Editorial de la Universidad de Puerto Rico, 1993.

Baker, Susan. *Understanding Mainland Puerto Rican Poverty.* Philadelphia: Temple University Press, 2002.

Baldrich, Juan José. "Class and State: The Origins of Populism in Puerto Rico, 1934-52." Ph.D. diss., Yale University, 1981.

————. *Sembraron la no siembra: Los cosecheros de tabaco puertorriqueños frente a las corporaciones tabacaleras, 1920-1934.* Río Piedras: Ediciones Huracán, 1988.

Baralt, Guillermo A. *Tradición de Futuro: El primer siglo del Banco Popular de Puerto Rico, 1893-1993.* Chicago: R. R. Donnelley and Sons, 1993.

Barret, Michéle. "Ideology, Politics, Hegemony: From Gramsci to Laclau and Mouffe," In Slavoj Žižek, ed., *Mapping Ideology,* pp. 235-264. London: Verso Books, 1994.

Barreto Velazquez, Norberto. "El ultimo de los tutores: la oposición enfrentada por el gobernador Rexford G. Tugwell, 1941-1946." M.A. diss., University of Puerto Rico, 1993.

Baudrillard, Jean. *In the Shadow of the Silent Majorities... Or the End of the Social.* New York: Semiotexte, 1983.

————. *America.* London: Verso Books, 1988.

Baver, Sherrie L. *The Political Economy of Colonialism: The State and Industrialization in Puerto Rico.* Westport, CT: Praeger, 1993.

Becker, Marjorie. "Lázaro Cárdenas and the Mexican Counter-Revolution: The Struggle over Culture in Michoacán, 1934-1940." Ph.D. diss., Yale University, 1988.

————. *Setting the Virgin on Fire: Lázaro Cárdenas, Michoacán Peasants, and the Redemption of the Mexican Revolution.* Berkekey: University of California Press, 1995.

Benítez Rexach, Jesús. *Vida y obra de Luis Muñoz Marín.* Río Piedras: Editorial Edil, 1989.

Benítez-Rojo, Antonio. *The Repeating Island: The Caribbean and the Postmodern Perspective.* Durham, NC: Duke University Press, 1992.

Bergad, Laird W. "Agrarian History of Puerto Rico, 1870-1930." *Latin American Research Review* 13 (1978): 63-94.

Bergquist, Charles. *Labor in Latin America: Comparative Essays on Chile, Argentina, Venezuela, and Colombia.* Stanford, CA: Stanford University Press, 1986.

Berman, Marshall. *All That Is Solid Melts into Air: The Experience of Modernity.* New York: Penguin Books, 1982.

Bernabe, Rafael Alberto. "Prehistory of the 'Partido Popular Democrático': Muñoz Marín, the Partido Liberal, and the Crisis of Sugar in Puerto Rico, 1930-1935." Ph.D. diss., State University of New York at Binghamton, 1989.

————. *Respuestas al colonialismo en la política puertorriqueña, 1899-1929.* Río Piedras: Ediciones Huracán, 1996.

————. *Manual para organizar velorios (Notas sobre la muerte de la nación).* Río Piedras: Ediciones Huracán, 2003.

Bernier, R. Elfrén. *Luis Muñoz Marín: Líder y Maestro, Anecdotario Mumarino I.* San Juan: Ramallo Bros. Printing, 1988.

————. *Luis Muñoz Marín: Anecdotario Mumarino II*. San Juan: Fundación Luis Muñoz Marín, 1999.

————. *Anecdotario Mumarino III (y el asunto de las carpetas)*. San Juan: Fundación Luis Muñoz Marín, 2002.

Bernier-Grand, Carmen T. *Poet and Politician of Puerto Rico: Don Luis Muñoz Marín*. New York: Orchard Books, 1995.

Besse, Susan K. *Restructuring Patriarchy: The Modernization of Gender Inequality in Brazil, 1914-1940*. Chapel Hill: University of North Carolina Press, 1996.

Bethell, Leslie, and Ian Roxborough, eds. *Latin America between the Second World War and the Cold War, 1944-1948*. Cambridge: Cambridge University Press, 1992.

Beverly, John, and José Oviedo, eds. *The Postmodernism Debate in Latin America*. Durham, NC: Duke University Press, 1993.

Bhana, Surendra. *The United States and the Development of the Puerto Rican Status Question, 1936-1968*. Lawrence: University Press of Kansas, 1975.

Biles, Roger. *A New Deal for the American People*. De Kalb: Northern Illinois University Press, 1991.

Bird Piñero, Enrique. *Don Luis Muñoz Marín: El poder de la excelencia*. San Juan: Fundación Luis Munoz Marín, 1991.

Blaut, J. M. *The Colonizer's Model of the World: Geographical Diffusionism and Eurocentric History*. New York: Guilford Press, 1993.

Bocock, Robert. *Hegemony*. London: Tavistock Publications, 1986.

Bothwell, Reece B., ed. *Cien años de lucha política en Puerto Rico*. Río Piedras: Editorial Universitaria, 1979.

————. *Orígenes y Desarrollo de los Partidos Políticos en Puerto Rico*. Río Piedras: Editorial Edil, 1988.

Bourdieu, Pierre. *Language and Symbolic Power*. Cambridge: Harvard University Press, 1991.

Boyer, Paul. *By the Bomb's Early Light: American Thought and Culture at the Dawn of the Atomic Age*. Chapel Hill: University of North Carolina Press, 1994.

Brenner, Y. S. *Looking into the Seeds of Time: The Price of Modern Development*. New Brunswick, NJ: Transaction Publishers, 1998.

Briggs, Laura. *Reproducing Empire: Race, Sex, Science, and U.S. Imperialism in Puerto Rico*. Berkeley: University of California Press, 2002.

Brinkley, Alan. *The End of Reform: New Deal Liberalism in Recession and War*. New York: Knopf, 1995.

Brunner, José Juaquín. *América Latina: Cultura y modernidad*. México, DF: Editorial Grijalbo, 1992.

Burbano, Felipe, ed. *El fantasma del populismo: Aproximación a un tema (siempre) actual*. Caracas: Editorial Nueva Sociedad, 1998.

Burbano, Felipe, and Carlos de la Torre, eds. *El populismo en Ecuador*. Quito: ILDIS, 1989.

Butler, Judith. "Restaging the Universal: Hegemony and the Limits of Formalism." In Judith Butler, Ernesto Laclau, and Slavoj Žižek, *Contingency, Hegemony, Universality*, pp. 11-43. London: Verso Books, 2000.

Byron Toro, Fernando. *Elecciones y partidos políticos de Puerto Rico, 1809-1976*. Mayagüez: Editorial Isla, 1977.

Cabán, Pedro A. "The State, Interest Associations, and Economic Change in Puerto Rico: 1948-1976." Ph.D. diss., Columbia University, 1981.

————. "Industrialization, the Colonial State, and Working Class Organizations in Puerto Rico." *Latin American Perspectives* 11 (1984): 140-172.

————. "El aparato colonial y el cambio económico en Puerto Rico: 1898-1917." *Revista de Ciencias Sociales* 1-2 (March-June 1987): 55-87.

————. "Industrial Transformation and Labour Relations in Puerto Rico: From 'Operation Bootstrap' to the 1970s." *Journal of Latin American Studies* 21 (October 1989): 559-591.

————. *Constructing a Colonial People: Puerto Rico and the United States, 1898-1932.* Boulder, CO: Westview Press, 1999.

Cabrera, Gilberto R. *Historia económica del comercio y la industria en Puerto Rico.* Hato Rey: Fundación Socioeconómica de Puerto Rico, 1980.

Camus, Albert. *Resistance, Rebellion, and Death.* New York: The Modern Library, 1960.

————. *The Rebel: An Essay on Man in Revolt.* New York: Vintage Books, 1991.

Cancel, Mario R. "Politización de la poesía: una propuesta interpretativa." In Cancel, *Antifiguraciones: Bocetos puertorriqueños,* chap. 8. San Juan: Editorial Isla Negra, 2003.

Cardoso, Fernando Henrique, and Enzo Faletto. *Dependencia y Desarrollo en América Latina: Ensayo de interpretación Sociológica.* México, DF: Siglo Veintiuno, 1969.

Carr, Raymond. *Puerto Rico: A Colonial Experiment.* New York: Vintage Books, 1984.

Carrión, Juan Manuel. *Voluntad de nación: Ensayos sobre el nacionalismo en Puerto Rico.* San Juan: Ediciones Nueva Aurora, 1996.

Carrión, Juan Manuel, Teresa C. Gracia Ruiz, and Carlos Rodríguez Fraticelli, eds. *La nación puertorriqueña: Ensayos en torno a Pedro Albizu Campos.* Río Piedras: Editorial de la Universidad de Puerto Rico, 1993.

Casimir, Jean. *La invención del Caribe.* Río Piedras: Editorial de la Universidad de Puerto Rico, 1997.

Castor, Suzy, et al. *Puerto Rico, una crisis histórica.* México, DF: Editorial Nuestro Tiempo, 1979.

Castro Arroyo, María de los Angeles, and María Dolores Luque de Sánchez. *Puerto Rico en su historia: El rescate de la memoria.* San Juan: Editorial La Biblioteca, 2001.

Chartier, Roger. *Cultural History: Between Practices and Representations.* Ithaca, NY: Cornell University Press, 1988.

————. *On the Edge of the Cliff: History, Language, Practices.* Baltimore: Johns Hopkins University Press, 1997.

Chatterjee, Partha. *Nationalist Thought and the Colonial World: A Derivative Discourse.* Minneapolis: University of Minnesota Press, 1986.

————. *The Nation and Its Fragments: Colonial and Postcolonial Histories.* Princeton: Princeton University Press, 1993.

Chiriboga, Jorge. *Historia de un retrato y el Puerto Rico de hoy.* San Juan: Editorial Colibri, 1994.

Chrisman, Williams, and Laura Chrisman, eds. *Colonial Discourse and Post-Colonial Theory: A Reader.* New York: Columbia University Press, 1994.

Clifford, J. Garry. "Bureaucratic Politics and Policy Outcomes." In Michael J. Hogan and Thomas G. Paterson, eds., *Explaining the History of American Foreign Relations,* pp. 141-150. Cambridge: Cambridge University Press, 1991.

Cohen, Lizabeth. *Making a New Deal: Industrial Workers in Chicago, 1919-1939.* New York: Cambridge University Press, 1990.

Cohen, Youssef. *The Manipulation of Consent: The State and Working-Class Consciousness in Brazil.* Pittsburgh: University of Pittsburgh Press, 1989.

Collier, David, ed. *The New Authoritarianism in Latin America.* Princeton: Princeton University Press, 1979.

Collier, Ruth Berins. "Combining Alternative Perspectives: Internal Trajectories versus External Influences as Explanations of Latin American Politics in the 1940s." *Comparative Politics* 26 (October 1993): 1-29.

―――. "Labor Politics and Regime Change: Internal Trajectories versus External Influences." In David Rock, ed., *Latin America in the 1940s: War and Postwar Transitions*, pp. 59-88. Berkeley: University of California Press, 1994.

Collier, Ruth Berins, and David Collier. *Shaping the Political Arena: Critical Junctures, the Labor Movement, and Regime Dynamics in Latin America*. Princeton: Princeton University Press, 1991.

Conniff, Michael L. *Urban Politics in Brazil: The Rise of Populism, 1925-1945*. Pittsburgh: University of Pittsburgh Press, 1981.

―――, ed. *Latin American Populism in Comparative Perspective*. Albuquerque: University of New Mexico Press, 1982.

―――, *Populism in Latin America*. Tuscaloosa: University of Alabama Press, 1999.

Cooper, Frederick, and Ann L. Stoler. "Tension of Empire: Colonial Control and Visions of Rule." *American Ethnologist* 16, no. 4 (1989): 609-621.

Cooper, Frederick, et al. *Confronting Historical Paradigms: Peasants, Labor, and the Capitalists World System in Africa and Latin America*. Madison: University of Wisconsin Press, 1989.

Cooper, Frederick, and Ann L. Stoler, eds. *Tensions of Empire: Colonial Cultures in a Bourgeois World*. Berkeley: University of California Press, 1997.

Córdova, Gonzalo F. *Resident Commissioner Santiago Iglesias and His Times*. Río Piedras: Editorial de la Universidad de Puerto Rico, 1993.

Córdova, Lieban. *Luis Muñoz Marín y sus campañas políticas: Memorias de su secretario-taquígrafo personal*. Río Piedras: Editorial de la Universidad de Puerto Rico, 1983.

―――. *Luis Muñoz Marín y sus campañas políticas: Memorias de su secretario taquígrafo personal*. Río Piedras: Editorial de la Universidad de Puerto Rico, 1983.

―――. *7 años con Muñoz Marín, 1938-1945*. Arecibo: Editora Corripio, 1988.

―――. *¿Cómo era Muñoz Marín?* 2 vols. Arecibo: First Book Publishing of Puerto Rico, 1996.

Coss, Luis Fernando. *La nación en la orilla (respuesta a los posmodernos pesimistas)*. San Juan: Editorial Punto de Encuentro, 1996.

Curet, Eliezer. *El Desarrollo Económico de Puerto Rico: 1940 a 1972*. San Juan: Management Aid Center, 1979.

―――. *Puerto Rico: Development by Integration to the U.S.* Río Piedras: Editorial Cultural, 1986.

Davey, William George. "Luis Muñoz Marín: A Rhetorical Analysis of Political and Economic Modernization." Ph.D. diss., Indiana University, 1974.

Dávila, Arlene M. *Sponsored Identities: Cultural Politics in Puerto Rico*. Philadelphia: Temple University Press, 1997.

―――. *Latinos, Inc.: The Marketing and Making of a People*. Berkeley: University of California Press, 2001.

de Heredia, Manuel. *Luis Muñoz Marín: Biografía abierta*. Río Piedras: Ediciones Puerto Rico, 1973.

de Ipola, Emilio. "Populismo e ideología. A propósito de Ernesto Laclau: Política e ideología en la teoría marxista." *Revista Mexicana de Sociología* 41 (1979): 925-960.

―――. *Ideología y discurso populista*. México, DF: Folios Ediciones, 1982.

de Jesús Toro, Rafael. *Historia económica de Puerto Rico*. Cincinnati: South Western Publishing Co., 1982.

de la Torre, Carlos. "The Ambiguous Meanings of Latin American Populisms." *Social Research* 59, no. 2 (Summer 1992): 385-414.

———. "Velasco Ibarra and 'La Revolución Gloriosa': The Social Production of a Populist Leader in Ecuador in the 1940s." *Journal of Latin American Studies* 26 (October 1994): 683-711.

———. *Un solo toque: Populismo y cultura política en Ecuador*. Quito: Centro Andino de Acción Popular, 1996.

———. "Populism and Democracy: Political Discourses and Cultures in Contemporary Ecuador." *Latin American Perspectives* 94, no. 3 (May 1997): 12-24.

———. *Populist Seduction in Latin America: The Ecuadorian Experience*. Athens: Ohio University Center for International Studies, 2000.

Delano, Jack. *El dia que el pueblo se despidio de Muñoz*. San Juan: Fundación Luis Muñoz Marín, 1987.

Derrida, Jacques. *Specters of Marx: The State of the Debt, the Work of Mourning, and the New International*. New York: Routledge, 1994.

———. "Remarks on Deconstruction and Pragmatism." In Chantal Mouffe, ed., *Deconstruction and Pragmatism*, pp. 77-88. London: Routledge, 1996.

———. *Limited Inc*. Evanston, IL: Northwestern University Press, 1998.

Díaz, Luis Felipe. *Semiótica, psicoanálisis y postmodernidad*. Río Piedras: Editorial Plaza Mayor, 1999.

Díaz, Luis Felipe, and Marc Zimmerman, eds. *Globalización, nación, postmodernidad: Estudios culturales puertorriqueños*. San Juan: Ediciones La Casa Puerto Rico, 2001.

Díaz Quiñones, Arcadio, ed. *Conversación con José Luis González*. Río Piedras: Ediciones Huracán, 1976.

———. "Recordando el Futuro Imaginario: La Escritura Histórica en la Década del Treinta." *Sin Nombre* 14, no. 3 (1984): 21-35.

———. "Tomás Blanco: la reinvención de la tradición." *Op. Cit.* 4 (1988-1989): 147-182.

———. *La Memoria Rota: Ensayos sobre cultura y política*. Río Piedras: Ediciones Huracán, 1993.

———. *El arte de bregar: Ensayos*. San Juan: Ediciones Callejón, 2000.

Dietz, James L. "The Puerto Rican Political Economy." *Latin American Perspectives* 10-3, no. 3 (Summer 1976): 3-16.

———. "Imperialism and Underdevelopment: A Theoretical Perspective and a Case Study of Puerto Rico." *Review of Radical Political Economics* 11 (Winter 1979): 16-32.

———. "Delusions of Development." *Revista/Review Interamericana* 11 (Winter 1981-1982): 472-475.

———. *Economic History of Puerto Rico*. Princeton: Princeton University Press, 1986.

———. ed. *Latin America's Economic Development: Confronting Crisis*. Boulder, CO: Lynne Rienner Publishers, 1995.

Di Tella, Torcuato S. "Populismo y reforma en America Latina." *Desarrollo Económico* 4, no. 16 (April-June 1965): 391-425.

Dirks, Nicholas B., ed. *Colonialism and Culture*. Ann Arbor: University of Michigan Press, 1992.

Dix, Robert H. "Populism: Authoritarian and Democratic." *Latin American Research Review* 20 (1985): 29-52.

Drake, Paul W. *Socialism and Populism in Chile, 1932-1952*. Urbana: University of Illinois Press, 1978.

Duany, Jorge. *The Puerto Rican Nation on the Move: Identities on the Island and in the United States*. Chapel Hill: University of North Carolina Press, 2002.

Duchesne Winter, Juan, ed. *Las tribulaciones de Juliá*. San Juan: Instituto de Cultura Puertorriqueña, 1992.

Duchesne Winter, Juan, et al. "La estadidad desde una perspectiva democrática radical." *Diálogo*, February 1997, pp. 30-31.

Edel, Mathew O. "Land Reform in Puerto Rico, 1940-1959." Part I and II. *Caribbean Studies* 2, no. 3-4 (1965): 26-61, 28-50.

Erickson, Kenneth Paul. "Populism and Political Control of the Working Class in Brazil." In June Nash, Juan Corradi, and Hobart Spalding, Jr., eds., *Ideology & Social Change in Latin America*, pp. 200-236. New York: Gordon and Breach, 1977.

Farley, Ena L. "Puerto Rico: Ordeals of an American Dependency during World War II." *Revista/Review Interamericana* 6, no. 2 (Summer 1976): 202-210.

Farr, Kenneth R. *Personalism and Party Politics: Institutionalization of the Popular Democratic Party of Puerto Rico*. Hato Rey: Inter American University Press, 1973.

Fernández, Ronald. *The Disenchanted Island, Puerto Rico and the United States in the Twentieth Century*. New York: Praeger, 1992.

———. *Cruising the Caribbean: U.S. Influence and Intervention in the Twentieth Century*. Monroe, ME: Common Courage Press, 1994.

Fernós Isern, Antonio. *Addresses of Antonio Fernós, Resident Commissioner of Puerto Rico to the United States*. Washington, DC: Office of Puerto Rico, 1947.

———. *El Estado Libre Asociado de Puerto Rico: Antecedentes, creación, y desarrollo hasta la época presente*. Río Piedras: Editorial Universitaria, 1973.

Ferrao, Luis Angel. *Pedro Albizu Campos y el nacionalismo puertorriqueño*. San Juan: Editorial Cultural, 1990.

———. "Nacionalismo, hispanismo y élite intelectual en el Puerto Rico de los años treinta." In Silvia Alvarez Curbelo and María Elena Rodríguez Castro, eds., *Del Nacionalismo al Populismo: Cultura y Política en Puerto Rico*, pp. 37-60. Río Piedras: Ediciones Huracán, 1993.

Flores, Juan. *"Insularismo" e ideología burguesa (Nueva lectura de A. S. Pedreira)*. Río Piedras: Ediciones Huracán, 1979.

———. "Cortijo's Revenge: New Mappings of Puerto Rican Culture." In George Yúdice, Jean Franco, and Juan Flores, eds., *On Edge: The Crisis of Contemporary Latin American Culture*, pp. 187-205. Minneapolis: University of Minnesota Press, 1992.

———. *Divided Borders: Essays on Puerto Rican Identity*. Houston: Arte Público Press, 1993.

Fonfrías, Ernesto Juan. *Historia de mi vida política en la fundación del Partido Popular Democrático*. Río Piedras: Imprenta ESMACO, 1986.

Foucault, Michel. "Truth and Power." In Colin Gordon, ed., *Power/Knowledge: Selected Interviews and Other Writings, 1972-1977*, pp. 109-133. New York: Pantheon Books, 1977.

———. *The History of Sexuality*, vol. 1. New York: Vintage, 1980.

———. *The Archeaology of Knowledge*. London: Tavistock, 1985.

———. *Discipline and Punish: The Birth of the Prison*. New York: Vintage Books, 1995.

Frambes-Buxeda, Aline, ed. *Huracán del Caribe: Vida y obra del insigne puertorriqueño Don Pedro Albizu Campos*. San Juan: Libros Homines, 1993.

Frank, André Gunder. *Capitalism and Underdevelopment in Latin America: Historical Studies of Chile and Brazil*. New York: Monthly Review Press, 1969.

Fraser, Steve. "From the 'New Unionism' to the New Deal." *Labor History* 25 (Summer 1984): 405-430.

Fraser, Steve, and Gary Gerstle, eds. *The Rise and Fall of the New Deal Order, 1930-1980.* Princeton: Princeton University Press, 1989.

French, John D. "Industrial Workers and the Birth of the Populist Republic in Brazil, 1945-1946." *Latin American Perspectives* 63, no. 4 (Fall 1989): 5-27.

———. *The Brazilian Worker's ABC: Class Conflict and Alliances in Modern São Paulo.* Chapel Hill: University of North Carolina Press, 1992.

———. "The Populist Gamble of Gertúlio Vargas in 1945: Political and Ideological Transitions in Brazil." In David Rock, ed., *Latin America in the 1940s: War and Postwar Transitions,* pp. 141-165. Berkeley: University of California Press, 1994.

Fromm, Georg. *César Andreu Iglesias: Aproximación a su vida y obra.* Río Piedras: Ediciones Huracán, 1977.

———. "La historia-ficción de Benjamín Torres (IV); la huelga de 1934, una interpretación marxista (1)." *Claridad,* June 24-30, 1977, pp. 6-7.

———. "La historia-ficción de Benjamín Torres (VI); la huelga de 1934, una interpretación marxista (2)." *Claridad,* July 1-7, 1977, pp. 4-5.

———. "El nacionalismo y el movimiento obrero en la década del 30." *Op. Cit.* 5 (1990): 37-103.

Galeano, Eduardo. *Open Veins of Latin America: Five Centuries of the Pillage of a Continent.* New York: Monthly Review Press, 1973.

———. *Patas arriba: La escuela del mundo al revés.* México, DF: Siglo Veintiuno, 1998.

Gallart, Mary Frances. "Mujeres, aguja y política en el Siglo 20 en Puerto Rico: Obdulia Velázquez de Lorenzo, Alcaldesa de Guayama, 1952-1956." Ph.D. diss., University of Puerto Rico, 1992.

———. "Political Empowerment of Puerto Rican Women, 1952-1956," In Félix V. Matos Rodríguez and Linda C. Delgado, eds., *Puerto Rican Women's History: New Perspectives,* pp. 227-252. Armonk, NY: M. E. Sharpe, 1998.

———. "Las mujeres en la discursiva de Luis Muñoz Marín: primeras décadas." In Fernando Picó, ed., *Luis Muñoz Marín: Ensayos del Centenario,* pp. 187-207. San Juan: Fundación Luis Muñoz Marín, 1999.

Galvin, Miles. "The Early Development of the Organized Labor Movement in Puerto Rico." *Latin American Perspectives* 10, no. 3 (Summer 1976): 17-35.

———. *The Organized Labor Movement in Puerto Rico.* London: Associated University Presses, 1979.

García, Gervasio L. *Historia crítica, historia sin coartadas: Algunos problemas de la historia de Puerto Rico.* Río Piedras: Ediciones Huracán, 1985.

García, Gervasio L., and Angel G. Quintero Rivera. "Historia del movimiento obrero puertorriqueño, 1872-1978." In Pablo González Casanova, ed., *Historia del Movimiento Obrero en América Latina,* pp. 358-412. México, DF: Siglo Veintiuno, 1984.

———. *Desafío y solidaridad: Breve historia del movimiento obrero puertorriqueño.* Río Piedras: Ediciones Huracán, 1986.

García Canclini, Néstor. *Hybrid Cultures: Strategies for Entering and Leaving Modernity.* Minneapolis: University of Minnesota Press, 1995.

———. *La globalización imaginada.* Buenos Aires: Paidós, 1999.

García Leduc, José Manuel. *Historia, historiadores, posmodernos y otros demonios.* San Juan: Editores Independientes Asociados, 2000.

———. *Apuntes para una historia breve de Puerto Rico.* San Juan: Editorial Isla Negra, 2002.

García Muñiz, Humberto. "El Caribe durante la Segunda Guerra Mundial: El Mediterráneo Americano." In Carmen Gautier Mayoral, Angel I. Rivera Ortiz, and Idsa E. Alegría

Ortiz, eds., *Puerto Rico en las relaciones internacionales del Caribe*, pp. 161-191. Río Piedras: Ediciones Huracán, 1990.

García Passalacqua, Juan Manuel. *Hegemón: Otredad y mismidad de la otra cara*. San Juan: Editorial Cultural, 1994.

———. *Los secretos del patriarca: Memorias secretas de Luis Muñoz Marín*. San Juan: Editorial Cultural, 1996.

———. *Invadiendo al invasor: Puerto Rico y Estados Unidos en el siglo veintiuno*. San Juan: Editorial Cultural, 1999.

———. "La carpeta de Luis Muñoz Marín, (1940-1960)." *El Vocero*, August 21-25, 2000.

———, ed. *Vate, de la cuna a la cripta: El nacionalismo cultural de Luis Muñoz Marín*. San Juan: Editorial LEA, 1998.

Gardner, Lloyd C. "Backing off the Colonial Issue." In Thomas G. Paterson and Dennis Merrill, eds., *Major Problems in American Foreign Relations, since 1914*, vol. 2, pp. 224-230. Lexington, MA: D. C. Heath Company, 1995.

Garzaro, Rafael. *Puerto Rico, colonia de Estados Unidos*. Madrid: Editorial Tecnos, 1980.

Gautier Mayoral, Carmen, Angel I. Rivera Ortiz, and Idsa E. Alegría Ortega, eds. *Puerto Rico en las relaciones internacionales del Caribe*. Río Piedras: Ediciones Huracán, 1990.

Gaztambide Géigel, Antonio, and Silvia Alvarez Curbelo, eds. *Historias vivas: Historiografía puertorriqueña contemporánea*. San Juan: Posdata, 1996.

Geertz, Clifford. *The Interpretation of Culture*. New York: Basic Books, 1973.

———. "Centers, Kings, and Charisma: Reflections on the Symbolics of Power." In Sean Wilentz, ed., *Rites of Power: Symbolism, Ritual, and Politics since the Middle Ages*, pp. 13-38. Philadelphia: University of Pennsylvania Press, 1984.

Gelpí, Juan G. "Las tribulaciones de Jonás ante el paternalismo." In Juan Duchesne Winter, ed., *Las tribulaciones de Juliá*, pp. 95-115. San Juan: Instituto de Cultura Puertorriqueña, 1992.

———. *Literatura y paternalismo en Puerto Rico*. Río Piedras: Editorial de la Universidad de Puerto Rico, 1993.

Germani, Gino. *Política y sociedad en una época de transición*. Buenos Aires: Editorial Pados, 1971.

———. *Authoritarianism, Fascism and National Populism*. New Brunswick, NJ: Transaction Books, 1978.

Gerstle, Gary. "The Protean Character of American Liberalism." *American Historical Review* 99 (October 1994): 1043-1073.

Giddens, Anthony. *A Contemporary Critique of Historical Materialism I: Power, Property, and the State*. Berkeley: University of California Press, 1981.

———. *A Contemporary Critique of Historical Materialism II: The Nation-State and Violence*. Berkeley: University of California Press, 1985.

———. *The Consequences of Modernity*. Stanford, CA: Stanford University Press, 1990.

Gil, Carlos. *El orden del tiempo: Ensayos sobre el robo del presente en la utopía puertorriqueña*. San Juan: Editorial Posdata, 1994.

———. "'Yo no me voy, yo regreso.' Luis Muñoz Marín y el montaje del leviatán." In Fernando Picó, ed., *Luis Muñoz Marín: Ensayos del Centenario*, pp. 209-232. San Juan: Fundación Luis Muñoz Marín, 1999.

Giusti Cordero, Juan. "La huelga cañera de 1942. Crónica de una huelga general." *Fundamentos* 5-6 (1997-1998): 82-96.

González, José Luis. *El país de cuatro pisos y otros ensayos*. Río Piedras: Ediciones Huracán, 1980.

———. *Nueva visita al cuarto piso*. Madrid: Exlesa, 1987.

González Díaz, Emilio. "Ideología populista y estrategias de desarrollo en Puerto Rico, 1940-1950." San Juan: CEREP, n.d.

———. "El populismo en Puerto Rico: 1938-1952." Ph.D. diss., UNAM, 1977.

———. "El estado y las clases dominantes en la situación colonial." *Revista Mexicana de Sociología* 40, no. 3 (1978): 1141-1152.

———. "Class Struggle and Politics in Puerto Rico during the Decade of the 40's: The Rise of PDP." *Two Thirds* 2, no. 1 (1979): 45-57.

———. "La lucha de clases y la política en el Puerto Rico de la década del '40: El ascenso del PPD." *Revista de Ciencias Sociales* 22, no. 1-2 (March-June 1980): 37-69.

———. "Muñoz, el populismo y el ELA." *Claridad*, July 25-31, 1980, pp. 2-3.

———. "La política, las clases y el cambio: algunos problemas de análisis social." In Eduardo Rivera Medina and Rafael L. Ramírez, *Del cañaveral a la fábrica: Cambio social en Puerto Rico*, pp. 131-137. Río Piedras: Ediciones Huracán, 1985.

———. "El populismo y la universidad." *Revista de Administración Pública* 18, no. 2 (March 1986): 21-33.

———. *La política de los empresarios puertorriqueños*. Río Piedras: Ediciones Huracán, 1991.

———. "Política, político, políticos." *Bordes* 3 (1996): 57-64.

———. *El Partido Popular Democrático y el fin de siglo: ¿Qué queda del populismo?* Río Piedras: Centro de Investigaciones Sociales, 1999.

González García, Lydia Milagros. *Una Puntada en el tiempo: La industria de la aguja en Puerto Rico, 1900-1929*. Río Piedras: CEREP, 1990.

Goodsell, Charles T. *Administration of a Revolution: Executive Reform in Puerto Rico under Governor Tugwell, 1941-1946*. Cambridge: Harvard University Press, 1965.

Gordon, Colin. *New Deals: Business, Labor, and Politics in America, 1920-1935*. Cambridge: Cambridge University Press, 1994.

Gould, Jeffrey L. *To Lead as Equals: Rural Protest and Political Consciousness in Chinandega, Nicaragua, 1912-1979*. Chapel Hill: University of North Carolina Press, 1990.

Gramsci, Antonio. *Selections from the Prison Notebooks*. Ed. and trans. Quintin Hoare and Geoffrey Nowell Smith. New York: International Publishers, 1971.

———. *Selections from Cultural Writings*. Cambridge: Harvard University Press, 1991.

———. *Pre-Prison Writings*. Cambridge: Cambridge University Press, 1994.

———. *Further Selections from the Prison Notebooks*. Ed. and trans. Derek Boothman. Minneapolis: University of Minnesota Press, 1995.

Green, W. John. "'Vibrations of the Collective': The Popular Ideology of Gaitanismo on Columbia's Atlantic Coast, 1944-1948." *Hispanic American Historical Review* 76, no. 2 (1996): 283-311.

Grosfoguel, Ramón. "Feminizando la política." *El Nuevo Día*, July 24, 1990, p. 51.

———. "Confesiones de un alienado." *El Nuevo Día*, September 29, 1990, p. 67.

———. "El Caribe y la 'Independencia realmente existente.'" *Diálogo*, May 1996, p. 26.

Grosfoguel, Ramón, and Ana Margarita Cervantes Rodríguez, eds. *The Modern/Colonial/Capitalist World-System in the Twentieth Century: Global Processes, Antisystemic Movements, and the Geopolitics of Knowledge*. New York: Greenwood Press, 2002.

Guerra, Lilliam. *Popular Expression and National Identity in Puerto Rico: The Struggle for Self, Community, and Nation*. Gainesville: University of Florida Press, 1998.

Guha, Ranajit. "Dominance without Hegemony and Its Historiography." In Ranajit Guha, ed., *Subaltern Studies IV*, pp. 210-309. Oxford: Oxford University Press, 1989.

Guha, Ranajit, and Gayatri Chakravorty Spivak, eds. *Selected Subaltern Studies*. New York and Oxford: Oxford University Press, 1988.

Hamilton, Nora. *The Limits of State Autonomy: Post-Revolutionary Mexico*. Princeton: Princeton University Press, 1982.

Harvey, David. *The Condition of Postmodernity: An Enquiry into the Origins of Cultural Change*. Cambridge: Blackwell, 1990.

Herzfeld, Michael. *Cultural Intimacy: Social Poetics in the Nation-State*. New York: Routledge, 1997.

Hobsbawm, Eric J. *Nations and Nationalism since 1780: Programme, Myth, Reality*. Cambridge: Cambridge University Press, 1995.

Hobsbawm, Eric J., and Terence Ranger, eds. *The Invention of Tradition*. Cambridge: Cambridge University Press, 1992.

Horowitz, Joel. "Industrialists and the Rise of Perón, 1943-1946: Some Implications for the Conceptualization of Populism." *The Americas* 47, no. 2 (1990): 199-217.

Hunt, Lynn. *Politics, Culture, and Class in the French Revolution*. Berkeley: University of California Press, 1984.

———, ed. *The New Cultural History*. Berkeley: University of California Press, 1989.

Hunt, Michael H. *Ideology and U.S. Foreign Policy*. New Haven, CT: Yale University Press, 1987.

Ianni, Octavio. "Populismo y relaciones de clase en América Latina." *Revista Mexicana de Ciencia Política* 18, no. 67 (1972): 25-51.

———. *La formación del estado populista en América Latina*. México, DF: Editorial Era, 1975.

———. *Teorías de la globalización*. México, DF: Siglo veintiuno, 1996.

Iggers, Georg G. *Historiography in the Twentieth Century: From Scientific Objectivity to the Postmodern Challenge*. Hanover, NH: Wesleyan University Press, 1997.

James, Daniel. *Resistance and Integration: Peronism and the Argentine Working Class, 1946-1976*. Cambridge: Cambridge University Press, 1988.

———. "October 17th and 18th, 1945: Mass Protest, Peronism, and the Argentine Working Class." *Journal of Social History* 22 (Spring 1988): 441-461.

Jameson, Fredric. *Postmodernism, Or, the Cultural Logic of Late Capitalism*. Durham, NC: Duke University Press, 1992.

Jenkins, Keith. *Re-thinking History*. London: Routledge, 1991.

———. *The Postmodern History Reader*. London: Routledge, 1997.

———. *Why History?: Ethics and Postmodernity*. London: Routledge, 1999.

Jenks, Chris. *Culture*. London: Routledge, 1993.

Johnson, Robert David. "Anti-Imperialism and the Good Neighbor Policy: Ernest Gruening and Puerto Rican Affairs, 1934-39." *Journal of Latin American Studies* 29 (1997): 89-110.

Joseph, Gilbert M., Catherine C. LeGrand, and Ricardo D. Salvatore, eds. *Close Encounters of Empire: Writing the Cultural History of U.S.-Latin American Relations*. Durham, NC: Duke University Press, 1998.

Joseph, Gilbert M., and Daniel Nugent, eds. *Everyday Forms of State Formation: Revolution and the Negotiation of Rule in Modern Mexico*. Durham, NC: Duke University Press, 1994.

Kaplan, Amy, and Donald E. Pease, eds. *Cultures of United States Imperialism*. Durham, NC: Duke University Press, 1993.

Kennedy, David M. *Freedom from Fear: The American People in Depression and War, 1929-1945*. New York: Oxford University Press, 1999.

Klaiber, Jeffrey L. "Prophets and Populists: Liberation Theology, 1968-1988." *The Americas* 46, no. 1 (July 1989).

Knight, Alan. "Populism and Neo-Populism in Latin America, Especially in Mexico." *Journal of Latin Amerian Studies* 30 (1998): 223-48.

Laclau, Ernesto. "Towards a Theory of Populism." In Laclau, *Politics and Ideology in Marxist Theory: Capitalism, Fascism, Populism*, pp. 81-198. London: NLB, 1977.

———. "Populist Rupture and Discourse." *Screen Education* 34 (Spring 1980): 87-93.

———. "The Impossibility of Society." *Canadian Journal of Political and Social Theory* 7, no. 1-2 (1983): 21-24.

———. "'Socialism,' the 'People,' 'Democracy': The Transformation of Hegemonic Logic." *Social Text* 7 (Spring-Summer 1984): 115-119.

———. "Psychoanalysis and Marxism." *Critical Inquiry* 13 (Winter 1987): 330-333.

———. "Populismo y Transformación del Imaginario Político en América Latina." *Cuadernos de la Realidad Nacional* 3 (1988), Quito.

———. "Metaphor and Social Antagonisms." In Cary Nelson and Lawrence Grossberg, eds., *Marxism and the Interpretation of Culture*, pp. 249-257. Urbana: University of Illinois Press, 1988.

———. *New Reflexions on the Revolution of Our Time*. London: Verso Books, 1991.

———. "Minding the Gap: The Subject of Politics." In Laclau, ed., *The Making of Political Identities*, pp. 11-39. London: Verso Books, 1994.

———. *Emancipation(s)*. London: Verso Books, 1996.

———. "Deconstruction, Pragmatism, Hegemony." In Chantal Mouffe, ed., *Deconstruction and Pragmatism*, pp. 47-67. London: Routledge, 1996.

———. "Identity and Hegemony: The Role of Universality in the Constitution of Political Logics." In Judith Butler, Ernesto Laclau, and Slavoj Žižek, *Contingency, Hegemony, Universality*, pp. 44-89. London: Verso Books, 2000.

———. "Constructing Universality." In Judith Butler, Ernesto Laclau, and Slavoj Žižek, *Contingency, Hegemony, Universality*, pp. 281-307. London: Verso Books, 2000.

———. *Misticismo, retórica y política*. México, DF: Fondo de Cultura Económica, 2002.

Laclau, Ernesto, and Chantal Mouffe. *Hegemony and Socialist Strategy: Toward a Radical Democratic Politics*. London: Verso Books, 1985.

———. "Post-Marxism without Apology." *New Left Review* 166 (November-December 1987): 79-106.

LaFeber, Walter. "The World and the United States." *American Historical Review* 100 (October 1995): 1015-1033.

Lange-Churión, Pedro, and Eduardo Mendieta, eds. *Latin America and Postmodernity: A Contemporary Reader*. New York: Humanity Books, 2001.

Langley, Lester D. *The United States and the Caribbean in the Twentieth Century*. Athens: University of Georgia Press, 1980.

Lenin, Vladimir. *El imperialismo, fase superior del capitalismo*. México, DF: Editorial Grijalbo, 1965.

Levine, Daniel H., ed. *Constructing Culture and Power in Latin America*. Ann Arbor: University of Michigan Press, 1995.

Levine, Rhonda F. *Class Struggle and the New Deal: Industrial Labor, Industrial Capital, and the State*. Lawrence: University Press of Kansas, 1988.

Lewis, Gordon. *Puerto Rico: Freedom and Power in the Caribbean*. New York: Monthly Review, 1974.

———. *Puerto Rico: Colonialismo y revolución*. Mexico, DF: Ediciones Era, 1977.

Lichtenstein, Nelson. *Labor's War at Home: The CIO in World War II*. New York: Cambridge University Press, 1982.

Lluch Vélez, Amalia. *Luis Muñoz Marín: Poesía, periodismo y revolución, 1915-1930*. San Juan: Universidad del Sagrado Corazón, Fundación Luis Muñoz Marín, 1999.

Lowell, Fiet, and Janette Becerra, eds. *Caribe 2000: Definiciones, identidades y culturas regionales y/o nacionales*. Río Piedras: Facultad de Humanidades - UPR, 1998.

López, Consuelo. "The *Memorias* of Luis Muñoz Marín." *Caribbean Quarterly* 37 (December 1991): 23-39.

López Rojas, Luis A. "Cambio ideológico de Luis Muñoz Marín: 1936-1940, 'He roto el arcoiris contra mi corazón.'" *Claridad*, December 17-30, 1993.

———. *Luis Muñoz Marín y las estrategias del poder, 1936-1946*. San Juan: Editorial Isla Negra, 1998.

Ludden, David. "India's Development Regime." In Nicholas B. Dirks, ed., *Colonialism and Culture*, pp. 247-287. Ann Arbor: University of Michigan Press, 1992.

Lugo, Kenneth. "Dos documentos perdidos de nuestra historia laboral." *Homines* 11, no. 1-2 (1987-1988): 164-177.

———. "Un peculiar manifiesto obrero puertorriqueño - época Confederación General de Trabajadores." *Homines* 13, no. 1 (February-July 1989): 226-235.

Lugo-Silva, Enrique. *The Tugwell Administration in Puerto Rico, 1941-1946*. Río Piedras: Editorial Cultura, 1955.

Luque de Sánchez, María Dolores. *La ocupación norteamericana y la ley Foraker*. Río Piedras: Editorial de la Universidad de Puerto Rico, 1986.

Lyon, David. *Postmodernity*. Minneapolis: University of Minnesota Press, 1999.

Lyotard, Jean-Francois. *The Postmodern Condition: A Report on Knowledge*. Minneapolis: University of Minnesota Press, 1993.

Maldonado, Alex W. "Muñoz y la época de la decencia." In Carmelo Rosario Natal, ed., *Luis Muñoz Marín: Juicios sobre su significado histórico*, pp. 64-67. San Juan: Fundación Luis Muñoz Marín, 1990.

———. *Teodoro Moscoso and Puerto Rico's Operation Bootstrap*. Gainesville: University of Florida Press, 1997.

Maldonado Denis, Manuel. *Puerto Rico: Una interpretación histórico-social*. México, DF: Siglo Veintiuno, 1974.

———. *Hacia una interpretación marxista de la historia de Puerto Rico y otros ensayos*. Río Piedras: Editorial Antillana, 1977.

———. *Puerto Rico: Mito y Realidad*. San Juan: Editorial Antillana, 1979.

Mallon, Florencia E. "The Promise and Dilemma of Subaltern Studies." *American Historical Review* 99, no. 5 (December 1994): 1491-1515.

———. *Peasant and Nation: The Making of Postcolonial Mexico and Peru*. Berkeley: University of California Press, 1995.

Malloy, James M., ed. *Authoritarianism and Corporatism in Latin America*. Pittsburgh: University of Pittsburgh Press, 1977.

Marx, Carlos. *El Capital*. 3 vols. México, DF: Fondo de Cultura Económica, 1986.

Mathews, Thomas. *Puerto Rican Politics and the New Deal*. New York: Da Capo Press, 1976.

———. "The Political Background to Industrialization." In Ronald J. Duncan, ed., *El Desarrollo Socioeconómico de Puerto Rico*, pp. 5-17. San Germán: Universidad Interamericana de Puerto Rico, 1979.

Matos, Félix V., and Linda C. Delgado, eds. *Puerto Rican Women's History: New Perspectives*. Armonk: M. E. Sharpe, 1998.

Mattos Cintrón, Wilfredo. *La política y lo político en Puerto Rico*. México, DF: Ediciones ERA, 1980.

Meléndez, Edgardo. *Movimiento anexionista en Puerto Rico*. Río Piedras: Editorial de la Universidad de Puerto Rico, 1993.

Meléndez, Edwin, and Edgardo Meléndez, eds. *Colonial Dilemma: Critical Perspectives on Contemporary Puerto Rico*. Boston: South End Press, 1993.

Meléndez, Hector. *Gramsci en la de Diego: Tres ensayos sobre cultura nacional, posmodernidad e ideología*. Río Piedras: Ediciones La Sierra, 1994.

———. *La identidad ausente: Credos, pueblos, capital, siglo*. Río Piedras: Ediciones La Sierra, 1996.

Milagros López, María, and Nalini Natrajan. "Colonial Discourse Analysis and the Puerto Rican Experience." *The Latino Review of Books* (Fall 1995): 32-36.

Miliband, Ralph. *The State in Capitalist Society*. New York: Basic Books, 1969.

Mintz, Sydney W. "The Culture History of a Puerto Rican Sugar Cane Plantation: 1876-1949." *Hispanic American Historical Review* 33 (1953): 224-251.

———. *Caribbean Transformations*. Chicago: Aldine, 1974.

———. *Worker in the Cane: A Puerto Rican Life History*. New York: W. W. Norton, 1974.

Montalvo Barbot, Alfredo. *Political Conflict and Constitutional Change in Puerto Rico, 1898-1952*. Lanham, MD: University Press of America, 1997.

Morales Carrión, Arturo. *Puerto Rico: A Political and Cultural History*. New York: W. W. Norton, 1983.

Morris, Nancy. *Puerto Rico: Culture, Politics, and Identity*. Westport, CT: Praeger, 1995.

Mouffe, Chantal. "Hegemony and New Political Subjects: Toward a New Concept of Democracy." In Cary Nelson and Lawrence Grossberg, eds., *Marxism and the Interpretation of Culture*, pp. 89-104. Urbana: University of Illinois Press, 1988.

———. "Democratic Citizenship, and the Political Community." In Mouffe, ed., *Dimensions of Radical Democracy: Pluralism, Citizenship, Community*, pp. 225-239. London: Verso Books, 1992.

———. *The Return of the Political*. London: Verso Books, 1993.

———. "Politics, Democratic Action, and Solidarity." *Inquiry* 39 (1994): 99-108.

———. "Deconstruction, Pragmatism and the Politics of Democracy." In Mouffe, ed., *Deconstruction and Pragmatism*, pp. 1-12. London: Routledge, 1996.

———. *The Democratic Paradox*. London: Verso Books, 2000.

———, ed. *Gramsci and Marxist Theory*. London: Routledge and Kegan Paul, 1979.

Mouzelis, Nicos. "On the Concept of Populism: Populist and Clientelist Modes of Incorporation in Semiperipheral Politics." *Politics and Society* 14, no. 3 (1985): 329-348.

Munslow, Alun. *Deconstructing History*. London: Routledge, 1997.

Muñoz Marín, Luis. *Luis Muñoz Marín: Pensamiento político, económico, social y cultural, segun expresado en los discursos oficiales*. Río Piedras: Corporación de Servicios Bibliotecarios, 1973.

———. *Mensajes al pueblo puertorriqueño pronunciados ante las camaras legislativas, 1949-64*. San Juan: Universidad Interamericana de Puerto Rico, 1980.

———. *Memorias: Autobiografia pública, 1898-1940*. San Juan: Universidad Interamericana de Puerto Rico, 1982.

———. *La Historia del Partido Popular Democrático*. San Juan: Editorial El Batey, 1984.

———. *Memorias: Autobiografia pública, 1940-1952*. San Germán: Universidad Interamericana de Puerto Rico, 1992.

———. *Diario, 1972-1974*. San Juan: Fundación Luis Muñoz Marín, 1999.

Nandy, Ashis, ed. *Science, Hegemony, and Violence: A Requiem for Modernity*. Tokyo: The United Nations University Press, 1988.

Nash, June. *We Eat the Mines and the Mines Eat Us: Dependency and Exploitation in Bolivian Tin Mines*. New York: Columbia University Press, 1993.

Navas Dávila, Gerardo. *La Dialéctica del Desarrollo Nacional: El Caso de Puerto Rico*. Río Piedras: Editorial de la Universidad de Puerto Rico, 1978.

———, ed. *Cambio y desarrollo en Puerto Rico: La transformación ideológica del Partido Popular Democrático*. San Juan: Editorial de la Universidad de Puerto Rico, 1980.

Negrón-Muntaner, Frances, and Ramón Grosfoguel, eds. *Puerto Rican Jam: Essays on Culture and Politics*. Minneapolis: University of Minnesota Press, 1997.

Ojeda Reyes, Félix. *Vito Marcantonio y Puerto Rico: Por los trabajadores y por la nación*. Río Piedras: Ediciones Huracán, 1978.

Oxhorn, Philip. "The Social Foundations of Latin America's Recurrent Populism: Problems of Class Formation and Collective Action." *Journal of Historical Sociology* 11, no. 22 (June 1998).

Pabón, Carlos. "De Albizu a Madonna: Para armar y desarmar la nacionalidad." *Bordes* 1 (1995): 22-40.

———. "De cómo se (de)construye el pasado." *Bordes* 6 (1998): 6-17.

———. *Nación Postmortem: Ensayos sobre los tiempos de insoportable ambigüedad*. San Juan: Ediciones Callejón, 2002.

Pabón, Carlos, and Arturo Torrecilla. "El capitalismo después del 'fin de la historia.'" *Bordes* 3 (1996): 19-28.

Pantojas García, Emilio. "Estrategias de desarrollo y contradicciones ideológicas en Puerto Rico, 1940-1980." *Revista de Ciencias Sociales* 21, no. 1-2 (March-June, 1979): 73-119.

———. "Reflexiones críticas en torno al uso del concepto de dependencia como categoria explicativa en el análisis del proceso de desarrollo en Puerto Rico." *Homines* 8, no. 1 (January-June 1984): 157-170.

———. "Desarrollismo y luchas de clases: Los limites del proyecto populista en Puerto Rico durante la decada del cuarenta." *Revista de Ciencias Sociales* 24, no. 3-4 (July-October 1985): 355-391.

———. "Crisis del modelo desarrollista y reestructuración capitalista: Hacia una redefinición del rol de Puerto Rico en la economía hemisférica." In Carmen Gautier Mayoral, Angel I. Rivera Ortiz, and Idsa Alegría Ortega, eds., *Puerto Rico en el Caribe hoy*, pp. 163-193. Buenos Aires: CLACSO, 1987.

———. "Puerto Rican Populism Revisited: The PPD during the 1940s." *Journal of Latin American Studies* 21 (October 1989): 521-557.

———. *Development Strategies as Ideology: Puerto Rico's Export-Led Industrialization Experience*. Boulder, CO: Lynne Rienner Publishers. Río Piedras: Editorial de la Universidad de Puerto Rico, 1990.

Paterson, Thomas G. "Defining and Doing the History of American Foreign Relations: A Primer." In Michael J. Hogan and Thomas G. Paterson, eds., *Explaining the History of American Foreign Relations*, pp. 36-54. Cambridge: Cambridge University Press, 1991.

Paterson, Thomas G., J. Garry Clifford, and Kenneth J. Hagan. *American Foreign Relations: A History since 1895*, vol. 2. Lexington, MA: D. C. Heath and Company, 1995.

Pérez, Louis A., Jr. "Intervention, Hegemony, and Dependency: The United States in the Circum-Caribbean, 1898-1980." *Pacific Historical Review* 51 (May 1982): 165-194.

Pérez Velasco, Erick J. *Bibliografía sobre el movimiento obrero de Puerto Rico, 1873-1996*. San Juan: Ediciones Cildes, 1996.

Perloff, Harvey S. *Puerto Rico's Economic Future, a Study in Planned Development*. Chicago: University of Chicago Press, 1950.

Picó, Fernando. *Historia General de Puerto Rico*. Río Piedras: Ediciones Huracán, 1986.

————. "La inconformidad, el respeto y la imaginación de Luis Muñoz Marín." In *Luis Muñoz Marín: Dos visiones universitarias*. San Juan: Fundación Luis Muñoz Marín, 1987.

————. "La incorporación del discurso del otro: La confrontación entre Vicente Géigel Polanco y Padrón Rivera en el Senado de Puerto Rico en marzo de 1941." In Fernando Picó, Silvia Alvarez Curbelo, and Carmen Raffucci, eds., *Senado de Puerto Rico, 1917-1992: Ensayos de historia institucional*, pp. 161-182. San Juan: Senado de Puerto Rico, 1992.

————. "La sociedad civil ante el Estado." In *Perspectivas sobre Puerto Rico en Homenaje a Muñoz Rivera y Muñoz Marín*, pp. 183-189. San Juan: Fundación Luis Muñoz Marín, 1997.

————, ed. *Luis Muñoz Marín: Ensayos del Centenario*. San Juan: Fundación Luis Muñoz Marín, 1999.

————. *Luis Muñoz Marín: Discursos, 1934-1948*, vol. 1. San Juan: Fundación Luis Muñoz Marín, 1999.

————. *Luis Muñoz Marín: Perfiles de su gobernación, 1948-1964*. San Juan: Fundación Luis Muñoz Marín, 2003.

Picó, Rafael. *The Geography of Puerto Rico*. Chicago: Aldine Publishing Company, 1974.

Pieterse, Jan Nederveen, and Bhikhu Parekh, eds. *The Decolonization of Imagination: Culture, Knowledge, and Power*. London: Zed Books, 1995.

Pike, Fredrick. *The United States and Latin America: Myths and Stereotypes of Nature and Civilzation*. Austin: University of Texas Press, 1992.

Plotkin, Mariano. "Politics of Consensus in Argentina (1943-1955)." Ph.D. diss., University of California, Berkeley, 1992.

————. *Mañana es San Perón: Propaganda, rituales políticos y educación en el régimen peronista, 1946-1955*. Buenos Aires: Ariel Historia Argentina, 1994.

Poster, Mark. *The Mode of Information: Poststructuralism and Context*. Chicago: University of Chicago Press, 1990.

————. *Cultural History and Postmodernity: Disciplinary Readings and Challenges*. New York: Columbia University Press, 1997.

Poulantzas, Nicos. *Classes in Contemporary Capitalism*. London: New Left Books, 1975.

————. *Political Power and Social Classes*. London: Verso Books, 1978.

————. *State, Power, Socialism*. London: Verso Books, 1980.

Pratts, Mary Louise. "Arts of the Contact Zone," *Profession* 91 (1991): 33-39.

————. *Imperial Eyes: Travel Writing and Transculturation*. London: Routledge, 1992.

Pumarada O'Neill, Luis. *La industria cafetalera de Puerto Rico, 1736-1969*. San Juan: Oficina Estatal de Preservación Histórica, 1990.

Quintero Rivera, Angel G. *El liderato local de los partidos y el estudio de la política puertorriqueña*. Río Piedras: Universidad de Puerto Rico, 1970.

————. "Background to the Emergence of Imperialist Capitalism in Puerto Rico." In Adalberto López and James Petras, eds., *Puerto Rico and Puerto Ricans*, pp. 87-117. Cambridge: Schenkman, 1974.

————. "La desintegración de la política de clases: De la política obrera al populismo," Part IV-2. *Revista de Ciencias Sociales* 20, no. 1 (1976): 3-47.

————. *Conflictos de clase y Política en Puerto Rico*. Río Piedras: Ediciones Huracán, 1977.

————. "Conflictos de Clase en la Política Colonial." In Gérard Pierre-Charles et al., *Relaciones internacionales y estructuras sociopolíticas en el Caribe*, pp. 22-57. México, DF: Universidad Nacional Autónoma de México, 1980.

————. "Bases sociales de la transformación ideológica del Partido Popular en la década del '40." In Gerardo Navas Dávila, ed., *Cambio y desarrollo en Puerto Rico: La transformación ideológica del Partido Popular Democrático*, pp. 35-119. San Juan: Editorial de la Universidad de Puerto Rico,1980.

————. "The Socio-Political Background to the Emergence of 'The Puerto Rican Model' as a Strategy for Development." In Susan Craig, ed., *Contemporary Caribbean: A Sociological Reader*, vol. 2, pp. 9-57. Trinidad and Tobago: S. Craig, 1982.

————. "Base clasista del proyecto desarrollista del 40." In Eduardo Rivera Medina and Rafael L. Ramírez, eds., *Del cañaveral a la fábrica: Cambio social en Puerto Rico*, pp. 139-145. Río Piedras: Ediciones Huracán, 1985.

————. *Patricios y plebeyos: Burgueses, hacendados, artesanos y obreros*. Río Piedras: Ediciones Huracán, 1988.

————. "La ideología populista y la institucionalización universitaria de las ciencias sociales." In Silvia Alvarez Curbelo, and María Elena Rodríguez Castro, eds., *Del Nacionalismo al Populismo: Cultura y Política en Puerto Rico*, pp. 107-145. Río Piedras: Ediciones Huracán, 1993.

————. "Puerto Rico, c. 1870-1940." In Leslie Bethell, ed., *Cambridge History of Latin America*, vol. 7, pp. 265-286. Cambridge: Cambridge University Press, 1995.

————, ed. *Workers' Struggle in Puerto Rico: A Documentary History*. New York: Monthly Review Press, 1976.

Quiñones Calderón, Antonio. *Trayectoria Política de Puerto Rico*. San Juan: Ediciones Nuevas de Puerto Rico, 1988.

————. *Historia Política de Puerto Rico*. 2 vols. San Juan: Credibility Group, 2003.

Raffucci de García, Carmen I. *El gobierno civil y la ley Foraker*. Río Piedras: Editorial Universitaria, 1981.

Rey, César A. "Parlamentarismo obrero y Coalición, 1932-1940." In Fernando Picó, Silvia Alvarez Curbelo, and Carmen Raffucci, eds., *Senado de Puerto Rico, 1917-1992: Ensayos de historia institucional*, pp. 137-160. San Juan: Senado de Puerto Rico, 1992.

Richards, Nelly. "Periferias culturales y descentramientos postmodernos." *Punto de Vista* 40 (July-September 1991): 5-6.

————. "Latinoamérica y la postmodernidad." In Herman Herlingaus and Monika Walter, eds., *Postmodernidad en la periferia*, pp. 211-222. Berlin: Langer Verlag, 1992.

Ricoeur, Paul. *Interpretation Theory: Discourse and the Surplus of Meaning*. Fort Worth: Texas Christian University Press, 1976.

————. *Time and Narrative*, vol. 1. Chicago: University of Chicago Press, 1983.

————. "History and Rhetoric." *Diogenes* 168 (1994): 7-24.

Rivera, José Antonio. "Political Autonomy and the Good in the Thought of Yves R. Simon and Luis Muñoz Marín." Ph.D. diss., The Catholic University of America, 1993.

————. *El pensamiento político de Luis Muñoz Marín*. San Juan: Fundación Luis Muñoz Marín, 1996.

Rivera, Marcia. *Tejiendo futuro: Los caminos posibles del desarrollo social*. San Juan: Ediciones Puerto, 2000.

Rivera Medina, Eduardo, and Rafael L. Ramírez, eds. *Del cañaveral a la fábrica: Cambio social en Puerto Rico*. Río Piedras: Ediciones Huracán, 1985.

Rivera Ramos, Efrén. *The Legal Construction of Identity: The Judicial and Social Legacy of American Colonialism in Puerto Rico*. Washington, DC: American Psychological Association, 2001.

Rock, David, ed. *Latin America in the 1940s: War and Postwar Transitions*. Berkeley: University of California Press, 1994.

Rodríguez, Nereida. *Debate universitario y dominación colonial, 1941-1947*. San Juan: N. Rodríguez, 1996.

Rodríguez, Neysa. "The Transformation of the Political Ideology of Luis Muñoz Marín." Ph.D. diss., University of Mississippi, 1992.

Rodríguez Beruff, Jorge. "Antonio S. Pedreira, la Universidad y el Proyecto Populista." *Revista de Administración Pública* 28, no. 2 (March 1986): 5-21.

———. *Política militar y dominación: Puerto Rico en el contexto latinoamericano*. Río Piedras: Ediciones Huracán, 1988.

———. "La Lija: La batalla contra la Coalición." *Fundamentos* 5-6 (1997-1998): 66-81.

———. "La pugna entre dos grandes sistemas: la guerra en el discurso político de Luis Muñoz Marín hasta Pearl Harbor." In Fernando Picó, ed., *Luis Muñoz Marín: Ensayos del Centenario*, pp. 127-152. San Juan: Fundación Luis Muñoz Marín, 1999.

———, ed. *Las memorias de Leahy: Los relatos del Admirante William D. Leahy sobre su gobernación de Puerto Rico (1939-1940)*. San Juan: Fundación Luis Muñoz Marín, 2002.

Rodríguez Castro, María Elena. "Tradición y modernidad: El intelectual puertorriqueño ante la década del '30." *Op. Cit.* 3 (1987-1988): 45-65.

Rodríguez Fraticelli, Carlos. "Rexford G. Tugwell, el Senado de Puerto Rico y el problema del status, 1941-1946." In Fernando Picó, Silvia Alvarez Curbelo, and Carmen Raffucci, eds., *Senado de Puerto Rico, 1917-1992: Ensayos de historia institucional*, pp. 183-206. San Juan: Senado de Puerto Rico, 1992.

Rodríguez Juliá, Edgardo. *Las tribulaciones de Jonás*. Río Piedras: Ediciones Huracán, 1981.

Rodríguez Vázquez, José J. "El Sueño que no cesa: La nación deseada en el debate intelectual y político puertorriqueño, 1920-1940." Ph.D. diss., University of Puerto Rico, 1998.

Rodríguez Vázquez, Manuel R. "Power and Development: The Puerto Rico Emergency Relief Administration and the Emergence of a New Colonial Order, 1933-1936." Ph.D. diss., Temple University, 2001.

———. "Representing Development: New Perspectives about the New Deal in Puerto Rico, 1933-36." *Journal of the Center for Puerto Rican Studies* 14, no. 2 (Fall 2002): 148-179.

Rosario Natal, Carmelo. *La juventud de Luis Muñoz Marín: Vida y pensamiento, 1898-1932*. Río Piedras: Editorial Edil, 1989.

———. *Muñoz Marín y la independencia de Puerto Rico*. San Juan: Producciones Historicas, 1994.

———, ed. *Luis Muñoz Marín: Juicios sobre su significado histórico*. San Juan: Fundación Luis Muñoz Marín, 1990.

———. *Luis Muñoz Marín: Servidor Público y Humanista (Cartas)*. San Juan: Producciones Históricas, 1998.

———. *Doña Inés María Mendoza y la batalla del idioma - Cartas, 1937-1938*. San Juan: Fundación Luis Muñoz Marín, 2004.

Rosado, Marisa. *Las Llamas de la Aurora: Acercamiento a una biografía de Pedro Albizu Campos*. San Juan: Editora Corripio, 1990.

Rosario Urrutia, Mayra. "'Mogollas, entendidos y malas mañas': La regeneración del partido político en el discurso muñocista, 1938-1948." In Fernando Picó, ed., *Luis Muñoz Marín: Ensayos del Centenario*, pp. 209-232. San Juan: Fundación Luis Muñoz Marín, 1999.

Roseberry, William. "Americanization in the Americas." In Roseberry, *Anthropologies and Histories: Essays in Culture, History, and Political Economy*, pp. 30-54. New Brunswick, NJ: Rutgers University Press, 1989.

Ross, David F. *The Long Uphill Path: A Historical Study of Puerto Rico's Program of Economic Development*. San Juan: Talleres Gráficos Interamericanos, 1966.

Roxborough, Ian. "Unity and Diversity in Latin American History." *Journal of Latin American Studies* 16 (May 1984): 1-26.

Ruíz Jiménez, Laura. "Peronism and Anti-imperialism in the Argentine Press: 'Braden or Perón' Was Also 'Perón Is Roosevelt.'" *Journal of Latin American Studies* 30 (October 1998): 551-571.

Said, Edward W. *Orientalism*. New York: Vintage Books, 1979.

———. *Culture and Imperialism*. New York: Vintage Books, 1994.

———. *Representations of the Intellectual*. New York: Pantheon Books, 1994.

———. "Identity, Authority, and Freedom: The Potentate and the Traveler." *Boundary 2* 21, no. 3 (Fall 1994): 1-18.

Safa, Helen L. *The Myth of the Male Breadwinner: Women and Industrialization in the Caribbean*. Boulder, CO: Westview Press, 1995.

Sánchez Olmeda, Marta. *Los movimientos independentistas en Puerto Rico y su permeabilidad en la clase obrera*. Río Piedras: Editorial Edil, 1991.

Santana Rabell, Leonardo. *Planificación y política durante la administración de Luis Muñoz Marín: Un análisis crítico*. San Juan: Editorial Cultural, 1984.

Santiago-Valles, Kelvin. *"Subject People" and Colonial Discourses: Economic Transformation and Social Disorder in Puerto Rico, 1898-1947*. New York: State University of New York Press, 1994.

Sartre, Jean-Paul. *Existentialism and Human Emotions*. New York: Citadel Press, 1987.

———. *Essays in Existentialism*. New York: Citadel Press, 1988.

Scarano, Francisco A. *Puerto Rico: Cinco Siglos de Historia*. San Juan: McGraw-Hill, 1993.

———. "La historia heredada: Cauces y corrientes de la historiografía puertorriqueña, 1880-1970." *Exégesis* 6, no. 17 (1993): 40-52.

Schlesinger, Arthur M., Jr. *The Coming of the New Deal*. Boston: Houghton Mifflin Company, 1959.

Silén, Juan Angel. *We, the Puerto Rican People: A Story of Oppression and Resistance*. New York: Monthly Review Press, 1971.

———. "Más sobre el movimiento obrero." In Silén, *Hacia una visión positiva del puertorriqueño*, pp. 97-103. Río Piedras: Editorial Antillana, 1976).

———. *Apuntes para la historia del movimiento obrero puertorriqueño*. Río Piedras: Editorial Cultural, 1978.

———. *Historia de la nación puertorriqueña*. Río Piedras: Editorial Edil, 1980.

———. *Historia de Puerto Rico*. Santo Domingo: SUSAETA, 1993.

Silvestrini, Blanca G. "Los obreros en la lucha social y política de Puerto Rico durante los años de 1932 al 1940." VI Annual Conference of the Association of Caribbean Historians, Universidad de Puerto Rico, April 4-9, 1974.

———. *Los trabajadores puertorriqueños y el Partido Socialista, 1932-1940*. Río Piedras: Editorial Universitaria, 1979.

———. *Violencia y criminalidad en Puerto Rico*. Río Piedras: Editorial Universitaria, 1980.

———. "La mujer puertorriqueña y el movimiento obrero en la década de 1930." In Edna Acosta-Belén, ed., *La mujer en la sociedad puertorriqueña*, pp. 67-90. Río Piedras: Ediciones Huracán, 1980.

————. "Women as Workers: The Experience of the Puerto Rican Women in the 1930s." In Edna Acosta-Belén, ed., *The Puerto Rican Woman: Perspectives on Culture, History, and Society*, pp. 48-66. New York: Praeger, 1986.

————. "Contemporary Puerto Rico." In Franklin W. Knight and Colin A. Palmer, eds., *The Modern Caribbean*, pp. 147-167. Chapel Hill: University of North Carolina Press, 1989.

————. "Igualdad y protección: La legislación sobre la mujer en Puerto Rico." In Fernando Picó, Silvia Alvarez Curbelo, and Carmen Raffucci, eds., *Senado de Puerto Rico, 1917-1992: Ensayos de historia institucional*, pp. 313-338. San Juan: Senado de Puerto Rico, 1992.

Silvestrini, Blanca G., and Maria D. Luque de Sánchez. *Historia de Puerto Rico: Trayectoria de un pueblo*. San Juan: Editorial La Biblioteca, 1988.

Skocpol, Theda. "Political Responses to Capitalist Crisis: Neo-Marxist Theories of the State and the Case of the New Deal." *Politics and Society* 10 (1980): 155-201.

Smith, Anna Marie. *Laclau and Mouffe: The Radical Democratic Imaginary*. London: Routledge, 1998.

Stein, Steve. *Populism in Perú: The Emergence of the Masses and the Politics of Social Control*. Madison: University of Wisconsin Press, 1980.

Sterling, Philip. *The Quiet Rebels; Four Puerto Rican Leaders: Jose Celso Barbosa, Luis Munoz Rivera, Jose de Diego, Luiz Muñoz Marín*. Garden City, NY: Doubleday, 1968.

Stern, Steve J. "Feudalism, Capitalism, and the World-System in the Perspective of Latin America and the Caribbean." *American Historical Review* 93, no. 4 (October 1988): 829-872.

Stoler, Ann Laura. "'In Cold Blood': Hierarchies of Credibility and the Politics of Colonial Narratives." *Representations* 37 (1992): 151-189.

Taller de Formación Política. *La cuestión nacional: El Partido Nacionalista y el movimiento obrero puertorriqueño*. Río Piedras: Ediciones Huracán, 1982.

————. *Huelga en la caña, 1933-34*. Río Piedras: Ediciones Huracán, 1982.

————. *No estamos pidiendo el cielo: Huelga portuaria de 1938*. Río Piedras: Ediciones Huracán, 1988.

Taussing, Michael T. *The Devil and Commodity Fetishism in South America*. Chapel Hill: University of North Carolina Press, 1980.

Torfing, Jacob. "A Hegemony Approach to Capitalist Regulation." In Rene Bertramsen et al., *State, Economy and Society*, pp. 35-93. London: Unwin Hyman, 1991.

————. *Politics, Regulation and the Modern Welfare State*. Basingstoke: Palgrave Macmillan, 1998.

————. *New Theories of Discourse: Laclau, Mouffe, and Žižek*. Oxford: Blackwell Publishers, 1999.

Torre, Carlos Antonio, Hugo Rodríguez Vecchini, and William Burgos, eds. *The Commuter Nation: Perspectives on Puerto Rican Migration*. San Juan: Editorial de la Universidad de Puerto Rico, 1994.

Torrecilla, Arturo. *El espectro posmoderno: Ecología, neoproletario, intelligentsia*. San Juan: Publicaciones Puertorriqueñas, 1995.

Trías Monge, José. *Historia constitucional de Puerto Rico*, 4 vols. Río Piedras: Editorial Universitaria, 1980.

————. *Puerto Rico: The Trials of the Oldest Colony in the World*. New Haven, CT: Yale University Press, 1999.

Trouillot, Michel-Rolph. *Silencing the Past: Power and the Production of History*. Boston: Beacon Press, 1995.

Tugwell, Rexford G. *The Stricken Land: The Story of Puerto Rico.* New York: Doubleday, 1947.

———. *The Art of Politics, as Practised by Three Great Americans: Franklin Delano Roosevelt, Luis Muñoz Marín, and Fiorello H. La Guardia.* Garden City, NY: Doubleday, 1958.

Velázquez Net, Ismaro. *Muñoz y Sánchez Vilella.* Río Piedras: Editorial Universitaria, 1974.

Vilas, Carlos M. "Latin American Populism: A Structural Approach." *Science and Society* 56 (Winter 1992-1993): 389-420.

Villaronga, Gabriel. "Puerto Rico and the United States: Sources for the Study of Populism and Inter-American Relations." In Gayle Ann Williams, ed., *Caribbean Studies: Bibliographic Access and Resources for the Past, Present, and Future,* pp. 145-152. Austin: SALALM, 2002.

Volek, Emil, ed. *Latin America Writes Back: Postmodernity in the Periphery.* New York: Garland Publishing, 2002.

Weffort, Francisco, and Anibal Quijano. *Populismo, marginalización y dependencia: Ensayos de interpretación sociológica.* Costa Rica: Editorial Universitaria Centroamericana EDUCA, 1973.

Wells, Henry. *La Modernización de Puerto Rico: Un Análisis Político de Valores e Instituciones en Proceso de Cambio.* Río Piedras: Editorial de la Universidad de Puerto Rico, 1986.

Whalen, Carmen Teresa. *From Puerto Rico to Philadelphia: Puerto Rican Workers and Postwar Economies.* Philadelphia: Temple University Press, 2001.

White, Hayden. *Tropics of Discourse: Essays in Cultural Criticism.* Baltimore: Johns Hopkins University Press, 1985.

———. *The Content of the Form: Narrative Discourse and Historical Representation.* Baltimore: Johns Hopkins University Press, 1987.

Williams, Patrick, and Laura Chrisman, eds. *Colonial Discourse and Postcolonial Theory.* New York: Columbia University Press, 1994.

Williams, Raymond. *Marxism and Literature.* Oxford: Oxford University Press, 1977.

Winn, Peter. *Weavers of the Revolution: The Yarur Workers and Chile's Road to Socialism.* New York and Oxford: Oxford University Press, 1986.

Wolfe, Joel. *Working Women, Working Men: Sao Paulo and the Rise of Brazil's Industrial Working Class, 1900-1955.* Durham, NC: Duke University Press, 1993.

Zapata Oliveras, Carlos R. *"Nuevos Caminos hacia Viejos Objetivos": Estados Unidos y el Establecimiento del Estado Libre Asociado de Puerto Rico, 1945-1953.* Río Piedras: Editorial Edil, 1991.

———. *De independentista a autonomista: La transformación del pensamiento político de Luis Muñoz Marín (1931-1949)* San Juan: Fundación Luis Muñoz Marín, 2003.

Zinn, Howard. *A People's History of the United States.* New York: Harper Collins, 2003.

Žižek, Slavoj. *The Sublime Object of Ideology.* London: Verso Books, 1989.

———. "Beyond Discourse Analysis." In Ernesto Laclau, *New Reflections on the Revolution of Our Time,* pp. 249-260. London: Verso Books, 1990.

———. *The Ticklish Subject: The Absent Centre of Political Ontology.* London: Verso Books, 2000.

———, ed. *Mapping Ideology.* London: Verso Books, 1994.

INDEX

ABOUT THE AUTHOR

GABRIEL VILLARONGA is Assistant Professor of History and the Humanities at the University of Puerto Rico in Bayamón.